THE KIMCHI MATTERS

The Kimchi Matters

Global Business and Local Politics in a Crisis-Driven World

*By Marvin Zonis,
Dan Lefkovitz, and Sam Wilkin*

Agate

CHICAGO

Printed in Canada.

Library of Congress Cataloging-in-Publication Data

Zonis, Marvin, 1936–
  The kimchi matters: global business and local politics in a crisis-driven age / Marvin Zonis, Dan Lefkovitz, and Sam Wilkin.
    p. cm.
  Includes bibliographical references and index.
  ISBN 0-9724562-1-X
  1. International trade—Cross-cultural studies. 2. International economic relations—Cross-cultural studies. 3. International relations—Cross-cultural studies. 4. Globalization—Cross-cultural studies.   I. Lefkovitz, Dan.
II. Wilkin, Sam.   III. Title.
  HF1359.Z66 2003
  337—dc22   2003017988

10 9 8 7 6 5 4 3 2 1

Agate books are available in bulk at discount prices.
Single copies are available prepaid direct from the publisher.

Agatepublishing.com

Contents

Preface

IN THE YEARS 1980 TO 1984, THE WORD "GLOBALIZATION" APPEARED in seventy-three articles in the *New York Times*. From 1990 to 1994, 325 articles. In the year 2000 alone, 517 articles. Of the books available on Amazon.com published from 1980 to 1989, only nine have as their subject or title "globalization." The years 1990 to 1994 yielded 49 books. From 1995 to 1999, 268 books. The first three years of the new millennium, 848 books.

So, yes, thank you, we get it. Globalization is Big, very Big: the defining story in business and international relations for the past two decades. In fact, so Big that some other stories were overlooked. For instance:

* Indonesia's economy grew so fast during three decades of uninterrupted rule by President Suharto that it seemed like sour grapes to point out that his family had amassed an ill-gotten fortune of perhaps $40 billion;

* Argentina privatized its economy so aggressively during the early 1990s that it seemed forgivable when, even as the country's economy boomed in the mid-1990s, government debt somehow ballooned from 29 percent to 41 percent of GDP;

* Saudi Arabia performed so well as the guarantor of cheap world oil prices that it seemed intrusive to comment on its sponsorship of fundamentalist Islam, and its falling per capita income (from $15,810 in 1981, on par with Spain, to $6,960 in 2000, poorer than Slovenia).

We now know that these stories should not have been overlooked. Indonesia's sudden collapse helped spread the "Asian flu" financial crisis around the globe. Argentina suffered the largest sovereign debt default in world history. And Saudi Arabia inadvertently exported its citizens' disappointment and anger to Afghanistan, Kashmir, and the U.S. in the form of Islamic terrorism.

An ironic side-effect of globalization is that relatively small, local stories—the budget policies of Argentina, the corruption of Indonesia, the stability of Saudi Arabia—matter more than ever before. They are played out in distant countries, but with the click of a mouse or the boarding of a plane their impacts are transmitted around the globe.

This book, in short, is about those small stories—why some countries succeed in achieving stability, why others fail—and why these stories matter.

∞

This book is also about unintended consequences, which in recent decades have sprouted in abundance. Rapid market reforms, for instance, unexpectedly led to the collapse of the Russian economy and the looting of Russian assets. Drilling operations in Nigeria inadvertently dragged Shell Oil into a nightmare of ethnic conflict that helped force a dramatic reorientation of the company toward greater social responsibility. A socialist revolution in Egypt unintentionally fueled the rise of Islamic fundamentalism there. Argentina's rapid opening to the world economy helped trigger its economic crisis. Each of these events was the result of well-intentioned actions that set off unexpected political dynamics. In each case, with the benefit of hindsight, one might wish that things had been done differently.

The central argument of this book is that to do globalization right, one must understand the local political realities of how individual countries work. This truth holds for companies venturing abroad and for policymakers contemplating foreign challenges, and no less for small investors, voters, and others whose lives and finances are increasingly affected by distant world events. This book lays out an intuitive framework for making sense of international economic and political developments, whether negative (why markets in Argentina collapsed, why Russia stumbled, why U.S. allies Saudi Arabia and Pakistan became sources of international terrorism and instability) or positive (why Singapore and Botswana, to name just two, became unlikely success stories). Investors contemplating buying foreign stocks or bonds or real estate can use the ideas here to analyze the countries in which they might commit time and money. Business executives who are contemplating expanding operations to other countries can use these ideas to determine the likelihood of those countries being politically stable and economically dynamic. Perhaps most importantly, readers should gain an understanding of what transpired in the globalization boom, why things did not work out as planned, and how they might be made to work better in the future.

This book has fifteen main chapters, sandwiched by an introduction and conclusion, and each section discusses a general principle of how countries work. That is not a comprehensive list, but in our view these fifteen are the most important. When understood, they provide a powerful tool for picking apart a country's economy and politics and assessing what makes it tick. In short, this book lays out a framework for understanding and forecasting local political dynamics, which, in this era of globalization, increasingly drive global markets, national economies, and indeed determine the stability and safety of our world. However, unlike the many widely read books on globalization, this book addresses local phenomena, not global phenomena. These local dynamics preceded globalization and will continue to operate even if the present globalization era falters in the face of growing security threats and public dissatisfaction.

∞

To this end, the book is organized around a simple model of political dynamics. Think of it as a cycle of demands and responses. The cycle begins with a political demand by the public. The government takes action, perhaps responding to this demand, perhaps ignoring it, perhaps aggravating the problem. A competent response leads to satisfaction. An incompetent response leads to dissatisfaction, possibly anger, and more extreme demands. The government response comes again. Either the situation settles or it escalates. Demands either become more extreme, and more directly political, or more moderate. At some point, a vicious cycle of escalating anger and incompetent responses will trigger a political crisis.

This basic political dynamic is influenced by many things: ethnic conflicts within the population; popular perceptions of the legitimacy of the government; the government's responsiveness to the people; the government's ability to make competent policies that address the sources of public anger; the dynamism of the economy in generating and preserving prosperity; the ability of the state to manage instability. Each of these is covered in this book's fifteen chapters.

We begin by addressing sources of public discontent and political demands. We cover corruption (in the Philippines), ethnic conflict (in Nigeria), social change (in Egypt), and economic crises (in Indonesia).

We then move to government responses to public discontent. We address opposition movements (in Venezuela and Sri Lanka), scapegoating (in Zimbabwe), responsive politics (in India), and government capacity to manage discontent (in Singapore and Iran).

Next we address political leadership: good leaders and bad (in Uganda), leadership succession (in Yugoslavia and Italy), and then we sum up the story so far with the idea of the ruling bargain (in Saudi Arabia and Peru).

The final section is on government policy. We show how instability affects policy (in Mexico), how vested interests distort policy (in Pakistan and Brazil), how state-led economic activity further distorts policy (in Turkey), how policy can be disrupted by external shocks (in Argentina), and how policies can imprison or unleash economic potential energy (in Russia and Botswana).

Our concluding chapter uses all of the principles covered in the book to assess China—quite possibly the country with the greatest potential to reshape the world's existing political and economic order. By then, the reader will have an intuitive framework for assessing political dynamics and an understanding of how to use the framework.

∞

Let us anticipate a couple of objections. First, some will complain, with justification, that our stories are too simplistic. And this is true. In our stories we strive for clarity at the expense of complexity, usually highlighting one determining factor at the expense of others. We hope specialists in a certain country or region will forgive us these histories, too neat by far. Our objective is to illustrate general principles rather than capture all the nuances of a particular country. If a story intrigues you, look to our endnotes for references to more nuanced tellings.

A second objection. What about geography, and what about culture? To the layperson, culture is probably the most common explanation for a country's stability and prosperity or turmoil and poverty. Too often, this kind of thinking devolves into pernicious racial stereotypes: "Japanese are industrious," "Mexicans are lazy," "Hindus are passive," and so on. There is, in fact, a great deal of evidence that culture and geography are important factors in a country's political and economic development.

However, our book focuses on the modern world, where culture and geography are no longer determinative. Scientific advances to boost agricultural production and combat disease are now available worldwide. (Singapore, in the heart of the tropics, managed to become one of the world's richest nations while South Koreans, seen as "lazy" by their colonial masters, produced some of the most rapid economic growth rates in world history.) Furthermore, the phenomenon of economic migration has demonstrated that people of any culture can become highly productive in the right environment. India is hardly a shining example of stability and economic development. But Indian-Americans are, in fact, the richest foreign-born immigrant group in the United States. Culture and geography are important, but other factors can overcome their importance.

The point is that advances in science and technology, legal codes, economic policymaking, and in countless other areas make it possible for all countries—irrespective of their cultures or geographies—to generate development. It is our firm belief that any country can be a material success story. The implication of this is that economic opportunities may be found in unlikely places and that no matter how desperate a country's situation, it is wrong to lose hope. The recent history of countless countries bears us out.

Finally, for those with an academic bent, let us comment on where our perspective fits into the broad range of writing on economic development. Many of the principles we have assembled will be familiar to students of political science, economics, history, and social psychology. These principles are not new. What is new is the combination of these principles to take a holistic view of a country—but then, that is the point of this book.

∞

Any book—and particularly this one—is a collaboration: foremost among the three of us, but also with a wider group without whose expertise and support this manuscript would never have been written or published.

We are greatly indebted to the members of the former country analysis team at Marvin Zonis + Associates. They contributed to the formation of this book's country analysis framework and originated many of the ideas for our country case studies. Evan Felsing provided superb insights on France, the Netherlands, and Nigeria; Kian Gohar, on South Africa and Vietnam; Jeff Greco, on Germany, Italy, and Turkey; Christy Griffin, on Mexico and Venezuela; Jin Kyu Joung, on China, Hong Kong, Taiwan, South Korea, and Microsoft in Korea; Kevin McGahan, on Malaysia, Indonesia, Thailand, and the Philippines; Kara Murphy, on Russia, the Czech Republic, Hungary, and Venezuela; Dwight Semler, on the Czech Republic, Hungary, Poland, Slovenia, Russia, and Central Asia; and John Thompson, on Argentina and Brazil. Analysts Alessandra Budnik, Dingding Chen, Eric Humphrey, Kristy Johnson, Steve Laymon, and Pete Wisner also provided useful insights.

Our intern Jessica Freedland compiled invaluable research on Zimbabwe, South Africa, Somalia, and South Korea. Maureen Loughnane and Leilei Shan provided crucial statistics and data points. Nick Howland contributed significant research on Singapore. Lisa Hughes copyedited the manuscript. And Jonathan Baskin provided extensive help on the index.

We would like to thank several friends, colleagues, and students who read the book in whole or in part and offered feedback: Matthew Canepa, Michael Denk, Eric Johnson, Larry Jones, Jeffrey Lang, Ken LaSala, Patrick Lohier, Thomas Mucha, and Matthew Percy. The fall 2002 and spring 2003 political risk classes at the University of Chicago's Graduate School of Business were not only "guinea pigs" for the book, but contributed insights and comments for which we are grateful.

Many others associated with Marvin Zonis + Associates also contributed to the ideas here. We would especially like to thank Dan Brumberg, Robert Egge, Dan Jones, Allon Ivri, Ethan Putterman, and Ivan and Monica Toft.

This book represents much of what Marvin Zonis has learned about emerging markets in the forty-plus years since beginning his graduate studies at M.I.T.'s department of political science. His mentors there,

Frederick W. Frey, Lucian Pye, and the late Daniel Lerner and Ithiel De Sola Pool, laid the foundation for his intellectual and academic growth. His fellow graduate students, especially William Quandt, Richard H. Solomon, Howard Wolpe, and Robert Melson helped shape his ideas over the years. His wife, Lucy Salenger, was both an intellectual and emotional support.

Dan Lefkovitz acknowledges the support of his family, Anne, Elliot, Aaron, and Jonathan Lefkovitz, Irving and Deana Richmond, and his grandmother Frances; his academic mentors, professors Lloyd and Susanne Rudolph of the University of Chicago; and his friends in Egypt, who were among his best teachers on the subject of political economy.

Sam Wilkin wishes to thank his teachers in world affairs, including Sid Reggie, Professor Diana Fuguitt of Eckerd College, Professor Helmut Norpoth of the State University of New York at Stony Brook, Professor Dali Yang of the University of Chicago, and his parents, Judy and Peter Wilkin.

We salute the hard work of Nancy Werner, our director of administration, who kept this work on track, and, finally, we thank our publisher, editor, and friend, Doug Seibold of Agate, for his diligence, energy, and abundant expertise. He believed in this project and his contribution to the manuscript is immense.

While much credit belongs to our colleagues, editors, and friends, any errors (and omissions), of course, remain our sole responsibility.

The Kimchi Matters:
An Introduction

IN THE SUMMER OF 1998—WELL INTO THE HEADY YEARS OF THE globalization era—Microsoft announced its expansion strategy for the Korean market. True to form, the strategy was bold, extremely aggressive, made use of the firm's comparative advantage of being stunningly rich, and seemed, to some, rather anticompetitive. Microsoft would make a $20 million investment in Hangul & Computer, which produced the Ah Rae Ah Hangul program that had locked up the market for word processing in Korea. In exchange, Hangul & Computer would cease development of Ah Rae Ah Hangul and focus on other software products.

The plan was not only bold but sophisticated. Microsoft had guessed, correctly, that in the wake of Korea's financial crisis, Korean assets were hugely undervalued. This was an opportunity to invest at knockdown prices. Better yet, Hangul & Computer, suffering serious financial trouble, would willingly sacrifice its flagship software in exchange for desperately needed cash. To be sure, the main cause of Hangul's problems was software piracy (people using illegal copies of Hangul's software instead of paying for it). A lesser firm than Microsoft might have been dissuaded from entering the market in the first place. But Microsoft had guessed—again correctly—that in a few years piracy would diminish sharply, spinning Korean market share from lead into gold. In business terms, the timing could hardly have been better.

Furthermore, Ah Rae Ah Hangul had, by some estimates, 80 percent of the Korean word processing market. Microsoft Word had about 15 percent. Hence, with Ah Rae Ah Hangul eliminated under the terms of the deal, Microsoft could expect to gain a nearly 100 percent market share in fairly short order. From underdog to near-monopoly with one well-judged trans-action: this was the kind of maneuver for which Microsoft was justly famed.

But Microsoft's irresistible commercial force was about to meet the immovable object of Korean politics. In the summer of 1998, Korea was wallowing in the aftermath of a punishing financial crisis. Decades of rapid growth had suddenly ended in an ugly recession (a one-year 6.5 percent economic contraction). Demonstrations and labor riots were commonplace, and some featured antiforeign undertones. Average Koreans may not have been quite sure what had gone wrong, but they knew that foreigners—actually, Korea's short-term debts to foreign banks—were somehow involved.

Which made it wise for foreign firms to tread lightly in the Korean market of the day. This applied doubly to high-profile behemoths like Microsoft, whose (at the time) $260 billion market capitalization approached the size of the entire Korean economy ($317 billion in 1998). Instead, far from tiptoeing, the company sallied forth intending to deliver a coup de grace to the local competition.

But there was much more going on than this. To understand the minefield into which Microsoft was charging, one must know the location and origin of the mines. These can be found in the Korean language itself. The Korean "alphabet" is unusual in that it did not evolve organically over the centuries, but was brought into being at a single stroke by royal decree in 1446. Until that time, Korean had been written using Chinese characters. But King Sejong, of the Chosun Dynasty, felt these foreign characters unsuitable. Declaring, "There have been many who, having something to put into words, have in the end been unable to express their feelings," he believed "Koreans are in great need of their own letters." Sejong issued a proclamation introducing an entirely new, and uniquely Korean, script.

This script, called Hangul, is something of a design miracle. It has the aesthetic look and feel of an ideographic language like Chinese, wherein each complex character has a distinct meaning. Yet the apparently complex characters are actually built from only twenty-four simple phonetic symbols, each of which indicates a single sound. Hence written Korean—despite its intimidating appearance—can be learned in a day. Contrast this with the 3,500 characters of written Chinese, the three alphabets of written Japanese, or, for that matter, the convoluted spellings of written English. In the Hangul system, there is only one way to spell each sound, so listeners immediately know how to spell any word they hear. All of which moved the British linguist Geoffrey Sampson to say, with some hyperbole, "Hangul must unquestionably rank as one of the great intellectual achievements of humankind."

This already potent history was made doubly so by the Japanese colonial occupation of Korea in the early 1900s. The Japanese almost immediately suppressed the use of Hangul, and then, in 1938, abolished Korean entirely, and declared that Japanese would henceforth be the country's only official language. In 1940, Koreans were forced to change their family names and use Japanese surnames instead.

These policies had the predictable effect of making Hangul a symbol of Korean national pride, independence, and patriotism. Once Korea regained independence at the end of World War II, the preservation of Hangul became a patriotic duty. Government policies to this end helped push Korean literacy rates to among the highest in the world. October 9, the anniversary of King Sejong's proclamation, was established as "Hangul Day." This likely makes Korea the only country on earth with an official holiday celebrating its alphabet.

Thus it was with no small pride that Lee Chan-jin, the man who would go on to found Hangul & Computer, announced in the late 1980s that he had become the first person in the world to adapt the Korean script for use on the computer. A survey of Korean college students, asking which celebrities they admired most, found that "Lee Chan-jin, who won national fame through his development of a unique Hangul word processor program," had taken second place. (The chairman of Hyundai came in first.)

It was into this minefield of nationalism that Microsoft charged. Hangul & Computer's Ah Rae Ah Hangul would disappear, and in its place would stand Microsoft Word; a foreign company would gain control of the primary means for representing the Korean script on a computer.

The backlash was immediate and intense. Outraged Korean newspaper editorials branded Bill Gates a colonialist and a grass-roots campaign against the deal quickly sprang up. The Korea Venture Business Association announced that it would raise funds to head off Microsoft's offer. The grass-roots opposition campaign took shape as the "Movement to

Keep Ah Rae Ah Hangul," which solicited donations from Korean citizens. It rapidly became clear that Microsoft's offer was doomed. It didn't help that Microsoft's software was unable to represent certain archaic character and word formations that were necessary to read pre-1900 texts.

In the face of public outcry, Hangul & Computer terminated the deal with Microsoft and accepted a smaller counter-offer from Korean venture capitalists. As the managing director of IDC Korea, a brokerage house, put it: "It was probably the first time that an entire nation, from the central government to corporations to private citizens, combined forces to save a local industry." In short, Microsoft's expansion strategy had inadvertently triggered a political opposition movement. Following Microsoft's retreat, Hangul & Computer revamped its word processing software and rereleased it under the name "Hangul 815." The "815" refers to August 15, the day that Korea was liberated from Japan's colonial rule.

∞

In the early, heady years of globalization, it was not unreasonable to imagine a world unified and stabilized by the growth of international markets. The logic went something like this: New technologies and porous national borders would foster the expansion of international linkages—between people, companies and governments—of unprecedented strength and complexity. Distant countries would come to be bound together in a web of shared prosperity, as their citizens traded, traveled and communicated across borders. An era of international stability and cooperation would inexorably ensue. Peace through commerce.

This was a historical moment of extraordinary optimism—at least in the West. "The movement toward a truly integrated global economy has already gone too far to be reversed," exclaimed a Phillips Petroleum executive in 1992. "We treat the world as a single nation," claimed the CEO of Gillette. In this new world order, politics and borders simply did not matter. "The world economy has become a single stage with leading roles played by multinational companies," said U.S. Deputy Secretary of State John Whitehead in 1989.

This was partially true. But countries that had opened themselves to global capital markets and into which investors had poured billions were

subject to violent crises (for instance, Argentina and Indonesia). Eager
market reformers often stumbled badly (Russia). Angry rhetoric against
the globalization system (Malaysia) sometimes turned into drastic action
(Venezuela and Zimbabwe). And an enraged and merciless few saw the
new global linkages not as a means to shared prosperity, but as a vulnerability to exploit in the pursuit of violence (al-Qaeda). It soon seemed
as if the globalization party had gone on too long. The euphoria of the
early years faded and then turned to dismay as the hosts realized they
had invited more than a few bad elements to the table. Globalization's
heightened intimacies became increasingly uncomfortable, as many of
the guests turned out to be angry, unpredictable, duplicitous, or violent.
What went wrong?

The answer is that the prophets of growing global stability had
ignored the fact that even as the globalization boom took hold, the
dynamics of local politics continued to operate. In fact, far from subsum-
ing local politics, globalization actually served to *amplify* local politics,
bringing the problems of distant, dysfunctional states uncomfortably
close to home, so that the lives and pocketbooks of people around the
world came to be buffeted by obscure political developments in faraway
lands. This was globalization's unintended consequence.

Writers are addicted to metaphors, and "kimchi" is ours. For the
uninitiated, kimchi is the unofficial Korean national dish: unassuming
cabbage soaked in chili, garlic, and ginger until fiery of flavor, pungent
of odor, and sharp red in color. To be sure, kimchi has its charms. But it
is, at least for now, an acquired taste, a very local dish.

Today, almost everyone eats Big Macs (118 countries at last count)—
which is unprecedented, amazing, revolutionary—in short, the Big story
of globalization. But one lesson of September 11, 2001 is that the small
stories, the regional politics and the local struggles, cannot be overlooked.
Everyone eats Big Macs; but the kimchi matters more than ever before.

∞

There is no denying that the globalization of business has, in the past
two decades or so, refashioned the world economy. Transactions such as
Microsoft's intended takeover in Korea, which not long ago could hardly
have been contemplated, are now commonplace.

And yet, in this seemingly uniform world marketplace, even unassailable commercial logic is no guarantee of success. South Korea may be just another market, but the unique history of Hangul is still the unique history of Hangul. Even in a relatively prosperous, high-tech, democratic country such as Korea, one has only to push the wrong buttons to trigger a political backlash against perceived colonialism. All of which proves that in this global marketplace, the kimchi matters more than ever.

This would be so obvious as to go without saying, were it not that the commercial logic of globalization is so universal and so overwhelming. In recent decades, growth in world trade has far outstripped growth in world production. During the 1970s and 1980s, international trade grew at about one and one-half times the pace of overall production. In the 1990s, this ratio jumped to three times the increase in production. According to the World Trade Organization, world merchandise trade expanded from $580 billion in 1973 to $1.8 trillion in 1983 to $6.2 trillion in 2000; foreign direct investment increased from just $57 billion per year in 1982 to $1.3 trillion in 2000. These volumes have fallen since their peak, but annual trade flows of around $6 trillion are still no small beer.

The sheer intensity of economic globalization has had the effect of producing political decisions that obey this commercial logic. For countries willing to open themselves to foreign trade and investment, the economic benefits are huge. And thus, as one would expect, economic openness has recently enjoyed a tremendous vogue. In 1975, only 8 percent of countries had open capital markets; by 1997, a full 28 percent did (and this in a post-Soviet world of many more countries). Everyone wants to get in on the benefits. The World Trade Organization now has 142 member states, and more are eager to sign up.

So it is tempting to conclude that—if politicians now obey commercial logic—politics matters less. This temptation is enhanced by the admirable desire to divorce business from politics; too much intimacy between businesspeople and politicians is almost inevitably unseemly. This is sometimes taken to extremes. One international businessperson, attending the April 2002 meeting of the World Economic Forum's Eurasian Summit held in Kazakhstan, was asked to comment on the recent arrests of opposition politicians in Kazakhstan, and revelations that Kazakh president Nursultan Nazarbayev had transferred $1 billion from the national treasury to an offshore bank account. His response: "I don't get involved in those issues. It has no impact on what we do at all." (It certainly impacted two Americans, one a former ExxonMobil executive, who were indicted for having paid bribes while securing oil deals in Kazakhstan.)

To the contrary. It may be tempting to discount the importance of local politics—after all, what does local politics matter when almost every country is a self-described "market economy"? But as Microsoft's Korean misadventure shows, the label "market economy" can obscure much that is crucial, including critical determinants of market movements and business success. During the week of July 28, 2001, for example, the official website for the government of Belarus boasted that investment in the country would be "profitable" and that Belarus is a "democratic...state governed by the rule of law." That same week, the last remaining British investor in Belarus quit the country, citing "a frustrating battle with bureaucracy and political interference." Behind every "market economy" hide unique local dynamics. This kimchi is ignored at our peril.

But how is it that Microsoft in Korea and bureaucracy in Belarus are related to crises in Russia and Indonesia, the economic policies of Argentina, or antiglobalization rhetoric from Venezuela? Simply, it is that in this age of globalization, the politics of foreign states matter not just to global businesses like Microsoft but to everyone.

It was not always this way. As Adam Smith famously contended in his *Theory of Moral Sentiments*, one might ordinarily prefer to hear of the death of millions in an earthquake in China than to lose one's own little finger. But globalization—especially advances in travel and communications—has changed this, quite possibly forever.

∞

Shortly after the tragedy of September 11, 2001, came a flood of new understandings; among these, that the rather obscure political dynamics of Saudi Arabia had a powerful and harmful impact on the lives of millions worldwide. Fundamentally, this was a result of globalization. In 1973, it took the actions of a global cartel of oil-producing states to focus world attention on the political dynamics of the Middle East. In 2001, it took only the actions of a few crazed individuals. Some have argued

that the events of September 11 could have occurred at any time since
the dawn of aviation. But this is untrue. The terrorists who struck the
United States were profoundly dependent on today's ease of global travel,
communications, and financial transfers.

Hence the world's attention extended far beyond oil prices and Middle Eastern military rivalries—issues that had concerned the West for
decades. Suddenly, local grievances—the motivations of a small group
of fanatics—were of crucial importance. The inner workings of Saudi
politics and society, hitherto the province of a few specialists, gained
global notoriety. Newscasters from Paris to Peoria bandied about terms
like "Wahhabi" and discussed the pernicious influence of oil wealth,
corruption in the monarchy, and the extremism of the country's Islam.
The most local of issues had come to preoccupy the globe.

Local dynamics now have global political, business and economic
repercussions. The recent barrage of emerging-market financial crises—
Mexico, Thailand, Indonesia, Korea, Russia, Brazil, Turkey, Argentina,
and Brazil, yet again—have led to effects felt both in corporate board-
rooms and by small investors. As a result of the Argentine crisis alone,
for example, Citigroup lost more than $1 billion, FleetBoston slightly less
than that, General Motors wrote off $97 million, and Xerox lost three
cents of earnings per share. The Asian financial crisis cost private investors an estimated $225 billion, and Russia's economic collapse a further
$100 billion. Unsurprisingly, a study by Mercer Consulting found that
"foreign macroeconomic issues" have become one of the top ten causes
of major stock price declines for Fortune 100 firms.

In foreign policy as well, the problems of the developing world
have assumed an outsized importance in recent years. Gone is the
fretting about China as a "strategic competitor" of the U.S. for global
dominance. We are now preoccupied not with threats from powerful
states but with threats from impoverished ones—the spread of religious
extremism, repression, and violence in the Islamic world, the export of
terrorism, and the proliferation of "weapons of mass destruction." The
war in Iraq is the most obvious example of these, but there are others:
SARS in Asia, AIDS in Africa, nuclear conflict in South Asia, political
strife and economic meltdown in Latin America. President George W.
Bush, who campaigned on a diminished international role for the U.S.,

has suddenly found himself focused on rebuilding Iraq and Afghanistan, increasing spending to fight AIDS in Africa, and dramatically increasing other U.S. foreign aid, all while watching the rest of the world like a hawk for other Iraq-type threats to American and international security.

A nineteenth-century satirist, Ambrose Bierce, observed dryly that war was God's way of teaching Americans geography. In this age of globalization, it no longer takes a war. Even the instability of small and distant states can have worldwide impact.

∞

All of this may sound horribly pessimistic. But this is not an argument that economic globalization should be stopped. Global flows of trade and investment have at least the potential to generate prosperity, and therefore improve the health and well-being of billions of people. Moreover, globalization today is based fundamentally on technological advances, notably in telecommunications. It won't go away even if global trade and investment flows decline. Today's globalization turns on the sheer ease of global travel, communications, migration, cultural exchange, and the like. It is globalization of an "I'm-connected-to-you-whether-I-like-it-or-not" variety.

To be sure, there have been and continue to be missteps. Too often, the superficial labels that globalization provides are relied upon to make crucial decisions. Simple questions are asked: Is a country a "market economy" or not? Is it a "democracy" or not? Is it "with us or with the terrorists," in the words of President Bush? There is a tendency to see the defining conflict of the new millennium as a struggle between the Big Mac countries and the few remaining "non-Big Mac" states (Iraq, North Korea, Iran, Afghanistan under the Taliban).

But this is a shortsighted view. September 11 demonstrated that "Big Mac or not" is too simple a formulation. By the Big Mac metric, Saudi Arabia was a U.S. ally. American foreign policy was conducted on this assumption. But at the same time, political dynamics in Saudi Arabia have produced much of the financing and extremist ideology that drove the September 11 hijackers. By ignoring Saudi Arabia's complex kimchi, observers overlooked a dangerous new phenomenon. The defining conflict of the new millennium is not about "Big Mac or not." It is about the struggle to get the kimchi right—to bring stability and prosperity to the Islamic world, for example, so it no longer exports terrorism. To make business decisions that respect and even take advantage of the political dynamics of the countries involved.

Consider, again, Argentina. The Big Mac metric said that this was one of the most aggressively reforming market economies on earth. Foreign investment poured into the country. The International Monetary Fund closely monitored Argentina's economic policies and lent money from the world's governments to support its reform efforts. But as in Saudi Arabia, there were complex and intense internal issues in Argentina, the kimchi of the country's flawed economic policymaking, that were ignored. Only a few years after it was the darling of global investors, receiving $24 billion in direct investment in 1999 alone, Argentina's economy collapsed, inflicting immense losses on the foreign businesses that had ventured there.

These kinds of challenges are not insurmountable. Rather than turn away from globalization, we need to do globalization better. Bad kimchi has thrown many Latin American countries into crisis. But during the same period, much of Eastern Europe has stabilized and bound itself firmly to the West. Indonesia, after years of rapid growth, plunged into a crisis from which it is having difficulty recovering. Yet Botswana, with impoverished and war-torn neighbors, somehow became the fastest-growing economy on earth for a span of more than two decades. And Microsoft, having adopted a business strategy that's far less aggressive and more attuned to local political sensibilities, is now doing quite well in the Korean software market.

More than anything, it's essential to move beyond the simple Big Mac metric. It is crucial to understand not just whether a country is stable or unstable—that may well be obvious after a casual inspection. Rather, it is crucial to understand how a country's stability is produced, and thus whether that stability is firm or fleeting and what byproducts are created in the process. There are dangers in globalization, yet there are also opportunities. Globalization can be done right if businesses and governments pay proper attention to the specifics of local political dynamics—the kimchi.

Part 1

Discontent

OUR INQUIRY BEGINS WITH THE PEOPLE, THE FOUNDATION UPON which a country's political stability is constructed.

Some might say that to accord the people such a primary role would be mistaken. After all, the United Nations estimates that repressive governments currently rule in 100 countries, home to 3.6 billion souls, and therefore a majority of the world's population. Surely, people living under such regimes, with little real say in how they are governed, do not represent the foundation of a country in any meaningful sense. And keep in mind that many of these countries are colonial fictions, their borders drawn arbitrarily by European mapmakers. In such countries, there are peoples, not a people—nations, not a nation. Without a common history, culture, or identity, individuals cannot feel the bonds of association or community.

Fair enough. But one of the countries most affected by a popular uprising in recent years was Indonesia, a repressive, dictator-led, postcolonial hodgepodge of thousands of islands and hundreds of languages. It is not as if the Indonesian public rose up as one to toss out a bad government during the crisis of 1997–1998. Rather, groups of angry Indonesians primarily set upon each other. But it was this turmoil that eventually led to the fall of the government. As such, the people played a crucial political role.

Public involvement in politics rarely if ever entails coherent action by an entire society. Yet a few small groups—for example, university students, Islamic fundamentalists, labor unions—can have a profound impact. The middle classes are perhaps the most powerful when it comes

I

to political action. Their education makes them both effective and aware, and their ranks frequently include the friends, neighbors, and families of civil servants and army and police leaders. Once the middle classes rise up, they are not so easily ignored or dispatched. (It was the middle classes that rose up first in Indonesia and, years before, in Iran.)

Hence we must pay close attention to understanding what moves the people. In particular, what compels ordinary people, those without personal political ambitions, to take political action, often at risk to life and limb? Basically, the chief motivation is anger and discontent. People who are basically content with their lives are unlikely to jeopardize house and home by taking political action. By contrast, angry people are easier to motivate, especially if they can be convinced that political action—which could range from organizing and taking part in anti-government demonstrations to killing neighbors from a different ethnic group—will, somehow, solve their problems.

It was popular discontent that drove such dramatic world-historical events as the French Revolution and the Free India movement. On a more mundane level, discontent drives labor strikes in Brazil, the Islamization of the Arab world, and separatist terrorism in Spain. Discontented people—sometimes very small numbers of discontented people—are capable of destabilizing countries and their economies.

But discontent also affects stability in a more indirect fashion. A government facing an angry public is an uncertain government. And uncertain governments are known for making bad decisions. An uncertain government may be afraid to undertake necessary but painful economic reforms. It may try to distract the public with foolish military adventures. It may try to buy off the public with wasteful handouts. It may print money in a desperate attempt to stimulate the economy. It may censor the media to stifle opponents. It may try to rally support by playing one ethnic group off another. It may blame the country's problems on foreign investors and take hostile action against them. All are cases of governments responding ineptly to popular discontent, and all can have disastrous consequences for the companies and individuals caught up in such dynamics.

CHAPTER ONE

"We Practically Own Everything..."

CORRUPTION

THE WALLS ARE THE FIRST SIGN ONE HAS STUMBLED UPON THEIR territory. High and often topped by fences or razor wire, these walls enclose a variety of buildings: whitewashed villas in the tropics, sprawling haciendas in Latin America, Black Sea dachas in Russia, the odd restored colonial mansion, the occasional faux Mogul Palace. This diversity may be cause for confusion. But then a gate opens and a gleaming silver Mercedes, windows tinted, speeds out on some urgent errand. And then you are certain. This home belongs to one of the *Wabenzi*.

The *Wabenzi* are an unusual "tribe." The name was coined by some disgruntled African, tired of seeing wealthy elites racing around in gleaming Mercedes. And so he dubbed them the "people of the Benz" (or, in Swahili: "*Wabenzi*"). The name traveled to Kenya, Tanzania, South Africa, and points beyond, to describe the rich in those countries, who share a fondness for German luxury cars. (In Nigeria, the same tribe is known as the "*Beento*," since they have *been to* exotic foreign locales on expensive vacations.)

Imagine a chance encounter between the proverbial Average Citizen of an impoverished country and one of the *Wabenzi*. A gleaming Mercedes flies past a rickety bicycle on a dusty street. In our simplified world, the man on the rickety bike thinks one of two things: "Those *Wabenzi* are successful. They worked hard for what they have. If I do the same that could be me, or my children." Those are the words of a man who believes in the system. David Brooks described the prevalence of just this sort of

3

sentiment in the United States: "Americans... have always had a sense that great opportunities lie just over the horizon, in the next valley, with the next job or the next big thing. None of us is really poor; we're just pre-rich."

But maybe the chance encounter does not go so well. Perhaps our Average Citizen lives in a country where rags-to-riches stories are not so common; where all of the *Wabenzi* are related to the president and the Average Citizen is not. Perhaps in this country one must pay bribes to obtain simple things like a driver's license or a permit to sell wares in the street. Perhaps, in order to obtain a phone line without waiting years, one must pay a hefty "gift." Perhaps, moments before this encounter, our Average Citizen has been shaken down by a corrupt cop, who threatened him with fines or imprisonment if he failed to hand over the money in his pocket. In this case our man on the rickety bike might have a very different reaction. He might think, "Those *Wabenzi* are crooks. The only people who make it in this country are corrupt or know somebody." That is a man who feels a profound sense of injustice. He feels that avenues of advancement are closed off for him and his family. He thinks the system is rigged.

Will our Average Citizen on his rickety bike be for the system or against it? Perhaps he is young, charismatic, ambitious and determined. In that case he is potentially one of society's greatest leaders, or one of its most dangerous. He is a budding Bill Gates or maybe a Mao Zedong. In this moment—repeated thousands of times every day for Average Citizens around the world—hangs the potential for growth or turmoil. Here begins, on a personal level, a kimchi dynamic of either prosperity or instability.

Certainly, that is one simplification too many. Different people have different reactions to the *Wabenzi*. Even if many Americans are "pre-rich" and many Indonesians joined violent protests against their country's wealthy elite, there are still American communists and Indonesian MBAs.

But anyone skeptical of the political power of corruption, or who thinks corruption is a sustainable political dynamic, or who believes that corruption does not matter for foreign businesses, must understand the story of the Philippines.

THE PHILIPPINES

When Ferdinand Marcos became president of the Philippines in 1965, he was a leader of great promise for a country on the brink of great things:

a brilliant lawyer, a political genius, and a war hero awarded more than thirty medals for his heroism fighting the Japanese in World War II (or so he claimed). His wife, Imelda Romualdez Marcos, a former Miss Manila, was beautiful and capable. His country was abundant in timber, sugar, coconuts, and minerals, and its manufacturing sector had grown by 12 percent per year during the 1950s. The "Asian Tigers"—Korea, Taiwan, Singapore, Hong Kong—were just beginning their own races to prosperity within a single generation. The newly independent Philippines was at the starting line with them.

But then Marcos made some expedient decisions. It's easy, in retrospect, to see how he fell into the first of these. Marcos won reelection to the presidency in 1969 just as things were coming undone. The crops had failed because of a bad monsoon. The Communist Party of the Philippines was launched in 1968; it sprouted a violent guerrilla arm in 1969. None of this was really the president's fault, but nobody likes bad news. Opposition to Marcos's rule grew.

Marcos's reaction to this opposition was perhaps excessive. But the late 1960s was the era when any anticommunist leader was considered, at least by the United States, a good leader, and the U.S.—the Philippines' main patron—was not too picky about human rights violations by its allies. Marcos faked a series of terror attacks and assassination attempts, and then declared martial law to calm the "crisis." He jailed opposition politicians, closed newspapers and radio stations, and gave sweeping authority to the military and police forces. A new constitution allowed Marcos to rule by decree, and few checks remained on the president's power.

But even a dictator needs friends. If his charisma was failing him, well, there was always the power of the purse. Marcos turned to time-honored values in the Filipino political system: *utang ng loob* (obligation through favors), *pakikisama* (smooth interpersonal relationships), and *pamilya* (kinship ties). He lavished patronage on politicians, the military, and the police force. He appointed natives of his home province of Ilocos Norte to key positions in the military and civil service. In short, he bought support. Through corruption and patronage, Marcos nurtured a Filipino political and economic elite that would be loyal to him.

To be sure, Marcos was corrupt before martial law had been imposed— he had opened his first Swiss bank account in 1967 with $1 million—but after 1972, Marcos's patronage created a tiny, close-knit elite with almost unimaginable economic power. Eduardo Cojuangco Jr., scion of one of the country's wealthiest landowning families, ended up with a monopoly over the country's lucrative coconut industry, by way of presidential decrees. Soon Cojuangco was running the United Coconut Oil Mills, the United Coconut Planters Bank, and the Coconut Planters Life Insurance Corporation. Roberto Benedicto, Marcos's former fraternity brother at the University of the Philippines Law College, was given the sugar industry as his personal fiefdom. Benedicto headed the National Sugar Trading Corporation, the Philippines Sugar Commission (the sugar regulatory body), and two banks that financed the sugar industry. Just for good measure, he also owned the Philippines' largest radio and television network. Others cronies included Lucio Tan, an immigrant from China who went from working in a cigarette factory to owning Fortune Tobacco a year into Marcos's term, and Rodolfo Guenca, who received lucrative government contracts as the head of the Construction and Development Corporation.

But above all, Marcos was a family man. Ferdinand and Imelda Marcos themselves had their fingers in almost every pie in the country. Marcos used his former fraternity brother, Benedicto, as a front man for his involvement in at least five communications companies. The Marcos family held stakes in 300 corporations by 1984; Ferdinand Marcos personally headed twenty-five of these. The Marcos holdings included one company brazenly called Sadlemi ("Imelda's" spelled backwards). Years later, Imelda would admit, "We practically own everything in the Philippines from electricity, telecommunications, airline, banking, beer, and tobacco, newspaper publishing, television stations, shipping, oil and mining, hotels and beach resorts down to coconut milling, small farms, real estate, and insurance."

∞

It is hard to say when corruption ceased to be a means to hold power, and instead became the only goal of the Marcos administration. But at some point, Marcos clearly ceased to care about his country, if indeed he ever did care. Marcos and his cronies needed a way to get their plunder out of the Philippines. They preferred Swiss bank accounts and pricey foreign real estate. Investigations by the U.S. Congress revealed that the Marcoses had properties in New York City worth some $350 million.

As a key U.S. ally, pumped with economic aid, Marcos was not about to run out of money, and this kept the Marcos bribeocracy afloat long after it should have run aground. But powerful dynamics had been set in motion. Patronage had bought Marcos powerful friends, but also created many more determined enemies. Filipino businesspeople struggled with a system rigged against their success. For those shut out of the Marcos crony network, the playing field was skewed. Filipino banks lent only to the well-connected. Foreign banks lent primarily to those businesses that had arranged government loan guarantees, which were, of course, only given to friends of the government. Businessmen were incensed, seeing the Marcos elite import millions of dollars' worth of foreign electronics gear and luxury goods each year, while honest businesses were denied the hard currency they needed to import supplies and capital goods on the grounds that there was a "foreign exchange shortage."

Stories of the Marcoses' ridiculous extravagance began to leak out, sparking anger among the middle classes. When Marcos's daughter got married in June 1983, the president flew in twenty-four planeloads of guests to his home province of Ilocos Norte, including the eighty-six-piece Philippine Philharmonic Orchestra. (An earthquake that struck the island two months later was called divine retribution for Marcos's wastefulness.) A slew of grotesque projects littered the country as literal monuments to the president's misrule, such as a Mt. Rushmore-esque Marcos bust carved into a mountain in northern Luzon. When asked how some of her family and friends had become so wealthy, Imelda Marcos answered, "Well, some are smarter than others."

∞

Those left out of this plunder were understandably enraged. Marcos's patron, the United States, began to pressure him in the early 1980s to loosen the reins and democratize the country. When Marcos did so, the anger of the middle classes began to bubble to the surface. An opposition movement began to grow. Then, in 1983, when popular opposition leader Benigno Aquino returned to the country after three years of exile in the United States, Filipino government forces gunned him down at the airport.

This only furthered the cause of the opposition. In 1984, opposition politicians captured 58 out of 183 seats in Congress, despite Marcos's efforts to fix the election. In 1985, the opposition legislators moved to impeach Marcos on charges of "graft and corruption." Though the impeachment failed, the opposition took the opportunity to air its claims in public: that Marcos had been siphoning funds from the Treasury, amassing ill-gotten wealth from foreign investments, and appointing cronies to influential positions.

This public airing of the dirty laundry served to harden opposition to Marcos and Imelda's rule. If the people could not work through the system, they would work around it. "People Power," one of the great nonviolent protests movements of the twentieth century, coalesced around Corazon Aquino, the slain opposition leader's diminutive widow.

The middle class and business communities were the first to join the opposition politicians in wearing the signature "People Power" yellow. They were incensed that the government had used billions of taxpayer dollars to bail out the bankrupt firms of Marcos's cronies. Jaime Ongpin, CEO of the Philippines' oldest mining company and a fierce Marcos critic, estimated that between $6 billion and $7 billion of the country's foreign debt was "wasted because of misallocation to crony-type projects." They were also furious that Marcos exempted well-connected companies from government audit. Using family connections in the Bureau of Internal Revenue, Marcos permitted family and friends to avoid taxes.

By 1986, political instability was sweeping the Philippines. Marcos called elections eighteen months early in 1986, hoping to catch the opposition unprepared. Though few believed Marcos would surrender power, even if defeated, Filipinos still flocked to the polls to lend Aquino their support.

By official count, Marcos defeated Aquino by a small margin. But observers alleged vote-buying, ballot-rigging, ballot-snatching, and voter intimidation. For four days after the election, People Power protested the poll result and demanded Marcos's resignation. The final blow came when the armed forces withdrew their support for the government. Younger officers had grown disillusioned with the corruption in the country and in the higher rungs of the army (where Marcos's cronies were clustered). Fidel Ramos, vice chief of staff of the Filipino armed forces (who would go on to become president of the Philippines from

1992 to 1998), was a crucial domino who fell in the direction of People Power. When it came time for officers to decide whether to shoot the protestors or hold their fire, they abandoned Marcos. With Imelda and a few choice cronies in tow, Marcos abandoned Malacang Palace in a U.S. Army helicopter and then hopped a U.S. airplane to Hawaii. Corazon Aquino was installed as president.

∞

The staggering reality of the Marcoses' corruption became known only after this ignominious departure. Aquino's investigators discovered two crates full of documents revealing Marcos's Swiss bank accounts. They estimated that he stole a total of $10 billion. The fleeing Mrs. Marcos left behind rooms at Malacang Palace filled with furs, gowns, and shoes. Thousands of pairs of shoes were discovered, as if to taunt the shoeless children who played on garbage heaps blocks away from the palace. Aquino, after taking the presidency, opened up the palace as a museum, where ordinary Filipinos could view Imelda's disco shoes with rechargeable lights in the heels, her collection of 935 gowns and dresses, her jewels, and her gallons of Christian Dior perfume—symbols of the Marcos's tragic and ridiculous legacy.

In the wake of the Marcos downfall, foreign businesses struggled to extract themselves from the unstable kimchi dynamic into which they had been pulled. Doing business during the Marcos years was about access, primarily access to the president. As early as 1977, the SEC filed a complaint against GTE citing payoffs of $4.5 million to well-placed Filipinos. Other U.S. companies accused of making illegal payments in the Philippines included McDonnell-Douglas, ITT, and Ford. But the worst such debacle involved Westinghouse. The Pittsburgh-based power company received a contract from the Marcos administration in 1976 to build a 620-megawatt nuclear power plant on the island of Luzon. Ten years and $2.1 billion later, the plant was completed. But after Marcos fled, it came out that Westinghouse had hired a "special sales representative" named Herminio Disini to assist on the deal. Hiring such a person was not unusual in the Philippines, where the bureaucracy could be unnavigable without the right connections. The criminality involved the specifics of Disini's connections. He was the president's golfing buddy and his wife was the president's doctor. The Aquino government alleged that Westinghouse and the engineering firm Burns & Roe had funneled $20 million to Marcos through Disini. Aquino sued in 1988, alleging that these bribes swayed Marcos to award the contract to Westinghouse despite major safety concerns. Then came the revelation from Westinghouse documents that Disini was described as a "bagman" and "front man" for Marcos.

The dispute was finally settled in 1995, nearly 20 years after the original negotiations had begun. Westinghouse agreed to pay $40 million in cash and $60 million in electrical power generating equipment to the Philippines.

∞

Surprisingly, this is not the end of the story of corruption in the Philippines—which illustrates something about political dynamics. There are clear patterns, patterns that repeat themselves across countries and throughout history, but these patterns often go unnoticed, or perhaps are underestimated, by those caught up in them.

And so, in 1998, twelve years after the downfall of Ferdinand Marcos, a populist former movie star named Joseph Estrada was elected to the presidency of the Philippines, and the country once again found itself in the grip of a patronage regime. The intervening administrations of Corazon Aquino and Fidel Ramos had made some—admittedly insufficient—progress on political and economic reform. But Estrada was different.

Like Marcos, Estrada surrounded himself with powerful allies, whom he further enriched through corruption. One of his first moves was to offer to transfer the since-deceased Marcos's remains from cold storage to the Heroes Cemetery in Manila. He also pulled from cold storage a number of old Marcos cronies. Two days after Estrada took power, Marcos confidant Eduardo Cojuangco Jr. drove his Mercedes to the boardroom of the San Miguel brewing corporation, his old fiefdom and the Philippines' largest company, and elected himself chairman and CEO. Estrada also dropped all criminal charges against Lucio Tan, another Marcos favorite, who had been accused of tax evasion to the tune of $612.4 million. Tan then took control of the Philippine National Bank, to which his Philippine Airlines owed nearly $120 million.

Why Estrada thought this would work is anyone's guess. Filipinos soon took to the streets. An unlikely combination of left-wingers and businesspeople marched through Manila dressed in yellow to evoke People Power. As Estrada's misrule continued, trade unionists and the urban middle class joined the movement. The president's approval ratings, once as high as 77 percent, fell to 31 percent by March 2000. People Power leaders came out of retirement for the anti-Estrada campaign. Corazon Aquino declared, "The issue is trust—not trust in the president but in the company he keeps."

When a corruption trial failed to bring about Estrada's impeachment, a series of increasingly angry protests swept the country. Stockbrokers wearing black armbands marched off the exchange trading floor to show their solidarity. Finally, with the people at the gates of Malacanang Palace, Estrada capitulated. But this time—unlike the end of the Marcos administration—there was no U.S. helicopter waiting, no retirement in Hawaii. Estrada was arrested and submitted for trial on charges of "economic plunder," with the death penalty a distinct possibility. Gloria Macapagal Arroyo was sworn in as the country's new president.

THE DYNAMICS OF CORRUPTION

Return for a moment to the tale of that encounter between the bicycle rider and the *Wabenzi*. Fundamentally, this is a story about legitimacy.

Corruption stacks the deck heavily in favor of those with connections, those who can become instant captains of industry by way of presidential decree. The odds are heavily against everyone else. Different cultures have different notions of what constitutes fairness (*utang ng loob*, obligation through favors, was a long-standing principle of Filipino politics), but a stacked deck is rarely a symbol of justice.

In nearly every society there are marked inequalities of power and wealth. And in many times and places, these inequalities are motivating forces. The question is, do they motivate enterprise or do they motivate rebellion?

In the United States, most believe in the doctrine of equality of opportunity—that whoever has the most talent, works the hardest, and makes the best choices, will come out on top. Sam Walton, Michael Jordan, Bill Clinton—individuals from humble backgrounds who became rich and powerful—are held up as examples of how equality of opportunity still works in the U.S. The rich deserve their wealth. They did the right things and made the right decisions to get it.

In corrupt countries, by contrast, wealth is seen as something beyond the reach of all but the well-connected. The rich are seen (by many) to have gotten where they are by entering into deals with the powerful. The powerful are seen to have accumulated power by entering into deals with the rich. In the extreme case, a majority of the people may come to see the distribution of wealth and political power, and indeed the political and economic systems, as illegitimate.

In the first case, the American case, every successful person in that country becomes an impetus for everyone else to work harder. In the second case, every "successful" person becomes a profound source of public anger at the ruling establishment.

This is exaggeration for effect, but the point is that corruption undermines the legitimacy of whatever it touches. This is extraordinarily corrosive for political stability. Power, whether the power of a leader or a system, depends fundamentally on legitimacy. People must accept the leader's commands and obey the system's rules. Whether they do so depends on if they see this power as legitimate. People may bow down before the barrel of a gun, but if they see a government's power as illegitimate, they may strike against it, as middle-class Filipinos did, even at risk to their own lives. And mass disobedience is a recipe for a dysfunctional political and economic system.

The past few decades have provided many dramatic examples of hyper-corrupt rulers who lived large and fell hard. Sani Abacha is thought to have pilfered $4 billion in just five years as president of Nigeria. Mobutu Sese Seko of Zaire stole $10 billion by some counts. And the Suharto family of Indonesia may have accumulated $40 billion. But Suharto was forced out by rioting pro-democracy demonstrators. Mobutu was exiled by rebel forces that overran his army. And Sani Abacha died (in a manner befitting his extraordinary lifestyle) from mysterious causes in the company of three Indian prostitutes.

To be sure, both corruption and legitimacy vary across cultures. In hereditary monarchies, being a member of the king's family may be seen as sufficient justification for wealth and privilege. Political leaders may be expected to use the government apparatus to reward their followers to some degree. Indeed, one could argue that the system of campaign contributions in the U.S. is—on a strict definition—a type of corruption. In practice, the definition of corruption is fluid—although the global spread of democracy and capitalism has certainly increased the worldwide consensus. Notwithstanding *utang ng loob*, Marcos was seen as a thief. Anticorruption movements—some more successful than others—have taken root worldwide.

Of course, every country has problems with corruption. Officials from Salt Lake City bribed International Olympics Committee members to land the 2002 Winter Olympics. Helmut Kohl was found to have accepted millions in illegal campaign contributions while head of Germany's Christian Democratic Party. French president Jacques Chirac has been implicated in sordid scandals dating from his tenure as mayor of Paris. Each of these scandals hurt the legitimacy of those they implicated. But when the scale of corruption is small, and more importantly, when those responsible are held accountable, a certain amount of corruption may be tolerated. This is especially true when growth is rapid (as was long the case in Indonesia) or when large numbers of people are enjoying the benefits (as was long the case in Saudi Arabia). However, this honeymoon can rapidly end if growth slows.

Profound corruption makes for a very unstable political dynamic. First, corruption has serious economic consequences. It was once fashionable to argue that corruption greased the wheels of the political machine, making government function more smoothly. No longer. Empirical evidence has found a direct link between high levels of corruption and low levels of foreign direct investment and economic growth. In countries rife with corruption, resources are not allocated to their most efficient use or to help those most in need. Instead, resources go to business enterprises started by relatives of the president (the Philippines), to projects in which army officers have taken the lead (Nigeria), or to projects in which princes play a role (Saudi Arabia). This directly reduces an economy's efficiency. In addition, corruption is like a tax to legitimate businessmen. The cost of bribes and kickbacks has to be figured into the bottom line. This further reduces economic growth.

Corruption also diminishes the efficiency of government. Laws and regulations meant to enhance efficiency, protect consumers, or ensure safety become meaningless if they can be bypassed with a bribe. In China in 1999, a bridge upstream from the Three Gorges dam collapsed. Investigations revealed that a contractor had bribed local officials to overlook faulty construction. In Turkey, thousands of *kaak* (contraband) buildings collapsed in the August 1999 earthquake. Builders had bribed inspectors to overlook their shoddy construction. Thousands died in structures that violated the Turkish building codes.

This dynamic of government inefficiency and economic decline fosters a vicious cycle. Corruption saps economic growth, diminishing a country's wealth. Hence there is less and less money for the government to hand out to its supporters. This reduces the number of supporters who get that money, and the economic opportunities available to those without connections diminish, making perceptions of a stacked deck that much more intense. The legitimacy of the government declines. The sense of popular discontent and disenfranchisement grows until a political explosion is imminent. Citizens who feel the economic system is illegitimate may be willing to trade a flawed capitalism for socialism or communism. Citizens who feel the political system is illegitimate may be willing to trade a flawed democracy for dictatorship.

There are exceptions. Extraordinary corruption can work in cases where, for some reason, the money keeps flowing despite high levels of corruption. This is true in oil-rich countries that are wealthy despite poor economies. It is also true for countries receiving huge amounts of foreign aid. Foreign aid has fostered the unnatural survival of more corrupt regimes than most western donors would care to admit—including that of Ferdinand Marcos, whose corrupt regime benefited tremendously from U.S. handouts. (George H.W. Bush, visiting Manila as U.S. vice president in 1981, told Marcos, "We love your adherence to democratic principles and to the democratic process.") And there are other examples.

For instance, stunning corruption in southern Italy has been financed in part by the stunning prosperity of northern Italy.

Even extraordinarily corrupt countries can be successful for a time. But, like Marcos in the Philippines, and Estrada after him, the day often comes when the bills must be paid. Even with generous U.S. aid, the kimchi cannot be ignored.

CHAPTER TWO

The Cake

ETHNIC CONFLICT

HERE IS A HEADLINE: "MANY DIE AS ETHNIC RIOTS DEAL NEW Blow to Nigeria." This does surprisingly little to orient the reader. It could just as easily have been written in 1962 or 1982. It so happens that the headline was filed on February 3, 2002, by Reuters, and it describes ethnic clashes between the Yoruba and the Hausa. The Yoruba and the Hausa are the biggest tribes in Nigeria. Most Yoruba are Christian. Most Hausa are Muslim. Surely this is a long-standing African tribal conflict? Or perhaps yet another example of the age-old struggle between Islam and Christendom?

But beware the obvious conclusion. To be sure, religious and ethnic conflicts throughout the world are often described as "age-old" and "intractable." Arabs and Jews in the Middle East; Croats, Serbs, and Bosnians in the Balkans; Hindus and Muslims in India; Hutus and Tutsis in Rwanda; Catholics and Protestants in Ireland. These conflicts are attributed to "ancient hatreds"—a term used by U.S. President Bill Clinton on his first inauguration day. According to this line of thinking, Arabs and Jews have been at each other's throats since biblical times. Hindus have always hated Muslims. The bloodshed in the Balkans can be traced back to "the Great Schism" in 1054, which divided the Christian world between Catholics and Orthodox, or perhaps 1389, when Serbia was defeated by the Ottoman Empire. By this logic, ethnically diverse states are destined to be unstable.

But, as pointed out by University of Chicago professors Lloyd and

Susanne Rudolph, this reasoning does not conform to the facts. At one time or another, most ethnic and religious groups have managed to get along peacefully for decades or even centuries—living side-by-side, doing business with each other, and even intermarrying. In fact, until the colonial 1800s, the Yoruba were not Christian and the Hausa and Yoruba had little interaction. By definition, there were no ancient hatreds here. But there are certainly modern hatreds, the groundwork for which was inadvertently laid by the British.

NIGERIA

In 1914, the British patched together modern Nigeria by merging a Muslim-populated region just south of the Sahara Desert with a territory populated by animists further to the south. The British respected the monotheistic northern Muslims, but thought the southern nature-worshipers needed to be civilized; missionaries were sent to convert them to Christianity.

At the time there was no particular animosity between the ethnic groups. The Muslim Hausa lived mainly in the north. The animist Yoruba dominated the southwest. And the Igbo tribe, also animist, populated the southeast of the country. All told, Nigeria was home to somewhere between 250 and 400 ethnic groups (depending upon how thinly one slices the categories). Where the groups mixed, they got along. Scholar Raufu Mustapha conducted a study of ethnic relations in precolonial Kano, the biggest city in the north. He found that each of the groups had a niche in the region's economy. The Wangarawa were traders of kola nuts, manufacturers of leather and textile products, caravan leaders, and financiers. The Beriberi traded in salt and horses and produced dyed cloth. The Nupe were weavers. Yoruba traders connected the city to the Atlantic Ocean. And Arabs living in the city were administrators and soldiers.

But social changes brought on by British colonial rule gave rise to ethnic consciousness. Prior to the arrival of the British, most Nigerians, living as they did in small, rural communities, rarely met large groups of people they did not know. Hence they identified themselves with their own families or villages, and outsiders with other families or villages. But the British built urban centers of administration, industry, and schooling. Rural Nigerians from both the north and the south flocked to the cities and the opportunities they offered. Streams of southerners—especially Igbo—left their homes and settled in the north. Igbo from the southeast and Hausa from the north also migrated to the capital city of Lagos, in the midst of the Yoruba homeland.

In the cities, recent migrants had no friends or family to fall back on. They had to form new support networks and they "discovered" ethnicity. They quite naturally turned to those who spoke the same language and practiced the same religion (even if they were from different villages or clans). Yoruba, Igbo, and Hausa began to form ethnic kinship associations—like the Pan-Yoruba Association, founded in 1942. These associations helped their members get established in the cities. They helped them find jobs. They provided credit. And they offered temporary shelter, financial support, and welfare.

Thus ethnic associations, and ethnic groups, began to take shape in the minds of Nigerians. And yet, these ethnic and religious understandings had only just been created. At the time, there certainly were no "ancient hatreds." So why all the bloodshed?

∞

To understand politics in Nigeria, you have to know about "cake." Nigerians talk about it all the time. By cake, they mean resources controlled by the government. Revenues. Jobs. Infrastructure projects. Spaces in the universities. Military employment. In Nigeria there is quite a lot of cake, and everyone wants a piece of it.

According to scholar Okwudiba Nnoli, a political dynamic rapidly emerged in Nigeria under British rule in which the newly minted ethnic associations began to compete for cake. Different ethnic groups, newly arrived in the cities, all wanted the same scarce housing, employment, and educational slots. Ironically, the formerly animist southerners (newly converted to Christianity) were at an advantage over the Muslim northerners, because the missionaries had taught them to read and write. According to a 1960 study by researcher Peter Kirby, Igbo from the south actually held the majority of the factory jobs in the north.

Ethnic consciousness was growing, and members of different ethnic groups had different levels of success in getting their share of the cake. The struggle therefore became an ethnic conflict. A political party soon emerged calling itself the Northern People's Congress. Its motto: "One North, One People, Under One God." It was a Hausa-dominated and pro-Islamic. It was also anti-southern and anti-Igbo. The Igbo and the Yoruba then came up with political parties of their own. Still, with the British running Nigeria, there were relatively few incidents of ethnic violence. The first major incident occurred in the town of Jos in 1945, touched off by a dispute over the sale of potatoes. Only two people died, but massive intervention by the military and the police was required to stem the resulting unrest.

When the British left, political power—the mother lode of cake—was transferred into the hands of native Nigerians. At this point, ethnic hatreds—new hatreds, not ancient ones—began to grow. Northerners, who had lost out to more-educated southerners during British colonial rule, feared that their subordination would continue when the British departed. But they soon realized they had a crucial trump card: they were more numerous. And so independent Nigeria's first government was dominated by the Northern People's Congress party.

With control of government, the newly empowered Northerners moved to take all the cake for themselves. In an assessment of Nigeria, the World Bank contended that "northern elites feared that they would lose in an unrestricted commercial contest, so they used the state to restrict the operation of market capitalism." In 1962, the government duly drew up a socialist-style six-year development plan that devoted most of the budget to the north, including the monumental Kainjin Dam, roads, railways, defense spending, healthcare, and education.

And this was only the beginning. The northerners set about their task with a racist hatred that was all the more shocking considering its recent vintage. As the architect of the "northernization" policy, Sir Ahmadu Bello, put it,

> The Northernization Policy does not only apply to clerks,
> administrative officers, doctors, and others. We do not want
> to go to Chad [an area in the north] and meet strangers [i.e.,
> southerners] catching our fish in the water, and taking them

away to leave us with nothing. We do not want to go to Sokoto and find a carpenter who is a stranger nailing our houses. I do not want to go to the Sabon-gari Kano and find strangers making the body of a lorry, or to go to the market and see butchers who are not Northerners.

∞

So the political dynamics of ethnic violence had been set in motion, and were about to get much worse. At first, after the departure of the British, the government's relatively meager revenues were generated primarily by international sales of cocoa. But then oil was discovered. The government quickly took control of the industry, and as it grew suddenly and extraordinarily wealthy, it expanded its grasp over the economy. The state moved into manufacturing, finance, and agriculture. It created public companies and bought shares in private-sector firms. Its bureaucracy expanded. This just meant more jobs, more contracts, more loans—in other words, day by day, more cake.

Enter some opportunistic politicians. Soon after independence, a Yoruba political leader named S.L. Akintola seized on ethnic hatred as a way to mobilize his followers. He told Yoruba that an era of Igbo "domination" was fast approaching. After the 1964 elections, the inevitable finally happened. The northerners attempted to fix the election by preventing Igbo politicians from campaigning anywhere but their native southeastern region. Voter intimidation, ballot theft, and the like were widespread. On January 15, 1966, Igbo soldiers from the south launched a coup d'etat. It started in the northern town of Kaduna, where the coup leaders killed the premier of the north, Sir Ahmadu Bello. Then it spread to Lagos, where the prime minister was killed. Twenty-seven political leaders were killed, including the premier of the west and many officers of northern origin, and the southerners were in power.

The northerners fought back, unleashing a wave of violence against Igbo living in their midst. Throughout cities in the north, Igbo were killed, raped, and maimed, and their property destroyed. Then came the counter-coup, known as the "return match." On July 29, 1966 northern officers deposed the government and seized power for themselves. Now that they were in control, the northerners inflicted even more vengeance on the Igbo. In the fall of 1966, more than 50,000 Igbo were killed and two million fled home to the south.

So the Igbo attempted to leave Nigeria. In 1967, they seceded from the country and declared the independent state of Biafra. The new government of Biafra expelled northerners from their newly created country. The northern-controlled federal government attacked the secessionist state (not least because Biafra was home to much of the country's oil wealth). The government predicted that the war would last only a few hours. But it lasted thirty brutal months—from June 1967 to January 1970. In the end, the secessionist Igbo were defeated. An estimated million lives were lost.

∞

All this may have sated the desire of many Nigerians for violence. But this political dynamic, of cake and ethnic consciousness, did not disappear. Rather, it moved underground, where it would fundamentally pervert the character of the Nigerian state.

One example is the Nigerian government's bizarre self-deconstruction. Every state and local government, of course, controls a small cake supply—public jobs and public funds—of its own. So when a smaller ethnic group finds itself a minority in a state dominated by a larger ethnic group, it may be excluded from the loot. But if the smaller group can get its own state, the problem is solved. This applied in the case of the Wawa, which is a dialect of Igbo. To Wawa speakers, it seemed that other Igbo always got a better deal. Thus an opportunity for ambitious Wawa politicians, who began to tell their constituencies that they were not getting their fair share of the cake. They began to analyze every ministry, every company, every educational institution, and every neighborhood to see if Wawa were fairly represented. And when they found that the Wawa were woefully underrepresented, they cried foul. After years of rabble rousing, the Wawa leaders were granted their own state in 1991. This pattern has been repeated all over the country. In the process, Nigeria has gone from two regions, to three regions, to four regions, to twelve states, to nineteen states, to twenty-one, to thirty, and finally to the thirty-six states that exist today.

These dynamics perverted the most well-intentioned policy initiatives. In the 1980s, the federal government, along with international multilateral institutions such as the World Bank, began to pour money into Nigerian agriculture. This made land much more valuable. Soon, rival ethnic groups in the border area between Gongola State and Benue State—who had historically coexisted peacefully—began to fight over the newly valuable farmland. The struggle spilled over into violence between November 1991 and March 1992. In the 1980s, foreign and domestic companies such as Lever Brothers, the Savannah Sugar Company, and the Nigerian Beverages Company started buying land in the Mambilla Plateau. Land prices went up, and people started killing each other. In 1990, a land dispute cost more than 100 lives among the Tiv and Jukun peoples. Property valued in the millions was destroyed. The dispute between the Jukuns and Tivs has resurfaced many times, including in 2001, in a clash that claimed 200 lives.

When political power is seen only as a means to get a slice of cake, corruption reaches staggering heights, nothing is built, and everything is plundered. In the fight over cake, any means are justified, including outright theft. Nigeria is vast and possesses tremendous natural resources. Yet unemployment is high and crime, disease, and infant mortality have all skyrocketed. Infrastructure is crumbling; electricity, water, post, and telecommunications are all unreliable; social services are often nonexistent. Today, with a per capita income of only $290 pear year, Nigeria is one of the twenty poorest countries in the world.

∞

This dysfunctional political dynamic has ensnared foreign investors. Oil companies such as ChevronTexaco, Mobil, and Shell are big players in Nigeria. Obviously, these firms would like nothing more than to stay out of the ethnic conflict, but, as investigative reporting by Norimitsu Onishi of the *New York Times* revealed, these companies have been made unwitting participants in Nigeria's dysfunctional kimchi.

Nigeria's oil is located in the Niger Delta, which is in the south, now populated mostly by Christian ethnic minorities. The southerners feel the oil is theirs, and indeed, tried to take it for themselves by declaring the independent state of Biafra in 1967. But since suppressing the secession, leaders hailing from the north have maintained a tight grip on the territory, keeping the Niger Delta underdeveloped in an effort to prevent any further secession attempts.

Foreign oil companies have traditionally entered into joint venture agreements with Nigeria's federal government—40 percent to the oil companies, 60 percent to the government. Little of the government's share—in total $275 billion from the 1960s up to the installation of democracy in 1999—has reached the Delta region. An estimated $50 billion was simply embezzled and shipped overseas. At the same time, the Delta's 7 million citizens live in appalling conditions—mud shacks, no telephones, unreliable electricity, no indoor plumbing, poor schools, limited health care. Citizens of the Delta frequently kidnap oil workers, sabotage pipelines, and raid oil company facilities. In some cases, foreign oil workers have been killed. At one point, militants shut down half of the country's oil production. The result is that oil service companies pay workers relocating to Nigeria the highest premium in the world. As one ethnic leader put it, "The development of the people is the responsibility of the federal government. We are angry at the government too. But we are angrier at Shell, because Shell is here."

On one level, the oil companies have been drawn into providing the services that Nigeria's dysfunctional government does not. As Kingdom Dateme, leader of a Delta town, put it, "Our government cannot assist us for anything. So in effect, we now make all our demands on Chevron." In July 2002, a group of Delta women staged a raid on ChevronTexaco's main facility, taking over docks, airstrips, office buildings, and residences. For ten days they held the oil workers hostage. The siege ended when ChevronTexaco agreed to a long list of demands, which included supplying water and electricity to the nearby community; building schools, a community center, and homes for tribal leaders; assisting women in setting up fish and poultry farms; and constructing a new village to replace the one that will be destroyed because of rising water levels. All told, Royal Dutch Shell, which accounts for about half of the 2.2 million barrels per day pumped in Nigeria, spends an estimated $53 million per year on social development projects in the Niger Delta.

But this is more than simply a difficult business environment. Nigeria's political dynamics have implicated the foreign oil firms in the country's dysfunction. In 1998, the Nigerian military used a Chevron helicopter to remove environmental activists who had occupied an off-shore oil rig. Two people were killed in the process, and Chevron now faces a U.S.-filed lawsuit.

Even more dramatically, Royal Dutch Shell's involvement in Nigeria has actually transformed the company. In 1995, the military government of Nigeria executed Niger Delta writer and activist Ken Saro Wiwa, whose crime was to demand that Shell compensate his Ogoni people for the oil they were pumping from Ogoni land. This event came right after a controversy in another part of the world, where Shell was being castigated over its attempts to dispose of the North Sea Brent Spar oil rig. A boycott by German consumers caused sales in that country to fall by 30 percent.

Shell Oil is no wilting violet. It is a $190 billion oil conglomerate with 1,700 subsidiaries, 91,000 employees, operations in 135 countries, and 20 million daily customers. The company can afford to operate in difficult business environments. But the death of Ken Saro Wiwa was something else entirely. This implicated the company in an execution. In this era of global media coverage that publicizes events in even the most distant regions, the death of this single man was a tremendous shock to Shell. Indeed, the intensity of Shell's response suggests that corporate leaders were not merely concerned about protecting their billions of dollars of brand value, but about the moral compromises that operating in Nigeria had forced upon them.

Shell launched a massive, transnational public relations campaign. Shell took out ads in *Time, Newsweek*, the *Economist*, and the *Financial Times* pledging its commitment to the environment and human rights and expressing regret over Saro Wiwa's death. It held public forums allowing its critics to air their complaints. It launched a "Tell Shell" campaign via the Internet, encouraging shareholders and customers to send questions and complaints. Shell then set about to change the way it operates. Executives of Shell's 130 subsidiaries were required to report on their adherence to corporate standards on the environment and human rights. The results are reviewed every year in annual reports the company produces on Shell's adherence to corporate social responsibility.

Family members of Saro Wiwa and other Ogoni activists killed by the Nigerian military are suing Shell in American courts. They are invoking the Alien Tort Claims act, which gives American courts jurisdiction over certain acts committed abroad. The U.S. Supreme Court has given a green light for the case to proceed. As of this writing, lawyers for the Ogoni are interviewing Shell executives as part of the discovery phase of the case.

And the issues underlying the oil company's problems in Nigeria have by no means dissipated. In 1999, the new democratic government of Nigeria razed the town of Odi after its citizens demanded a bigger share of the oil cake. But solved or not, these events have certainly transformed the companies that were caught up in Nigeria's kimchi. Nigeria's ethnic battles again made the headlines not long ago when the country attempted to host the 2002 Miss World pageant. Some Muslims protested the pageant as an affront to religious sensibilities. A Christian journalist responded with an article in the newspaper *ThisDay*, at one point asking, with humorous intent, "What would Muhammad think? In all honesty, he would probably have chosen a wife from among them." This wisecrack sparked riots in the northern town of Kaduna. Muslim youths burned the newspapers, then the newspaper offices, then set out after their Christian neighbors. And the Christians retaliated. In the end, more than 200 were dead, thousands were left homeless, churches and mosques lay in rubble, and the Miss World pageant was relocated to London. As for the journalist, she was forced to flee the country after some officials called for her death.

This kind of thing sounds like another case of "ancient hatred," specifically Muslims versus Christians. But at its heart, the conflict is about ethnic competition. Another bout of religious violence that erupted near the town of Kaduna swept out of control, spreading to Kaduna and the town of Kafanchan. The cause of the conflict was forgotten as Christians burned Muslim homes, killed Muslim-owned cattle, and set out after their Muslim neighbors. Meanwhile, Muslims destroyed Christian churches and businesses. Dozens of lives were lost and property was destroyed. A committee set up to investigate the violence found that the causes were not ancient hatreds, they were economic: "lack of equitable distribution of social amenities in southern Zaria," "domination of economic activities by the Hausa-Fulani groups," "unfair land disposition," "inequitable appointment and posting of villages and district heads," and on and on. In short, most causes cited had to do with struggles over cake.

One might hope these distant problems would not trouble residents of rich, industrialized countries. Especially those who, unlike executives at Shell, are not seeking to operate in the Niger Delta. But the United States, seeking to diversify its oil supplies away from the Middle East, has focused on Nigeria as well as other African producers like Angola and Equatorial Guinea. Nigerian oil is free of sulphur, making it ecologically preferable to other varieties. Africa's share in U.S. oil imports is expected to rise from its current 15 percent to roughly 25 percent in the next decade. But those who believe that the situation in Africa cannot get as bad as that in the Middle East are fooling themselves. If the U.S. is not to give rise to another Middle East, to local hatreds that come to be directed firmly against it, Americans must take great care. The kimchi here is volatile.

THE DYNAMICS OF ETHNIC CONFLICT

Ethnic and religious conflicts, even the most violent, are often neither "intractable" nor "ancient." But what these conflicts lack in vintage is more than made up in the sheer power and inevitability of their political logic.

The first part of this logic is the logic of competition. It is no small thing for ordinary people to attack and maim their neighbors. Rarely do abstract concepts such as racism or historical injustices, or stories learnt in school or told around the dinner table, trigger the kind of concrete hatred that incites a person to violence. (A fact that accounts for the success of many groups in living together after previously fighting bitterly.) A definable injustice must exist. Many people from one ethnic or religious group must feel—simultaneously—that they have been wronged, concretely, by members of another ethnic group.

But just introduce a little competition. There are few things more important and universal than providing for one's family. In poor countries like Nigeria, migrants to unfamiliar cities find that jobs and housing are hopelessly scarce. No job means insufficient food. No house means insufficient protection from the elements. And before one imagines it possible, a child has died. Few injustices are more concrete than that. Now suppose that one lives not far from members of another ethnic group, and these "strangers" have plenty of food for their families.

Suppose that these people have homes, safe and dry, offering protection from malaria-carrying mosquitoes. There is not enough to go around, and they have what the migrant wants: it's no great leap of logic to resent them for this.

It is little wonder, then, that economic competition so often creates ethnic conflict where none previously existed. Susan Olzak unearthed this pattern in statistical research on the turn-of-the-century United States. During this time, immigrant Irish, Italians, and Poles lived side by side, competing fiercely for jobs and struggling to fend off poverty. These newly arrived groups held no "ancient hatreds," but like the Igbo and Hausa in Nigeria, they often set upon each other. Olzak's statistical analysis shows that ethnic violence between these groups was most frequent in cities with the most acute labor market competition. Philadelphia, where competition over jobs and housing was especially intense during the 1880s and 1890s, witnessed a good deal of violence between Italians and Eastern Europeans during that time.

A study comparing black-white relations in the U.S. and Brazil focused on the period after both countries freed their slaves in the late nineteenth century. While Brazil was relatively violence-free, the U.S. experienced bloodshed and lynchings. The difference is explained by the fact that after slavery was abolished in the U.S., black and white small farmers found themselves in frequent competition, but in Brazil, Portuguese plantation owners were not in direct competition with ex-slaves. The Portuguese were in a clearly dominant position. Hence the groups did not come to blows. Studies have found similar patterns among Hindus and Muslims in India. Communal violence is most likely to break out where Muslims and Hindus are competing for the same jobs. (And thus, ironically, communal violence tends to increase when a city's rising prosperity attracts Muslim migrants into Hindu-dominated areas—it is the curse of success.)

Throwing political competition in with economic competition just makes things worse. In Nigeria, the better educated southerners had all the factory jobs, but the more populous northerners had all the political power. A showdown was inevitable. This logic reaches its zenith in the competition over cake. When the government controls all the worthwhile resources—jobs, funds, projects, university spots—economic competition inevitably becomes political conflict. In the extreme, this produces civil war. Even when the conflict is more civilized, it is a recipe for dysfunctional politics.

Just how dysfunctional is shown by the experience of postcolonial black Africa. The colonizers had no intention of creating unworkable states, but the structures they founded made this almost inevitable. These were multiethnic states drawn up arbitrarily by European mapmakers, designed for natural resource extraction, with rich governments and poor people. Even at the abstract level of statistics, the legacy there is astounding. A study by the World Bank found that countries with rich supplies of natural resources—in other words, richer cake—were far more likely to suffer from civil wars than resource-poor countries, because competing groups inevitably battled for political control. A study of postcolonial Africa found that nearly 90 percent of the 45 independent black African states had experienced a military coup, an attempted coup, or a coup plot between 1960 and 1982. Almost all of these cases were driven by competition between ethnic groups for resources linked to political power.

But this logic of competition is not the whole story. Competition can give rise to ethnic struggles where none had existed before, but things really get out of hand with the addition of one more ingredient: the political dynamic of ethnic mobilization.

Consider for a moment the thankless job of a would-be Nigerian politician. The politician wants to rally support, but what does he have? Everyone in his district wants different things. What can the politician say that will appeal across all income levels, age groups, and occupations? As soon as a concrete policy platform is articulated, someone is unhappy. Then our politician has a moment of inspiration. By appealing strictly to ethnicity, he can mobilize everyone, young and old, rich and poor, men and women. There are very few things that any sufficiently large group of people can agree on. But one of them is that "the Igbo are stealing our jobs." Or that "the northerners have too much of the cake." One would wish for restraint on the grounds of morality, but this is too much to ask. If there is any ethnic or religious consciousness, an enterprising politician is likely to attempt to exploit it. It is one of those very few things that bind together people who in reality have nothing in common. This political logic of appeals to ethnicity or religion has unfolded in countries around the world. Serbia, Rwanda, Lebanon—the list of disasters goes on. Relatively prosperous societies are not immune, although there demagogues have less appeal—Pauline Hansen in Australia, Jean-Marie LePen in France, Jorge Haider in Austria.

Scholar Amy Chua noted that this logic is particularly compelling in countries where there are "market-dominant minorities." In these countries, national wealth falls into the hands of a few wealthy businesspeople from one particular ethnic group—the Chinese in Southeast Asia, the Lebanese in West Africa, the whites in Southern Africa and Latin America, and the Jews in postcommunist Russia. This is an extraordinary political opportunity. The vast majority of the people are from other ethnic groups, and they are impoverished while the elites flaunt their wealth. There could hardly be a better target. This circumstance allows opportunistic demagogues to mobilize supporters who would otherwise have little in common, and spur them to often violent political action.

The tragic lesson of the Nigerian case is that these political dynamics of ethnic competition can create terrific hatred where none had previously existed, rapidly and on a tremendous scale. Their recent vintage does not make them any less destructive.

∞

But modern hatreds can have modern cures. One is so-called social capital. Consider India, with its history of bloody ethnic and religious violence. Note that ethnic violence plagues only certain parts of India. The cities of Ahmedabad and Godhra in Gujarat—where much recent violence has occurred—are notorious for religious strife. But in other areas, Hindus and Muslims continue to live together peacefully. Why?

Political scientist Ashutosh Varshney sought to answer this question by studying all Hindu-Muslim riots that occurred in India between 1950 and 1995. He found that eight cities—Ahmedabad, Bombay, Aligarh, Hyderabad, Meerut, Baroda, Calcutta, and Delhi—accounted for nearly 46 percent of all deaths, even though they comprised just 18 percent of India's urban population. Varshney found that the main factor distinguishing these violence-prone cities from their peaceful counterparts was the presence of civil institutions, including businesses, labor unions, professional associations, civic organizations, charities, and the media.

As a stark example, Varshney presented a tale of two cities, one peaceful and one the scene of ghastly violence. Aligarh is located in the north Indian state of Uttar Pradesh; Calicut is located in the south Indian state of Kerala. Both cities have Hindu majorities and Muslim minorities that comprise roughly 36 to 38 percent of the urban population. There the similarities end. Aligarh has been the site of repeated Hindu-Muslim riots; Calicut, by contrast, experienced not one riot in the twentieth century. And Varshney found striking differences in their civil institutions. In Calicut, citizens are organized into business, labor, and professional associations. The town's Lions and Rotary clubs are active, as are the associations of porters and rickshaw-pullers, and film, sports, theater, and reading clubs. These civic institutions bring people into constant contact with each other, and membership cuts across religious and ethnic lines. As a result, Hindus and Muslims had frequent personal interactions. Nearly 83 percent of those surveyed by Varshney reported a recent experience of dining with a person or persons of a different religion; 84 percent reported regularly meeting people of other religions.

In Aligarh, by contrast, trade associations and civic groups are few. As a result, people are more isolated. Only 54 percent of Hindus and Muslims reported regularly socializing with members of other religions. Instead, their main experience of other ethnic groups was as competitors for jobs and housing. Indeed, two of Aligarh's strongest civic groups were the "Hindu protection committee" and the "Muslim protection committee."

In short, because of well-developed civic institutions, Calicut's Hindu and Muslim populations knew each other, associated with each other, and even depended on each other. They had an interest in preserving the status quo and preventing their society from being ripped apart by communal rioting. Politicians in Calicut calculated that trying to polarize the two communities would only lose them votes. Following recent communal violence elsewhere in India, Calicut's citizens organized grassroots peace committees that coordinated law and order efforts between the city administration and neighborhoods. The peace committees squelched rumors and allowed citizens to air their grievances and concerns. Aligarh, on the other hand, erupted once again into violence.

CHAPTER THREE

Neon Allah

SOCIAL CHANGE

MODERNIZATION BRINGS TREMENDOUS BENEFITS. EDUCATION, improved health care, plumbing, soap operas, cell phones. Not to mention guns and industry, the tools of national power. Who could turn it down? Today the countries that, as a matter of deliberate national policy, actively resist modernization, can be counted on one's fingers—indeed only reclusive Bhutan springs to mind.

Yet modernization is fundamentally destructive. Modernization demolishes social orders that have existed for hundreds if not thousands of years. This gives rise to phenomenal social stresses, such as when residents of rural communities, their ways of life having scarcely changed for millennia, migrate to cities where they must cope with internal combustion engines and tenement housing. Normally such processes form part of the scenery before which political dramas are played out. The social stresses remain hidden, although they may be uncovered in statistical indicators: rising alcoholism in Russia following the transition to capitalism, dramatically higher suicide rates in Japan as bankruptcies and redundancies replace stability and lifetime employment. But every so often, not content with a supporting role, social change steals the show. The thousands of tiny dramas that make up each statistic suddenly become a political movement. Instead of drinking, instead of killing themselves, people take to the streets.

Or to the churches. Such is the case of the rise of political Islam, which was driven, in part, by drastic social change.

EGYPT

When Gamal Abdul Nasser and his fellow military officers overthrew a British-allied monarch and seized power in Egypt in 1952, they fully intended to transform Egyptian society—and they succeeded. Their policies unleashed a social transformation of tremendous speed and scale. But the universal law of unintended consequences applies: the grander and bolder the scheme, the more likely that its results will be both extraordinary and completely unexpected.

Nasser's grand plan was a secular socialist revolution, erasing the legacy of colonialism and feudalism. For the first time since the days of the Pharaohs, Egypt was ruled by Egyptians. Nasser planned to modernize his country, catapulting a backward, north African state suddenly and dramatically into the ranks of the great powers. The core of his government's policy was a bold land reform program, giving peasants title to their land and at a stroke dismantling the country's feudal structure.

Enter the unintended consequences. The land reform reduced farmers' holdings to tiny tracts that were unprofitable to cultivate and could not support large peasant families. At the same time, rising subsoil water made the land far less fertile. The result was a migration, not of opportunity but of necessity, by peasants fleeing en masse from land that could no longer sustain them. This was urbanization at a catastrophic pace and scale, turning towns into mega-cities in a matter of decades. Cairo shot from a population of 2 million to 18 million.

Thus Nasser unleashed a far-reaching social transformation—and not the one he had intended. By the thousands, Egyptian peasants accustomed to living in tiny villages where most neighbors were relatives were thrown into vast slums with people from across the country. Young couples began to move to distant suburbs of Cairo, putting enormous strains on extended families. Agricultural jobs that had been unchanged for generations were suddenly replaced by unfamiliar factory labor or construction work. The new peasant shantytowns in Cairo, such as the sprawling Imbaba, were slums with open sewers and staggering overcrowding. Even those lucky enough to get an education saw their hopes of advancement dashed. Millions of Egyptians benefited from Nasser's socialist education system. In 1952, only 42,485 Egyptians were

attending institutions of higher education; by 1977, that number had
grown to 500,000. Within a generation, Nasser had produced scores of
new doctors, engineers, and lawyers, whom he lauded as leaders of a resurgent Arab nation. But the job market could not provide employment
to match their qualifications. A glut of professionals and a dearth of jobs
left engineers driving taxis and lawyers working as electricians. In 1991,
the average engineer earned 336 Egyptian pounds per month, doctors 332
pounds, and lawyers 292 pounds—all less than $100.

Perhaps the most profound social change in Egypt was in the status of
women. Rent controls fed a housing shortage in Cairo; making the rent
on an apartment became a monumental struggle for most Egyptians. A
lower-middle class family simply could not afford to buy items such as
a refrigerator, television, or a car on the husband's salary alone. Wives
often had no choice but to work.

This was not what the women wanted. The traditional Egyptian ideal
for womanhood is the *sitt-al-bayt*, the housewife whose responsibilities
center on child rearing, cooking, and running the household. Many
Egyptians believe further that Islam designates the home as the woman's
realm, out of the sight of unfamiliar men and protected by her male family
members. Women who leave the home are in this view morally unfit, and
sure to bring about the rapid degeneration of their households. Unlike
in the U.S. or Europe, Egyptian women did not eagerly leave the home
to take advantage of new opportunities. Rather, Egyptian women were
forced out by economic desperation. Only 8 percent of Egyptian women
say that working outside the home is acceptable or proper according
to Islam. But they have little alternative. So women entered the world
outside the home in a culture where, even today, women seen walking
alone are thought of as immoral and fair targets for harassment.

∞

The working-class section of Imbaba is home to millions of Egyptians
whose lives have been upended by their country's epic social transformation—long-time Cairenes who can no longer afford to live in central
neighborhoods; recent migrants from rural Egypt; black-skinned refugees from the Sudan. On the sidewalks such men crouch over huge tarps
hawking parts of transistor radios, bicycles, and hand irons. In the streets

deformed people are a common sight, blind or with clubbed feet, as they cannot afford medical care. The coffee shops overflow with men sipping sugary tea, playing dominoes, smoking water pipes, and speculating endlessly on the Jewish conspiracies and U.S. acts of imperialism that they suppose to be the cause of their problems. There are men in their early thirties with university degrees but who remain so poor that they cannot afford to marry, and therefore remain frustrated virgins. There are older men who grew up on a steady diet of Arab nationalism, only to see their country humiliated by Israel in 1967. There are teenagers, sent from the countryside to make a living in Cairo, where they squeeze into illegally constructed apartment buildings that lack telephone services or running water.

Indeed, some lives have been distorted to the point where they become surreal. In 1992, one notorious section of Imbaba had only open sewers, shantytowns, and hastily built apartments. Indeed it was not recognized by the government; the one million people who lived there and survived on a pittance did not, officially, exist. But then a militant Muslim leader, Sheikh Gaber, declared the foundation of *"El Goomhooriyah Imbaba,"* (the "Republic of Imbaba") and imposed strict Islamic law. Soon Sheikh Gaber and his lieutenant, a national karate champion nicknamed "Hassan Karate," headed a miniature "government" and police force composed entirely of slum residents. One of their favorite pastimes was shooting up wedding parties (music and dancing were strictly prohibited according to their version of Islam). When the (real) Egyptian government finally got wind of this, the situation was already well out of hand. It took a bloody invasion involving 15,000 Egyptian troops to reoccupy the slum and overthrow the upstart "Islamic regime." Sheikh Gaber and most of his fighters were killed. Hassan Karate, however, disavowed extremism, was rehabilitated, and now runs a successful sandwich stand.

∞

In short, for millions of Egyptians, modernization has meant shattering disruptions, new forms of misery, and diminishing opportunities. But for those who have fallen through the cracks, and those bewildered by the pace of change, there has always been one support network willing to take them in: Islam. Islamic movements, with their urban network of mosques, schools, and charitable organizations, have seen their ranks swelled by the millions.

In the decades since Nasser launched his "revolution" of unintended consequences, membership in religious associations has soared. The Muslim Brotherhood—founded in the 1920s—has become a significant national force, despite frequent harassment by the government. Egyptians have flocked to the mosques in droves. Religious literature and audiotapes proliferate in the streets and souks. Student unions and professional syndicates (similar to unions or professional associations) have come to be dominated by Islamists. And, in perhaps the most powerful symbol, Egyptian women have donned the *hijab*, the religious head covering that covers the hair, or, in more extreme cases, the *niqab*—a full-length black garment that conceals all but the eyes. A rare sight in the 1960s, it's common in the new millennium.

For confused Egyptians unable to understand or plot a way out of their dismal situations, Islam provided prescriptions for what had to be done. And for people discouraged that Arab nationalism had failed to build Egypt into a great power, or that socialism had failed to bring prosperity, Islam was the attractive alternative. From the 1960s onward, more and more Egyptians took up the battle cry "Islam is the Solution." In a survey taken by the Cairo Center for Criminal and Social Studies, 90 percent of young people living in Imbaba said that Islam would solve their problems, ranging from open sewers to the housing shortage.

Islam also explained who was to blame for the Egyptians' suffering: the secular government of Egypt, which had allied itself with Western powers; Egypt's nouveau riche, who had adopted immoral consumerist attitudes and overtly sexual Western styles of dress; and of course Israel, Egypt's perennial enemy.

It was not long before Egypt's Islamist movement turned violent in its quest to punish those blamed for the people's suffering. Militant Islamists gunned down Egyptian President Anwar al-Sadat in 1981. Many militants went to Afghanistan to join the holy war against the Soviets. When they returned, they led an all-out insurrection against the Egyptian state. More than 1,200 lives have been lost in the conflict, Egyptian President Hosni Mubarak was nearly assassinated, and cabinet ministers have been shot. Militants have also terrorized Egypt's Coptic Christian minority, who make up an estimated 10 percent of the population.

∞

This political dynamic has ensnared foreigners venturing into the country. The principal terror group, the Gamaa al-Islamiya, announced, "Anyone who helps a regime that is opposing Islam should receive the same punishment as the oppressors." Under this logic, they set out after the tourist industry, starting in the fall of 1992. With every terrorist attack, tourism declined. An assault on a tour bus in Cairo's old Christian quarter that left eight Australians dead caused a two-year decline in tourism. Just as the industry was recovering, militants gunned down seventeen Greeks and then nine Germans, and there was a 20 percent falloff in tourist business. Then the Luxor Massacre, which left fifty-eight tourists dead—mostly Japanese, German, and Swiss—cost the country about $1 billion in tourist revenue.

These were not the only foreigners targeted. Religious leaders have encouraged Egyptians to boycott foreign products and retailers, such as British supermarket chain Sainsbury's, for alleged anti-Islamism or collusion with Israel. Sainsbury's ended up leaving Egypt in 2001. Religious leaders have helped fan rumors that "Coca Cola," when held to a mirror, allegedly reads "No to Allah, No to Muhammad," and that "Pepsi" stands for "Pay Every Penny to Save Israel." It was an Egyptian spiritual leader, Sheikh Omar Abdul Rahman, who orchestrated the attack on the World Trade Center in 1993, and two Egyptians, Ayman al-Zawahiri and Mohammad Atef, who rose to the top ranks of Usama bin Laden's al-Qaeda network.

Nasser achieved a social transformation, but not the one he wanted. His policies led to an Islamic Egypt, not the secular, socialist, and modern Egypt he had envisioned. Nasser's successors have presided over a thorough Islamization of the country. State TV runs frequent religious programming, and the government bans books and movies not approved by Islamic clergy. Islam has even affected economic policymaking—the insurance and mortgage industries have both been blocked because they offend religious sensibilities.

And atop the headquarters of the National Democratic Party—the party that launched Nasser's secular revolution—sits a prominent neon green sign reading, "Allah."

THE DYNAMICS OF SOCIAL CHANGE

Modernity and tradition; neon and Allah. Their relationship is not necessarily a happy one.

The dynamic of social change in Egypt illustrates the importance of kimchi. Social change is subtle, even hidden, to the point that it often goes unnoticed. Social change is also an inevitable counterpart to the modernization brought on by economic globalization. And yet social change can give rise to political dynamics with entirely unexpected and unintended consequences.

This is basic human psychology. It is human nature to identify oneself with persons, groups, symbols, values, and institutions in one's environment. When any of these are maligned, that injury is transferred to those who identify with it. Events that diminish the prestige of one's alma mater, for instance, diminish one's own prestige, causing a person to become hurt and upset.

Inevitably, social change displaces or defiles institutions, values, and symbols with which people identify. The Egyptian peasants living in the slums of Cairo had identified the dutiful stay-at-home wife as a sign of virtue. But economic necessities forced them to act against their most profound values. Similarly, bonds of family loyalty and duty were broken by the need to work in factory jobs or live in distant suburbs. People broke these bonds and turned their backs on their extended families because, practically, they had no choice. But they were not happy about doing so. In 1949, the great social theorist Karl Polanyi identified this process at work in the Industrial Revolution in seventeenth and eighteenth century England. He argued that discontent among laborers was not driven by a perception that they were being exploited, but rather, by the wrenching social change to which they were subjected, which forced them to act against their cherished cultural values.

In many cases the outcome of these psychological injuries is anger and confusion. Millions of Egyptian peasant farmers were uprooted from their traditional ways of earning a living. Millions of Egyptians were educated and promised great things, then found themselves driving taxicabs. Millions of Egyptians were told they should identify with their nation and then saw that nation humiliated on the battlefield and forced to ally with sworn enemies. All of these changes have proven to be profoundly disorienting and debilitating.

The extreme case of this scenario has been dubbed a "sense-making crisis." At some point, change is so abrupt that people literally have trouble making sense of the world around them. At the same time, values and institutions with which they identify are discarded or defiled. The result is profound psychological stress. This helps to explain a critical truth about popular discontent. Angry and confused people are very susceptible to any ideology or leader who can explain their misery and how to overcome it. The rise of political Islam in Egypt is one example of this. Organized religion not only provides a support network that replaces lost community and family ties and comforts distressed people, it also explains what these distressed people should do to address their problems (pray, don veils, attend services), and it often explains who is to blame for their suffering (the West or Israel or immoral government officials). Religion provides these comforting explanations with a certainty that can only be found in holy writ.

Social change and its accompanying distress occur in almost every country. Urbanization and industrialization are worldwide phenomena. But in cases where the social disruption is extremely rapid and far-reaching, as in Egypt, and not compensated by rising wealth, social change can produce powerful political dynamics.

But will it result in instability? In Egypt, this has been limited. The Islamic guerrillas are for the time being under control. (Although, as shown by Afghanistan's formerly U.S.-funded "freedom fighters," Pakistan's uncontrollable Kashmiri jihadis, and Saudi Arabia's fundamentalist Wahhabi clerics, political Islam is a genie not easily bottled.) To produce instability, the dynamic of social change may need only a small further push.

CHAPTER FOUR

"They Transform Themselves into Tigers"

THE J-CURVE

SOMETIMES A COUNTRY'S POLITICS GOES SPECTACULARLY AND horrifically wrong. Millions of citizens take to the streets and violently attack their rulers and each other. Property is destroyed on a massive scale. Economic activity ceases. Organized political activity is overwhelmed by mob violence. The government—sometimes even the entire political system—collapses in on itself.

Of course, dramatic leadership struggles do not necessarily bring people onto the streets. The fall of a government in Italy is hardly noticed. The most recent military coup in Pakistan took place almost without bloodshed. Assassinations, riots, and even military takeovers occur with regularity around the world. But incidents of mass political upheaval are—fortunately—quite rare.

Yet, surprisingly, these incidents tend to occur in countries whose prospects had—until that moment—seemed the brightest. Iran in the late 1970s was an emerging market with a promising future, a favored destination for U.S. investment. The same was true of Indonesia in the late 1990s. Yet both countries subsequently succumbed to extreme political chaos. A kimchi dynamic is at work here. In the phenomenon of rapid economic success hide the seeds of catastrophic political failure. Consider the case of Indonesia.

INDONESIA

Not long ago, Indonesia was considered a stable "sure thing" for foreign investors seeking dazzling returns. In those days, foreigners had certain notions about Indonesians. They considered them soft-spoken, docile, and industrious. Even their religion was described as "tropical Islam," far more moderate and tolerant than its Middle Eastern counterpart. The foreign businesses that employed cheap Indonesian labor were charmed by their workers. Risk premiums in markets for sovereign bonds in July 1997 declared to the world that Indonesia was less risky than, for instance, the Czech Republic.

How naïve those notions now look. Over the following months and years, the "meek" Indonesians have been responsible for an ongoing stream of bloodletting—from the rape and murder of ethnic Chinese to the bloody separatist struggle of East Timor to the bombing of a Bali nightclub by homegrown Islamic militants. Risk premiums on Indonesian debt increased by 400 percent, vastly higher than the Czech Republic and most of the rest of emerging Europe. Meanwhile, foreign investors left the country, complaining that their docile and industrious workers had suddenly become unruly and unproductive. Indonesia today is a lesson in the dangers of cultural stereotyping and the power of popular discontent.

∞

Back in 1965, a gambler wanting to bet against Indonesia would have had little trouble finding someone to accept his wager. This was an artificial patchwork nation of more than 6,000 inhabited islands and hundreds of languages and ethnic groups, improbably cobbled together by Dutch colonial ambitions. The Dutch, fixated on their canals, had built them even here, where the stagnant ditches promptly clogged and became breeding grounds for malaria-carrying mosquitoes. President Sukarno, the first postcolonial leader, had appointed himself president for life. Declaring, "I am not an economist...I am a revolutionary," he proved this by driving the economy to hyperinflation and nationalizing the valuable foreign investments. His disastrous policies soon engineered a breakdown in law and order. Rioters took to the streets in an orgy of looting and ethnic violence.

This being the 1960s, the communists were quick to arrive, followed closely by Americans hoping to get rid of them. The United States latched onto a man named General Suharto, who had fought in the Japanese colonial army during World War II. Toward the end of the war, he joined a rebellion against the Japanese. After the war, he fought against the Dutch, who had returned to retake their former colony. He was also anticommunist. Good enough. With U.S. backing, Suharto seized power from Sukarno in the spring of 1966. He then set out to crush what was, at the time, the world's third largest Communist Party after those of Russia and China. Sukarno was deposed, an estimated 500,000 Indonesians were killed, and bodies floated in those Dutch-built canals.

Suharto called his political movement the "New Order," and indeed it was. Sukarno had been a populist, a dazzling orator oozing charisma from every pore, a believer in Indonesia's "nonaligned" status during the Cold War. General Suharto, by contrast, had no time for ideologies. He allied his country with United States, stiffly read out his speeches, and affected the persona of a traditional Javanese king—detached and seemingly above the fray. He embarked on the radical market-oriented reform plan recommended by his advisors, American-trained technocrats nicknamed "The Berkeley Mafia" for their University of California degrees. They stabilized the currency, privatized state-owned industries, returned nationalized businesses to their owners, and successfully courted foreign investment in the country's vast natural resources.

Indonesia's fortunes soared. In return for Suharto's allegiance, the U.S., along with Japan and Western Europe, pumped money into the country's economy. Indonesia joined OPEC, benefiting handsomely from the oil price hikes of the 1970s. The country was soon a dazzling "emerging market." Western banks and mutual funds poured capital into Indonesia's stock exchange, bonds, and banks. Foreign investors, eager to take advantage of cheap labor and a welcoming business climate, built factories in Indonesia to make textiles, footwear, toys, and furniture. Jakarta became a destination for an emerging class of global businessman and investors.

No big success story is without its smaller failures. Suharto was intolerant of political opposition. The parliament was a rubber stamp, the army and police were used to beat down separatist activity and political Islam, and most "opposition" leaders were actually appointed by the government. Suharto ruled not only through fear but also through patronage. Suharto's wife, Tien, earned the nickname "Madame Tien Per Cent" for her habit of taking cuts of big projects. Suharto's three sons and three daughters had their hands in everything from petrochemicals to airlines to fisheries to an ill-fated scheme to build a national car. Alarming inequalities in wealth began to form along ethnic lines. Suharto cultivated Indonesia's ethnic Chinese business class, which made up four percent of the population but came to control an estimated 60 percent of the country's wealth.

Still, Indonesia's boom was no mirage. Between 1970 and 1996, the economy grew by an average of 7 percent per year. Per capita income rose from less than $100 in 1970 to around $900 in 1996. With the boom came improved living standards. The percentage of poor people in the country declined from 60 percent of the population at the beginning of Suharto's rule to 10 percent in 1996. In 1975, there were 87.2 million people living in poverty. By 1985, that number had fallen to 52.8 million, and by 1995 to 21.9 million.

It was one of the most rapid reductions of poverty in history. Fishermen and subsistence farmers became upwardly mobile. Millions flocked to the cities, where employment in manufacturing plants boomed. Over the course of Suharto's rule, primary schooling became virtually universal in Indonesia, with the poor just as likely to attend school as the rich. In 1975, only 11 percent of Indonesians had access to safe water. By 1996, that had increased to 62 percent. Life expectancy jumped from 49 years to 65. Millions of Indonesians saw their lives materially enhanced.

And along with this economic boom came remarkable political stability. Although Suharto's Golkar Party retained a virtual monopoly on political power and the president and his family remained above the law, opposition to the regime was negligible. For three decades, Suharto maintained political stability on an archipelago rife with religious and ethnic divisions.

Then, with unexpected viciousness, Indonesia's boom came to a catastrophic and bloody end.

∞

The proximate cause was the 1997 exchange rate crisis in Thailand. Financial contagion spread and both foreign and local capital fled the country en masse, causing the collapse of the currency and the stock market and triggering bank failures. Teams of economists-cum-bureaucrats from the International Monetary Fund arrived in the Indonesian capital. They delivered to General Suharto a list of humiliating demands, telling him that his government could only qualify for the loans it needed to stave off a financial crisis by agreeing to a series of painful economic reforms.

The IMF economists—some would later admit—were advised by Indonesians who saw their country's economic crisis as a golden opportunity to clean out the corruption built up in three decades of Suharto's crony-capitalist administration. Among the IMF's demands: that Suharto overhaul state-owned banks, including banks owned by regional governments; that he immediately halt major infrastructure projects; and that he dismantle state-sponsored cartels that controlled key domestic industries. These demands were not chosen at random. The IMF took aim at policies that disproportionately benefited Indonesia's political and business elites. The state-owned banks lent easily and excessively to the well connected (with little concern about being repaid). The government-backed cartels allowed influential businesspeople to reap extraordinary profits without fear of competition. The huge infrastructure projects provided lucrative contracts and kickbacks that enriched Suharto's political allies.

President Suharto likely understood what the IMF was up to. He also probably understood that his policies were damaging Indonesia's economy. The state banks had run up $90 billion in bad loans lending to friends of the government. Many of the infrastructure projects had been wasteful or unnecessary. And the cartels drove up prices and limited competition in key domestic industries. But—and even today these assertions remain controversial—fixing these structural problems, while good for Indonesia, may not have eased the country's financial difficulties. More importantly, these policies were how Suharto kept himself in power. He handed perks to Indonesia's richest citizens for a reason—he relied on their support to hold the country together. For three decades, Suharto maintained political stability by employing a combination of generous patronage and brutal repression. And the IMF, in effect, ordered him to dismantle this political system.

Suharto refused the IMF conditions, making tepid commitments and reneging on most of them. The IMF complained loudly and refused to disburse the loans. The crisis quickly spread from financial markets to the real economy. The precipitous decline of the currency (the ruppiah) sent prices soaring and real wages into free fall. In the six months before the crisis, the ruppiah traded around 2,400 to the dollar, and the Consumer Price Index, measuring the prices of food, housing, clothing, and healthcare, was stable. In July 1997, the ruppiah crashed, losing 20 percent of its value—trading at 3,035 to the dollar. For the next six months, the currency depreciated steadily. Then, on January 8, 1998, the ruppiah plunged to 16,000 to the dollar, and the price of food rose as much in the month of January as it had the previous six months.

This economic meltdown had a staggering impact on Indonesia's poor. The cost of living for the most impoverished urban households increased by an average of 128 percent between January 1997 and October 1998. For the rural poor, the cost of living rose by 136 percent over the same time period. Urban workers saw their real wages fall substantially. In 1997, the real wage was nearly 700 ruppiah per hour; by 1998, the wage had fallen to less than 500 ruppiah per hour. The central bank was forced to hike interest rates in response to the crisis. With declining access to capital, businesses shed workers. The plants that had served as a magnet for workers from the countryside embarked on massive layoffs. It is estimated that 50 percent of the pre-crisis workforce was affected. The construction sector saw 75 percent of its pre-crisis workforce lost. A running joke that the construction crane was Indonesia's national bird turned to mockery, as half-finished skyscrapers dotted the Jakarta skyline.

On the ground, Indonesians suffered mightily. The number of beggars on the streets of Jakarta surged. In rural areas, people scavenged for roots. The poor began to cut back from three meals per day to two. Expectations were shattered. One statistic is especially telling. The Asian Development Bank estimates that, as a result of the crisis, 6.1 million children were pulled out of school to help their families earn money. As peoples' concerns turned to day-to-day living, dreams of future wealth evaporated.

∞

It did not take long for collective shock and dashed expectations to turn to rage. Indonesians soon had targets for their anger: other ethnic groups, and the Suharto regime. In the wake of the crisis, ordinary Indonesians—farmers, factory workers, students, and shopkeepers—became capable of extraordinary savagery. Muslims rampaged against the mostly Christian Chinese minority in May 1998, killing at least 1,100 people. Student protests triggered a three-day orgy of violence and destruction that left 500 dead and thousands of buildings leveled. No one was more surprised by this transformation than the Indonesians themselves. Amien Rais, a key figure in the opposition to Suharto who would later became speaker of the upper house of parliament, said of his countrymen: "They look friendly, they look innocent, they look patient, but all of a sudden they transform themselves into tigers and do very destructive things."

Popular unrest eventually undid the Suharto regime. A series of protests came to a head on May 20, the "Day of National Awakening," which recalls the founding of the nationalist movement against Dutch rule. Some 30,000 students converged on the parliament building, waving banners and singing songs of "reformasi." The tipping point may have come when the speaker of the house, once one of Suharto's closest allies, called for his resignation. Seeing the writing on the wall, Indonesia's top general, its vice president, and half Suharto's cabinet followed suit. The next day, Suharto went on TV from the royal palace and resigned. True to Indonesian form, the resignation was brief and understated. Suharto apologized for his "shortcomings"; his successor, Vice President B.J. Habibie, was sworn in, and the commander of the armed forces pledged his support to the new regime. In a matter of weeks, a leader who had maintained a vise-like grip on power for thirty years was unceremoniously deposed.

∞

Foreign investors who had been intimate participants in Indonesia's boom also shared in its collapse. Some fled for the exits. Sony yanked its audio plant from West Java and relocated to Malaysia. Matsushita traded in Indonesia for Vietnam as its favored plant location. More than thirty Korean firms closed their facilities in Indonesia, leaving 30,000 Indonesians unemployed.

Many firms in the labor-intensive industries that had helped fuel the Indonesian miracle left for other low-cost destinations. Ironically, countries now seen as more stable than Indonesia included China, Vietnam, and even Myanmar (Burma). A third of the 300 shoe manufacturers located in Indonesia left in the three years prior to 2002. Nike and Reebok both cut loose thousands of workers. Whereas 38 percent of Nike shoes were once made in Indonesia, only 26 percent are now. Payless Shoe Source has cut its Indonesian orders in favor of other Southeast Asian producers. Ikea has begun buying from Vietnam. Procter and Gamble, while still selling in Indonesia, bases its manufacturing for the region in Thailand.

Perhaps most notably, the crisis caught up several energy companies, including Enron, GE, and MidAmerican, giving rise to the largest political risk insurance claims in history. In the wake of the crisis, Indonesia's state-owned energy distributor refused to pay negotiated prices for the power generated by the foreign-owned plants. Many of the resulting losses were insured. In fact, the Indonesian crisis led to the first claim payment in its history by MIGA, the Multilateral Investment Guarantee Agency, the political risk insurance arm of the World Bank. (Previously, the World Bank had always been able to pressure countries and investors into settling their disputes amicably.) All told, MIGA and OPIC, the U.S. Overseas Private Investment Corporation, paid out $290 million in insurance claims.

Indonesia has the chance to recover, to adopt a better and more sustainable kimchi dynamic, but doing so will not be easy. Protesters brought down Suharto's replacement, B.J. Habibie, in 1999. He yielded power to a government led by Abdurrahman Wahid, who failed to restore order and was himself impeached. Wahid was replaced by his vice president, Megawati Sukarnoputri, whose chief qualification was that she was the daughter of Sukarno. The former Portuguese colony of East Timor, which Indonesia invaded in 1975 and eventually annexed, seized on the chaos to make a push for independence. In 1999, the mostly Roman Catholic Timorese voted for independence in a U.N.-backed referendum, and in 2002, the independent country of East Timor came into being. (But not before a bloody battle with pro-Indonesian militias that left 1,000 dead, 250,000 displaced, and Indonesian General Wiranto indicted by the U.N. for crimes against humanity.) Meanwhile, Irian Jaya, Aceh, Ambon, and Kalimantan have provided grisly scenes of Muslims killing Christians, Christians killing Muslims, and Indonesia's military either complicit in the violence or helpless to stem it. Militant Islam even reared its ugly head, most tragically in the October 2002 bombing in Bali, which killed nearly 200.

None of this means that Indonesia is a hopeless case. The country's fledgling democracy has, at least, held together. But in its sudden instability, and collapse of central control, Indonesia powerfully illustrated the kimchi dynamics of popular discontent.

THE DYNAMICS OF THE J-CURVE

The Indonesian students who challenged Suharto were not, by and large, trained insurgents. The rioters who killed hundreds of ethnic Chinese were not career criminals. They were ordinary students and farmers and factory workers. Yet they were willing to do the nearly unthinkable: risk their lives, and take the lives of others, for political ends.

Political uprisings require coordinated action by thousands of people. What can generate such mass rage that private citizens by the thousands are suddenly and simultaneously pushed to a breaking point, ready to stand up to the government thugs, water cannons, trigger-happy police, and all the other formidable instruments of repression that governments can muster?

Of course, no mass political movement has a single cause. This is easy to forget when thousands of rioters take to the streets, seemingly set on a single goal—but in reality, each person has his own motivations. As David Gilmour, describing the causes of the Indian Mutiny against British colonial rule, wrote: "…while one man may rebel on account of the cartridges, another may join him for the prospect of loot, a third may support them because of a grudge against an officer, and a fourth may fight because he resents the annexation of Oudh."

So it was in Indonesia. One thing that made the Indonesian situation so volatile was the fact that so many sources of discontent were present in the country: rapid social change, resulting from extraordinary economic growth; severe corruption, including outright embezzlement by the Suharto regime; and ethnic conflicts, as an ethnic Chinese business class, making up only 4 percent of the population, came to control a majority of the country's wealth. All of these factors, mixed together with the odd personal grudge or criminal urge, helped motivate a mass uprising.

But what takes all of these disparate individual motivations and sources of anger and brings them together in collective political action?

One answer is the rather innocuous-sounding "J-curve effect," which was originated by political scientist James Davies. Examine the graph below, which charts Indonesia's economic performance over time. With a little imagination, one can see the chart describe an inverted "J," especially in the pattern of growth from 1988 to 1998.

Indonesia's Gross Domestic Product
Billions of U.S. Dollars

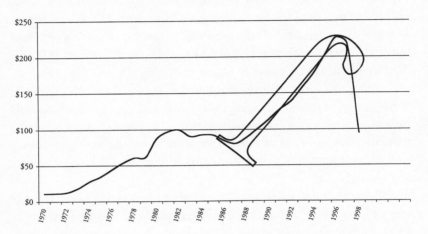

If a country has always been poor, this poverty is not necessarily destabilizing. Citizens are likely to perceive their lot as fated—people in Cuba and North Korea have never expected that they would become rich, at least not any time soon, and are less likely to become disappointed when they remain poor. Indonesia, however, experienced years of economic growth and increasing prosperity. Expectations were on the rise. Even ordinary farmers and factory workers began to formulate hopes and dreams based on economic betterment. True, rising growth increased economic inequality. But ordinary people understood that, while others were getting richer faster than they were, they could point to real improvements in their own well being and their own chances for becoming more prosperous were increasing. Relatively little attention was paid to widening inequalities; eventually, everyone would benefit.

Then, suddenly, people accustomed to becoming steadily better off found themselves stricken by poverty. This was profoundly traumatizing. After years of witnessing their society's rising prosperity, people began to hope that they—or their children—would eventually get rich. Then when the crash came, those hopes were shattered, and lives based on the promise of continued growth were altered dramatically.

The J-curve is also called the "revolution of falling expectations." A gap opens up between inflated expectations and a shockingly dismal reality. When a national economy collapses as rapidly as did Indonesia's, a powerful political dynamic is unleashed. Expectations are shattered and anger arises, in thousands of people, all at the same time. The result is often rage directed at the regime and its leaders. The rage also tends to be directed against those who had gotten rich most quickly. Income inequality suddenly becomes politicized. Corruption becomes objectionable. The newly rich, many of whom have been the businesspeople and entrepreneurs driving the economic development, become targets of the rage along with the regime itself. Individual injustices—people who are upset that their wives must work outside the home; people who feel they have been wronged by members of another ethnic group; people who feel the system is corrupt and the deck stacked against them—suddenly become actionable. Cumulative psychological stress drives people onto the streets.

Perhaps the most extraordinary thing about this dynamic is that it feeds on success. Countries that are perennial failures will never experience a J-curve. This is all the more reason to understand a country's kimchi. A country whose dynamics of stability are not firmly rooted, yet for the moment is experiencing rapid growth, is a country that may suffer a dramatic upheaval.

It is worth nothing that the Indonesian case could have been much worse. Popular discontent never really took on a political direction. There were attacks against ethnic Chinese and protests against the government, and some moderate Islamic parties took power. Indonesia's discontent triggered chaos, but no coherent mass movement. This was a far cry from the Chinese or Iranian revolutions, when charismatic leaders peddling attractive ideologies mobilized discontented citizens to overthrow governments and install totalitarian and extremist regimes. Indeed, when public anger is harnessed and directed, that is often when it is most dangerous.

Part 2

Managing Discontent

THE SINGLE GREATEST FORCE FOR POLITICAL STABILITY IS, SIMPLY
put, material wealth, widely distributed.

Prosperity makes people happy. This is not to say that all people are
greedy, or even necessarily care about wealth. But people almost universally
care about the things that wealth provides, including housing, food, transportation, medical care, and education. Hence rising wealth can mitigate
the discontent caused by, for instance, corruption and social change.
Wealth gives people the ability to solve their own problems—instead of
expecting the government to provide a solution and then becoming angry
if the government fails to deliver.

Furthermore, prosperity gives people a stake in "the system." People
with material wealth are people with something to lose. These people
may be discontented, even angry, but they will think twice before they
attempt to bring about destabilizing political or economic change, and
risk sacrificing what's been granted to them by the existing political and
economic order. Wealth is a powerful stabilizing influence.

The relatively prosperous middle classes do sometimes lead demonstrations, and even riots. But the causes for which middle-class citizens
tend to agitate are not usually catastrophic ones. "People Power" in the
Philippines sought to overthrow a corrupt government, not usher in
Communism. But whatever the stakes (a lost election or a bloody revolution), governments rarely wish to be overthrown, and so they seek to
manage discontent. They do this in many ways. They may try to distract
the public by demonizing foreign enemies or minority ethnic groups.
They may attempt to imprison or outright eliminate—murder—any

actual or potential opposition leaders. Or they may in fact deliver excellent policies that address the sources of public discontent and satisfy them, breaking the political dynamic of escalating public anger and botched government response, and thereby achieving stability.

In this section we deal with the management of discontent. We show how opposition leaders capitalize on public discontent (the infamous Hugo Chavez of Venezuela) or access to resources (the Tamil Tigers in Sri Lanka); how countries can manage even extreme discontent by providing channels for its nonviolent expression (India); how governments can turn discontent away from themselves by scapegoating (Zimbabwe); and how extraordinarily competent governments can alleviate discontent (Singapore) and incompetent governments can inadvertently increase it (Iran). And in each case, we show the consequences for international investors and global stability.

CHAPTER FIVE

Toppling Punto Fijo

OPPOSITION

POLITICAL OPPOSITION MOVEMENTS ARE AT TIMES HEROIC AND at times terrifying. When Gandhi led Indians in a peaceful uprising against British rule, he gave extraordinary testimony to the power of popular discontent mobilized for political aims. When Hitler toppled the Weimar democracy and propelled Germany to both war and genocide, he did the same.

When witnessed firsthand, political opposition is almost uniformly frightening. No one likes to be confronted by angry crowds banging pots, throwing rocks, and yelling slogans. Markets fall and the wealthy ship their money offshore. But distance breeds comfort. Gandhi was seen as a menace by India's colonial administrators but has, with time, joined the ranks of history's great heroes, not just in India but worldwide. Viewed in retrospect, not all instability is bad—the fall of the Marcos regime was almost certainly good for the Philippines, and so was the toppling of the Estrada government.

Whether for good or ill, when public anger grows, political opportunity grows with it. Governments that fail to manage public discontent often find that an opposition movement steps in to do just that. Opposition movements succeed by grasping public anger and directing it towards concrete political goals. Managed by gifted leaders, whether Gandhi or Hitler, a mobilized public can make quick work of seemingly insurmountable political obstacles. Two instructive examples of political

movements that overcame enormous odds are before us today: Hugo
Chavez in Venezuela and the Tamil Tigers in Sri Lanka.

VENEZUELA

The amount of risk, I won't say there's no risk, because there's risk
everywhere, but the amount of risk in Venezuela has been declining in
an objective, visible, appreciable way...Political risk? What risk? What
political risk is there in Venezuela? I don't see any. God willing, we
will be governing, this government, at least until 2007.
HUGO CHAVEZ, FEBRUARY 2001

In 1958, Venezuela's two main political parties, struck by the realization
that contesting elections was a hard way to make a living, decided instead
to collude. In theory, Venezuela was, and remains, a democracy. But in
1958, in the town of Punto Fijo, the two parties got together and inked an
agreement in which they agreed to share power, no matter what the result
of the 1959 election. Thus was born the "Punto Fijo system." This bizarre
power-sharing arrangement persisted despite all manner of political and
economic turmoil, surviving incredible corruption, severe economic
mismanagement, and even violent riots. The two main parties together
held onto power for three uninterrupted decades.

Between 1958 and the 1970s, with the Punto Fijo system in place,
Venezuela became one of the world's leading exporters of oil. In 1958,
government oil revenues per capita were $450. By 1974, revenues had
reached $1,650. The capital city of Caracas became, briefly, one of the
most expensive cities in the world. In those days, Venezuelans were the
world's foremost consumers of champagne. It was not uncommon for
middle-class Venezuelans to fly to Miami for a weekend of shopping.

And then this prosperity collapsed. The oil price crash of 1986 threw
the country into a deep recession. Worse yet, the government was at the
same time facing a crippling debt burden that had been created by wasteful government spending during the boom years. Political leaders were
forced to add to the pain by adopting harsh fiscal austerity measures.

Venezuela's economic output, which had grown rapidly from 1975 to 1985, suddenly declined sharply.

In other words, Venezuela was experiencing a classic J-curve. The people took to the streets. In 1989, protests and riots paralyzed the country for several weeks. Shortly thereafter, polls indicated that 75 percent of all Venezuelans believed their economic situation to be hopeless, and that nothing they could do would raise their standard of living.

And yet Punto Fijo survived. The two main parties, bloated by years of uncontested control over state spending, still had the funds necessary to buy off anyone who posed a threat to them. By the early 1990s, the two parties had such an extensive patronage network that more Venezuelan towns had party branch offices than had Catholic churches. Hence the only political candidates with any chance of electoral success were Punto Fijo candidates. And therefore, despite their anger, Venezuelan voters continued to elect—in relatively free and fair contests—leaders from the establishment parties.

∞

In 1992, a charismatic young colonel named Hugo Chavez, thinking creatively, tried to bring down Punto Fijo by extraordinary means—launching a military coup. But too many of the generals had bought into the system. The coup failed and Chavez was carted off to prison, to salve his wounds and ponder where he had gone wrong.

Then, toward the end of the 1990s, oil prices plunged again, to the point that per capita government oil revenues slipped to $330—one-fifth of their 1974 levels in real terms. The country's economy contracted by 7 percent in one year. The downturn was so painful that real per capita wages at the end of the 1990s were actually 60 percent lower than they had been in the 1970s. Unemployment doubled to almost 20 percent and crime rates rose quickly. The percentage of Venezuelans living in poverty ballooned from 44 percent to 86 percent.

Once again, the result was rising public anger against the ruling establishment. But even then, the grip of the Punto Fijo parties on Venezuelan politics was so tight that it was hard to imagine that they could ever lose power. It would not be a great exaggeration to say that nearly every politician in Venezuela with any significant amount of power was a beneficiary of the Punto Fijo system.

But Hugo Chavez, newly released from prison, had a plan. He saw the weak point in the armor. He understood that the only way to defeat a system with such a firm hold on professional politicians was to propel hitherto passive Venezuelans into politics. And this is precisely what he did. Abandoning his coup plotting, he entered the 1998 elections as a presidential candidate.

And he told a good story. Known as "El Commandante," Chavez wore a red paratrooper's beret and invoked militaristic jargon, giving impassioned and lengthy speeches that were especially well received by the poor. A fiery orator, he sought to explain to Venezuelans why they had to act. He sought to take unfocused public anger and concentrate it on a single political goal—the toppling of Punto Fijo. He claimed that Venezuela was an inherently rich country suffering from a mysterious malaise: "So much riches—the largest petroleum reserves in the world, the fifth-largest reserves of gas, gold, the immensely rich Caribbean Sea. All this, and 80 percent of our people live in poverty. What scientist can explain this?"

A "scientist" might not be able to explain this seeming paradox—but Chavez did. He claimed that Venezuela's vast wealth had been stolen by its corrupt elite. He pointed to the lavish lifestyles and patronage networks of establishment politicians as evidence that the riches of the 1970s had disappeared into the pockets of the government. To an amazing degree, Venezuelans believed him. Opinion polls revealed that 91 percent of the public believed that corruption was the only factor preventing all Venezuelans from living "very well." A full 78 percent of respondents believed that Venezuela was "one of the richest nations in the world." Chavez cast himself as the heir to the famous liberator of colonial South America, Simon Bolivar. He promised a "Bolivarian Revolution" that would restore honesty, integrity, and social justice to government. Bolivar, of course, had liberated the country from the yoke of Spanish colonialism; Chavez would liberate Venezuela from the yoke of corruption, cronyism, and neglect by the Punto Fijo establishment.

His strategy was a stunning success. The poor flocked to his political rallies. In 1998, Hugo Chavez won the presidential election, with a landslide victory of 56 percent to 40 percent over his opponent. Voter turnout was an astounding 95 percent, compared with the usual turnouts of 30 percent for Venezuelan polls. Chavez had mobilized more ordinary—and hitherto passive—Venezuelans to take part in the political process. And he did not stop there. For the first two years of his administration, Chavez enjoyed success upon success. Riding widespread public support, he disbanded the opposition-dominated legislature, wrote a new constitution for the country, and passed an endless succession of controversial laws. His popularity was unmatched, and his personal domination of Venezuelan politics nearly complete. Whenever he met opposition from the establishment, he would appeal through the media to the masses, and they would respond by taking to the streets.

∞

Chavez appeared to be an unstoppable political force—especially after creating a new constitution that solidified his grip on power. But it turned out that he was not unstoppable. What Chavez had told the Venezuelan public was fundamentally untrue. To be sure, the Venezuelan ruling establishment was tremendously corrupt. But Venezuela, contrary to Chavez's claims, was not a rich country. Per capita oil revenues of $330 per year could not bring riches to the general public, no matter how well distributed. Truly oil-rich states such as the United Arab Emirates or Kuwait have yearly per-capita oil revenues of more than $9,000. So Chavez was simply unable to deliver on his extravagant promises. Four years into Chavez's administration, the Venezuelan people were still poor. In fact, they found themselves 20 percent poorer than at its start. Attendance at pro-Chavez rallies began to dwindle. By February 2002, his approval rating had fallen to only 35 percent.

Chavez catapulted himself to power and toppled the Punto Fijo system by mobilizing ordinary Venezuelans into politics. Establishment politicians simply could not manage the level of discontent that Chavez had tapped. That was his strength but also his weakness. Without public support, he was suddenly vulnerable. Chavez had made all kinds of enemies: he battled with the labor unions; caused outbreaks of violence in the countryside with a bold land reform program; attempted to assert control over PDVSA, the country's powerful oil monopoly; angered business leaders with anticapitalist rhetoric; and even tangled with the Catholic Church.

The establishment decided to bring Chavez down. At first they sniped from the sidelines. Hoping the military would do their work for them, some Chavez opponents mailed ladies' underwear to 140 top military officials, implying that they were not macho enough to overthrow Chavez. The episode came to be known as *El Pantaletaxo*, "The G-String Revolt." Then a general strike was called. But the strikers and demonstrators who took to the streets were firmly middle-class. Rather than actually banging pots and pans, some protesters purchased a CD recording of pots and pans called "*Caserolas Contra Chavez*" (The Anti-Chavez Casserole) and played it on handheld boomboxes. They mocked the poor Chavez loyalists who came out to challenge them. "The worse they look," one anti-Chavez civil engineer suggested, "the more they are with Chavez. I mean, if they do not have teeth, they are Chavistas."

∞

Ultimately, the increasingly high-stakes battle that began once Chavez's popular support diminished came to international attention. Pro-Chavez troops opened fire on protesters, killing thirteen and injuring more than 100. Military leaders stepped in to oust Chavez and installed a businessman named Pedro Carmona as president, sending the stock market up by 8 percent. But Carmona immediately dissolved the legislature and the Supreme Court, suggesting authoritarian ambitions of his own. Popular support began to swing back to Chavez. His poll ratings jumped. A counter-coup began in the interior of the country and culminated in Chavez's return to the presidential palace. The stock market promptly lost the 8 percent it had gained

The battle between Chavez and the middle class then took the form of a general strike led by oil workers. This brought the economy to a grinding halt. Between mid-1999 and early 2003, the Venezuelan economy contracted by 10 percent. Unemployment rose to 17 percent. United Airlines shuttered its Caracas office and halted its daily Miami-Caracas flight. American Airlines suspended several flights to Caracas and rearranged schedules so that its crews and planes would not have to overnight in Venezuela. Microsoft temporarily closed its offices in Caracas. So did IBM, Ford, Shell, and

Coca-Cola. A Coca-Cola bottling plant was seized by pro-Chavez military officers. Oracle and Avon were operating at reduced capacity.

It was not just foreign investors who suffered. In the end, the entire global economy was pummeled by Venezuela's dynamic of conflict and struggles to capture and manage discontent. With Venezuela's oil production sharply reduced, global oil prices shot up. According to the U.S. Energy Department, in the winter of 2003, U.S. crude oil supplies fell 14 percent, and heating oil inventories were down 26 percent on the previous year. (Although this was also partly attributed to fears of a looming war in Iraq.)

Whatever the final toll of the Chavez legacy, he exemplified this crucial dynamic: Opposition movements that can mobilize public support can overcome impossible odds. Where the Punto Fijo establishment had failed, Chavez succeeded, stunningly, in managing the discontent of the Venezuelan public and harnessing it to his own political ends.

At least for a time. Eventually, Chavez also demonstrated the corollary of this: when the public support is gone, even powerful opposition movements falter.

SRI LANKA

The Liberation Tigers of Tamil Eelam are another opposition movement that, going strictly by the numbers, had little hope of success. The minority Tamil ethnic group makes up only 3.4 million of Sri Lanka's 19 million inhabitants. The government army is ruthless and government troops have at times outnumbered the Tigers by as many as 45 to 1.

And yet, the Tigers prosecuted a guerrilla war against the Sri Lankan government for more than two decades. This conflict has claimed an estimated 64,000 lives. Scores of prominent politicians, military leaders, and journalists have been killed. The Tigers assassinated Sri Lankan president Ranasinghe Premadasa in 1993, and former Indian prime minister Rajiv Gandhi in 1991. They tried to kill Sri Lankan prime minister Chandrika Bandaranaike Kumaratunga, but only managed to get one of her eyes. The Tigers have destroyed a third of the Sri Lankan navy, grounded half the aircraft belonging to the national airline, and blown up the central bank. The Tigers have achieved an extraordinary degree of success—to the extent that killing people, including innocents, can ever be defined as "success."

The seeds of the Sri Lankan struggle were planted, inadvertently, by Britain (again, unintended consequences), whose colonial policy of "divide and rule" promoted the minority Tamil Hindus over the majority Sinhalese Buddhists. In colonial Sri Lanka (then called Ceylon), Tamils enjoyed the easiest access to education and staffed the British administration. Predictably, when Sri Lanka achieved independence in 1948, the majority Sinhalese set out to correct the historical imbalances. The new constitution gave the Sinhalese privileged status over the minority Tamils. A preference system favored Sinhalese for jobs and places in the educational system. The government forced Tamils to use the Sinhalese language and study Sinhalese history and culture. Severe anti-Tamil riots broke out in 1956, 1958, 1961, 1974, 1977, 1981, and 1983; thousands of Tamils were killed or fled into exile.

Tamil militants decided to take up arms against the majority Sinhalese and launched a guerrilla war. A short fight, one might expect. And it would have been, but for one thing: the Tamils had access to outside resources.

∞

The outside aid to the Tamils came at first from neighboring India. In the early 1970s, Sri Lankan Tamils had set up shop in the Indian state of Tamil Nadu (a one-hour boat ride from Sri Lanka). Tamil Nadu was home to 60 million ethnic Tamils sympathetic to their Sri Lankan brethren. Indian Tamil political parties allowed the main guerrilla group, the Liberation Tigers of Tamil Eelam, or LTTE, to set up military training camps in their state. In 1983, this support increased when Indian prime minister Indira Gandhi decided to use the Tigers as a stick with which to beat the Sri Lankan government. Sri Lanka had allied itself with the West during the Cold War, which meant that it forged links with Pakistan—the sworn enemy of India. In an effort to destabilize Sri Lanka, Gandhi trained, armed, and financed the LTTE. The strength and intensity of the guerrilla war increased proportionately. By the end of 1983, there were 32 LTTE training camps in Tamil Nadu, and by 1987, more than 20,000 Sri Lankans had been trained by either the central government of India, the state government of Tamil Nadu, or the militant groups operating there.

But the Cold War was coming to an end and relations warmed between India and Sri Lanka. In 1987, India decided to pull the plug on its support for the LTTE. Indira Gandhi's son and successor, Rajiv, reversed his mother's policies, signed an accord with Sri Lanka, and even sent Indian "peacekeeping" troops to fight against the Tigers. (The Tigers did not overlook this betrayal. Rajiv Gandhi's 1991 murder came at the hands of a Tiger suicide bomber.) Indian money had been the Tigers' lifeline, and with that lifeline cut, the Tigers appeared isolated, abandoned, and outmatched. The Sri Lankan government expected an easy victory.

But they could not have been more wrong. Incredibly, after India withdrew its support, the Tigers' access to external funds actually grew. In 1983, major anti-Tamil riots had left 3,000 Tamils dead. Seeing no future in Sri Lanka, 100,000 Tamils fled the country. Countries around the world, especially in the West, granted asylum to fleeing Tamils and extended them refugee status. Where Tamil communities were established, the Tigers also set up shop. The international wing of the LTTE came to operate in fifty-four countries, most prominently in Canada, the U.S., the U.K., Australia, Switzerland, and Scandinavia.

When India cut off funding and support, the Tigers turned to this Tamil diaspora. By one estimate, internationally based Sri Lankan Tamils in 2000 were contributing an astonishing $2.75 million per month to the LTTE. The largest single contributor was a U.S.-based doctor, who donated roughly $4 million during the 1990s. One bank in the Jaffna Peninsula reportedly collected funds from expatriate Tamils equivalent to one-half the government's annual war budget. In addition to contributions, the Tigers set up a plethora of legitimate businesses: gas stations, restaurants, trucking companies, computing companies, and investments in gold, financial markets, and real estate. The LTTE also engaged in human trafficking, heroin smuggling, passport forging, welfare scams, and extortion. Resulting profits were channeled back to Sri Lanka and the guerrilla war.

The story of the Sri Lankan Tamil community in Canada is especially telling. Canada is home to some 200,000 Tamils, most of whom have refugee status. Canadian authorities estimate 10,000 former guerrillas live in the country. Several known leaders in the movement are among them—a former LTTE intelligence squad chief, an ex-LTTE zone commander, and a senior leader from a faction called the Eelam Revolutionary Organization. Pro-LTTE demonstrations in Canada have drawn upwards of 20,000 people, and Tamils hold frequent contribution drives. While many Canadian Tamils voluntarily contributed to the Tigers, there are also many reports of intimidation and extortion used to extract funds from the community. Some Canadian Tamils complained that militants, many of whom belong to Tamil street gangs in Toronto, levy a 6 percent annual tax that goes directly to Tiger coffers. In total, Canada's Tamil community contributed roughly $22 million per year to the LTTE.

This money funded a resource supply chain of staggering sophistication. K. Pathmanathan, the LTTE arms procurement officer, was thought to be based in Kuala Lumpur and in possession of no fewer than twenty passports. The LTTE purchased at least ten ships to ferry weapons from North Korea, Myanmar, Africa, and arms dealers in the Middle East and Eastern Europe. The ships were registered in Panama, Honduras, and Liberia and owned by front companies. The Indian army once seized a boat carrying $1 million worth of weapons. The largest known shipment transported 50 tons of TNT and 10 tons of the explosive RDX from a Ukrainian Black Sea port. The RDX was eventually used in a truck bomb that destroyed a large section of Colombo's financial center in 1996.

Money gave the Tigers access to military technology that enabled them to overcome their numerical inferiority. The LTTE fielded an army of three brigades and a guerrilla cadre in the Eastern province specializing in ambushes and mortar attacks. The Sea Tigers were considered the world's most sophisticated guerrilla navy, equipped with high-powered ships that frequently sunk Indian and Sri Lankan vessels. The Air Tigers consisted of light aircraft used for suicide bombing missions. And the Black Tigers were notorious for highly efficient suicide bombings often carried out by teenage girls (foreshadowing later events in Israel). The Tigers acquired night-vision goggles, rocket-propelled grenade launchers, and global positioning systems even before the Sri Lankan army. The Tigers are known to have purchased surface-to-air missiles from Cambodia that cost $1 million apiece.

With extraordinary access to funds, the Tigers managed to stage ambitious terrorist attacks and chalk up military victories. In 1996, a suicide bomb attack at the Sri Lankan central bank killed 90 and injured 1,400. In 1997, thirty foreign tourists were injured in a bombing of the Galadari Hotel in Colombo. In April 2000, the Tigers overran the crucial Elephant Pass, before being driven back by the Sri Lankan army. And on July 24, 2001, the Tigers struck the island's only international airport and an adjoining air force base, destroying eleven planes and crippling Sri Lanka's tourist economy (and causing one of the ten largest catastrophic insurance losses of 2001).

These military successes allowed the Tigers to create a de facto mini-state in the country's northeast, ruled by their leader Velupillai Prabha-karan. The Tigers run their own customs and tax collection service, their own judiciary and police, their own newspapers, and their own depart-ments of health, education, and finance. They even set their clocks one half hour behind official Sri Lankan time.

∞

This has been a war with real costs. In 2001, Sri Lanka's economy contracted by 1.4 percent thanks partly to the Tigers' attack on the in-ternational airport. Sri Lankan government spending on energy, roads, and other infrastructure were all preempted by the government's single-minded pursuit of military victory. The World Bank estimates that Sri Lanka's civil war has lowered the country's GDP growth by 2 percent per year, as military expenditure crowded out private sector lending, tourism was scared off, and capital and brainpower fled the country.

The Tigers also set an unfortunate precedent. Their success in sui-cide bombings—more than 200 to date—has been studied by Middle Eastern groups. Experts believe that the al-Qaeda attack in Yemen on the *USS Cole* in the year 2000 was modeled after a 1991 Tiger attack on the Sri Lankan navy.

For anyone unconvinced that outside resources have been crucial to what the Tamil Tigers have "achieved," consider what has transpired since the September 11 terror attacks in the U.S. Prior to that point, many world governments tolerated the Tigers' fundraising efforts in their countries, partly out of lack of interest and partly out of a feeling that the Tigers—as representatives of a minority group harshly treated in the past—were in some way justified in their violence. In the post-September 11 environment, however, fundraising for terrorism, no matter how "justified," is not tolerated. Authorities in the U.S. and other Western countries have located and frozen Tiger bank accounts totaling $4 billion. The U.S. officially declared the LTTE a "foreign terrorist organization" in October 1997, but it was only after September 11 that it began shutting down its U.S. activities. President George W. Bush issued an executive order blocking assets belonging to the Tigers and 188 other terror-linked groups. The U.K., Canada, and Australia quickly followed suit. The tragedy of September 11 also deeply affected the overseas Tamil community. Now that their adopted countries had become victims, the terror of suicide bombings was brought home. The relativism inherent in "one man's terrorist is another man's freedom fighter" no longer seemed to hold.

And so, the Tigers realized the tap was being turned off: better to negotiate now, from a position of strength. In February 2002, a cease-fire was declared. Tiger leader Velupillai Prabhakaran emerged from his jungle redoubt to hold his first press conference since 1990 and announced, "We will seriously consider renouncing armed struggle if a solution acceptable to the people is worked out." The two parties met in Thailand in September 2002, where the Tigers agreed to accept regional autonomy and the Sri Lankan government responded positively. Since then, life has improved in Sri Lanka. Domestic flights, which had been completely halted for fear of hijacking, have resumed. The main road between the Tamil stronghold of Jaffna and the Sri Lankan capital of Colombo has been reopened. And the two parties are actively recruiting international aid donors to help rebuild the shattered island state. This is no guarantee of peace; but the odds are better than they have been for many years.

THE DYNAMICS OF OPPOSITION

Hugo Chavez and the Tamil Tigers make for compelling stories, but bad examples, because they make challenging the established political order look easy. In reality, for every Chavez whom the government of Venezuela failed to "manage," there are hundreds of would-be opposition leaders killed by government thugs, thrown in jail, or still languishing in obscurity, ignored by the people they had hoped to mobilize. Would-be opposition leaders often have few resources, and must build a movement from scratch. Put it this way: they are ordinary citizens, taking on governments. And keep in mind Max Weber's famous definition: "A state is a human community that (successfully) claims the monopoly of the legitimate use of physical force within a given territory." If incumbents are willing to misuse the resources of their office to suppress opposition, as they so often are, this makes governments all the more formidable.

For this reason, opposition movements often fail to emerge even when the groundwork of public discontent has been amply prepared. Russia is one example. In the ten years after the fall of the USSR, Russians saw their country go from mighty superpower to troubled "emerging market." The economy contracted by 40 percent. State-owned industries closed down, especially in the hinterland. This forced workers into the cities. But strict residency and work permit requirements blocked many urban migrants from access to resources. Furthermore, the educational system and healthcare services were in rapid decline, and infrastructure was crumbling. Deadly pollutants frequently turned up in populated areas. Workers in many professions—including miners, teachers, and soldiers—all too often went without pay for months at a time. Not surprisingly, signs of extraordinary discontent were everywhere. In December 1999, the Institute of Psychiatric Research reported that in the past decade, incidents of neurosis had increased by 10 percent, alcoholism by 30 percent, and depression by 35 percent. Between 1995 and 2000, drug addiction leapt a staggering 600 percent. Partially as a result of rising alcoholism, the life expectancy of the average Russian dropped from 69 years in 1990 to 64 years, and to only 57 years for males.

And yet, there has been no successful opposition. Partially this can be attributed to the success of the Russian government in managing discontent. But another reason a successful opposition failed to emerge is that all of the would-be opposition movements in Russia lacked some crucial attribute. Three main factors—besides government ineptitude—seem to make an opposition movement successful: charismatic leadership, potent ideology, and access to political resources.

CHARISMATIC LEADERSHIP

For an opposition movement to succeed, people must be willing to follow its leaders, even at great peril to their lives. A successful opposition movement therefore benefits greatly from charismatic leadership. Charisma is extremely hard for outsiders to judge. Was Hitler charismatic? Of course, in his time and place. But judged by the standards of today? One man's charisma is another's ridiculous demagoguery. The elements that make a leader charismatic differ based on time, culture, and circumstance. Cubans were taken—some would say taken in—by Castro's fiery rhetoric. Bulgarians were thrilled by the regal aloofness of prime ministerial candidate Simeon Saxe-Coburg-Gotha—a former king who refused most media requests for interviews during his political campaign. Tamil Tiger military leader Velupillai Prabhakaran inspired new recruits by telling them they had the right to kill him if he settled for anything short of Eelam—a Tamil homeland.

Charismatic leadership requires extraordinary communication. The individuals who would exercise it must convince followers that they embody their aspirations; that they understand their deepest longings and have dedicated themselves to realizing those longings. This requires extraordinary empathy. Charismatic leaders demonstrate an almost uncanny ability to grasp the psychic state of their followers and then convince them that they have been understood. The root of Chavez's power was his ability to convince the poor that he truly understood and represented them, and that the Punto Fijo government of Venezuela did not.

An opposition leader's charisma is most effective when preceded by a sense, on the part of the people, that the government has lost all touch with the concerns of the masses. Whether it was the Westernization and disdainful remoteness of the Shah of Iran, or the corrupt idolatry of Batista in Cuba, King Idris in Libya, or Louis XVI in France, the people had lost all faith in the ability of their governors to relate to them. Profound discontent and a deep-seated sense of not being heard prepare a nation's people for the rise of a charismatic opposition leader.

Perhaps the most successful opposition movement in postcommunist Russia has been the Communist Party itself, which has constantly tried to re-take power through democratic means and, in the process, became the largest party represented in the Duma. The Party even came close to capturing the presidency in 1996, when Gennady Zyuganov took second place in the first round of voting, making it into a runoff against incumbent Boris Yeltsin. But Zyuganov was unable to convince angry

Russians that he understood and truly represented them. One reason is that after seventy years of Soviet rule, Russians were extraordinarily distrustful of political organizations. During the time of the USSR, no organizations independent of the state were allowed to exist. The social organizations that did exist under the Soviets were nothing more than extensions of the party itself. When Russians are asked to rate their trust in institutions, political parties still rank near the bottom of the heap. Fully three-quarters of the population do not identify with a political party. And Zyuganov, lacking charisma, was unable to overcome this. Russians did not like the system, but were unimpressed by its opposition. In the 1996 elections, of the 108 million registered voters, 34 million did not vote. And close to 4 million chose the bizarre ballot option "against the two candidates."

POTENT IDEOLOGY

A successful opposition movement needs more than a charismatic leader to mobilize people—it also must be able to mobilize their anger for political ends. Truly effective leaders propel hitherto passive citizens into political action by propounding an effective ideology. Psychologically, an ideology resolves the kind of "sense-making" crises that can plunge people into popular discontent. People undergoing severe trauma brought on by rapid social change or sudden material hardships often cannot understand or come to grips with their suffering—not simply in the physical sense of what is causing their suffering, but in the moral sense of what has gone wrong that they should suffer in this way. A successful opposition ideology presents a worldview that identifies the cause of people's suffering, and even more critically, explains how their suffering can be ended through political action.

In revolutionary Iran, the culprit identified by the Ayatollah Khomeini and his Islamic fundamentalist ideology was the materialist influence of the West. Hence, he and his followers argued, suffering could be resolved through the whole-hearted rejection of the West and all it stood for—materialist prosperity, human rights, democracy, and the like—and the whole-hearted embrace of what he defined as the basic beliefs and practices of Islam. In Hitler's Germany, the culprit was initially identified as the Jews, who were to be killed or deprived of their property. In Venezuela, the enemy was a thieving and corrupt elite, who needed to be thrown from power.

As these cases suggest, it is tragically rare that the culprit identified by an opposition ideology is the real root cause of the country's troubles. It is even rarer that the solution propounded by the ideology will actually solve the country's problems. Two vital and powerful examples are Marxism and political Islam. As history shows, these opposition ideologies are profoundly appealing to distressed people but offer little in the way of working solutions to poverty and deprivation.

Another reason post-Soviet Russia's Communists have thus far failed as an opposition movement is their tired ideology. The power of communist ideology to explain Russians' misery and solve their problems has been sorely diminished by the humiliating decline and fall of the USSR. Zyuganov tried to overcome this problem by toning down his socialist rhetoric and making some forays into anti-Semitism, famously remarking, "Too many people with strange-sounding family names mingle in the internal affairs of Russia." But fortunately, this did not catch on. The party's support was limited mostly to the elderly and to the rural poor, earning it a reliable, but stagnant, 20 percent of the national vote.

ACCESS TO RESOURCES

Even with both a charismatic leader and a compelling ideology, a political opposition movement will flounder without resources. Opposition leaders have to be able to disseminate their messages and organize and mobilize their followers.

Technology has made it far easier both to disseminate messages and organize followers, giving people the ability to communicate both widely and secretly. Even in the 1970s, Iranian revolutionaries were able to make use of three new technologies—photocopiers, direct-dial phone service, and audiocassette tapes—to communicate to followers. Groups opposed to the Soviet regime relied on the fax machine. More recently, the cellular telephone—in particular, the ability of cell phones to send text messages—played a large role in bringing down the government of Estrada in the Philippines, helping thousands to gather in protest at a moment's notice. In China, in the spring of 2003, text messages by the millions were sent from cell phone to cell phone, contributing to the decision of the Politburo to abandon its efforts to keep the SARS epidemic under wraps. The Internet also poses opportunities to protest movements. The Chinese Communist Party has closed thousands of Internet cafes, while the government of Syria allows only limited access to the Internet. While governments can make it difficult to get the message out—most commonly by controlling the media—a determined opposition (everywhere, it seems, but in North Korea) can usually find a way.

Opposition movements are also aided by good organization. This was one advantage of Russia's Communists; Zyuganov was a capable administrator and the party had good discipline. But other Russian opposition movements were almost ridiculously disorganized. Nationalist leader Vladimir Zhirinovsky could work crowds into a frenzy on command, preaching the building of a Russian empire so vast that "Russian soldiers could wash their boots in the Indian Ocean." Zhirinovsky came in third place in voting for the 1991 presidential election and his Liberal Democratic Party won the second-highest number of seats in the December 1993 Duma elections. But the Nationalist legislators squabbled amongst themselves, failed to adhere to a party platform, and could not present a united front. Some Nationalists praised Lenin and Stalin and spoke of the reformation of the USSR. Others were diehard monarchists and more interested in the return of the czars. In the end, Zhirinovsky's movement fell apart; from 1993, when his party first won representation in the Duma, to 1996, when he ran for president, his popularity fell fourfold to a mere 5.7 percent of the popular vote.

But political parties are not the only means to power. Indeed, if they were, opposition movements would never succeed in the many countries where parties are outlawed or repressed. One way for opposition leaders to achieve effective organization without the backing of an organized political party is to piggyback on an existing, theoretically apolitical, institution. The church is often a source of opposition support and succeeds in organizing and mobilizing political movements—the mosque in Iran, for example. This is one reason why repressive governments, such as the government of China, are so leery of any kind of organized religion. Labor unions (such as Solidarity in Poland) and the military have also historically provided opposition movements with organizational backing.

Then there is the question of funding. Political opposition is expensive, especially when bribery is common and media airtime expensive, or opposition may mean buying costly weapons. Indeed, a recent study by the World Bank found that countries with an abundance of natural resources or a large international diaspora (as in the case of Sri Lanka), are more likely to suffer civil wars. This is the curse of natural abundance. Since natural resources are relatively easy to sell internationally for hard currency, and tend to be located in rural areas, they can quickly become a key source of funding for rebel groups that want to take up arms against the government. In Sierra Leone, rebel groups have been funded by diamonds; in Cambodia, by timber; in Colombia, by cocaine. Indeed, one Colombian rebel group, the FARC, which has fought the government for thirty years and fields roughly 50,000 soldiers, earns an estimated $500 million per year from its cocaine trafficking business.

Cases of ethnic or religious diasporas funding civil war are also common. Sikh separatists who staged a violent confrontation with the Indian military in the 1980s received their support from overseas Sikhs, mostly in the U.K., U.S., and Canada. The Kosovo Liberation Army was able to mount a serious challenge to the Serbian military with the assistance of overseas Albanians. The Irish Republican Army depended, throughout its struggle, on the assistance of the Irish diaspora in the U.S. And Hamas, Islamic Jihad, and other Palestinian terrorist organizations have been supported by Arab and Muslim groups in the U.S., Canada, and the U.K.

Deprived of access to resources, opposition movements often falter. When the Communist Party candidate took second place in the first round of voting in the 1996 presidential elections, Russia's new elites, especially those who had prospered from "free-market" reforms, were terrified by the prospect of a communist president. They opened their wallets to support incumbent President Yeltsin. They had purchased, and therefore controlled, most of Russia's television, radio, and newspaper media outlets. They prevented the Communists from getting out their message and took every opportunity to label their candidate a dangerous renegade. A tired ideology, a leader lacking charisma, and a lack of access to resources—the communists had virtually no chance to succeed.

But then, any opposition movement faces long odds. Political Risk Services, a country risk analysis firm, in a disarmingly honest assessment of its success, found that they had been successful in predicting changes of government 80 percent of the time. However, if they had simply predicted "no change," they would have been right 86 percent of the time. The examples of Hugo Chavez and the Tamil Tigers notwithstanding, political opposition is not easy. Many governments *do* succeed in managing discontent.

CHAPTER SIX

Tony Blair's Gay Gangsters

CHANNELS FOR DISCONTENT

IN THE SPRING OF 1999, SHORTLY AFTER THE FALUN GONG HAD organized its large and unexpected demonstration in Beijing, the Chinese government had a problem. The Chinese leaders were in the midst of WTO membership negotiations, and were hoping to host the Olympics in Beijing. Another highly visible incident of public unrest and repression would be most unwelcome. And the tenth anniversary of the June 4 student protests at Tiananmen Square was fast approaching.

Then the Chinese leadership received an unexpected gift in the guise of a tragedy. On May 7, as part of its campaign against Yugoslavia, NATO accidentally bombed the Chinese embassy in Belgrade, killing three people and injuring twenty.

The Chinese government immediately threw the propaganda machine into high gear. Spokesmen angrily refused to accept U.S. explanations that the bombing was accidental, fanning the flames of public anger. The *People's Daily* ran editorials comparing NATO to the government of Nazi Germany and declaring that the bombing of Yugoslavia reflected the U.S. ambition to become "Lord of the Earth." On the street, the authorities allowed angry protesters to throw rocks, paint, and chunks of concrete at the U.S. embassy in Beijing, and burn the U.S. consulate in Chengdu.

If your people are angry, better they be angry with someone else. On this theory, the Chinese authorities redirected a tide of resurgent nationalism. America became, temporarily, public enemy number one—and it was hard for the U.S. to complain because its planes had, after all, bombed the Chinese embassy. All this was marvelously distracting. The June 4 Tiananmen anniversary passed without incident.

∞

For a moment, spare a thought for the world's political leaders. From their point of view, politics is something like a pressure cooker: economic downturns, ethnic tensions, corruption, and social change can heat a country's politics to the boiling point. How many leaders—in straits so much more dire than the Chinese—must have prayed for some sort of distraction, some *deus ex machina*, to soak up public anger?

Such mechanisms do exist. Turn down the heat, and the pressure dissipates; open a hole in the container, and often, the steam escapes harmlessly. Some political systems—most notably democracies—have built-in outlets for political pressures. Governments that enrage their citizens are quickly voted out of office, which turns down the heat. There is nothing more cathartic for disgruntled citizens than "throwing the bums out." In addition, the discontented can let off steam by freely complaining— writing letters to the editor, joining opposition movements, and even demonstrating if necessary. Furthermore, some governments—democratic or otherwise—are particularly adept at channeling away popular anger. The Chinese employed this strategy to good effect. Malaysian Prime Minister Mahathir Mohammed's crusade against currency "speculators" is another example. Arab governments' habit of identifying Israel as public enemy number one is yet another. All of these help an angry public to let off steam.

In this regard, different countries have very different kimchi dynamics: India is more stable than it should be, because of channels wide open; Hong Kong is less stable than it should be, because of channels slammed shut; and Zimbabwe is led by a failed regime that nonetheless demonstrates an uncanny ability to channel anger away from itself.

INDIA

India, birthplace of the Buddha, is, ironically, a very angry place. Each year, without fail, the country leads the world in the reported number of major riots, strikes, and demonstrations. Many (often thousands) die annually in horrific incidents of religious, ethnic, and caste violence. Various low-level guerrilla wars rage, primarily in the northeast and in the Muslim-majority state of Jammu and Kashmir.

In some sense, this is not surprising. Like Nigeria, India is a maze of religious, regional, linguistic, and caste divisions. Roughly 400 distinct languages are spoken—114 of which are each spoken by more than 10,000 people. The country's 850 million Hindus are divided into 900 castes and subcastes, not to mention regional and linguistic groupings such as Bengali, Tamil, Oriya, Telegu, and Gujarati. The 120 million-person Muslim community makes India the world's third most populous Muslim country. Add Sikhs, Christians, Jains, Zoroastrians, and Jews, and India is a volatile mix of cultures and religions often at each other's throats. As Winston Churchill once remarked, "India is a geographical expression. It is no more a united nation than the Equator."

Add to this ample reasons for discontent. Per capita income is a paltry $460 per year. As of the last World Bank survey year, 1997, 44 percent of the population lived on less than $1 per day and 35 percent lived below the established poverty line. Infant mortality rates are high and disease is rampant. Basic infrastructure, such as electricity, roads, and telecommunications, is often in appalling condition. Political corruption reaches epic proportions, while day-to-day corruption—in the bureaucracy and the legal system—serves as a persistent tax on daily life. Cyclones, earthquakes, and fires frequently leave death tolls in the thousands, their natural destructiveness worsened by ignored building codes and absent emergency services.

The Indian government has also deliberately brought about tremendous social disruptions. At the time of independence, residents of rural India (some 80 percent of the population) lived in a quasi-feudal system, with landowning *zamindars* and *jagirdars* at the top of the pecking order. The landlords were upper-caste, while the landless laborers belonged to lower castes. But India's first prime minister, Jawaharlal Nehru, introduced land reform in 1951 that overturned the feudal order in much, but not all, of the country. Upper-caste landlords suffered an instant and radical loss of wealth and social status. Stories abound of Brahmin (upper-caste) families, especially in northern India, who were reduced to the status of beggars, common criminals, or—the greatest humiliation—laborers for lower castes. And lower castes grew bold and defiant, no longer willing to accept their deprived economic and social status. Nehru introduced a quota system in the early 1950s that gave the lowest castes and tribes preference in government jobs and school admissions. In 1990, these quotas were extended to all "backward" castes—a full 52 percent of Indians.

The wonder is that India, unlike Nigeria, has suffered no civil wars, and has survived as a unified country. Indeed, British colonial rulers confidently predicted that India would soon disintegrate after they departed. And yet, despite extraordinary levels of political discontent, the country has held together, for more than fifty years, as the world's largest democracy. What accounts for India's surprising longevity?

The answer can be found in the country's political system. The people elect leaders at the national, state, and village levels in relatively free and fair contests. Angry Indians (and there are many of them) are free to express their feelings on the streets, at the ballot box, or even by forming their own political parties. This they have done again and again. When farmers felt they were not being heard, they formed a political movement to articulate their demands and force politicians to cater to their interests. When workers in new state-owned industrial enterprises felt they were being exploited, they formed communist parties. When regional and linguistic groups decided that India's centralized political structure squelched their distinct identities, they rallied for the creation of their own states, and formed political parties that aired their grievances on the national level. When lower-caste groups became more assertive, they formed caste-based political parties that have altered the political landscape, especially in northern India. Today, forty political parties are represented in the Lok Sabha, the national parliament, and 600 distinct political parties have registered nationwide. In India's volatile and vibrant democracy, almost all voices can be heard. When India's last government was sworn in, in 1999, its president was an untouchable, the speaker of the house was a member of the Telegu-speaking minority from the southern state of Andhra Pradesh, the defense minister was a Christian, and the coal minister a Muslim. Since then, a Muslim has assumed the office of president. He rose to fame as the father of India's nuclear program.

As a result, India's flawed but functional democratic system has tremendous legitimacy. Since 1947, fourteen national elections have been held. And, while allegations of vote-buying, ballot-rigging, and unfair uses of incumbency are not uncommon, election results are widely seen as legitimate. Voter turnout has consistently hovered around 60 percent since 1962, handily exceeding turnout in the United States. In a 1996 poll taken by the newsmagazine *India Today*, 59 percent of Indians said their vote makes a difference, while only 21 percent claimed the opposite.

Even the habitually cynical journalist Pankaj Mishra—observing an Indian election in October 1999—was moved to comment:

> At village after village that afternoon, people waited patiently in long queues, under the harsh monsoon sun, the normally impassive faces brimming with excitement—images stereotypical of Indian elections and democracy—which ignored so much of what was not seen, the caste consolidations, the regimented votes, the feudal decrees, the ignorance and brutality. And yet it was hard not to feel the strength of the hopes and desires of the people lining up to vote; hard not to see poignancy in the devotion they brought to their only and very limited intervention in the unknown outside world; hard not to be moved by the eagerness with which they embraced their chance to alter the world that wielded such arbitrary power over their lives.

Perhaps the most stabilizing feature of India's democracy is that the lower classes and lower castes—those groups most likely to agitate for drastic change—buy into the system the most. The lower castes, the dispossessed, and the illiterate have been the most active in joining political parties and participating in the political process. Voter turnout among untouchable voters is higher than that among other sections of society. And India's poorest people, from northern, Hindi-speaking states such as Uttar Pradesh and Bihar, are also the most represented in parliament.

∞

This is certainly not to suggest that India's political system is flawless. Governments rise and fall with extraordinary speed. The fractured parliamentary system makes it easy for special interest groups to block needed economic reforms. And personalities and parties at the state level have been able to create mini-fiefdoms, often by playing ethnic groups off against each other. (This was the case in Gujarat, where Hindu-Muslim rioting killed 1,000 people in spring 2002.) But India's political system is extraordinary, maintaining fundamental stability in the face of tremendous tensions. India's politics may be constantly at a boil, but here is a dynamic that lets the pressure escape.

Hong Kong

While India's citizens lead the world in discontent, Hong Kong's lead the world in privilege. Per capita income is $25,920 per year, higher than that of Germany. Yet surprisingly, since Hong Kong's 1997 transition from British colony to Special Administrative Region of China, popular unrest has reached unprecedented levels. In 1997, the territory saw 448 public protests and 425 assemblies for political purposes. Admittedly, 1997 was a tumultuous year—the year of both the handover to Chinese rule and the Asian financial crisis. But with the crisis over and the handover complete, the protests continued—in only the first ten months of 2000, there were more protests than in all of 1997 (518, and 479 assemblies).

Opposition is always unnerving, yet these protests are not driven by extremists. In fact, the protests have targeted fairly prosaic issues such as air and water pollution, residency rights for mainland children, housing, English requirements for teachers, civil service reform, welfare budget cuts, academic freedom, medical reform, and even the construction of a Disneyland on Lantau Island. Groups such as teachers, doctors, lawyers, and social workers have also taken to the streets.

Why? Are Hong Kongers bored? Pollution is one thing, but are English requirements for teachers really worth a march? In the words of Gloria Chang, president of the student union at the University of Hong Kong and an avid protester, "There is simply no other way to pressure the authorities toward change." As Mei Ng, leader of Friends of the Earth, an environmental activist group, put it, "We have exhausted peaceful means of communication with the government."

But how did it come to this? To be sure, Hong Kong under the British was by no means democratic. But the British did build a political framework (a Westminster-style parliament, a free press, and a legal system) in Hong Kong that was intended to form the foundations of democracy once they departed. In 1991, the British allowed some seats in Hong Kong's parliament to be contested in direct elections; in 1995, more than 1 million voters elected a new legislature.

All of which was promptly trod underfoot by China, which had no interest in flowering democracies. Hong Kong's new chief executive would be Tung Chee-hwa, a pro-Beijing shipping magnate and a self-confessed admirer of long-time Singapore leader Lee Kwan Yew's "Asian Values" philosophy of social control before civil liberties. Which was good for him, because after one term in office, Tung was extremely unpopular. Polls showed that only 16 percent of Hong Kongers wanted to see him stay in power. But it was not their decision. In July 2002, Beijing appointed Tung for another five-year term.

As with the executive, so with the legislature. China fiddled with the election laws so that in the Legislative Council (LegCo), only twenty seats would be popularly elected, while thirty would represent functional constituencies (businessmen and professionals) and ten would, in effect, be appointed by Beijing. China also changed the eligibility requirements for functional constituency voters, reducing the number of eligible voters from 2.7 million to 200,000. So when the opposition Democratic Party (DP) won 60 percent of the popular vote in 1998 elections, it only got 30 percent of the seats in the LegCo.

All of which sent rich, but angry, Hong Kongers out onto the streets. Most of their protests were peaceful, but they could still spin out of control. In a protest over residency rights for mainland-born children, protesters set fire to the Immigration Department office, killing two. In the summer of 2002, tens of thousands of protesters took the streets over civil service pay cuts. It was the largest demonstration since the 1989 protests against the Chinese crackdown in Tiananmen Square.

During the same year, Hong Kong's leadership began to contemplate a dubious "Anti-Subversion Law," which was promptly condemned by human rights groups and even drew raised eyebrows from the Bush administration. Under the law, subversion would be broadly interpreted to include anything that would excite disaffections against the Central People's Government, the People's Republic of China, or the Hong Kong

Special Administrative Region Government. Ten foreign banks voiced concerns that the new law could prevent the free flow of economic information and therefore jeopardize Hong Kong's status as Asia's premier financial center.

The citizens of Hong Kong reacted in unprecedented fashion; half a million angry protesters took to the streets in July 2003, in the territory's largest demonstration since the 1989 Tiananmen Square protests. Tung was forced to shelve the law and even sacked two unpopular ministers. Seen positively, the government had at last shown itself to be responsive to popular demands. Seen negatively, it is alarming that this responsiveness came only after discontent had built to the point that so many of the territory's citizens would make public protests. Even for a place as rich as Hong Kong, there are dangers inherent in closing channels for discontent.

ZIMBABWE

The infamous Robert Mugabe, president of Zimbabwe, has, for all his stunning failures, a certain panache. In the face of all the concentrated hatred the international community can muster, he has held on to his patch. Too bad for Zimbabwe; but a testimony to what can be accomplished by channeling discontent.

Zimbabwe, once called Rhodesia, was known as the "Jewel of Africa" for its rich farmland and mineral and gem deposits. Even today Zimbabwe has the highest literacy rate in Africa (90 percent) and a decent network of roads and telephones. Zimbabweans and foreigners alike had high hopes for the erudite Mugabe when, in 1980, he replaced the racist white regime of Ian Smith. He had a fine Jesuit education and had obtained six college and university degrees. He wore exquisitely tailored Western suits and was a mesmerizing public speaker. Most importantly, he said all the right things about democracy and liberty.

But twenty years after independence, the jewel sparkles no more. Zimbabwe has achieved the dubious honor of being one of only five countries in the world whose social indicators—education, healthcare, and prosperity—have actually declined since 1980. Zimbabwe also has the third-highest AIDS infection rate in the world, and the quality of its healthcare system was ranked dead last among 191 countries surveyed by the World Health Organization.

Mugabe has also presided over staggering economic mismanagement. Zimbabwe spent $3.2 million per day servicing its debt in 2000, and unemployment and inflation were both hovering around 60 percent. This is not one of those regimes that inherited the debt of corrupt and spendthrift predecessors. Mugabe, who has ruled since 1980, spent most of that money himself. Over half the population lives below the poverty line; many commodities are in perennial shortage, and many others simply unaffordable.

So how does this man stay in power? First of all, he is no democrat. He inherited a political system that already gave the ruling party excessive power. In 1987, he created the office of executive president, which allowed him to appoint all senior officials of the civil service, the army, and the police force. Additional advantages for the ruling party were also written into the constitution, skewing the electoral process to prevent opposition parties from staging a meaningful challenge.

Still, it is amazing that Mugabe has hung on. A government as incompetent as his inevitably sparks determined opposition. Yet Mugabe has one streak of extraordinary brilliance. He is a master at channeling away discontent—at scapegoating and shifting blame.

∞

It is hard to say when Mugabe first realized the potential of this tactic. But he achieved one great success early on. At the start of his rule, he faced an uprising by rival Joshua Nkomo, leader of the N'debele people. He promptly explained to the international community that South Africa's apartheid regime was trying to undermine his rule using Joshua Nkomo as a proxy. The claim that the N'debele were South African stooges was a good one, because South Africa's racist leaders were international pariahs. Merely invoking their name justified Mugabe's colorful warning—"We might very well demand two ears for one ear and two eyes for one eye." Such was the South African threat that "an eye for an eye" was evidently not good enough. Mugabe sent his Fifth Brigade, trained by the North Koreans, into the N'debele territory of Matabeleland. His troops butchered an estimated 20,000 civilians in acts of horrific atrocity. But the international community, focused on the South African bogeyman, was willing to look the other way.

Another favorite enemy for Mugabe is the British, Zimbabwe's colonial rulers. It is much easier to shift the blame to a scapegoat that is already hated. And the British have much to answer for concerning their historical misconduct in Zimbabwe. When the British colonized the territory in 1897, the colonists forcibly removed blacks from their homes and resettled them onto stony land in arid climes. The white rulers of Zimbabwe continued this process until as late as 1980, earning huge profits from the country's most valuable resources and creating a relationship of dependency with the African natives.

So, as one might expect, the British are unloved in Zimbabwe. It cannot be said that the British have really done anything to undermine Zimbabwe since independence in 1980—successive economic disasters have been mostly of Mugabe's making. But Mugabe casts every crisis as some kind of British plot. Zimbabweans "cannot continue to exist as though we were an extension of the British Empire," he has said. To Tony Blair: "Keep your England and let us keep our Zimbabwe." Mugabe implausibly blamed the British for a recent fuel shortage, accusing the British navy of "trapping tankers on the high seas."

Zimbabweans are culturally homophobic, so Mugabe has developed into one of the world's foremost gay bashers. His most virulent remarks, labeling gays "lower than pigs and dogs," came when he was facing criticism for his second marriage and extravagant wedding to a far younger woman. Mugabe has also blamed the rampant spread of AIDS in Zimbabwe on gays, ignoring the fact that AIDS in Africa is spread predominantly through heterosexual activity.

Since 1999, when a gay activist in London attempted to perform a citizen's arrest on Mugabe for his homophobic comments, the president has identified a British-gay conspiracy bent on undermining his rule. He calls Tony Blair's administration a group of "gay gangsters," memorably calling it "the gay government of the gay United gay Kingdom." Mugabe explains the cutoff of aid and loans to Zimbabwe as a response to his government's sensible antigay policies: "We are being told we must accept gay rights. If we do not, we risk losing millions of dollars in foreign aid."

Over the years, Mugabe has blamed everyone and everything but himself for Zimbabwe's economic malaise: acts of nature like droughts and floods; the British colonial regime; South Africa; the International Monetary Fund and World Bank, which attempted structural adjustment programs in the country starting in 1991; even that age-old scapegoat, the Jews ("Jews in South Africa, working in cahoots with their colleagues here, want our textile and clothing factories to close.").

But above all others, Mugabe's favorite scapegoats are his country's white farmers, obvious targets who first gained their property under the colonial regime. Despite this, at first Mugabe extended the olive branch to whites, saying, "The wrongs of the past must be forgiven and forgotten. It could never be a correct justification that because the whites oppressed us when they had power, the blacks must oppress them today because they have power." But then Mugabe realized that the whites could be a great boon to his faltering government. First, they could provide tax and export revenues, since they controlled the most productive and profitable segments of the Zimbabwean economy (and generated jobs for some 65 percent of the population). And second, even more importantly, they could take the blame for everything that went wrong.

This required some delicate maneuvering. When Mugabe announced that he wanted to redistribute white land, the British, moved by justifiable postcolonial guilt, agreed to support the programs. But in his first two decades in power, Mugabe ultimately did very little about the land issue. No doubt he recognized that the whites were more help to him on their farms than off them—they could continue to run their farms productively, and at the same time provide an excellent scapegoat. In 1992, legislation was passed allowing the government to seize land owned by white farmers without compensation. At that time, there were roughly 4,500 white-owned commercial farms in Zimbabwe. Oddly, up until 1998, there were still nearly 4,500 white-owned commercial farms in Zimbabwe.

But political dynamics have a way of developing their own momentum. The dynamic of scapegoating is no exception. At some point, Mugabe's approach to managing discontent began to spiral beyond his control.

∞

By the late 1990s, younger Zimbabweans who did not remember Mugabe's charismatic leadership during the independence movement had grown tired of his failures. A grassroots opposition movement took shape to limit the president's authority. Unionists, lawyers, journalists, human rights groups, and a women's movement formed a party called the Movement for Democratic Change (MDC). The leader of the MDC was Morgan Tsvangirai, a former manual laborer who had risen to become leader of Zimbabwe's trade unions. Tsvangirai is known for his casual dress and straight talk—a vivid contrast to Mugabe's business suits and flowery rhetoric. In February 2000, the MDC rallied Zimbabweans against Mugabe's attempt to expand his own powers through a new constitution, defeating the measure in a referendum. Mugabe now found himself faced with serious opposition—an opposition that threatened to defeat him in parliamentary elections scheduled for June 2000.

So Mugabe started acting on his scapegoating rhetoric. Calling the white farmers "greedy, greedy, greedy colonialists," Mugabe encouraged the veterans of Zimbabwe's independence war to seize white-owned farms starting in 1998. (The irony was that many of these "veterans" were far too young to have actually fought in the war.) By 2001, over 1,600 farms had been invaded and their owners expelled and often assaulted. The so-called veterans disrupted factories, assaulting employees of white owners. By 2002, nearly all the 4,500 white farmers had been evicted. This had a devastating impact on the economy, which contracted by 7 percent in 2000, 10 percent in 2001, and 12 percent in 2002. An estimated quarter of a million jobs were lost. Foreign investment collapsed. Exports dropped by 40 percent from their peak in 1996 and inflation ran to triple digits. Per capita incomes declined by about one-third since Mugabe started his land resettlement policies. Tourism, which was once the country's leading earner of foreign exchange, all but dried up.

Whether land reform to redress colonial wrongs was morally justified or not isn't the point. This was no way to go about it. Highly productive, high-tech farmers who produced profitable crops of tobacco, citrus, beef, and flowers (much of which were exported) were evicted, and subsistence farmers resettled on their land (that is, the land which did not go to Mugabe cronies). Human rights issues aside, this was an economic disaster. Food production fell by a third. As of this writing, the World Food Program has arrived in the country in hopes of averting starvation. There is the potential for a severe humanitarian crisis, one on a scale that again compels the involvement of the world community, in an effort to avert an even greater tragedy.

∞

Mugabe achieved his immediate objective, which was to win the March 2002 presidential election. Though independent opinion polls taken before the election showed Tsvangirai beating Mugabe, the president pulled out all the stops to ensure his victory. His thugs, mobilized by antiwhite rhetoric, turned against opposition supporters. One nongovernmental organization estimated that three quarters of the population either suffered from or witnessed state violence designed to intimidate voters. Mugabe won, but independent observers, including the United States, denounced the polls as neither free nor fair.

In its chaos, Zimbabwe may remind the observer of Indonesia, but it is not. This is a political crisis wholly manufactured by Zimbabwe's government. Mugabe may not, in the end, survive. But it is his supporters, with his backing, who have violently taken to the streets, not some kind of opposition movement. The collapsing economy, rising unemployment, and runaway inflation are all byproducts of an intentional political strategy. This is truly dysfunctional kimchi.

THE DYNAMICS OF CHANNELING DISCONTENT

The best way to turn the heat down on boiling national politics is to throw out poorly performing governments with faltering popular support. Democratic systems, in all their myriad varieties, are usually quite good at this. In India, for instance, bad governments (and admittedly good ones as well) are easily disposed of; this has unfortunate consequences for policy— producing frequent changes and even reversals—but it gives angry Indians the feeling that their voices have been heard. When a government that people hold responsible for their problems is thrown out, the public's anger at least temporarily dissipates. Fundamentally, democracy is exceptional because it can channel discontent constructively through the political system. This makes for good kimchi. By contrast, in an authoritarian state, discontent is forced outside (and often against) the political system.

Democracy also offers people a voice in policymaking. Governments will tend to implement the policies that the people want, for fear of being voted out of power. If they fail in this, unresponsive governments can be tossed out and replaced by new regimes with better policy agendas. Thus democratic political systems, while by no means guaranteeing great policy, do at least respond to people's demands and thereby ease the sources of their discontent. (Of course, a very competent authoritarian regime can do this as well.)

But liberal democracy also provides freedom of expression. By forming or supporting opposition movements, writing letters to the editor, or taking to the streets, people can relieve their anger. Some of their anger may dissipate instead of building toward an eventual explosion. These people are less apt to feel that their only way of pressing for political change is through violence. Hong Kong may not be democratic, but it is liberal. While the people have no real vote, they are still free to express their opinions by demonstrating. If a nervous China closes even that safety valve, it risks making its problems considerably worse.

But democracy is no panacea. The democracies of Western Europe and North America tend to exclude many voices because their systems favor centrist parties. This is tyranny of the majority, and it can leave the minority with bottled-up anger (the Basques in Spain, for instance). Yet far more worrisome—and more likely to drive instability—is the tyranny of the minority. In some "democratic" systems, an elite group effectively controls political power while the majority has little voice. This closes off democracy's safety valves—a situation long true in Pakistan, where the grip of agricultural landlords is strong. It was true of pre-Chavez Venezuela, where the system was dominated by the two Punto Fijo parties. And it is true of Venezuela under Chavez, because the president modified the Constitution so that he is effectively unimpeachable.

States that are not democracies, or are poorly functioning democracies, run serious risks with popular discontent. In the short term, they may appear very stable (as Indonesia did), because the discontent is kept below the surface. Instead of dissipating, the discontent tends to grow.

Authoritarian regimes are by no means helpless in the face of public anger. Despite Zimbabwe's disastrous example, scapegoating can be an astonishingly effective way to manage discontent. One example can be found in Malaysia. Of all of the high-growth "Asian tigers," Malaysia was the only one that kept its government in the wake of the 1997 Asian financial crisis, despite the fact that its GDP fell by 7.5 percent in 1998, after having grown at roughly 8 percent a year for the previous nine years.

Malaysia's prime minister, Mahathir Muhammad, was able to deflect much of the blame for the crisis onto foreigners. Most notably he blamed Western currency speculators, and specifically one single, larger-than-life individual: "The Government has definite evidence that the pressure on the ringgit and other Asian currencies was caused by George Soros." Mahathir explained that Soros had attacked the ringgit in retaliation for Malaysia's decision to allow dictatorial Burma into the Association of Southeast Asian Nations. "We have spent our time—thirty to forty years—building up our nation, giving our people a good life, raising their income levels, and this man in a few days destroyed everything," he said. "And the world doesn't regard him as a criminal...just as much as people who produce and distribute drugs are criminals, they destroy nations, undermine economies." Mahathir also took note of the fact that Soros is Jewish, declaring that "We are Muslims and the Jews are not happy to see the Muslims progress." This comment was aimed especially at Malaysia's Muslim Malay majority, which had increasingly drifted away from Mahathir and to an opposition Islamic party. This strategy was not completely successful—he lost ground to the Islamists in November 1999 parliamentary elections—but he retained his hold on power.

Other masters of deflecting discontent are found in Arab regimes across the Middle East. In Egypt, state newspapers pay disproportionate attention to foreign affairs, especially the Arab-Israeli conflict, and give scant heed to the country's severe social and economic problems. Syria's Hafez al-Asad portrayed his state as being under constant threat of Israeli aggression and used the long-running conflict with Israel to divert attention from economic decline, internal ethnic conflict, and power struggles in Damascus. Saddam Hussein managed to redirect some of the Iraqi people's attention away from Iraq's many problems by using threats to attack Israel, and monetary rewards offered to Palestinian "martyrs." University of Maryland Professor Shibley Telhami conducted an opinion poll in five Arab states (Egypt, Saudi Arabia, the United Arab Emirates, Kuwait, and Lebanon), revealing—amazingly—that the majority of the citizens in each country ranked Palestinine as "the single most important issue to them personally." (Egyptians were most adamant—a full 79 percent of the population agreed that Palestine was the issue most important to them.) While no one denies that the Palestinian problem is an intensely emotional one, it is startling that an issue that has no direct impact on the day-to-day lives of citizens in these other countries is of such concern. For their governments, of course, this is a very good thing. The more they can keep their citizens' attention focused outward, the less attention will be paid to their own failings at home.

While it works, this kind of kimchi is useful for political survival but not for political stability. A more sound approach is taken by those countries that are able, through competent policies, to preempt the root causes of discontent.

CHAPTER SEVEN

The World's Most Powerful Man

STATE POWER

IT IS THE TYRANT'S FAVORITE MODEL.

To governments unwilling to relinquish power, Singapore's approach to development has obvious appeal. Singapore is both an extraordinary success story and, in essence, a one-party state. Political freedoms are substantially curtailed. But year after year, the government has delivered political stability and phenomenal economic growth. On the whole, the Singaporean people have accepted this tradeoff. To other authoritarian governments, Singapore's example offers a justification for political oppression. The ends (growth and stability) justify the means. China's Communist Party is walking this path, as are the leaders of Malaysia and Tunisia; Indonesia, of course, attempted this and failed, with tragic consequences.

What makes the difference between success and failure? What will determine whether China ends up facing Indonesia's future of economic and political turmoil or Singapore's achievement of greater per capita wealth than most of Europe? One key is state power, specifically the capacity of state institutions (the political leadership, the civil service, the police, the army, and so on) to achieve the goals of the ruling regime. Powerful states can either defuse discontent by addressing popular demands, or suppress discontent that turns into opposition. They can therefore deliver the growth and stability so crucial to their survival.

What makes a powerful state? To answer this question, consider Iran, where the Shah's government once appeared indestructible.

IRAN

The Shah of Iran reached the pinnacle of his power in the 1970s. His visage stared down at the people of Iran from every street corner, public place, office, and shop wall. He was the *Shahinshah*, the King of Kings, and the *Aryamehr*, Light of the Aryans. The world came to see the Shah through a mythical lens. A pulp novel was published in 1976 called *A Bullet for the Shah: All They Had to Do Was Kill the World's Most Powerful Man*. On New Year's Eve 1978, just one month before the start of revolution, visiting U.S. president Jimmy Carter infamously toasted the Shah's grip over his state: "Iran, because of the great leadership of the Shah, is an island of stability in one of the most troubled areas of the world." And the U.S. Defense Intelligence Agency confidently predicted in September 1978 that the Shah would remain in power for the next ten years.

It is not hard to understand how the Shah inspired such confidence. His grip on Iran was absolute. He banned all opposition and reigned supreme atop his own Rastakhiz Party. His State Security and Intelligence Organization (SAVAK) maintained tight control over society, cultural institutions, and all forms of communication. With oil revenues reaching $25 billion by 1974, the government had more money than it knew what to do with. And the Shah seemed to have the support of his people. A full 99 percent of voters approved a referendum on his "White Revolution," a series of reforms including the Family Protection Act, which gave women unprecedented rights; the Anti-Land Speculation Bill, which was a response to real estate speculation; an antiprofiteering campaign designed to attack inflation; and privatization. The Shah even claimed dominion over time itself: with the stroke of a pen, he reworked the Iranian calendar so the years would be counted from the founding of the first Iranian kingdom, rather than from the flight of the Prophet Muhammad from Mecca to Medinah.

And this was no paper tiger. The Shah had shown mettle under real duress. A popular prime minister named Mohammad Mossadegh had forced the Shah into exile in the early 1950s. With help from the CIA and the British, the Shah returned to power, with a new intolerance of opposition. He dealt harshly with his opponents, and in so doing demonstrated his not inconsiderable capability as a leader. He crushed the opposition Tudeh party and exiled most of its leaders from the country. Factions within the army loyal to Tudeh were purged. The Shah, dismayed with the results of 1960 parliamentary elections, simply voided them. Riots swept many Iranian cities, as opposition to the Shah's dictatorial rule grew. But the Shah repressed the uprisings. He arrested the spiritual leader of the opposition movement, the Ayatollah Khomeini. His troops stormed the religious schools where the demonstrations originated. The Shah then eliminated the National Front, a coalition of opposition groups. When a guerrilla uprising struck a police outpost near the Caspian Sea, the Shah's forces tracked down and captured the insurgents, arrested their associates in Tehran, and proceeded with a round of executions and jailings that decimated the group.

The Shah's secret police, SAVAK, maintained a watchful eye over all activity in the kingdom, repressing opposition and promoting the Shah's dictatorship. SAVAK ordered newspapers to celebrate the Shah and feature the activities of the royal couple on every front page. SAVAK agents infiltrated opposition groups to root out "black and red reactionaries"—the religious and communist opposition. Along the way, the Iranian regime was complicit in human rights violations that included detention, assassination, execution, beatings, and torture. All this is what Carter saw, when he made his infamous toast. But behind the façade, visible to those who cared to look, was a weak state incapable of realizing the Shah's grand ambitions.

∞

Despite his American connections, the Shah of Iran decided initially to follow a socialist state-planning economic model, so popular at the time. A Plan Organization (PO) was duly established to build infrastructure and guide Iran's development. The government had the money—as oil prices rose, more than enough of it. But it simply lacked the institutional capacity to make state planning work. As a result of corruption and mismanagement, a staggering 45 percent of the oil revenues intended to fund the PO was diverted. The corruption didn't stop there. In order to import, export, or expand, companies were required to obtain licenses, which often entailed bribery reaching the highest levels of government.

There were a few extraordinary prestige projects; visitors to Tehran were impressed by large-scale, mechanized industrial plants clustered around the capital. But most of the Shah's economic vision for an Iran that would come to rival Japan was simply inappropriate, decreeing that uneducated and unskilled Iranians would produce high-tech goods for competitive markets. Cheap credit was extended to large firms but denied to the kind of small-scale operations that could have generated significant employment gains and promoted entrepreneurship. The PO devoted much of its resources to constructing impressive dams. The dams were grand to look at, but often failed to serve their functions of irrigation and power generation; the government generally neglected to build local irrigation systems that would deliver water from the dams to farms.

Bad planning is worse than no planning at all. The Shah's policies were highly inflationary. Government spending was unrestrained. The endless credit supply to large-scale domestic enterprises encouraged frenetic expansion. Prices for essential commodities such as grain skyrocketed, hitting the poor in their bellies. Rural peasants began to flood into the cities, which were not equipped to handle the surging number of migrants. Rising discontent was further fueled by the Shah's evident disregard for the cultural sensibilities of his people. The Shah never missed an opportunity to display his wealth and grandeur. And the Shah's close relationship with the U.S., his Western ways, and his opening of the country to legions of Western businessmen was unsettling to many Iranians. Many perceived—with justification—that the Shah was more focused on impressing his foreign friends than with delivering material prosperity to the masses at home.

Sooner or later, the people of Iran were going to react to what they saw as the Shah's callous indifference. In the late 1970s, the Shah's renowned leadership ability began to fail him. The Shah withdrew from meetings of the cabinet and decisions about the day-to-day running of the kingdom. Those who spoke with the Shah during this period described him as "no longer functioning." Prime Minister General Gholem Reza Azhari told the American ambassador, "The country is lost because the king cannot make up his mind."

And then the true weakness of the Iranian state became clear: an institutionally underdeveloped government was unable to do much about its subjects' wide-ranging discontents other than repress them. And this just made them madder. When the Shah faltered, it suddenly became dramatically obvious that the Iranian regime was fundamentally dependent on this one man. In 1978, antiregime demonstrations began to mount. Initially, the Shah sought to suppress the uprisings. In September 1978, on a day that would come to be known as Black Friday, military units opened fire on 20,000 demonstrators who had gathered in Jhaleh Square. This filled people with fear but also anger. After the trauma of the killings, the Shah shied away from using force. On November 2, 1978, crowds roamed the streets burning symbols of "Western decadence and corruption," including liquor stores, banks, government offices, and a wing of the British embassy. The Shah did nothing.

This was the beginning of the end. Protesters mobilized by the charismatic Ayatollah Khomeini challenged the Iranian government, which then collapsed. The Shah fled into exile, Khomeini returned from his own exile to lead the new Islamic government, and radical students urged to action by the aging ayatollah seized the American embassy and U.S. citizens who had taken refuge there. Fundamentalist hardliners ousted the moderates and secularists and still control the levers of power to this day.

The U.S. government, so intimately tied to the Shah, could not extract itself from this political cataclysm. U.S. businesses had participated eagerly in Iran's oil-driven boom, which was seen as one of the world's hottest developing markets. The revolutionary regime confiscated all U.S. investment in the country, resulting in more than $4 billion in losses. U.S. citizens living in Iran lost their homes and their property when they fled. This catastrophic event fueled the rise of the newly developed political risk insurance industry (which insures businesses against threats such as war, rebellion, and government seizure of assets). OPIC, the U.S. government political risk insurer, had a $1 billion book of business in the 1970s; by 1983, this had ballooned to $4 billion. The Iranian case had demonstrated how much damage politics could do.

Perhaps even more importantly, the U.S. was profoundly implicated in Iran's dysfunctional dynamics. A regime sprang up whose very reason for existence at times seemed to be to oppose "the Great Satan." Indeed, "Death to America" remains a knee-jerk refrain in Iranian politics to this day, two decades later, while so much else in geopolitics has changed. This lesson of long memories and strong hatreds is worth remembering as, in the pursuit of the war on terrorism, the United States props up other unsteady and dictatorial regimes.

SINGAPORE

If not through repression, how does one build a super state?

Anyone seeking the answer to this question would hardly have expected to find it in the Singapore of 1959—an impoverished, stagnant swamp with unpaved roads, abundant slums, a raging tuberculosis problem, and an exploding population. Labor unrest was common. Race riots broke out between the island's Chinese, Malay, and Indian communities. The departing British closed their military base on the island and, at a stroke, Singapore lost a fifth of its GDP.

But something unusual was happening there in the tropics. Singapore's first prime minister, Lee Kwan Yew, had a business-oriented sensibility. He focused on a sound strategy—becoming an attractive location for manufacturing—and provided incentives for foreign investors. Lee established an Economic Development Board to build industrial estates and infrastructure. He put together a program to control population growth that mixed education, incentives, and coercion. This sounds like any number of countries—most of which have achieved nothing near Singapore's level of success. Not so very different from Iran, in fact.

But there were crucial differences. Most countries pay lip service to these basics; Singapore poured money into them. During its first nine years in power, the government spent an incredible amount—nearly one-third of its budget—on education. Lee just did things better. Fewer prestige projects; more well-maintained roads. Mass transit was also good, indeed soon among the world's best, as was the international airport. The government drew up strict health, safety, and building codes, and then actually enforced them.

But the true key to Lee's success was a civil service of ruthless competence. A typical developing-country bureaucracy is used as a means of distributing political favors. Being a civil service employee is like being a waiter in the United States: the base salary is low, but there is ample opportunity to collect tips (more bluntly: to abuse one's position of authority—as a building inspector, driver's license examiner, or construction project supervisor—by collecting bribes and kickbacks.) The government can thereby put more cronies on the payroll than would be possible if wages were strictly out-of-pocket. In Singapore, however, the civil service selection process was highly meritocratic, and civil servants were given excellent salaries (current prime minister Goh Chok Tong earns ten times the salary of his Malaysian counterpart). This reduced incentives for corruption. It also attracted talented people into government. Those who were nevertheless corrupt were punished ruthlessly. No one was exempt from scrutiny, and penalties for even small offenses were harsh. Corruption was excised to the point that, in 2002, Singapore ranked as the fifth least corrupt country in the world—less corrupt than the United States and United Kingdom, and surpassed only by Finland, Denmark, New Zealand, and Iceland.

Lee built a civil service that could deliver results, and then involved that civil service in every aspect of Singaporean life. Even today, fully 75 percent of Singaporeans live in government-built housing. Government-linked companies (GLCs) account for a sizable majority (60 percent) of Singapore's annual economic output. The state minutely directs economic activity through a mix of laws, regulations, and fiscal incentives. This is state planning, truly Big Government. But it has worked.

Lee's civil service was given a mandate to deliver law and order. Spitting, chewing gum, and watching pornography were made illegal. Taxis were equipped with bells that ring automatically when the driver is exceeding the speed limit. Singapore became one of Asia's safest cities. Gates are left unlocked, and mail carriers frequently drop packages on doorsteps without fear of theft. Parked motorcyclists leave their helmets and jackets resting openly on their bikes and walk away. Lawbreakers are subject to notoriously harsh prison terms and stiff fines; caning is the punishment for thirty different offenses, from vandalism to drug trafficking. So yes, Singapore is boring. But to investors—who want to minimize risks to their personnel and capital—boring is good.

Lee's government has also been repressive. His People's Action Party (PAP) maintains an unquestioned monopoly on power. Even today it controls eighty of the eighty-four seats in the parliament. In 2001, the PAP took 75 percent of the votes—which is not surprising, when one considers that opposition parties did not even try to contest 55 of the

84 seats. Certainly, opposition is kept down. The Internal Security Act (ISA) provides for arrest without warrant and was used against the PAP's early communist opponents. The ISA also restricts the media. Reporting usually conforms to the government line, reflecting intimidation of the press and self-censorship. Public assemblies must be state-sanctioned, and the Societies Act has outlawed religious movements deemed to be dangerous. And the PAP is not above coercion. In 1997, the prime minister warned voters that constituencies electing opposition parliamentarians would be given lowest priority for government housing renovations. Opposition politicians are hit with defamation suits that leave them bankrupt and impotent and deter others from challenging the PAP.

But is this what has made Singapore stable? Or is it the fact that the government has been able to deliver results? Virtually 100 percent of children are enrolled in school (mostly at the government's expense), and more than 92 percent of the people are literate. Infant mortality—an excellent measure of basic sanitation and health care—is a mere 3.6 deaths per 1,000 live births (below North American and at European levels). The country's per capita income is $24,740, richer than Canada, Germany, or Belgium. Ninety percent of Singaporeans own their own homes—tops in the world (the government, after building homes for most of the country's citizens, let residents buy their homes—frequently at reduced prices). As a result, nearly everyone has a stake in the system. There has been no political violence in Singapore in thirty years. The island's last strike was in 1986. Singapore has created such world-class companies as Singapore Airlines (frequently named the world's top airline), Singapore Telecommunications, and DBS, the largest bank in Southeast Asia. This is a government of extraordinary effectiveness. It is a government capable of identifying and addressing sources of public anger, and thereby managing discontent.

∞

But some will say the shine has worn off the "Singapore Miracle." In 2001, Singapore was struck by its worst recession since independence. To be sure, these economic difficulties are more the result of current global conditions—Singapore's reliance on high technology and its dependence on the United States as an export market—than anything that is structurally wrong with the country. But there is nothing like a recession to inspire self-doubt. There are some things that a government bureaucracy, no matter how sharp, simply does not do well. To stay at the top of the value chain, and move into creativity-dependent industries such as biotech and software, Singapore needs to learn how to cultivate more innovation and risk-taking. Michael Porter has recommended that the government tolerate a more "chaotic and heterogeneous" society. Easier said than done. Venture capital firms are springing up, political leaders can frequently be heard praising risk taking, and there has even been some talk of privatizing or at least diluting government stakes in GLCs. But Prime Minister Goh Chok Tong has said that he does not want to be remembered as "Goh-bachev," the leader who opened the Pandora's Box of reform.

Whatever the country's future course, Singapore has shown what can be accomplished by a truly powerful state. It is staggering to think that a young Singaporean who started work in 1959, when Lee Kwan Yew took power, might just now be retiring. From poverty to prosperity in a single generation.

THE DYNAMICS OF STATE POWER

To this day many analysts mistake dictatorial authority for power. This is not surprising—repressive regimes *look* stable. Unlike democracies, there is minimal public protest and dissent. The government stays in power for years, unchallenged. Iran looked stable in 1977. Indonesia looked stable in 1996. Repression can deliver a superficial calm. But it cannot deliver fundamental stability—a stability that can survive determined opposition, unexpected external shocks, or an economic crisis. What has made Singapore fundamentally stable was its government's ability to deliver the goods, time and time again—not its curtailing of political freedoms, but its ability to address most sources of public discontent. What made Iran unstable was the government's inability to accomplish these things. The Shah of Iran was powerful in obvious ways but weak in a more profound sense. He could order the execution of any person, anywhere in his country, on a whim, while the president of the U.S., for instance, could not. Yet the Shah, no matter how hard he tried, could not order the building of an effective transport infrastructure or an educational system, or even a noncorrupt police force.

The Iranian state, simply put, lacked the organizational power to do such things. It therefore lacked the ability to deal with a determined opposition movement. More fundamentally, it lacked the ability to make policies that would alleviate the sources of the public's discontent. Weak states all too often fall into a dynamic of instability that acquires its own momentum. It begins with some element of public discontent—perhaps not great discontent, perhaps just dissatisfaction that's been created by the weak state's own corruption. But when this discontent is expressed, the weak state responds in a way that raises public anger. Incompetent policies, ineptly administered, make all problems worse. So do heavy-handed crackdowns. The people, now even angrier, begin to express their dismay publicly. The state responds again, still ineptly, further worsening the situation in a vicious cycle.

∞

The most sophisticated and effective states have the ability to regulate, direct, and implement highly complex activities. These states can maintain law and order in all regions of the country. Their civil service is top-notch. They can regulate even the most sophisticated economic behavior—preventing corruption and white-collar crime, and collecting taxes and punishing tax evaders. These states, when they wish, can deliver essential services—transportation networks, communications infrastructure, school systems, health care, and so on. All states—even the most effective—have failures in some areas. But some, like Singapore, can achieve things that in most countries are considered impossible—for example, state-owned corporations that operate with efficiency and profitability.

Less-effective states may suffer occasional random breakdowns in their control of political and economic activity. Corruption scandals may plague an administration, or criminal activity may flourish in some areas. Some types of difficult regulation (antitrust enforcement, say, or tax collection) may have costly shortcomings. Complex national systems (education or infrastructure) or state-run enterprises may have serious failings. Most "industrialized" or "First World" states exhibit such occasional shortfalls.

Farther down the scale of state competence are countries whose shortcomings have direct and substantial economic costs. Failures are systematic, not random. Public order breaks down in some areas of the country. Tax evasion runs rampant. Corruption is widespread in the civil service. Regulations and legal codes are not well enforced. Indeed, the very rich or powerful may repeatedly flout the law without punishment. The state may have little alternative but to resort to the threat of force to accomplish its goals.

Even farther down the scale are those states that lack the capacity to control major aspects of political and economic activity—short of resorting to the use of force. The state may be superficially stable but extremely repressive, and with a dismal record in building infrastructure, providing public services, educating its people, ensuring their health, and so on. The civil service and state-run companies are usually a haven for patronage and incompetence.

∞

But delivering the goods is only half the story. Powerful states are also able to keep opposition elements under control. With rare exceptions, even the best-run states may face disgruntled elements of society—the economically disadvantaged, ethnic or religious minorities, groups backed by hostile foreign powers, and so on.

The most powerful states deal with opposition using highly legitimate and transparent rules. These legal codes are not arbitrary or totalitarian, but are enforced with due process and subject to appeal. Such states have the ability to suppress illegal opposition without triggering more discontent. A weak state, through heavy-handed tactics, usually creates more popular anger every time it tries to deal with dissent. (Certainly, this was the case when the Shah of Iran attempted to deal with opposition to his rule.) Demonstrators, when faced with arrest, rigged courts, and harsh prison sentences (or worse), can turn into revolutionaries. Unjustified violence against the public can swell the ranks of the government's foes. Singapore, for all its state power, has failings in this area, while the democratic states of North America and Europe are the most effective in using legitimate and transparent rules for dealing with opposition. Less admirable are those states with highly effective police and intelligence forces that deal effectively with discontent, but with somewhat question-able legitimacy.

Below these states are countries that try to control dissent but fail. The judiciary may be distrusted by the public. The police may be in-competent or violent and feared by the citizens. The state may exercise little control over some geographic areas or social groups. Illegal acts, and their perpetrators, may be widely known but unpunished. Illicit gains—from corruption or criminal activity—may be publicly flaunted. Guerrillas may control large areas of territory. Short of the use of force, these states can accomplish little. Rising discontent or a charismatic and well-funded opposition may be the breath of wind that causes these states to collapse.

State power—along with material prosperity—is one of the great de-terminants of long-term political stability. Ultimately, powerful states have the ability to manage popular discontent in a constructive fashion. In effect, they can address the underlying causes of the public's discontent. But whether the leaders of these states choose to do so is another story.

Part 3

Leadership

OUR FIRST TWO SECTIONS FOCUSED ON THE GENERAL PUBLIC—
when, why, and how "the masses" become involved in politics. Section
One identified the drivers of popular discontent, Section Two the ways
in which governments attempt to manage that discontent.

The influence of the general public on politics—even in a dictatorial
system—is profound. Mass political action can bring down governments
(Indonesia, Iran, Venezuela, the Philippines) or render a government
dysfunctional (Nigeria). The threat of mass action can compel governments to adopt policies that support religious fundamentalism (Egypt)
or bring about economic disaster (Zimbabwe). Even countries that successfully channel public discontent through the political system may
have volatile politics as a result (India).

Which is why we did not start this book with leadership—though in
the chapters that follow, we now turn to bad leaders (Uganda) and good
(Uganda, again); leadership succession (Yugoslavia and Italy); and the
"bargain" between the leadership and society (Peru and Saudi Arabia).
We did not start with leadership because even the most forceful and
independent-thinking leaders must pay close attention to the public's
disposition. To be sure, explosions of mass political violence are very rare.
But this is because governments constantly make decisions that reduce
discontent or channel it or head off opposition. These decisions may
not be the best in economic terms, or even be consonant with the goals
of the leadership. But they are political necessities. Governments that
fail to heed these necessities are generally rapidly deposed. Leadership is
always constrained.

CHAPTER EIGHT

Good Leaders and Bad

QUALITY OF LEADERSHIP

LEADERSHIP IS NOT EVERYTHING. THIS MAY HAVE SUPPLIED SOME small comfort to Americans, when it suddenly came to light that Bill Clinton, the president of the United States, the commander-in-chief, the so-called "leader of the free world," had been (at least figuratively) caught with his pants down in the company of a twenty-four-year-old intern.

From the moment the news broke, Washington, D.C. was obsessed with Monica Lewinsky. Surviving the scandal soon became the main focus of the Clinton administration. The president was forced to meet constantly with his lawyers. By the time the Supreme Court ruled that he did not have immunity from a civil suit, he had constructed elaborate defenses—famously questioning the meaning of the word "is"—for a grueling video cross-examination. In the Congress, partisanship escalated to the point where little could be accomplished. The Senate blocked campaign finance reform and a treaty to ban nuclear testing. The Republicans stymied Democratic spending initiatives in education, health care, and environmental protection. A delegation of American legislators, with more important things on their minds, failed to turn up at a meeting with European heads of state in Munich over the future of NATO.

And nobody outside of Washington seemed to care. Crime rates dropped sharply. There was no major civil unrest. The economy grew a whopping 4.2 percent in 1998 (5.6 percent in the last quarter, when the impeachment trial took place), inflation fell to 1.6 percent (the lowest yearly rate since 1986), and unemployment was 4.5 percent (the lowest rate since 1969 and the lowest peacetime rate since 1957). A full 72 percent of Americans say 1998 was a good year for them.

Proving, clearly, that America's government is quite capable of running itself. The same day Clinton testified on closed circuit television before a grand jury, the Treasury Department, located across the street, was dealing effectively with the threat from the Russian ruble devaluation and debt default. Over the next several weeks, the Federal Reserve, the Treasury, and the White House crafted a crisis response plan. When Clinton—seeking an escape from Monicagate—tried to get involved, he was told everything was under control. The Federal Reserve cut interest rates three times within seven weeks, and Treasury coordinated an international response. In short, the American government continued to function effectively regardless of its rather distracted leadership.

Which seems odd. The emphasis in media coverage is almost always on political leaders. They seem to be single-handedly responsible for all sorts of world events—from peace ("African Leaders Meet to Push Burundi Peace Process Forward"); to war ("Sharon and Arafat Stumble Toward the Abyss"); to economics ("Putin Promises Seven Percent Rise in Russia's GDP"); to medical breakthroughs ("Clinton Vows to Develop AIDS Vaccine within Ten Years"). (Reading such a headline, one might fully expect to see President Clinton in a lab suit manning the centrifuge.)

"But can one person really make a difference?"—a question that is inevitably and earnestly posed by the latest Hollywood thriller, shortly before the hero or heroine heads off to save the world. The lesson of this tried-and-true Hollywood formula is that heroism makes a good story. True at the movies, and no less true in politics. Journalists and analysts, when assessing a country's prospects for future stability and growth, almost inevitably focus on the top leaders—their backgrounds, ideologies, policies, capabilities, and goals.

But leadership is only part of the story. In some countries, it's not a very important part; in others, it can make a significant difference. Consider the case of Uganda.

UGANDA

Uganda got off to a bad start—indeed, it would not be a great exaggeration to say it was designed to fail. Consider the characteristics that make a good colony: pliant local elites; political leaders unable to organize to challenge their colonial masters; and borders drawn not to reflect existing tribal territories, but rather, the colonists' concerns with power politics, climate, and geography. Uganda was just such a place: ideally suited for the efficient extraction of coffee, cotton, and tea, but highly dysfunctional as a country.

The pliant elites were imported from the far corners of the British Empire (mostly from India). Tens of thousands of Asians were brought to Uganda to serve as the country's commercial class. The geographic borders were drawn in a room of European mapmakers, randomly slicing through the territory of some twenty ethnic groups, the largest being the Buganda, Banyankole, and Basoga. The disorganization of local political leaders was ensured by the creation of convoluted political institutions. The constitution specified a bizarre arrangement in which four semiautonomous kingdoms existed within a federal state. Of these four kingdoms, the Bugandans were given privileged status. The constitution was then made extremely difficult to amend.

When Uganda gained independence in 1962, groups from the north, who were economically deprived and resentful of the wealthy Bugandans, made up the bulk of the armed forces. The military mutinied in 1964, demanding higher pay and faster promotions. Uganda's first president, Milton Obote, called on the British for help. They bailed him out, but in the end Obote was forced to concede to the military's demands, and from that point on, the military was in charge. Obote promoted and relied on an illiterate officer named Idi Amin to maintain his hold on power.

The country's already tenuous democracy fell apart in November 1966. Obote and Amin had been implicated in a smuggling scheme involving ivory and gold from the Congo. Parliament passed a motion of censure against Obote and pressed for a full investigation into Amin's activities. Obote reacted as so many African despots have done: he declared a state of emergency, arrested political rivals, and seized all powers of the state "in the interest of national unity and public security and tranquility." Two days later he suspended the constitution.

Obote then drafted a new constitution that placed an inordinate amount of power in the office of the presidency. With military support, Obote forced the new constitution through parliament without a reading and without the required quorum. He then politicized the civil service and the judiciary and manipulated local governments to do his bidding. He dismantled the opposition parties and promoted his own UPC Party, which would eventually penetrate the religious establishment and the trade unions. Obote abolished the traditional tribal kingdoms. The troublesome Buganda region was administered under martial law.

Then, in his notorious "Move to the Left," Obote embraced socialism. He extended state control over the economy and tried to create an indigenous commercial class. The government placed roughly 85 companies under its direct control, many of which were mismanaged. Predictably, these economic policies proved disastrous. Shortages of food caused dramatic price rises. Crime skyrocketed. Soon Uganda was teetering on the brink of disaster. The army's support for Obote began to wane. Fearing a putsch, Obote attempted to arrest his one-time protégé, Amin. But he was too late. Amin preempted the arrest by orchestrating a military coup. Obote fled into exile. But Amin's coup and Obote's flight were only the beginning of Uganda's problems. During his years in power, Obote had dismantled democratic institutions and created a constitution that placed all power in the hands of the president. And unfortunately, Uganda had extraordinarily bad presidents.

∞

Of which the infamous Idi Amin soon proved to be the worst. To assert control over the army, he whipped up popular hatred of the Acholi and Langi peoples, who had been the majority in Obote's armed forces. He then set out to massacre them. An estimated 300,000 were killed during Amin's eight-year reign. The illiterate Amin terrorized his own government. Bureaucrats listening to his rambling speeches could not decipher what policies he wanted them to implement. Afraid of retribution for making the wrong decisions, they most often did nothing at all. Amin's first cabinet was technocratic and competent, but he felt threatened by them and quickly replaced competent ministers with docile loyalists. Amin became a pariah in the West, and the subject of a U.S. trade embargo for accepting military aid from Muammar Qadhafi of Libya.

Amin expelled the country's 70,000-person Asian community. This was a disastrous move. Asians owned 90 percent of Ugandan businesses;

they were the country's traders, bankers, teachers, and artisans. Their expulsion caused an economic collapse. Cement factories closed; sugar production ground to a standstill. Uganda's economy plummeted. Between 1971 and 1978, Uganda's real GDP per capita fell by 4.4 percent. By 1980, real GDP was only 62 percent of its 1971 level. Of the 930 public enterprises registered in 1971, only 300 remained in operation by the early 1980s. The central bank was commanded to print money to cover government expenditure, and, predictably, inflation skyrocketed.

Amin's incompetence finally got the better of him when he invaded Tanzania, which had been harboring some of his political opponents. The Tanzanians fought back and soon had invaded and conquered Uganda. Amin was thrown from power. Unfortunately for long-suffering Ugandans, Tanzania reinstalled Milton Obote, who dedicated his second presidency, from 1981 to 1985, to creating even more of a disaster than he had in his first. He exacted revenge against the Bugandans of the south. In an effort to undermine support for rebels fighting his government, he uprooted 750,000 people living north of Kampala, placing them in internment camps. Obote's army killed as many as 300,000 civilians. Once again, Obote soon found himself facing a popular rebellion, and he lost control of the military. He fled the country—but not before taking much of the national treasury with him.

Given the disaster that had befallen the country, Uganda seemed a hopeless case. But this was a country that had degenerated into one-man rule. Hence, to correct the mistakes of its bad rulers, what Uganda needed was a good ruler. And, in 1986, this is what it got.

∞

Yoweri Museveni, a former guerrilla leader, had a very different style from his predecessors. Rather than purging and slaughtering his political rivals, he invited them into his government, offering them positions in the military or his cabinet. He resolved some ethnic tensions by restoring special privileges to the Buganda. He invited back the Asians who had been expelled under Amin. He disbanded the corrupt and despised police force of 20,000 and tried to develop one that was more professional and accountable. He drastically reduced crime. He demobilized 35,000 soldiers and reintegrated them into civilian life.

Museveni also made a 180-degree turn on economic policies. At first he continued to promote import substitution, an artificially high exchange rate, and state socialism. But he quickly changed course, and started to listen to the counsel of the World Bank, IMF, and the Paris Club of sovereign lenders. Uganda's economy took off. From 1990 to 2000, growth averaged a respectable 6.9 percent. Museveni devalued the Ugandan shilling and introduced one of Africa's most liberal exchange rate policies. In a monetary miracle, he reduced inflation from 230 percent in 1991 to 0 percent in 1993. The economy grew at a rate of 7.2 percent that year. Housing boomed; private investment soared; revenue collection nearly doubled. Museveni adopted an IMF reform plan aimed at achieving monetary stability, reducing government spending, and reforming the public sector. Thanks to his efforts, the once bustling black market for foreign currency disappeared.

The international community was overjoyed. Here was an impoverished country, struggling to improve its lot, under a crippling debt burden for which it could not be blamed—the money had been borrowed by Obote and Amin. (Who, it seems fair to say now, should never have been lent to in the first place.) International donors showered Uganda with money. By the late 1990s, a full 40 percent of Uganda's annual budget was financed by contributions from abroad. In December 1998, the IMF and bilateral donors pledged $2.2 billion, to be dispensed over a three-year period. Uganda became the first state to receive debt relief under the Highly Indebted Poor Country initiative.

Most Ugandans saw their lives materially improve under Museveni's leadership. The poverty rate fell from 56 percent in 1992 to 44 percent in 1998. Consumption per capita rose by 16.5 percent between 1992 and 1997. Hospitals obtained doctors and medicine. Primary school attendance doubled. And the roads were paved. (Indeed, in a 1990 survey, asked about the biggest single improvement in their lives since 1985, 34 percent of rural Ugandans said "peace," but almost 50 percent said "improved roads.")

Furthermore, Uganda became a rare African success story in the international fight against AIDS. From the first year he took power, Museveni breached African etiquette by openly discussing sexual behavior and AIDS prevention. On his radio program, he exhorted women to take control of their sexuality and protect themselves. He required all cabinet ministers to make speeches about AIDS and enlisted religious leaders to spread awareness in their communities. Museveni's efforts won him financial and logistical support from the UN and other international organizations. This paid dividends. From 1990 to 2000, the infection rate dropped from 15 percent of the population to 8 percent.

Perhaps there is more to this story than good leadership. Perhaps competent legislators have passed good laws? Perhaps a sophisticated bureaucracy makes and implements policy? Far from it. Uganda is still a one-man show. Museveni drew up a constitution in 1995 that outlaws political parties and bans political activity. The bureaucracy and civil service are still phenomenally corrupt (Uganda rated 93rd out of 102 countries on the 2002 Transparency International Corruption Perception Index). The minister of state for finance and economic planning recently resigned for impropriety. Though parliament has shown some autonomy—principally by delaying economic reform bills—Museveni has proven that he is able to enforce his will with a combination of the carrot and the stick. As Billy Okadimiri, a Ugandan journalist, put it, "The stability of Uganda hinges on one man. National sanity and international respect revolves around one man."

In sum, in Uganda, one man has made a difference.

THE DYNAMICS OF LEADERSHIP

There is no magic formula for good leadership—or even for determining who is likely to be a bad leader. Legacies are often debated endlessly, for decades or even centuries after a leader's departure from office. However, the following observations reflect a few general lessons offered by history and current events.

Lesson One: What a leader says is not, on its own, a very good indicator of a country's stability. In general, political leaders are taken at their word. The arrival of a new, pro-reform government is almost always (prematurely) hailed as a turning point for a country. Speeches made by chief executives and cabinet ministers are carefully examined for hints about the future. But even dictatorial leaders are constrained by political necessities and interest groups. Policy programs quickly fall victim to these types of political pressures. Furthermore, speeches and policy announcements are part of the game of politics. A leader may intentionally sound more antiforeign than he really is, because he is trying to channel discontent (for instance, Mahathir in Malaysia); or more pro-market than he really is, because he is trying to curry the international community's favor (for instance, Suharto in Indonesia). A country's kimchi can rarely be understood with a superficial review of a leader's public pronouncements.

Lesson Two: Even bad leadership will not necessarily undermine stability. In this regard, the relative strength of a country's political institutions matters. In countries with weak political institutions, where one person completely dominates the government (such as Uganda), the quality of that country's leadership will indeed have a big impact on stability, at least in the short-term. But the stronger a country's institutions—including an independent legislature and judiciary, the rule of law, and a competent civil service—the less value there is in trying to figure out what a particular leader is capable of doing, or actually intending to do. In highly developed countries with effective institutions, such as the U.S., the quality of leadership has very little impact on stability.

Lesson Three: Leaders come and leaders go. Suppose a leader does accomplish what he says he is going to do and completely dominates a country's politics. As a result, observers may mistakenly identify a country very strongly with that leader. (Museveni is a success in Uganda. Therefore—by this line of reasoning—Uganda is a successful country.) It is difficult, with a larger-than-life leader in office, to envision what that country would be like in his absence. But this feat of imagination is absolutely critical for understanding a country's fundamental stability.

Lesson Four: In times of transition, the impact of leadership is vastly magnified. When South Africa's first-ever black government assumed power in 1994, no one knew which direction the country would take. Most of those who had trodden similar paths, such as Zimbabwe, offered only cautionary examples of what not to do. It therefore fell to the extraordinary Nelson Mandela to push South Africa in the right direction. Mandela did this in part by producing a seemingly endless supply of powerful symbolic gestures. Guests at his inauguration speech included many one might have expected to be there: heads of state, friends, family, political supporters, and colleagues. But also, unexpectedly, there were members of the apartheid regime he had spent his life fighting, and the former prison wardens who had imprisoned him.

Even before he was elected, Mandela reached out to the white community. During a televised debate in the election campaign of 1994, after a particularly lively exchange with F.W. de Klerk, then the white president of apartheid South Africa, Mandela said "…in spite of my criticism of Mr. de Klerk, sir, you are one of those I rely upon…we are going to face the problems of this country together. I am proud to hold your hand and go forward." On one particularly striking occasion, when Betsie Verwoerd, the frail, ninety-four-year-old widow of Hendrik Verwoerd (the architect of apartheid), faltered while attempting to read a speech demanding the creation of a separate white-ruled state, Mandela stood by her and helped her continue the speech. This earned him grudging respect from even his political enemies. General Constand Viljoen, an Afrikaner leader, said of Mandela, "He created a way for the Afrikaner community to participate in the new South Africa." Perhaps most famously, Mandela set the tone by delivering part of his inaugural address in Afrikaans, the native language of many white pro-apartheid South Africans. "*Wat is verby is verby,*" he proclaimed. What is past is past.

Lesson Five: Leaders also make a big difference in institutionally weak states. Good examples of this are Uganda, and also Tunisia under President Zine El Abidine Ben Ali. When Ben Ali took power in 1987, he faced a rising Islamic opposition movement. He crushed it, passing broad antiterror laws that gave his security services a free hand. Islamist leaders were imprisoned and exiled and their movement was banned. Mosques were nationalized and put under strict government control. It was a familiar story from the Arab world—an Islamic threat followed by government repression, followed again by a long and bloody campaign against the Islamists as the economy stagnates.

What separates Tunisia from the rest is that Ben Ali did not stop there. He realized that poverty, unemployment, and lack of opportunity were the social ills that gave the Islamists their strength. So he set out to develop the Tunisian economy. Ben Ali went to the IMF and instituted a strict IMF-sponsored program to deregulate the economy, reduce state meddling, and open up to the outside world. As a result, Tunisia's economy grew by over 4.7 percent per year during the 1990s. Rampant inflation was reined in. Ben Ali also made sure that as many Tunisians as possible saw tangible benefits from the growth. The government pursued an active social welfare agenda: villages were given electricity and running water, basic healthcare was made available to all, and home ownership was encouraged. By the early 1990s, three quarters of Tunisians lived in a home that they either owned or were in the process of buying. Ben Ali had calculated, correctly, that people who own homes have a real stake in the system. Tunisia is still a one-man show; Ben Ali wins elections with an implausible 99 percent of the vote, and opposition of all kinds—secular democratic as well as Islamist—is repressed. But certainly, Ben Ali has made a difference. This is a rare Arab success story.

CHAPTER NINE

After Tito—Tito

SUCCESSION THREAT

"A government of laws and not of men."
JOHN ADAMS

"L'etat c'est moi." ("I am the State.")
LOUIS XIV

BRUTUS, SLAYER OF JULIUS CAESAR, HAS BEEN CONDEMNED BY history as the eternal symbol of betrayal and disloyalty. But had the rules of politics functioned differently, Brutus might now be remembered as one of history's great role models. After all, Caesar was by no means a model leader. A man of staggering political ability, he had captivated soldiers, politicians, and the public with his charisma, while seizing absolute power for himself. In his determination to dominate his political opponents and suppress dissent, he was very much a dictator, a role model for Lenin and Mao. Like Louis XIV, he *was* the state.

And remember that Brutus had the best of intentions: to restore the Roman Republic, the constitutional system of government that had kept the political peace within Rome for roughly 500 years. ("Not that I love Caesar less, but that I love Rome more," as Shakespeare had him say.) To be sure, the Republic was not a full-fledged democracy by today's standards, but it was certainly more democratic than the absolute rule of Caesar. Had Brutus been successful in his ultimate goal, we might remember him very differently, as the heroic re-founder of the Roman Republic.

But of course, that did not happen. Brutus failed to understand that killing Caesar was no solution; he failed to understand that when one person is the state, leadership changes tend to wreak havoc on political stability. In countries with weak political institutions, or a divided political spectrum, leadership succession is fraught with danger. Brutus's action unleashed a civil war—great theater to us, today, but a bloody political and historical tragedy (and yet again, unintended consequences). The constitutional peace of the Roman Republic was gone forever. During the time of the Roman Empire, some leadership transitions went smoothly but many were accomplished by treachery, murder, and further civil war (most notably during the "Year of the Four Emperors," 69 A.D.).

Of course, Brutus was probably not the first person—and he was certainly not the last—to underestimate the havoc that follows leadership struggles and transitions. But then again, some leadership transitions go so smoothly they pass almost unnoticed. What distinguishes a routine succession from a potentially dangerous one?

YUGOSLAVIA

Tito—president, supreme commander, and marshal—humbly born "Josip Broz" to a Croatian father and a Slovene mother, was in many respects larger than life. Smartly dressed in military uniforms bedecked with medals, or expensively tailored Italian suits; owner of thirty-two homes; shown on television hunting bears or wild boar; ruling his people with empathy and charisma; hiding his advancing age with toupees and hair dye; well known for his extraordinary and infamous appetites for luxury, fine food, expensive cars, and women. Larger than life—and in the end, larger than the country he ruled, Yugoslavia.

Yugoslavia, "land of the South Slavs," was created shortly after World War I out of a religious and ethnic patchwork of different peoples, but it never really functioned successfully. Political violence was a staple of public life until before World War II, when Croatia came under the control of brutal, Nazi-allied fascists who massacred Serbs, Jews, and whomever else they thought were in their way. Bosnia-Herzegovina—

a multiethnic region composed of Muslims, Serbs, and Croats—was sucked into a vortex of ethnic violence. A lesser man might have been discouraged. But not young Josip. Tito rallied his forces, an antifascist, communist rebel group called the Partisans, around the slogans "Death to Fascism, Freedom to the People," and "Brotherhood and Unity." He welcomed people of all ethnic groups into his army. After much slaughter, Tito found himself in charge.

But in charge of what? Never to be accused of lacking vision, Tito decreed that the post-civil-war mess over which he presided was actually a budding federation of six republics: Serbia, Croatia, Slovenia, Macedonia, Montenegro, and Bosnia-Herzegovina. The first five republics would be ethnic homelands. The last, Bosnia, was a multiethnic republic comprising Muslims, Serbs, and Croatians. There were also two areas within Serbia that received special status: Vojvodina, a multiethnic enclave, and Kosovo, a region dominated by Albanian Muslims. Tito had the determination and ability to make this improbable vision a reality. "We have spilt an ocean of blood," he said, "for brotherhood and unity of our nations—and we shall not allow anyone to touch this or destroy it from inside, to break this brotherhood and unity." His first task was to spill a little more blood—he tried and punished war criminals, and eliminated his political opponents. Then Tito set about building a nation.

This required a bit of wishful thinking. The true story, that a civil war had claimed a tenth of Yugoslavia's population, was officially forgotten. Those who had worked for or collaborated with the Croatian fascists were welcomed into the new Yugoslavia, so long as they disavowed their past. In Tito's official version of history, all Yugoslavs had come together as one to drive out the fascist oppressors, making the creation of Yugoslavia an historical inevitability.

In the early years, this "historical inevitability" required a good deal of prodding. The interests of the republics, the autonomous units, and the minority groups were diverse and often contradictory. Slovenia and Croatia were wealthy and Christian. Kosovo was impoverished and Muslim. Multiethnic Bosnia was inherently troubled. And the Serbs suspected that Tito (who was part Croat) was preventing them from accumulating power commensurate with their status as the country's most populous ethnic group.

Tito could be ruthless when necessary. His secret police were numerous and feared. He stifled economic reforms that might diminish central control. He often dealt harshly with his political opponents both inside and outside the Communist Party. But he could also be magnanimous. One example was his treatment of Kosovo. The majority of Kosovo's population was Albanian and Muslim. But the Serbs saw Kosovo as their Jerusalem—it was the site of Serbia's culturally defining battle against the Ottomans in 1389. The Kosovar Albanians, fearing that they would be oppressed in the new Yugoslav state, rebelled against Yugoslav rule in 1944. Tito responded by sending 30,000 troops to crush the uprising. The Kosovars lived as a subjugated people for two decades. But then, in 1966, Tito decided to integrate them. He gave in to many of the Kosovars' demands for autonomy. They would be educated in the Albanian language. They would run their own judiciary and police force. Their capital city of Pristina would be developed. A university would be constructed. Cultural exchanges with Albania would be allowed. Billions in federal funds would go toward developing the province. In fact, during the 1970s, federal aid comprised three-quarters of Kosovo's budget. It was no surprise that many Kosovar Albanians adored Tito.

The carrot and the stick; while the Kosovars were coddled, restless Croatians got a beating. In the late 1960s and 1970s, the Croatian republic's politicians demanded more autonomy—including the right to secede from Yugoslavia, the right to a separate defense force, and the right to keep all their tax revenue for themselves. Intellectuals wanted the Croatian language to be considered distinct from Serbian, instead of being designated "Serbo-Croatian." On the street level, Croatians rioted against Serbs at football matches and destroyed signs written in Serbian Cyrillic characters.

Tito would have none of it. He went on national TV and accused Croatia's leadership of pandering to nationalism and separatism. He purged prominent Croatian politicians, banned nationalist publications, and executed Croatian fascists who had infiltrated the country. When he was done, he carried out a similar purge in Serbia. He sought to protect the minorities, like the Kosovars, and contain the jingoistic tendencies of the larger groups.

But Tito's Yugoslavia was not simply a creation of power politics and delicate balancing acts. Tito succeeded in creating a genuine "Yugoslav" identity. Every Yugoslav schoolchild was fed a steady diet of propaganda about the importance of respecting other ethnic groups. Croatian schoolchildren were made to study and revere Serbian heroes and vice versa. The "National Liberation War" was studied intensely and school trips were taken to neighboring republics. Television in each of the republics and provinces included programs from other locations, complete with subtitles. The evening news was broadcast from a different republic or province each day: one day from Slovenia, the next day from Montenegro, the next from Vojvodina, and so on. Yugoslavs responded genuinely to this prompting. Intermarriage was common in the big cities, producing a generation of Yugoslavs of mixed ethnicity. Tito of course, embodied this phenomenon. He was half Croat, half Slovene, and his wife was a Serb.

A huge personality cult arose around Tito. His visage adorned posters, shop windows, stamps, and currencies. Hundreds of biographies—many of them basely sycophantic—lauded his bravery and his exploits. When Tito traveled the country on his trademark "Blue Train," many of the villages in which he stopped bore his name. Streets across the country were named for him. Schoolchildren were given tours of his boyhood home. Many Yugoslavs genuinely adored their leader. Tito-worship transcended nationality and religion.

Most importantly, the country was peaceful during his tenure. Ethnic clashes were rare. Tito accomplished something extraordinary and unprecedented in living memory, and for that matter, never reproduced since: a Yugoslavia in which a person of any ethnicity could travel from one end of the country to the other without being harassed.

∞

But Yugoslavia had a problem. Tito may have been larger than life, but he was not immune to death. As he grew older, the problem of succession became more urgent. Predicting Tito's successor became a favorite parlor game in Yugoslavia and abroad. Scholar Gavriel Ra'anan tried to lay out the qualifications for Tito's successor in a 1977 book: (1) not a Serb, because the other nationalities resented Serb domination; (2) acceptable to the Serbs, because the Serbs were in fact dominant; and (3) supported by the army, because the army would be needed to hold the country together.

Tito's solution to this intractable problem was to attempt to rule from beyond the grave. He drew up a new constitution in 1974, the world's longest at the time, containing 406 articles, 100,000 words, and 205 pages. In this remarkable document, Tito attempted to specify, in minute detail, all aspects of how Yugoslavia should function after his departure. But this bizarre plan—rule by Ouija board?—was never going to work. The terrified Yugoslav government attempted to avoid the problem by keeping Tito alive as long as possible. Tito became incapacitated at some time around January 1980, but was kept alive on machines (and officially remained President of Yugoslavia) for five months, until May 4.

At first, a collective denial set in. Sloganeers dutifully churned out pithy mottos reflecting Tito's attempt to continue to rule, even in death. As Tito's corpse traveled the country on the Blue Train, from Ljubljana in Slovenia to Belgrade in Serbia, crowds of mourners held signs reading: "Tito we will follow you. From your path, we will not stray," "What will there be now? There will be Tito." And most poignantly: "After Tito—Tito."

Not a chance. Tito's grand constitution specified a decentralized state, giving each republic and province of great deal of autonomy. This central government, in charge of foreign affairs and defense, would be led by a "collective federal presidency." In practice, this meant an eight-person executive, made up of one representative from each of the eight federal units. The top position would rotate annually among the representatives. Executive actions had to be taken by consensus.

The system was mocked as "Tito and the Eight Dwarves." There was a gaping hole at the center, a vacuum of authority that simply could not be filled by a dead Tito. In the early 1980s, the system's impracticality became obvious when Yugoslavia suffered an economic crisis. Foreign debt surpassed $20 billion, inflation soared, and wages fell. The Eight Dwarves could not agree on a solution. Croatia and Slovenia favored free-market reforms. Serbia and others wanted more state control. Without Tito, there was no way to forge a consensus, and the leadership vacillated.

With the weakness of the Yugoslav Federation conspicuous, it was not long before opportunists arose. Shortly after Tito's death, Kosovo's

Albanians demanded even more autonomy. They took to the streets demanding that Kosovo become a full republic, completely separate from Serbia. Kosovo's Serb minority, which had not fared well under Albanian rule, was terrified. In 1987, Serbia's new leader, a rather color-less bureaucrat named Slobodan Milosevic, sensed the opportunity of his lifetime. Why should he struggle to balance the conflicting interests of Serbia's rich and poor, young and old, communists and reformers, when at a stroke, all Serbs could be rallied to the cause of ethnic unity? Milosevic visited Kosovo and the province's Serbs staged a large protest, demanding that Milosevic protect them. It was then that Milosevic made the speech that first marked his transformation into a rabid Serbian nationalist. "Nobody must ever again dare to beat this people!"

The rest of this story is by now well known. Under Milosevic, Serbia extended its control over Kosovo, Montenegro, and Vojvodina. Serbian nationalists sowed fear and hatred among Serbian minorities outside the republic in a quest to forge a "Greater Serbia." A similar process was un-derway elsewhere in Yugoslavia. When elections were held in each of the provinces in 1990, nationalists won in every republic. This quickly led to conflict. The four subsequent wars that ravaged the Balkans from 1991 to 1999 were aptly known as the "Wars of Yugoslav Succession." First Slovenia, then Croatia, then Bosnia-Herzegovina, and then Kosovo, were plunged into ethnic violence and civil war that recalled some of the worst images of World War II. Yugoslavia was ripped apart until all that remained were the republics of Serbia and Montenegro under the rule of Slobodan Milosevic. This European humanitarian catastrophe was too close at hand, and too horrifying, for the world to sit on the sidelines. The United States and its allies intervened in Bosnia and launched a war against Serbia. These military actions achieved their aims, but at a cost to American taxpayers in excess of $20 billion. By 2002, peacekeeping operations in Bosnia had cost $2.4 billion and in Kosovo, $1.9 billion.

There is one hopeful postscript. In 2000, in a remarkably peace-ful revolution, the people of Serbia rose up and forced the removal of Slobodon Milosevic, who was then tried for war crimes by a U.N. tribunal. His replacement was the democratically minded Vojislav Kos-tunica. With Kostunica's agreement, the European Union brokered the creation of a new state, called Serbia and Montenegro, and "Yugoslavia" thereby formally disappeared from the map. As part of this process, Kostunica voluntarily agreed to step down. He left office so that the new state might—rather than inheriting a ruler—start with a clean slate of democratic elections. His concern was the succession process. "We need a democratic transition of power," he said. "We must not allow the transition process to be undignified and ugly."

ITALY

Contrast this with the Italians, heirs to ancient Rome and undisputed masters of the art of leadership succession. Judged solely by the numbers, Italy is one of the most unstable countries on earth. In all, fifty-nine Italian governments have held power since World War II. No Italian government has yet lasted to the end of its five-year mandate. The average Italian government survives a paltry eleven months before collapsing.

But what looks like chaotic instability is hard to reconcile with the fact that Italy is a stunning success story. Since the end of World War II, Italy's national income has grown fivefold and individual income fourfold. From postwar devastation, Italy's gross domestic product has now grown to $600 billion—close to that of the United Kingdom.

Clearly there is more—or more accurately, less—going on here than meets the eye. Not all "government crisis" headlines herald actual political crises. What is the Italians' secret?

To answer this question, look behind the headlines to discover some surprising truths about Italy's politics. The first of these is that the Italians use the word *immobilismo* to describe their political system. Wry humor, one might think, but actually, not. Postwar Italian politics really were immobilized by the incredible dominance of the Christian Democratic Party. In fact, from 1946 until 1981, as governments rose and fell, the prime minister was always a member of the Christian Democrats.

This seems odd, given the huge number of parties represented in the Italian parliament. Until recently, members of the lower house of parliament were elected through a pure proportional representation system; parties could win seats with just 2 percent of the national vote. Ten parties won seats in 1948. By 1992, there were sixteen parties; today, twenty-four parties occupy the Italian parliament. These new parties found it extremely easy to attract members, receive state funding, and consistently win (a few) seats in the legislature.

Fortunately something more important than party politics was going on in postwar Italy. The goal that unified Italy's fractionalized political spectrum was preventing the communists and the neofascists from ever attaining political power. Italy had the largest and most powerful Communist Party outside the Soviet bloc. So the U.S., the Vatican, and even the Mafia funded the Christian Democrats, the largest noncommunist party, to counterbalance the Communists' strength.

This both helped to create Italy's instability problem and provided the solution. The problem was that the communists and neofascists together usually controlled about 40 percent of the seats in parliament. Yet they were political untouchables, and therefore could not be included in government. As a result, Italian prime ministers were left with little choice but to cobble together unwieldy coalitions of tiny parties. This was a recipe for governmental instability. Even the tiniest of parties could defect from the coalition and bring down the government, as they have happily done many times over the last fifty years.

But Italy's small parties were always willing to band together—in coalition with the large Christian Democratic Party—to keep the Communists out. As a result, the Christian Democrats dominated postwar Italian politics, even though they consistently won only about a third of the popular vote. This was the Italians' secret. What looked like instability was not really instability. Governments rose and fell with head-spinning rapidity, but since the same political party was in power, the same set of people were always in government. Amintore Fanfani, Giulio Andreotti, Mariano Rumor, and Aldo Moro each served as prime minister no less than five times. Between 1946 and 1976, governments rose and fell so rapidly that a total of 1,331 ministerial and sub-cabinet jobs were created. But, incredibly, 152 oft-reappointed people held almost two-thirds of these jobs; and 31 people were reappointed so often that they held 489 jobs between them.

Therefore, it is not surprising that changes of leadership in postwar Italy occurred smoothly. When a government fell, there was no mass panic or riots on the streets (and certainly no danger of the collapse of the Italian state). Instead, a well-practiced constitutional process kicked in. Either the president simply dissolved parliament and called new elections, or, far more commonly, the outgoing prime minister simply resigned and the president selected a new prime minister behind the scenes and oversaw the formation of a new government. Usually, it took about six weeks to form a new government. The longest it has ever taken is five months. A far cry from the bloodshed that followed changes of leadership in ancient Rome.

THE DYNAMICS OF SUCCESSION

Extraordinary leaders are capable of extraordinary achievements—as in Yugoslavia, Uganda, and South Africa. A great leader can take a "basket-case" country and, seemingly through sheer force of will, make it appear to work. But political leaders, no matter how great, inevitably die, and replacements must be found. Usually, "choosing" the next leader involves a bitter struggle for power. Few themes in human history are more well established. The Biblical patriarch Isaac's family was divided when his sons Jacob and Esau feuded over who would inherit the Hebrew birthright. A disagreement over succession to the Prophet Muhammad caused a (still ongoing) rift in Islam between Sunnis and Shiites. The Hundred Years War started because of a succession struggle. The list goes on.

This is one problem. Another is the impermanence of a political stability that is dependent upon one extraordinary person. Even if a successor can be found, there is no guarantee that the successor will be able to replicate the achievements of his predecessor. (A general rule: the greater the leaders, the harder they are to follow.)

Governments that appear stable and powerful often crumble quickly upon the leader's departure. Muhammad Siad Barre, who ruled Somalia as military dictator from 1969 to 1991, said, "I am sitting on a volcano and the day I go it will explode, and no one will be able to stop it." Siad Barre understood his country. When he was deposed, Somalia disintegrated. Rivalries broke out between the country's two major clans. Two warlords rose to prominence: Ali Mahdi Mohamed and the now-infamous Mohamed Farrah Aidid. Somalia ceased to be a country and degenerated into rival gangs fighting for turf. Inter-clan violence reached a fever pitch. Roving bands of militiamen, hopped up on khat—a narcotic leaf chewed by Somalis—pillaged and looted with reckless abandon. Before long, nearly three-quarters of Somali children were facing starvation. This led to the U.S. humanitarian intervention of 1993. The military action cost American taxpayers $1.5 billion—a spectacular figure, three times the size of the entire Somali economy—and resulted in twenty-nine U.S. deaths.

This particular Humpty Dumpty has yet to be reassembled. A "Transitional National Government" was formed in 2000, but it managed only to extend its authority over parts of Mogadishu and some strips of land along the coast. To date, there have been fourteen attempts to bring peace to Somalia. The most recent peace talks, in Kenya, have been typically contentious—the factions squabbled for three days over the words "We the undersigned." Worryingly, in the vacuum left by the collapsed Somali state, fundamentalist Islam has grown. Funded by Arab states, especially Saudi Arabia, religious organizations have set up schools, clinics, and courts. Only 10 percent of Somali children now have access to education that is not Koranic in nature. Since 1991, *shariah* (Islamic law) is the only real law to be enforced in Somalia. Though Somalis are not traditionally strict Muslims (in Siad Barre's days, women served in the army), these days, few women can be seen without a headscarf. The United States, worried about new militant Islamic groups, has frozen the assets of Somali financial institutions and held talks with warlords opposed to the central government.

∞

What are the magic ingredients that make leadership succession a matter of little consequence rather than the harbinger of catastrophe? Two are most important.

The first is the succession mechanism: how will the next leader be chosen? Leadership succession is a delicate process that can be likened to the mating practices of the praying mantis (when copulation is complete, the female often eats the male). A political leader has every incentive to nominate a friendly successor, to ensure that his legacy and the fortunes of his family are protected upon his departure from power. Indeed, like the male praying mantis, the political leader has every incentive to find a strong partner, one who can successfully fend off opposition. The problem is that strong successors are, by definition, hungry. The stronger the successors, the more likely they are to grow impatient, depose the existing leader, and seize power.

In China, for instance, Deng Xiaoping chose his own successor and then spent years slowly and gracefully fading from power. (At the end of his life, he had only one formal title: vice-chairman of the National Bridge Club.) His successor-in-waiting, Jiang Zemin, dutifully bided his time, protecting Deng's legacy and taking orders. (Jiang is now attempting to repeat the process with his newly elected successor as president and secretary general of the Communist Party, Hu Jintao.) But things do not always work out this well. President Suharto of Indonesia, for example, deposed and exiled his mentor, Sukarno. Idi Amin of Uganda ousted his political patron, Milton Obote. Slobodan Milosevic turned on his mentor Ivan Stambolic to seize power in Serbia.

Because succession is so inherently difficult, leaders in countries with no well-established succession mechanism are more likely to attempt to rule until they die. Worse yet, they are more likely to die in office having named no successor—the worst possible situation for stability. As Ghana's ex-president Jerry Rawlings put it, lamenting his perceived mistreatment after leaving office, "When I used to travel it would take hours for my motorcade to pass through the throngs of well-wishers. Today, they yell out, 'thief!' I am ignored. I am humiliated. I gave my life to this country and now I am being maligned. If this is what happens when you leave office, well, no one will agree to leave."

The most venerable method for overcoming this pitfall has been to keep things in the family. The Aztecs, the Mayans, and the Egyptian pharaohs all relied on dynasties, as did feudal Europe and Japan. Korea's Choson Dynasty reigned for a remarkable five centuries—power passing predictably from father to son. Today the Middle East clutches determinedly to this time-worn succession mechanism—in the six Persian Gulf states, for instance, as well as Jordan, Morocco, and Syria. When done well, with elaborate rules, long traditions, and independent oversight bodies, dynastic succession can be fairly reliable.

But it is not always done well. Ad hoc dynastic succession is prone to catastrophe. Feuds surface within the ruling family. Sons betray fathers. Challengers to the throne arise. Without rules to govern these feuds, they are often bloody or destabilizing (as in ancient Rome). Perhaps even more importantly, the dynastic succession process does not necessarily select competent leaders or, for that matter, leaders with any public support. Democracy solves this problem. Unlike dynastic succession, it is a merit-based process. The newly chosen leader has just demonstrated his political competence by winning an election and, at least at the beginning, has the public's support. Disputes are fought at the ballot box and in the legal system, instead of with guns and on the streets.

This fact often mystifies observers from nondemocratic countries. Prince Bandar Bin Sultan, Saudi ambassador to the U.S., once recalled his reaction upon awakening on the morning of Nixon's resignation in 1974. He fully expected to see tanks and soldiers on the streets of Washington, D.C. Instead he saw daily life continuing uninterrupted, Nixon meekly flying off to retirement in California, and Vice President Gerald Ford calmly assuming power—just as prescribed in the American constitution. In other words, democracy, while not perfect, helps ensure that the succession process goes smoothly and that a worthy successor is chosen.

Some caveats apply. Until a democracy has seen a change of power, it has not truly proved its credentials. When push comes to shove, some long-ruling regimes will obey election results (Mexico, Taiwan), while some will not (Algeria, Peru). Furthermore, many "democracies" with weak institutions actually function more like dictatorships. If political leaders can break the law at will, there is no guarantee they will obey election results. This is true today in Central Asia, for instance, as well as in Egypt (under President Hosni Mubarak). In these countries, the current leaders are reluctant to name successors.

∞

But choosing a new leader is only half the story when it comes to succession. The other main consideration is whether the new leader is up to the job. Even if the succession is both smooth and democratic, a country's stability may quickly evaporate when a new leader—someone less competent, less respected, or less ruthless—takes power. This was true in the case of Yugoslavia. It was also true of Alexander the Great, whose death ushered in a civil conflict that consumed Greece for forty years, and Charlemagne, whose empire folded soon after his death, and more recently of Indonesia and Iran.

The way around this problem is for a country to build strong political institutions. A country overcomes the succession problem when its government can run itself. This requires the rule of law, checks and balances, and a sophisticated state apparatus. A sophisticated state apparatus helps to ensure that policy is of high quality, and the business of government is accomplished, even if the political leadership is less than inspiring. The rule of law and division of power ensure that stability is maintained and power struggles do not get out of hand, even in the absence of firm leadership. "A government of laws and not of men," as John Adams put it.

To be sure, this is not glamorous stuff. Yet, dull as they may be, states with strong political institutions are far more stable and permanent. Fidel Castro often gloats publicly about his ability to outlast multiple U.S. presidents (and, until his disposal in the spring of 2003, so did Saddam Hussein). But this longevity is a sign of his country's weakness, not strength. Castro's departure is almost certain to be catastrophic for Cuba. Conversely, when countries with strong political institutions have a "crisis," it rarely matters. Recall that in May and June of 1999, the Netherlands suffered its worst political crisis in eighteen years. If you cannot recall this event, you are not alone. The story received scant international attention.

At the height of the crisis, as the coalition government nearly fell, the Dutch stock market climbed by ten points. During the quarter in which the instability occurred, Dutch unemployment hit its lowest level since 1980, economic growth was among the highest in the EU, and inflation was negligible. Eventually the Netherlands' constitutional monarch, Queen Beatrix, coaxed the parties back into the coalition and resolved the crisis. But it really did not matter. If the government had fallen, the Dutch would have calmly gone to the polls for an early election. Holland's political institutions are rock-solid. The constitution is strong, succession mechanisms function smoothly, and the rule of law is well established. (Indeed, the Netherlands consistently ranks as one of the

world's least corrupt states in rankings by Transparency International.)
Yes, politics in rich countries can be boring. But boring is good.

LEADERSHIP POSTSCRIPT: CENTRAL ASIA

The issue of leadership succession applies directly to foreign policy and
global trade, since Western governments have an unfortunate habit of
building close ties with leaders of countries almost certain to have a succession crisis. This is understandable. From a short-term point of view, it
certainly eases the mind when a U.S.-allied leader is able to ward off the
opposition. The problem is that this ability frequently involves undermining succession mechanisms—interfering with democratic elections,
diminishing the independence of the legislature or the courts, and so
on. All of this increases the likelihood of an eventual political crisis. It
also increases the likelihood that the United States will become a target
of resulting popular discontent. Perhaps the most extreme example has
been Iran. The Shah, with U.S. support, sought to crush all opposition
and seize absolute power. This helped produce the anti-Western extremism that guides Iran to this day.

This logic informs a stark threat evident in post-Soviet Central Asia.
In that region, the West has befriended a number of authoritarian leaders who have deliberately undermined their countries' institutions. One
example is Kazakhstan. Former Communist Party leader Nursultan Nazarbayev won election with an improbable 98 percent of the vote in 1991.
He then appeared to repent, holding democratic parliamentary elections
in 1994. His repentance was short-lived. A year later Nazarbayev dissolved parliament and held new elections, this time with political parties
he himself had created. He granted himself sweeping powers to dissolve
parliament, amend the constitution, call referenda, and appoint heads
of cities and regions. He passed a law granting himself permanent immunity from prosecution.

Likewise in Kyrgyzstan. President Askar Akayev knows how to soothe
the consciences of his Western allies. He quotes John Locke, allows some
multiparty democracy, and has even shown some enthusiasm for market
reforms. But his actions speak more loudly. When parliament became
too meddlesome, Akayev held referendums to reduce its authority and

granted himself the power to appoint all top officials. He jails political opponents and uses the docile press to bolster his accomplishments and castigate his opposition. There is even a touch of feudalism. Like a medieval European monarch, President Akayev married off his son to the daughter of President Nazarbayev of Kazakhstan.

And Uzbekistan. President Islam Karimov, who bizarrely and famously built a surreal state-of-the-art tennis complex in Tashkent that's said to outshine the U.S. National Tennis Center in Flushing Meadows, has banned the country's opposition parties and sent their leaders either to prison, exile, or the grave. Rather than face election in 1995, Karimov held a national referendum to extend his term another five years, in which he won—to no one's great surprise—99.6 percent of the vote. In the 2000 elections, Karimov repeated the feat; his handpicked opponent, a little-known philosophy professor, later admitted he himself voted for Karimov. Karimov then extended his own term to 2007.

Then, in Turkmenistan, this scenario takes a turn from the alarming to the surreal. Known by his self-granted title, "Turkmenbashi" (leader of the Turkmens), President Saparmurat Niyazov traces his family tree back to Noah. (Yes, the same Noah who built the Ark.) In the capital city of Ashgebat, Niyazov has erected a seventy-five-meter-high column topped by a gold statue of himself. The statue revolves with the sun. Niyazov has renamed some days of the week and months of the year after himself, and April has been changed to his mother's name. On one memorable occasion, he claimed to be able to control the weather. True to a leader of his stature, Niyazov has no time for political opposition. The president's misleadingly named Democratic Party is the only legal party in Turkmenistan. Turkmenistan's parliament only meets for a few days every year to rubber-stamp Niyazov's mandates. During one session, lawmakers reportedly refused to adjourn until Niyazov accepted their offer to make him "President for Life." He was then adorned with flowers and treated to twenty minutes of uninterrupted applause.

Finally, Tajikistan. Like leaders in neighboring states, Tajikistan's President Imomali Rakhmanov is no democrat. In 1999, the president was reelected to a seven-year term, taking 96 percent of the vote, with 98 percent of the population voting. (Someone should point out to Central

Asia's leaders that election victory percentages in the high 90s look bad, not good, to international observers.)

Given this litany of misbehavior, it may be surprising to find that these rulers are almost uniformly close allies of the United States. One motivation for this, of course, is oil. Companies including ChevronTexaco and ExxonMobil have already invested $13 billion in Kazakhstan. (And thus far, Nazarbayev has reportedly transferred more than $1 billion in oil revenues to bank accounts in his own name.) It is estimated that the combined oil and gas deposits of the five Central Asian "stans," plus Azerbaijan, are equal to the remaining reserves of Saudi Arabia and Iraq combined. U.S. troops are also in the region, staging operations in Afghanistan and seeking to head off Islamic rebels. By 2003, at least 1,000 U.S. troops were part of a multinational force on the Kyrgyz-Afghan border. For the 2002 invasion of Afghanistan, the United States stationed 2,000 troops in Uzbekistan. President Karimov, once considered an unredeemable dictator, now receives invitations to the Oval Office and offers of U.S. aid. Tajikistan is also home to an American military base.

The problem, of course, is that these leaders have all crippled what independent political institutions were set up following their transition from Soviet communism. For the moment, these leaders are firmly in charge. But with succession mechanisms undone, troubles down the road are inevitable.

At bottom, it's fair to say that frequent changes of leadership are desirable in and of themselves. To be sure, leadership changes create uncertainty. And it's not only military coups that are unsettling; when firmly democratic governments are toppled at the ballot box, it can spook foreign governments. Brazil's presidential election in the fall of 2002—featuring the left-leaning frontrunner (and eventual winner) Luiz Inacio Lula da Silva—so unnerved foreign investors that they almost forced the country into debt default. But spare a thought for the alternative. The longer a leader stays in power, the harder he is to replace. Long stays in power generally require that succession mechanisms are dismantled—otherwise, the leader might be thrown out. Long stays in power frequently cause political institutions—the courts, the police, the army, the legislature—to atrophy and become directionless without the leader's iron guidance.

The increasingly conspicuous problems that come with such long-lived governments have led to term-limit movements in many countries. Perhaps it was this awareness that motivated the president of the Dominican Republic, Hipolita Mejia, when he rejected the Congress's attempt to give him another term in office. "I want institutions, not people," said Mejia. "I do not want people to perpetuate themselves in office by reelection. I do not want history to treat me as a tyrant." Unfortunately, Mejia then changed his mind, attempted to stay in office, and became embroiled in a scandal over the failure of the country's second-largest bank. He would have done far better sticking with the original plan.

CHAPTER TEN

Fujishock

The Ruling Bargain

*"Ask not what your country can do for you,
but what you can do for your country."*
John F. Kennedy

Kennedy's famous sentiment is both inspirational and perplexing. Inspirational as an eloquent expression of the emotion of patriotism; perplexing because, at a fundamental level, one already does quite a bit for one's country.

There are laws to be obeyed, governing everything from the conduct of business to the institution of marriage; taxes to be paid, gobbling up a fair-sized chunk of one's income; police and civil servants, whose often unwelcome authority must be respected; and in extreme cases, an army into which one may suddenly be conscripted. Above all, there are politicians whose power must be accepted.

That's a lot to swallow. In some countries, it is rammed down one's throat, and the people have no choice in the matter. Such regimes, however, find that they cannot both preserve stability and foster economic growth while threatening their citizens at gunpoint. It is dysfunctional kimchi. A successful government is founded on willing cooperation from its citizens.

Thus politicians of a far more common breed than Kennedy are wont to ask: "what can your country do for you?" Fortunately, governments can do quite a lot. They can provide physical security, the common defense, policies and regulations that promote economic prosperity, protection of human rights, the right to vote, social welfare benefits, infrastructure, public education…the list goes on. By providing these things they can earn the public's enthusiastic support.

Thus the idea of the "ruling bargain"—a deal between the government and the governed. Think of it as a (usually) unwritten contract, by which the people (at least some of the people) consent to be ruled so long as the government fulfills certain conditions. This is a time-honored theme in Western politics. The thirteenth-century Magna Carta, for instance, was a ruling bargain that the king of England was, in effect, forced to sign. British noblemen demanded guaranteed political rights in return for accepting and funding the king's rule.

Things are not always so amicable. Governments must continually justify their hold on power. An unstable ruling bargain unleashes powerful dynamics—almost overnight a state can make the transition from stability to mass civil disobedience. A dramatic historical example is the French Revolution. For more than 250 years, the Bourbon dynasty had ruled the country, power passing predictably within the same family. Then in 1789, the French people effectively rejected the right of Louis XVI to rule based solely on his bloodline. The country erupted in violence and Louis lost his throne and his head.

The ruling bargain addresses much that is fundamental in the conduct of politics: the management of discontent, the government's ability to satisfy the public's demands, and the skill of political leaders, among other crucial issues.

SAUDI ARABIA

When it turned out that fifteen of the nineteen September 11 hijackers were citizens of Saudi Arabia, many Americans were stunned. Wasn't Saudi Arabia a long-time U.S. ally? Hadn't American troops risked their lives defending Saudi Arabia against potential aggression from Iraq?

To understand this extraordinary political dynamic—how citizens of a U.S.-allied country transformed themselves into suicidal terrorists—one must understand the Saudi ruling bargain. The side effects of this bargain and its failings provided Usama bin Laden with motives, resources, and recruits. As dissected by scholar Joshua Teitelbaum, the Saudi ruling bargain has two components: Islam and oil.

The Islam came first. In 1745, Muhammad Ibn Saud was the ruler of a small oasis town in the central Arabian desert. He allied himself with Muhammad Ibn Abd al-Wahhab, a religious leader who preached a return to a stricter form of Islam. Together they spread both the Wahhabi religious doctrine and the Saud family's political power. Ibn Saud provided the tactics and political organization. Al-Wahhab produced holy warriors committed to the cause. Piling success upon success, the House of Saud expanded its territory to include Islam's two holiest cities, Mecca and Medina, where the prophet Muhammad received his revelations from Allah and founded the Islamic faith in the seventh century.

To this day, the government of Saudi Arabia maintains the alliance founded in that desert oasis. The power of the descendents of Ibn Saud—the *umara* (princes) of the Saud family—is wedded to the doctrine of the followers of al-Wahhab—the *ulama* (religious scholars) of the Wahhabi sect. Hence the government's "mission statement" does not lack ambition: to "protect the principles of Islam, enforce its *shariah* [religious laws], ordain what is good, and forbid what is evil." To fulfill this duty, Saudi Arabia's modern government bases the country's official constitution on the Koran and the teachings of the prophet Muhammad. It is an unabashedly fundamentalist regime. The Ministry of Justice oversees not secular but religious courts. The government pays for the printing and distribution of holy texts. Religious scholars have access to the state-controlled media for religious instruction and proselytizing. Mosques, religious schools, Islamic scholarly organizations—even thuggish stick-wielding religious police—are all funded directly by the Saudi state. Most crucially, the Al Saud oversees and protects Mecca and Medina, and manages the annual *hajj* pilgrimage, required of all able-bodied Muslims once in their lifetime. The royal family has poured untold millions of dollars into the upkeep of holy sites, and King Fahd has officially adopted "Custodian of the Two Holy Mosques" as part of his title. It is the Al Saud's sworn duty to defend these sites at all costs.

∞

But fundamentalist Islam is not the only thing the Al Saud had to offer. Oil was discovered in the kingdom in the late 1930s, although significant production had to wait until the 1970s. The state has monopolized the oil business. It controls the extraction and sale of oil and claims sole authority to distribute the revenues. And "money is the great lubricant," goes the famous Saudi saying. Saudi politics is certainly well lubricated. Between 1974 and 1990, the government spent $800 billion in oil money on development projects (45,000 miles of paved roads, 3,000 hospitals, 99 colleges, 29 airports, and so on). Bread, rice, sugar, flour, meat, electricity, water, gasoline—all were subsidized by the state. A staggering 50 percent of the Saudi labor force was employed by the free-spending public sector. During the 1970s and 1980s, education through the university level was free to all citizens. Students received $270 per month in pocket money. University graduates were guaranteed a well-paid, undemanding government job.

This was the Al Saud's end of the bargain: an oil-funded good life. But there are always unintended consequences. Saudi Arabia's first problem was a social inevitability. Take billions of dollars in oil money and hand it out to people previously accustomed to poverty, whose conservative religion and culture celebrates large families, encourages women to be homemakers, and discourages their education. What happens? Saudi Arabia soon had one of the world's highest birth rates. The annual population growth rate during the 1990s was 2.8 percent, compared with 1.2 percent for the U.S. and 0.2 percent for Spain. In 1981, the population was 9.8 million. In 1990, 14.9 million. In 2001, 21.4 million.

To these numbers factor in the fluctuating price of oil: as oil accounts for 75 percent of Saudi budget revenues, 35 percent of GDP, and 90 percent of export earnings, it is no exaggeration to say that the Saudi economy is wholly reliant on the price of petroleum. Prices peaked around 1982 at roughly $42 per barrel, but then came the "Oil Bust." The big fall of 1986 sent prices below $10 per barrel. Prices remained below $20 per barrel for years after the Gulf War.

Now do the math. 9.8 million people in 1981, and a GDP of $155.1 billion. That is a per capita income of $15,810. That is fairly rich—on par with Spain today. Add a lot more people. The population in 2001 was 21.4 million. Add cheaper oil, so total national income falls to $149 billion in 2001 (in other words, *less* than in 1981). Divide a bit less money by a lot more people: a per capita income of $6,960. That is less than half of the country's per capita wealth in 1981—and poorer than Slovenia or Brazil. For the Saudis, that adds up to quite a shock.

Unsurprisingly, the Al Saud could no longer afford its elaborate system of political patronage. By the early 1990s, Saudis were forced to pay more for government-subsidized water, electricity, oil, and domestic airfares. During the fat years, thousands of young Saudis had gone to study in the West on the Al Saud's dollar. In the lean years, students had no choice but to take their education in the predominantly religious Saudi educational system. The Al Saud downsized the state, shutting down ministries and bureaucracies. A university diploma no longer guarantees a young Saudi a government job. In fact, many university graduates cannot find desirable employment no matter where they look, leading them to apply for welfare. Western sources estimate that the unemployment rate in the kingdom may be as high as 25 percent.

Rags to riches and back to rags. Beggars can now be seen on the streets of Riyadh. According to dissidents, a chief source of information about the secretive kingdom, a shanty town of 60,000 sits near the Kuwaiti border, its residents without benefit of sewage or electricity. Indeed, where water and electricity were once cheap and abundant, Saudis must now contend with rolling blackouts and water rationing. The 1999 budget enforced a hiring freeze, a 30 percent cut in defense spending, and a 50 percent increase in the price of gas. Crown Prince Abdullah, who has taken over the day-to-day running of the kingdom from an ailing King Fahd, has stated in blunt terms: "The boom period is gone for good and...we have to become used to a different lifestyle in which every individual should perform their effective role and not totally rely upon the state." That was never part of the bargain.

But that is not the Al Saud's only headache. Oil money and puritanical Islam were never going to be an easy combination. The Saud family has thousands and thousands of princes and princesses, and tales abound of royal excess. King Fahd has one son who lives in a $300 million palace in Riyadh and pocketed an alleged $1 billion commission on the kingdom's $4.5 billion telephone contract with AT&T. Reports of the princes indulging in the many pleasures offered by Western cities—gambling, drinking, prostitution—filter back to the kingdom. To say the least, this does not sit well with the puritanical code of Wahhabi Islam.

Furthermore, strict interpretations of Islam conflict with modern economics. The kingdom's banking system uses interest (*riba*), which is strictly forbidden by Islamic doctrine. The royal family invests the kingdom's money in interest-bearing instruments abroad and borrows with interest. Indeed, many state regulations directly contravene *shariah*.

Over the years, these tensions have led to protests. In 1965, radical Islamists opposed to the introduction of television into the kingdom stormed a TV station in Riyadh. The Iranian revolution in 1979 presented an even bigger challenge. Iran's supreme religious leader, the Ayatollah Khomeini, mocked the Saudi royal family's claim to have founded an Islamic state, declaring: "There is no king in Islam." This touched a nerve in Saudi Arabia. In November 1979, a Saudi militant group occupied the Grand Mosque in Mecca, accusing the Al Saud of abandoning the principles of Islam. The militants defiantly stated that they would obey "only those who lead by God's book," and hence the Al Saud had "no claim on our obedience and their mandate to rule is nil." The Al Saud removed the invaders, but only after a protracted and brutal confrontation.

That said, things did not get really bad until Iraq invaded Kuwait. The Al Saud, fearing they might be Iraq's next target, turned to the U.S. for assistance. Some 600,000 soldiers—mostly American—were based in the Kingdom during Desert Shield and Desert Storm. For the Al Saud, this was a deal with the devil. The Saudi government had entered into an alliance with Christian "infidels" against Iraq—a Muslim Arab state. The Al Saud had invited non-Muslims—including female soldiers—onto the holiest grounds of Islam. (Wahhabis have always separated themselves from non-Muslims, and some radicals oppose any contact at all with Christians and Jews.) But most critically, the Al Saud had failed in its sacred duty to protect Islam's holy cities of Mecca and Medina. Menaced by Iraq, the Al Saud had shown its impotence, humiliatingly calling on the United States to guard the sacred cities. Militant leader Usama bin Laden reportedly offered to rally his own Islamist troops to defend Saudi Arabia and even depose Saddam Hussein's secular regime. The Saudi government scoffed at his offer and instead invited the Americans onto Saudi soil. For Usama bin Laden—whose band of militants had previously been funded by the Saudi government—this was the last straw. He openly turned against the regime and against the arriving Americans.

∞

Thus cracks began to spread through the pillars supporting the Al Saud's rule. With diminishing funds for patronage, the Saudi government could no longer justify its hold on power by providing an oil-funded good life for its citizens. At the same time, the increasingly visible security relationship with the United States undermined the al-Saud's claims to be constructing a pure Islamic state.

Opposition to the government spread. Following the Gulf War, 400 members of the state-sponsored *ulama*, along with university professors and others, sent a petition to the king urging him to embrace a more "Islamic" policy. The petition cited non-Islamic banking practices in the kingdom (especially the use of interest), the country's ties to the U.S., and corruption. The next year, more than one hundred Islamists signed a "Memorandum of Advice" to the king, which lambasted the al-Saud's "lack of seriousness" in enforcing the *shariah*. The signatories demanded the creation of religious institutions that operated outside of the corrupting influence of the degenerate Saudi state.

Two radical Wahhabi shaykhs, dubbed the "Awakening Shaykhs," attracted large followings by blasting the regime and its corruption, its ties to the West, and its failure to adhere to Islam. They accused the Al Saud of promoting *shirk* (polytheism), in opposition to the Wahhabi doctrine of *tawhid* (unity of God). They even called for the Al Saud to be branded "unbelievers"—the most serious charge a Muslim can face. Like the signers of the petition, the Awakening Shaykhs demanded that the Al Saud truly incorporate Islam into the state: "Our religion was not meant to be only confined to corners of a particular mosque. It came to teach us how to structure our economy and how to invest our money."

The Al Saud eventually arrested the Awakening Shaykhs, but they did not go quietly. When security forces came for Shaykh al-Awda, 500 of his followers occupied the governor's quarters in the town of Burayda and protests lasted several days in Riyadh. A militant group later threatened to "destroy Western institutions, kidnap U.S. citizens, Saudi royal family members, and security personnel, and attack corporations owned by the

Saudi royal family" if the shaykh was not released. The group added: "It is never acceptable that Christians and Jews are wandering freely in the peninsula while the *ulama* are held in prison."

While these militants hold extremist views, their critique of the Al Saud's rule has gained a wide audience. In Saudi Arabia, opinion polls are rare, the media is tightly controlled, and organized opposition is not allowed. But an informal poll conducted by Interior Minister Nayef in November 1994 produced unnerving results: 10 percent of Saudis supported Al Saud, 10 percent were hostile, 40 percent indifferent, and 40 percent unsure. Hardly a ringing endorsement of the regime.

∞

All this could have been, frankly, inconsequential. The Saudi government does not appear to be in immediate danger of collapse. It maintains a tight grip on society and tolerates little opposition. In a less globalized world than today's, the dynamics unleashed by the dwindling legitimacy of the Saudi regime might have been little concern to anyone. But times have changed. Saudi Arabia's political dynamics now have the attention of the world.

Partially this is because of one infamous man, Usama bin Laden. And certainly, bin Laden, a self-described follower of the Awakening Shaykhs, turned against the Saudi regime after the Al Saud rejected his offer of an Islamic defense force during the Gulf War. It was this that helped push bin Laden into opposition and exile. But without resources and recruits, bin Laden would pose little threat to anyone. And the phenomenon of al-Qaeda could never have existed absent Saudi Arabia's troubled ruling bargain. To deflect increasing domestic criticism, the Al Saud has financed Muslim causes around the world—ranging from the construction of mosques in Europe, Central Asia, and elsewhere to support for Islamic liberation struggles in Afghanistan and Bosnia. It was these international activities that nurtured the "Arab Afghans," many of whom would become the core of al-Qaeda. It is estimated that between 5,000 and 10,000 Saudis attended Afghan training camps. More generally, the Saudi regime's encouragement of fundamentalism at home—also an attempt to ward off criticism—has helped provide these organizations with recruits. Religious education has created a class of young Saudis who are quick to buy into the anti-Western message peddled by violent extremists.

Perhaps more importantly, the declining legitimacy of the Saudi regime has allowed al-Qaeda to mobilize support. Usama bin Laden has appealed to his followers by declaring his aim to abolish the Saudi regime and divide the entire Arabian Peninsula into two large states—"Greater Hijaz" and "Greater Yemen." Bin Laden has also invoked the religious decrees of the antiregime Awakening Shaykhs. The failing ruling bargain has lent power to such messages. Bin Laden is personally popular in Saudi Arabia, his idealistic decision to throw away enormous family riches contrasting with the opulence of the Saudi princes. His arguments have the most resonance with Saudis who feel betrayed by their government: most militant Islamists come from the lower rungs of Saudi Arabia's socioeconomic ladder—precisely the people who have been hit hardest by cutbacks in the government's social spending. It is no coincidence that most of the September 11 hijackers came from the 'Asir, one of Saudi Arabia's poorer regions.

Usama bin Laden is certainly a menace, but just as menacing is the political dynamic at work in Saudi Arabia, without which Usama bin Laden would be far less menacing than he is. (Acknowledging this, the U.S. government recently announced that it would move its military bases out of the country.) And this is worth remembering. For as long as this political dynamic persists, the resources bin Laden has employed are always available to someone else willing to take up the cause. Globalization has provided the mechanism for Saudi Arabia to export its citizens' rage to the world.

PERU

In 1990, Mario Vargas Llosa, the country's most acclaimed novelist, ran for the presidency of Peru. It is not every day that a novelist runs for president. But even stranger than Llosa's unusual candidacy was what happened next. Indeed, the events that followed had an almost surreal quality that would not have been out of place in one of Llosa's own "magical realist" novels.

First, Llosa found that his main opponent was, oddly enough, of

Japanese ancestry. Second, despite the support of the ruling party, Llosa lost the election. Third, this ethnic Japanese candidate, who won the election, launched a military coup and installed himself as the country's dictator. Fourth, genuinely delighted Peruvians gave their new dictator an 80 percent approval rating. Fifth, this dictator, seeking to legitimate his rule through an election, ran against and defeated Javier Pérez de Cuéllar, a former secretary-general of the United Nations. Sixth (and finally), a few short years later, this dictator, facing out-of-control public protests, fled the country in fear for his life and ended up living in Japan in exile. Stranger than fiction? Not if you understand the crucial role of the ruling bargain of Peruvian politics.

In 1990, Peru was a basket case. Earlier governments had built inefficient public industries, triggered runaway inflation, and run up a colossal national debt. Political institutions had decayed to the point where the government was unable to collect taxes. Over the course of the 1980s, tax receipts contracted from 17 percent of national economic output to less than 7 percent. While promising socialist wealth redistribution, the government actually cut back on social spending, from 4.9 percent of GDP in the 1980s to 2 percent in 1990. As a result, living standards plummeted. The real value of the minimum wage fell by nearly 85 percent over the course of the decade.

President Alan Garcia, who held office from 1985 to 1990, did an especially poor job. Overwhelmed by debt, he came up with the ultimately self-defeating idea of unilaterally capping foreign debt repayments. This helped trigger years of recession. Between 1985 and 1990, government revenues plunged by 70 percent in real terms. Far from growing, the economy actually contracted by a third in the late 1980s. Inflation reached a staggering 40 percent per month.

As the economy sank, a Marxist insurgency plunged the country into turmoil. During years of military rule in the 1970s, a guerrilla group called the *Sendero Luminoso,* the "Shining Path," had first attracted widespread support in the Peruvian countryside. A former philosophy professor named Abimael Guzman rallied rural Indians and *mestizos* (Peruvians of mixed ethnicity) who were angry with the country's feudalistic, white-dominated social order. During the 1970s the Shining Path launched a "People's War" that at the time was responsible for scattered killings and kidnappings. This insurgency exploded in the 1980s. The Shining Path escalated their struggle into a brutal civil war that was to cost the lives of more than 30,000 Peruvians and cause roughly $25 billion in economic damage. Guzman's troops discovered the money-making potential of drug smuggling, using their profits to purchase sophisticated weaponry and intelligence-gathering equipment. Nearly every Peruvian government institution was targeted with bombings and assassinations. As part of a campaign to rid the country of foreign influence, the Shining Path also targeted the diplomatic missions of several countries and inflicted damage on foreign businesses. Soon another guerrilla force—the Tupac Amaru Revolutionary Movement (MRTA)—joined the struggle, pursuing similar goals. To his credit, Garcia attempted to avoid human rights violations when combating the guerrillas. But his approach rendered the army ineffective and the country threatened to descend into chaos.

∞

Enter Alberto Fujimori. Fujimori's Japanese-immigrant parents, proud owners of a tire-repair shop in Lima, had never even dreamed that their son would grow up to become president of Peru. But Peruvians desperately wanted change. And they identified Fujimori as an outsider separate from the white establishment (with which the fair-skinned Vargas Llosa was identified) that had run the country into the ground. It helped Fujimori's cause that many rural Peruvians mistook his Asian features for those of an indigenous Andean. Fujimori played up this status. He repeatedly and emphatically promised change and vowed to restore both economic and political stability.

In 1991, Fujimori won the presidency with 62 percent of the vote. Upon taking office, Fujimori set out to implement the changes he had promised. A series of bold initiatives known alternatively as "tsunamis" or "Fujishock therapy" abolished capital controls, freed the currency, and rapidly privatized state-owned industries. To bring government finances under control, Fujimori slashed wages, cut social expenditures, and raised taxes. The resulting economic pain took a political toll. Fujimori's approval rating plummeted to 38.6 percent during the first nine months of 1991 as the legislature bickered about his plans.

Then Fujimori did something entirely unexpected. In April 1992, he

launched an *autogolpe,* a military coup—against himself. Fujimori sent
tanks to shut down Congress, suspended the constitution, and gave himself
the power to rule by decree. In a stroke, Fujimori demolished the country's
democracy. As he did so, he made some promises: that the government
would be more "direct, responsive, and efficient," and that stability and
growth would be restored. Perhaps even more unexpected was the public's
reaction. After years of economic decline and growing violence, Peruvians
were willing to listen. Instead of plummeting, Fujimori's popularity soared
to an astonishing 80 percent approval rating after the self-coup.

Why? Because Fujimori made good on his word. Inflation was
brought down to double digits in 1992 and to around 8 percent by 1995.
Fujimori aggressively deregulated the economy, sold off state enterprises,
and dismantled the Byzantine regulatory framework that stifled business
activity. In 1993, Peru's economy grew 6.4 percent. The next year, it grew
by a whopping 12.9 percent, tops in the world. Fujimori had turned Peru
into a dazzling "emerging market."

Fujimori was a canny politician. He took the proceeds from privatization and channeled them directly to the neediest Peruvians. Measured on
a per capita basis, the poorest regions of the country received the greatest
poverty relief. The impoverished Southern Andean states of Ayacucho,
Apurimac, and Puno saw their regional economies expand by more than
75 percent between 1993 and 1994. In only three years, from 1991 to 1994,
the national poverty rate declined from 55.1 percent of the population to
49.6 percent. Over the same period, consumer spending by the poorest
tenth of the population jumped by 36 percent.

Fujimori set upon the Shining Path with the same brutal zeal he
brought to economic reform. Unlike past administrations, Fujimori had
no qualms about violating human rights. The president allowed military
commanders free reign to impose martial law within their jurisdictions.
He gave military units the right to enter universities and prisons, which
until then had been fertile recruiting grounds for the guerrillas. Fujimori's
intelligence chief and armed forces leader created death squads, tortured
captured guerrillas, and held summary executions. For better or worse,
these tactics worked. In 1992, the army captured Guzman, decapitating
the Shining Path, and the intelligence service captured Victor Polay,
chief of MRTA. The number of political killings dropped rapidly. In

1992, there had been 3,102 deaths due to political violence. In 1994, there were only 297. And by 1995, the Shining Path was a spent force.

In December 1996, a desperate MRTA staged the boldest guerrilla action in Peruvian history. Twelve guerrillas infiltrated the Japanese ambassador's residence in Lima, seizing the building and taking seventy-two hostages, among them prominent foreign diplomats and members of the Peruvian government. The rebels demanded the release of MRTA's top leadership. But Fujimori would not budge. After nearly five months of stop-and-start negotiations, Fujimori sent in a crack commando team that burst into the building while the rebels were playing soccer. The soldiers mowed down the guerrillas and extricated all but one of the hostages. Fujimori's approval ratings soared. In April 1995, in a relatively fair election, he won with 64 percent of the vote. Peruvians had traded their "democratic freedoms" for "stability and growth"—a bargain they were willing to accept.

∞

But by the late 1990s, Fujimori seemed to have lost his touch. The guerrilla problem had become a distant memory. Peruvians were taking the security Fujimori had promised them for granted. On top of that, the Peruvian economy was slowing to a halt. In 1998, Peru was devastated by the dual effects of El Niño and the Asian financial crisis. Scores of Peruvians lost their livelihoods as freak weather patterns ravaged the fishing and farming industries. Total economic growth for 1998 was a meager 0.7 percent, and growth for 1999 was similarly anemic. To be fair, El Niño was not Fujimori's fault. But economic stability had been part of his ruling bargain, and Fujimori was not delivering. The deal that gave an autocratic leader his legitimacy began to unravel. With security a forgotten concern and the economy in the tank, Peruvians began to wonder what exactly Fujimori was doing for them. They paid more attention to his autocratic excesses—like military courts with anonymous, hooded judges. They became angry when Fujimori harassed Peru's largest television station after it exposed human rights abuses and the military's involvement in drug trafficking. Scattered street demonstrations erupted, as Peruvians protested everything from Fujimori's "neoliberalism" and "excessive centralism" to unreliable supplies of electricity and water.

On April 28, 1999, a massive anti-Fujimori strike was staged—the largest protest under his rule. Labor unions, the intelligentsia, and newly vocal political leaders began to attack Fujimori and question his dictatorial style.

Then Fujimori made a grievous error. Thinking the protests were temporary setbacks, he bullied a constitutional court into allowing him to seek a third presidential term. Before the election he spent lavishly to buy-off key constituencies and made populist promises to anyone who would listen. Then, in true dictatorial style, he stole the election. His opponent, a Harvard-educated academic of ethnic Andean origin named Alejandro Toledo, garnered substantial support. After a first round of votes, Toledo boycotted runoff elections when it became clear that Fujimori was going to win, no matter what. After a highly flawed electoral process with widespread voting irregularities, Fujimori was inaugurated for a third term in July 2000. But by this point the bargain had collapsed. Peruvians took to the streets to demand Fujimori's ouster. The street protests expanded and started to turn violent. A beleaguered Fujimori fled the country, turning up in Tokyo.

The collapse of the Fujimori regime has had severe costs for Peru. Floundering without leadership, the country suffered a macroeconomic crisis. A caretaker government did an admirable job stabilizing the economy, but Peru still has a long way to go. Alejandro Toledo was elected president in June 2001 and now faces the difficult task of rebuilding Peru's battered institutions. The judicial system, military, bureaucracy—all have lost their integrity and must be reconstructed.

Meanwhile, Fujimori, once the country's savior, lives in exile in Japan, which has refused to extradite him. Fujimori is said to have started a new life with a young Japanese girlfriend, but he is clearly haunted by his stunning descent. He can be found desperately trying to defend his reputation on FujimoriAlberto.com.

The Dynamics of the Ruling Bargain

Is any ruling bargain truly stable? Sadly, no. But the ruling bargain in liberal democracies has much to recommend it. The ruling bargain in a democratic state is very fundamental: the government earns its authority by representing the people. The citizens obey the laws and pay their taxes, and in return, the state puts the citizens in charge of the government and upholds their civil and political rights. In a sense, the democratic system allows numerous small bargains to be made and broken while the larger bargain remains intact. Political parties come into power making promises; if they fail to deliver, discontented people are allowed to "throw the bums out." And democratic governments agree to abide by the same laws that govern the people—politicians who abuse their power face impeachment or legal action. Elections and impeachment proceedings create instability, to be sure, but the system as a whole retains its legitimacy. After all, politicians must win office through the legitimate electoral process. People who dislike a particular government will still obey the laws, and pay their taxes, as long as their faith in the system remains intact. This critical feature—the separation of the current government from the larger system—is essentially unique to democratic politics.

This is not to say that democracies are invulnerable. Elections are a necessary evil—conferring legitimacy on leaders, but at the same time encouraging vices such as short-term thinking and poor public policies, ethnic demagoguery, and pandering to special interests, all to cultivate public support. And as the case of Peru demonstrates, the democratic ruling bargain falls apart when enough people feel that the system cannot deliver an effective and representative government. Before Fujimori, successive governments failed to deliver security, stability, and prosperity; Peruvians were willing to accept Fujimori's alternative, however repressive it was.

In fact, this is another type of ruling bargain—dubbed the "developmental state" by scholar Chalmers Johnson. The government earns its authority by delivering the goods—usually, stability and prosperity, but also social welfare spending, infrastructure, protection from crime, and so on. This "developmental state" is exemplified brilliantly by Singapore, in terms of the way its citizens accepted authoritarian rule in return for comfortable stability and rapid economic growth. The Chinese government is attempting to replicate Singapore's approach. To some extent, Chilean military dictator Augusto Pinochet successfully emulated this model. And he inspired his own imitators—Fujimori in Peru and, more recently, Pervez Musharraf in Pakistan.

The problem with "developmental state" regimes is that when they fail to deliver the goods, their legitimacy is undermined. This is true even when the failure is not their fault. The underlying deal that supports democratic states is absent. People are not going to wait for the next election and obey the laws and pay their taxes in the meantime. They are more likely to decide that everything the government does is totally illegitimate. When the ruling bargain utterly collapses, the resulting dynamics can cause a breakdown of political, social, and economic order; Indonesia is a tragic example.

The oldest type of ruling bargain is probably the one based on the charismatic leader. People are willing to follow someone whom they believe understands them and is capable of realizing their ambitions. By exuding charisma, these leaders convince the people to follow. This dynamic likely propelled many leaders to power in the earliest human societies, before formal governments or political institutions were even conceived. And this dynamic still operates in many places. It is often the foundation for opposition movements, and when these opposition movements take power (e.g. Chavez in Venezuela), they tend to rely on their charisma to maintain support. As Norberto Ceresole, a controversial Argentine sociologist, said of Chavez: "If my analysis is correct, the people's wish is clear . . . they voted to be led by a concrete person, not an idea or generic political party." Of course, over time, charisma can fade, as the Shah of Iran and Robert Mugabe of Zimbabwe have learned. Charismatic regimes that seem out of touch with their people can lose even their most ardent supporters.

There are still other ruling bargains. Countries that earn their revenues from some form of economic "rents," rather than from taxing their citizens, have been dubbed "rental income states." Saudi Arabia, for instance, earns its income from oil exports. Other sources of rental income include money from foreign aid, remittances from overseas workers, and so on. But to qualify as a true "rental income state," the government must be able to rely almost totally on these sources of revenue—not some of these revenues plus taxes.

Rental income does bizarre things to the ruling bargain. As scholar Hossein Mahdavy noted, the relationship between citizen and state is altered because citizens do not pay taxes. Political scientist Gregory Gause III compared the ruling bargain of a rental income state to the founding American principle of "no taxation without representation." In rental income states, he noted, the equation is reversed: "no representation without taxation." In other words, the people do not pay any taxes. Rather, they rely on handouts from the government. So why should they have a say in how they are governed?

In short, rental income states are almost always authoritarian regimes that "buy" the loyalty of their people by distributing generous social services. Nothing, sadly, seems to diminish a country's prospects more than the discovery of oil. The Persian Gulf states—Saudi Arabia, Kuwait, Oman, Qatar, Bahrain, and the United Arab Emirates—have delivered astounding benefits to their citizens. Living conditions in these countries—measured by indicators such as income levels, caloric intake, literacy, and life expectancy—have all improved dramatically since the 1970s. Citizens—more precisely, subjects—of these countries have enjoyed lavish subsidies on health care, food, utilities, housing, and they often work for the state. But the tradeoff is that citizens of the oil monarchies have almost no political rights or freedoms. Indeed, to the best of our knowledge, no rental income state has ever become a democracy.

"Rental income" ruling bargains have an Achilles heel: to retain their legitimacy, governments must continue to distribute the "rents." When the money dries up, the bargain implodes, the legitimacy of the system collapses, and the kimchi becomes unstable. Fortunately for the Gulf States, the sharp decline in oil prices has been offset by the sheer amount of oil money available. But Saudi Arabia shows that even a declining—as opposed to collapsing—ruling bargain can have severe negative effects both at home and on the international stage. The entire world has been caught up in this tortuous Saudi political dynamic.

The rental income state is, in a sense, an extreme case of another ancient ruling bargain: the patronage regime. Simply put, patronage works because those with wealth are able to convince others to follow by distributing handouts. In their most primitive modern form, patronage regimes tax some segments of the population and use the revenues to buy off other groups by distributing political favors and government funds. This is one step above rule by force, but it is not a big step. The resulting phenomenally corrupt governments usually fail to promote economic development and, therefore, may eventually run out of patronage to distribute. Not to mention that corruption angers those who are left out of the patronage system (as illustrated by the Philippines). Yet this type of bargain is common in the developing world. In many countries, leaders distribute favors to agricultural landlords who in turn keep the peasants in check. (The Philippines and Pakistan are two examples.) The government of Indonesia used an extraordinary patronage system for village chiefs in order to maintain control of its vast archipelago of 6,000 inhabited islands.

Indeed, patronage regimes can themselves be taken to the level of high art—not just by the clumsy distribution of rental income, but by the building of sophisticated institutions. The Soviet Union may have been founded on raw charisma and ideology, but it grew into an extraordinarily sophisticated state, as the Communist Party exerted control over organizations ranging from trade unions to professional associations to religious groups. Through these organizations, the Communist Party was able to promote people who were politically loyal and demote those with a tendency for free thinking. The Party also employed force—shipping dissidents to the camps of the dreaded *gulag*—but in most cases this was unnecessary. Those loyal to the Party were rewarded with state-controlled resources (and the economy was almost entirely state-controlled); those lacking in loyalty saw their fortunes dwindle.

Such sophisticated one-party regimes can achieve centrally-planned economic growth and, for a time, maintain stability. But—as in the case of the USSR—this growth is extraordinarily inefficient, and thus tends not to last. As scholar Samuel Huntington noted, such regimes also collapse if the ruling party falters. (Americans have had ring-side seats to the collapse of the Iraqi state following the removal of Saddam Hussein's Ba'ath Party.)

Other types of ruling bargains are predicated on ideological, religious, cultural, or historical concerns. The Al Saud, for instance, pledge to establish a purer form of Islam. Ethnic divisions are a highly effective, yet destructive way to gain popular support: in the former Yugoslavia, Slobodan Milosevic justified his rule by pledging (disastrously) to create a greater Serbia; in Kenya, Daniel arap Moi justified his tight hold on power by playing up the majority Kikuyu tribe's fears of what other ethnicities might do in a more open democracy. True communist ruling bargains are hard to find these days. Communist ideology can inspire revolutionaries, but does less well in convincing people to accept the long-term rule of a repressive, often corrupt, one-party regime. Instead, nominally communist regimes tend to rely on patronage, charisma, or sheer repression (e.g., North Korea) to stay in power. What once may have been the most common bargain—the hereditary monarchy—still thrives in some states. King Abdullah of Jordan and King Muhammad VI of Morocco base their authority on their bloodlines.

At the bottom of the pile are those governments that completely lack legitimacy. These regimes—the warlords of Somalia come to mind—rule purely by organized terror. These types of governments can never create prosperity for their people. They may enforce a repressive form of stability, but sophisticated regulation of political and economic activity is impossible when people will obey laws only because of the threat of immediate punishment. Perhaps a central planning regime can survive under such circumstances to some extent. But free markets are impossible, because people without respect for the rules will flout them. This is a tragic lesson of many failed states.

But were not many of the warlords of Somalia charismatic, and did they not use their charisma to mobilize their followers? This hits at a crucial point about the ruling bargain. In actuality, there are often many bargains in a single country, as in the case of Saudi Arabia. There are democratic regimes that offer patronage to key supporters; religious regimes that also provide rental income; charismatic leaders in monarchies; democratic governments that promise to deliver the goods to their people; and the list goes on. The Somali warlords are no doubt charismatic, and generous suppliers of patronage, to their gun-toting followers, but not to many of the terrorized Somali people. For some in Saudi Arabia, the oil is important. For others, only Islam matters. It might be more accurate to talk about "ruling bargains" rather than "the ruling bargain."

Rather than a single, defining principle with which to understand an entire country, the ruling bargain is a way to dissect its kimchi, analyze its stability. What conditions must continue to hold for the sake of stability, because these conditions convince the public that the government has the right to rule? When these bargains fail for politically powerful groups (militant Islamists, the middle class, agricultural landlords), the results can be disastrous. Indeed, many histories can be viewed through the ruling bargain lens. The rise and fall of charismatic patronage regimes in the Philippines. Providing patronage (the cake) to one's own ethnic group in Nigeria. An increasingly Islamic government in Egypt. Delivering the goods (or failing to) in Indonesia. Charismatic opposition (and governments) in Venezuela. A fundamentally democratic bargain in India. Failing charisma in Zimbabwe and Iran. Delivering the goods (very well) in Singapore. What happened to stability in each of these countries depended in some way on the government's ability to fulfill its bargain with the people—sometimes the poor, sometimes the middle class, sometimes members of only one ethnic group, sometimes society at large.

Even more importantly, understanding these ruling bargains helps one forecast not just how stable a country will be, but what policies the government will follow in the future. After all, to survive, the government has to uphold its end of the bargain. For example, in Saudi Arabia, the government tried to shore up its credentials by supporting fundamentalist causes, much to the dismay of the Western world. In Indonesia, Suharto refused to agree to IMF reform demands that would have dismantled his patronage regime, again with disastrous consequences. This—the all-important subject of policymaking—determines a country's true prospects for achieving prosperity over time.

Part 4

Policy

In some respects, everything up to this point of the book has been a prelude. Discontent (covered in Part 1), how it is managed (Part 2), and leadership (Part 3)—these are the ground rules for how countries work. Admittedly, this is also where the drama can be found: the violent revolutions, the riots and demonstrations, the political intrigue, the unexpected military coups, the ethnic and religious conflicts. Political instability is exciting, but what really matters is a country's ability to generate prosperity for its people. Ultimately, this makes the difference between a state that succeeds and a state that fails. South Korea, despite endless violent demonstrations, produced real wealth for its people. Italy, despite constant changes of government, grew prosperous. Thailand, despite regular military coups, enjoyed years of rapid growth. These states are not without their failings, but who would trade their fortunes for the "stability" of Cuba or North Korea?

In this section, we address what is most critical to a country's fortunes— its ability to generate prosperity over time. We argue that this ability is fundamentally contingent on how a country "works": the sources and level of popular discontent, how the discontent is managed, and the stability of a country's leadership. All of these have a profound effect on the types of policy decisions that can be made, and whether these policy decisions will be implemented, ignored, sustained, or overturned. It is these policy decisions—about budgets and exchange rates, war and peace, openness and protectionism, markets and government intervention, price controls and judicial independence, property rights and subsidies—that will determine if a country becomes and remains prosperous and stable.

There is always room for freedom of choice. A superb leader can accomplish things that are nearly impossible. But think of the political pressures we have so far discussed—discontent, the various strategies to manage it, and constraints on leadership—as a powerful current pushing a country's policymakers in a certain direction. A poor leader may be overwhelmed by this current. A good leader can fight it. A great leader may even alter its flow. But the current is always there, and its influence is strong.

In this section, we demonstrate how this current of political necessity influences government policy. We will explain why unstable states have such a hard time making good policy (Mexico). We will show how the interest groups on which political leaders depend to maintain power can twist policy to their own ends (Pakistan and Brazil). We will assess the external shocks of economic globalization (Argentina and Eastern Europe), examine state involvement in the economy (Turkey), and assert that all countries contain economic potential energy and describe how they can unleash it (Russia and Botswana).

A Brief Note on Economics

This section on policy necessarily delves into a bit of economics. For readers unfamiliar with the discipline, we provide here a brief explanation of some basics.

First, rapid economic growth tends to raise wages and prices—to push up the rate of inflation. Too much inflation is undesirable because it has the potential to undermine continued growth. So there needs to be some balance in order to limit the rate of inflation.

Second, low interest rates tend to fuel faster growth, and government spending also tends to fuel faster growth. But increased government spending may be financed by increased taxes, which tend to sap the vitality of the private sector; or through government borrowing that can starve the private sector of funds; or through the government's creating credit, which means more inflation. Here also, a balance is needed.

Add to these balances the balance of international transactions. Many things flow across a country's borders—people, ideas, goods, services, money. Money, "capital," may flow out in order to pay for imported goods and services. Some capital may be headed to foreign stock markets, or to Swiss bank accounts, or to pay interest on foreign loans. Capital may flow in to finance investment, or as foreign aid, and so on. The sum total of the financial value of all the transactions crossing the borders, in both directions, is called a country's "current account balance."

A country can run a current account deficit, importing more capital than it exports, by borrowing from abroad or attracting foreign investors. If a lot of net borrowing and investment is going on, the current account deficit can be high, fueling growth if the imported capital is invested productively. But imports of capital are often wasted, funding the import of goods, often luxury goods for the elites; building show projects; or fueling bubbles in real estate or stocks. Eventually, a country that does not use its imported capital wisely will, usually, come to grief—growth will falter, foreign banks will refuse to lend, and foreign investors may pull their money out. A crisis is likely to follow. Once again, a balance—between closed borders and excessive imports of capital—is good.

To complete this story, one further factor must be addressed: the exchange rate. The "real exchange rate" is just what it sounds like—the current exchange rate, adjusted for inflation, to reflect the true purchasing power of a country's currency. If inflation (rising prices) erodes the value of a currency (i.e., the same amount of currency buys fewer goods) the real value of the currency plunges. A currency whose market rate is high but real value is low is "overvalued." This makes it easy for the country to import goods—a benefit in the short term. But it also makes it hard to export, enlarging the current account deficit and risking a crisis.

Finally, a word about the mechanics of a troubled country. A country that seems in danger of suffering a financial crisis will likely raise its interest rates in an effort to attract more foreign capital and improve its current account balance, as well as to reduce inflation, thereby increasing the real value of its currency. Unfortunately, higher interest rates will slow growth, which will be politically unpopular at home and will also make foreigners nervous about sending more money. Far better to keep the current account balance at manageable levels. But there is, unfortunately, great temptation to do otherwise.

CHAPTER ELEVEN

Clockwork Crises

THE INSTABILITY TRAP

IMAGINE A PECULIAR RACE OF PEOPLE WHO COMPLETELY LACK foresight. Consider the dysfunctional patterns of behavior that would result. With no concern for the future, these people would cease to save, to invest, or to care about education—because all of these things involve present sacrifice for future payoffs. Instead, they would spend all that they have, and indeed, borrow what they could and spend that as well. They would try to get rich by redistributing wealth (less diplomatically, by stealing it), because redistribution is immediate, while the creation of wealth requires long-term effort. The less these people cared about the future, the more they would become venal, untrustworthy, and corrupt. In the extreme case, nothing would be built and everything plundered.

These patterns of behavior are not purely hypothetical. In certain circumstances, political leaders—though they are entrusted with decisions that affect the lives of millions—will cease to care about the future consequences of their decisions for the countries they rule. This is kimchi that undermines prosperity and begets financial crises.

MEXICO

1976: After twenty years pegged at the same rate, Mexico's currency, the peso, undergoes a sudden 60 percent devaluation. This economic shock leads to recession and soaring inflation.

1982: Once again, the Mexican economy collapses. The peso is devalued by nearly 100 percent and the Mexican government announces a unilateral moratorium on foreign debt repayments.

1988: The Mexican inflation rate reaches 150 percent. The stock market plummets. A well-timed bailout package arranged by the U.S., IMF, and World Bank keeps the country afloat.

1994: The Mexican government bungles an attempt at a controlled peso devaluation, causing the infamous "Mexican peso crisis" and sending inflation and interest rates soaring. The banking system totters near collapse and the country lurches into its worst recession in fifty years.

Twice is a coincidence. Three times a pattern. Four times a conspiracy. Readers will note that each of these events was separated by a span of six years. Why did the Mexican economy crash, with clockwork regularity, every six years? Here is a hint: in Mexico, 1976, 1982, 1988, and 1994 were all election years.

∞

By the late 1960s, Mexico's Institutional Revolutionary Party (PRI) had already been in power for longer than most Mexicans had been alive—despite the fact that Mexico was at least nominally a democracy. Every six years, as mandated by the constitution, there were elections, and the PRI candidate always won. One reason this was possible was that the PRI tried to appeal to the entire political spectrum, and sat at the center of Mexican politics.

And so, when Mexican politics—in tune with the times—took a sharp leftward turn in the late 1960s, the PRI turned left with it. Student radicals took over campuses, going on strike along with their professors, holding raucous protests denouncing electoral fraud, and invoking leftist icon Che Guevera. The PRI, eventually—after blundering into a Tiananmen-style massacre of student protestors in 1968—heeded these calls. President Luis Echeverria blasted the "tragic complacency of previous regimes," and doubled public spending during his *sexenio* (six-year presidential term). Under a socialist-style "Shared Development" program, state enterprises multiplied and millions of Mexicans found jobs as public-sector workers.

This leftism was good politics but bad economics. Mexico's government deficit trebled as a percentage of GDP during the Echeverria *sexenio*. New public borrowing expanded by a factor of 11, from $443 million to $5.1 billion. At this point, something odd happened—something that was to happen again and again in Mexican politics. It became fairly obvious, even to many in the government, that an economic disaster was imminent. Yet there was no attempt to change course. The government rushed eyes-wide-open into a crisis.

Inflation shot up, thanks to out-of-control government spending. Echeverria raised workers' salaries, which, in turn, caused more inflation. Soon the overheating economy and rising inflation had undermined the real value of Mexico's currency—the nominal exchange rate was pegged, and had been set at the same value since the 1950s. This opened a yawning current account deficit. Mexico was living well beyond its means. Fearing the inevitable collapse, Mexicans with money shipped it offshore for safekeeping. Still playing the leftist, Echeverria railed against "the little rich Mexicans who buy dollars," who "are despised by their own sons, because they are not strengthening the fatherland."

A way out still existed at this point. The government could have cut spending and clamped down on inflation. But to cut spending and raise interest rates would have brought about an economic downturn during an election year. Echeverria was not about to commit electoral suicide. His handpicked successor, Jose Lopez Portillo, who was serving as the Minister of Finance, instructed his aides not even to mention the word "devaluation." "We're not going to devalue anything here," Portillo explained to a cabinet minister, "because we've got a lot of balls."

Lopez Portillo won the 1976 election, but at great cost. In September of that year, facing a balance-of-payments crisis, the Mexican government abandoned its currency peg. The peso collapsed, falling by 60 percent, and the Mexican economy sank into recession. U.S. speculators who had believed the Mexican government's claims that it would not devalue were trapped in the mess as well. Mexican businesspeople, angered by the PRI's leftist rhetoric and stunning economic mismanagement, founded a new organization, the Coordinating Enterprise Council, to voice their outrage.

∞

But the PRI had not held onto power for five uninterrupted decades by making enemies. President Lopez Portillo set about winning back business support. He promptly invited the International Monetary Fund into the country and arranged a standby loan. Austere policies brought down inflation and, in just one year, Lopez Portillo slashed the budget deficit from 9.9 percent of GDP to 6.7 percent.

But this era of responsibility did not last, because, one year into the new president's *sexenio*, Mexico discovered oil. Over the next few years, oil production tripled to 2.4 million barrels per day and known hydrocarbon reserves rose elevenfold. Suddenly, Mexico's budget held enough money for everything: housing, education, health care, public works, more government jobs. As the government's wallet expanded, so did its appetites. Pumping oil out of the ground took time, and impatient politicians did not want to wait. But waiting was unnecessary—foreign banks were only too happy to lend against future revenues, providing the Mexican government with hundreds of millions of dollars in easy credit. The public sector deficit skyrocketed from 7.3 percent of GDP in 1980 to 12.5 percent in 1981. But Lopez Portillo was not worried, and neither were foreign lenders. The government had oil revenues to pay for its borrowing and these were only growing.

And then, with spectacularly bad timing, the world price of oil plummeted, just as Mexico was heading toward another presidential election. This time, the approaching crisis was going to be a lot worse than a simple recession. Mexico had become one of the developing world's most indebted countries, having borrowed approximately $52 billion. The country was facing an outright default. Global interest rates spiked, making debt payments even harder to make. As disaster neared, Mexicans sent their money offshore at a frantic pace—between 1980 and 1982, an estimated $17 to $23 billion left the country. A Federal Reserve Bank study found that by 1981, Mexicans had stashed almost $25 billion in assets in Texas alone.

Even in an election year, one might expect that the specter of debt default would compel responsible action. But this time, election pressures were further complicated by a pitched battle over who would succeed Lopez Portillo. Some in the Mexican government—notably Finance Minister David Ibarra—warned that a crisis was imminent. His finance ministry forecast an unsustainable budget deficit and recommended immediate spending cuts. But Minister for Planning and Budget Miguel de la Madrid, hoping to force Ibarra out and become the PRI's official presidential candidate, produced only implausibly good news. On the logic that "birds of ill omen never win," his ministry forecast a small deficit and said big cuts were not necessary.

Lopez Portillo evidently liked yes-men, because de la Madrid was appointed the PRI's official candidate. By election day, the Mexican economy was spectacularly out of control—with a budget deficit in excess of $20 billion and current account deficit of $13 billion. But, with Lopez Portillo promising to defend the overvalued peso "like a dog," de la Madrid won.

Even before the new president could take office, disaster struck. Lopez Portillo devalued the peso by 100 percent and declared that Mexico could no longer make payments on its foreign debts. This had the consequence of suddenly pushing the entire U.S. banking system to the edge of collapse. Never suspecting that foreign governments might actually become insolvent, U.S. banks had loaned so much that their cross-border exposures exceeded 500 percent of their capital. If Mexico and other sovereign borrowers ceased payment, many of the banks might collapse. A panicking U.S. government, hoping to save the U.S. financial system, extended a $600 million line of credit to Mexico. But Mexico was already melting down. Lopez Portillo nationalized fifty-nine private banks and froze foreign currency deposits in Mexico. With a U.S. financial crisis looming, the U.S. government had no choice but to intervene directly. Treasury Secretary James Baker III devised a scheme to let debtors defer or reschedule debts, so the loans would not be completely in default, and the international banks that had lent billions to Mexico would survive. Eventually, Baker's successor as treasury secretary, Nicholas Brady, came up with a plan whereby private banks wrote off a portion of developing country debt. Debtor countries then bought thirty-year "Brady Bonds" financed by richer countries. The international banking system was, for the moment, saved.

∞

The next crisis, brought on by the 1988 election, was comparatively mild. The PRI, still eager to please, embarked on another quixotic attempt to win back business support. De la Madrid, now installed as president, set up a generous subsidy scheme to repair some of the damage Mexican businesses had suffered as a result of the debt crisis. This was financed by a ruthless austerity towards the poor. At the beginning of de la Madrid's term, spending on health, education, and social welfare consumed 24 percent of government spending. By the end of his *sexenio*, social spending was a paltry 10 percent of the budget.

But Mexican businesspeople were not impressed. The middle class had by this point realized the PRI was probably incapable of shaping up. They increasingly abandoned the PRI for the right-wing National Action Party (PAN). The PAN was backed by powerful industrialists in Monterrey and other more-developed regions, who wanted to reduce state participation in the economy. The PAN won control of several large cities in the 1983 elections.

Facing growing political threats, the PRI resorted to its usual pre-election tactics. The new minister of budget and planning, a Harvard Ph.D. named Carlos Salinas, used his power over the purse strings to boost public spending before the 1985 state elections. Even with inflation running over 60 percent, Salinas increased funding for subsidy programs. This boost in spending pushed inflation over 100 percent. Eventually, Salinas made a clean break from his fiscally responsible past, declaring: "We have cut spending right down to the bone. We can't cut any more." As the presidential polls approached, Salinas (supported by President de la Madrid) dramatically expanded the money supply. He channeled funds to key constituencies, such as the rural sector and Mexico City.

Once again, this strategy, combined with substantial electoral fraud, worked for the PRI in the elections, and once again, the economy collapsed. Inflation exceeded 150 percent in 1987. In November 1987, the Mexican stock market crashed and private capital fled the country. But this time, people knew what to expect. The outside world understood Mexico's dynamics, and the U.S., the IMF, and World Bank rushed in with bailout funds that kept the country afloat.

∞

At this point, one might expect that the world had pretty much figured out Mexico's clockwork crises. But another spectacular crash was still to come. In fairness, this next crash was uniquely hard to anticipate, because Mexico became, suddenly and unexpectedly, a tremendous economic success. Mexico's new president, Carlos Salinas, whose free-spending ways as finance minister had nearly caused a disaster, became, in office, a textbook economic reformer. Salinas adhered rigidly to fiscal discipline, restructured Mexico's economy, and dismantled the state sector. He reduced the number of state-run companies from 1,110 to 220. He brought inflation down from triple digits to just 7 percent in 1994. Under Salinas, Mexico even began recording budget surpluses. Salinas privatized state industries, deregulated the economy, and negotiated the NAFTA trade pact with the U.S.

Thus the "Mexican Miracle" was born. Foreign investment flooded the country, to the tune of $30 billion per year in the early 1990s, while the stock market rose. *Euromoney* magazine reported that Mexico's country risk rating had improved dramatically. Between 1990 and 1993, Mexico received more than half of all investment headed for Latin America, a total of $91 billion. From the devastation of the debt crisis in 1982 and the stagnation of the de la Madrid *sexenio*, Salinas built Mexico into a shining "emerging market."

To be sure, while Mexico was booming, it was still borrowing. This time most of the funds went to the private sector. The current account deficit rose to 6.8 percent of GDP in 1993, and 8 percent in 1994. Investors began to feel a sense of deja vu: the peso was overvalued, it was an election year, and the president clearly had no intention of letting the peso fall. (In the words of Lopez Portillo, "The president who devalues is devalued.") Still, there seemed to be little cause for concern. Mexico was attracting investment and government debt seemed under control.

But the world was about to get the first of many lessons in the volatility of cross-border portfolio capital flows—so-called "hot money." Two unpleasant surprises materialized in quick succession. First, in the early part of 1994, an Indian uprising in the southern state of Chiapas led to bloodshed. Then, the PRI's presidential candidate, Luis Colosio, was assassinated. Foreign investors panicked and sent their money streaming out of the country. Salinas spent $10 billion defending the peso's value, and also increased government spending just before the election, showering money on districts where the PRI faced its most significant opposition. At the same time, to keep growth moving, the Central Bank extended $8 billion in domestic credit in March and April, hoping to keep Mexican businesses afloat. But much of this money was used by the private sector to buy foreign assets. This just worsened the gaping current account deficit.

History repeats itself. The eventual PRI candidate, Ernesto Zedillo, won the presidential elections in August 1994. Shortly thereafter, the Mexican economy imploded. Zedillo initially pledged to stick to the currency peg, but days later the government ran out of money to defend the peso and the currency lost 30 percent of its value, driven down by Mexican businessmen close to the new government who fled the peso after being tipped off on the coming currency plunge. This was a new type of crisis: a liquidity crisis, brought on by sudden capital flight, as opposed to a balance-of-payments crisis brought on by a structural inability to service the country's debts. The Mexican economy crashed, suffering its worst recession in fifty years.

And once again, despite ample lessons of history, the world got caught up in Mexico's political dynamics. U.S. banks, with improved country risk management procedures, were better poised to handle the crisis, but Citicorp still had an estimated $5 billion invested in Mexico. American portfolio investment in the Mexican stock market was estimated at $1 billion, with another $2.2 billion in the Mexican debt market. U.S. traders felt the pain as the Mexican stock market lost an astounding half of its value in 1995. The United States ultimately extended $50 billion in bailout funds, saving Mexico from a debt default. This was politically unpopular in the U.S., but considering the 2,000 mile border between the two countries, the prospect of fervent anti-Americanism, mass immigration, and political instability in Mexico terrified the Clinton administration.

A complete meltdown was averted. But this was now the age of globalization. Mexico's crisis created the "Tequila Effect"—as the peso plunged, markets around the world trembled. Emerging markets were battered everywhere: Malaysia, Singapore, Thailand, the Philippines, Russia, Poland. Hardest hit were markets in Latin America. Argentine stocks lost 7.5 percent of their value in 1995, Brazil lost 28 percent, Colombia 26 percent, and Peru 20 percent.

So, one may wonder, what happened in 2000? Did Mexico succumb to another crisis? As it turned out, no. For one thing, government policies leading up to the election were dramatically better. The current account deficit, budget deficit, and inflation rate were all manageable. This, plus NAFTA and a freely floating peso, reduced Mexico's vulnerabilities. Whereas in 1994, 75 percent of foreign investment in Mexico was in volatile bonds, in 2000, 70 percent was in long-term foreign direct investment.

And for another thing, the PRI was finally willing to lose. Zedillo lost the election, and peacefully ceded power to Vincente Fox of the opposition PAN party, breaking the PRI's seven-decade monopoly on Mexican politics. None of this completely insulates Mexico from this clockwork crisis dynamic. But it does make the odds for 2006 quite a bit better.

THE DYNAMICS OF INSTABILITY TRAPS

A fundamental insight into good governance: it all depends on the long term.

This is true at a very basic level. Consider the puzzle of why governments exist at all. Anarchy is rare in today's world, but when it does occur, governments (admittedly, very often despotic governments) tend to arise quickly and restore some semblance of order. Scholar Mancur Olson explained this phenomenon by considering the alternative. In lawless areas, bands of marauding thugs typically prey upon the people, periodically sacking villages and stealing everything they can get their hands on. These thugs are a curse on progress since their looting is unrestrained. The people are miserable, because everything they produce is likely to be stolen. Most importantly, the thugs are miserable. People who know their wealth will eventually be stolen generally do not bother to produce much, so even the thugs make a poor living.

At some point, an enterprising group of thugs realizes they are better off settling down. The motivation for doing so is not immediately obvious, since the life of a government, which must provide its people with order and security, seems more difficult than the life of a thug, who need only take care of himself. But the key is to think about the long term. Unlike a roving bandit—a short-term opportunist who loots all that he can and then leaves town—a stationary government loots with more of a long-term view. The government is better off if it takes (in the form of taxes) only a portion of the people's income, because then the people will have an incentive to work hard and produce more income in the future. Almost immediately, everyone is better off. The thugs who have set up a government collect more taxes than they did in their roving days, because they have harder-working subjects. The people, for their part, gain peace, security, and the luxury of keeping some of their income.

But the promotion of prosperity is a trickier business than the simple imposition of public order. It is one thing to convince a thug to forbear from absolute plunder in return for almost immediate rewards. It is another thing entirely to convince this thug that short-term pain is warranted for long-term gain.

Yet this is what modern economic reforms require. Many economic policies that promote prosperity tend to require sacrifice in the short run and pay off only over the long term, and all too often to people who did not make the original sacrifices. Hence these policies are difficult to implement. Call it the "the time distribution problem." A classic example is cutting the budget deficit. With one exception—providing stimulus during an economic downturn—there is no justification for running high deficits. There is no ideology—on the right or the left—that claims that chronic deficits are good. Chronic deficits build up government debt, which future generations must pay off, and excessive government borrowing sucks up scarce capital, starving the private sector of funds. In short, large and chronic budget deficits are, in the long-term, indisputably bad, and the truth of this fact is almost universally acknowledged.

The fact that governments around the world—not just in poor countries, but also in the U.S., Europe, and Japan—often run chronic deficits is testament to the intractability of the time distribution problem. Cutting the deficit hurts now and pays off in the future. Running a deficit boosts growth now and primarily hurts future generations. Fortunately, while running a chronic deficit is bad, it can be considered an acceptable evil as long as it not extraordinarily large. In some countries, however, the time distribution problem is so extreme that unacceptable evils result. Chronic deficits grow into debt crises. Inflation becomes hyperinflation. An overvalued currency causes a balance of payments disaster. The government opportunistically expropriates private property rather than protecting private property rights. Politicians implement extremely shortsighted policies that undermine prosperity and refuse to implement policies that could nurture growth. The result is that the people remain impoverished.

This "instability trap" happens when political leaders cease to care about the long term. One obvious reason for this phenomenon is that the leaders may not expect to be around for long. In the extreme case, political leaders revert back to their original role as roving thugs. They plunder and then leave, as so many despots have done, with large Swiss bank accounts. Essentially, this is a disease of governments that expect to be rapidly deposed. When political leaders believe their political survival is immediately threatened (due to rising discontent, perhaps, or powerful opposition), the goal of seeing off an immediate challenge tends to override all other considerations. Desperate governments will take desperate actions. In such cases a harsh dynamic quickly develops. The more short-term the government's policies, the more the economy plunges; the more the economy plunges, the more stability is threatened; and the more stability is threatened, the more the government has trouble thinking beyond the short term. Hence the "trap."

The classic example is pre-election policymaking. In the run-up to elections, leaders face an immediate threat—they, or their chosen successors, might be voted out of office. Hence they favor policies that engineer a short-term economic boom, and may abandon economic reforms that have short-term costs and long-term benefits. The result is the so-called "political business cycle." Growth (and budget deficits, and inflation) tends to peak in election years. And elections are sometimes followed by an economic crash. As the World Bank observed of Mexico, with characteristic dispassion: "In the election year and the year before presidential elections, growth in per capita GNP is nearly always significantly higher than in the year following the elections. In fact, this pattern of behavior can be seen in every one of the eight presidential elections held since 1950, except one (1988). The probability of this recurring pattern being mere coincidence is close to zero."

∞

Another example is Thailand. Between 1985 and 1995, Thailand had produced an economic miracle: an average of 9.4 percent growth per year. But a dangerous short-termism had set in, because Thailand during the 1990s was a country in perpetual campaign mode. If elections were not being held, they were on the verge of being held. Four elections took place in five years. Bangkok was a virtual revolving door of prime ministers, finance ministers, and central bank governors.

In the summer of 1997, the government of Prime Minister Chavalit Yongchaiyudhi was in no position to take a principled stand. Chavalit was fighting for his government's short-term survival. At the start of his administration, Chavalit acknowledged Thailand's economic difficulties—a current account deficit at 8.1 percent of GDP and short-term debt totaling $41 billion, a 40.7 percent increase over the previous year. He attempted to give his finance minister authority over five economic ministries. But Chavalit's coalition partners rejected this plan and Chavalit was forced to back down. In an effort to gain favor and ward off challenges, the prime minister gave contracts to his friends, awarded commercial banking licenses to cronies from the military, and propped up weak financial institutions. Worst of all, fearing he would be thrown from office, he refused to devalue the currency. He instead ordered the government to spend its exchange reserves in a futile attempt to fight off currency speculators.

Chavalit's government finally had no choice but to float the currency in July 1997. The Thai government had run through its foreign exchange reserves; the currency plunged by nearly 100 percent and the banking system collapsed. Thailand suffered a devastating financial crisis. The country received a $17.2 billion bailout package from the International Monetary Fund, but refused to follow the fund's harsh policy recommendations. The financial crisis quickly spread throughout the region: Indonesia, South Korea, and, to some extent, Malaysia and the Philippines all suffered.

Thus political stability has its own rewards. As Lee Kwan Yew, former prime minister of famously stable Singapore, once stated, "The governments with political strength to do the unpleasant quickly and thoroughly will reap the best rewards." Many political leaders have wished for that luxury.

CHAPTER TWELVE

Powers Behind the Throne

ENTRENCHED INTERESTS

*"Nobody is saying that...the custody...ought not go to the father.
If the father says on free soil that he believes the son should go back...
that of course...will be determinative."*
U.S. VICE PRESIDENT AL GORE SPEAKING ABOUT ELIAN GONZALEZ
(APRIL 4, 2000, MORNING)

*"Let's focus on what's in the best interest of this child and let's don't let Fidel
Castro manipulate the situation, speaking for the father, intimidating the
father, not allowing the father to come here to see his child..."*
U.S. VICE PRESIDENT AL GORE SPEAKING ABOUT ELIAN GONZALEZ
(APRIL 4, 2000, AFTERNOON)

IN NOVEMBER 1999, A YOUNG CUBAN BOY NAMED ELIAN GONZALEZ
floated from a beach in Cuba into the middle of a political maelstrom.
Elian and his mother were following a dangerous but well-traveled route
when they fled Cuba in a rickety boat for political asylum in the United
States, but their vessel sank before they reached the coast of Florida.
Elian's mother drowned. Miraculously, the six-year-old boy survived.

Thus was born a foreign policy dilemma. Cuban refugees who do
not make it to Florida, usually because they are picked up by the U.S.
Coast Guard, are sent back. Elian, now seemingly an orphan, was instead
delivered into the care of his Florida-based relatives. Miami's Cuban

community, fervently opposed to the Castro regime, seized on Elian as a powerful symbol of liberation from oppression. Here was a boy whose miraculous survival seemed to suggest a North American destiny.

But Elian's Cuba-based father declared that he wanted the boy back. International law was fairly clear on the issue: as the closest living relative, the father's wishes were, as Al Gore initially said, "determinative." Furthermore, opinion polls revealed that an overwhelming majority of Americans supported returning the boy. It is therefore tempting to condemn Al Gore for his unprincipled flip-flops and waffling.

But what then-presidential candidate Gore apparently remembered, sometime during the lunch hour on April 4, 2000, was that Miami Cubans form a powerful voting block in Florida and that delegate-rich Florida would likely be a key battleground state in the upcoming presidential election. Gore suddenly found himself in possession of hard line anti-Castro convictions. He even went so far as to express support for the idea of giving Elian permanent resident status.

As it turned out, the 2000 U.S. presidential race did in fact come down to Florida. And Miami Cubans did not believe Gore's change of heart (especially not after armed federal agents seized Elian and sent him back to Cuba). A gleeful George W. Bush heckled loudly from the sidelines, declaring firmly that Elian should stay in the U.S. no matter what his father said. The Miami Cubans, who had been giving more support to Democrats in recent elections (an estimated 35 percent voted for Clinton), turned firmly against Gore. They called the 2000 polls *el voto castigo,* "the punishment vote," and cast their ballots for Bush in overwhelming numbers. A *National Journal* headline, "Elian Gonzalez Defeated Al Gore," is probably not so wide of the mark.

Future presidential candidates will doubtless pay the Miami Cubans more attention. Although a small minority, as a powerful "special interest" group they punch above their weight in U.S. politics. Of course, they are only one of many. Special interests have strong influence in many areas of U.S. policy, ranging from environmental law to trade policy to foreign affairs. Even individual companies can benefit, if they are large and free-spending enough. The now infamous Enron, a generous contributor to election campaigns, got good value for its money. In one instance, acting on Enron's behalf, the Clinton administration threatened to cut foreign aid to Mozambique if the country did not award Enron a lucrative pipeline contract.

This is deplorable, but it could be worse. In some countries, special interest groups—the "powers behind the throne"—exert such control that they can dictate the most fundamental of government decisions: everything from exchange rate policies and government budgets to the conduct of the courts and the police. In extreme cases this leads to a political dynamic that destabilizes a country and impoverishes its people.

PAKISTAN

For most people, in most countries, the word "feudal" has a distinctly archaic ring. Not in Pakistan. Those nostalgic for the Middle Ages, an era of all-powerful landlords and penniless serfs, need only visit South Asia, where they can see those dynamics reflected in Pakistan's present-day political and economic structure.

Like many developing-world political tragedies, this story begins in colonial times. The British, searching for a simple means to maintain law and order in the vast northern region of India, had no desire to install an expensive military and administrative apparatus. Instead they won the allegiance of local nobles by granting them vast landholdings and absolute power over their land, so long as they maintained order among the landless peasants who lived there.

But the assets of a successful colony are the liabilities of an independent country. When Pakistan became independent in 1947, it was dominated by the landlord class created by the British. To this day, a feudal elite—the top 5 percent of agricultural households—owns 64 percent of all Pakistan's farmland. A 1997 study found that the top 800,000 landlord families owned roughly 11 million acres between them. These feudals, as they are called in Pakistan, are a tiny minority, and, on their vast estates, a very visible target. It seems to defy logic that throughout the upheavals of Pakistan's history, including flirtation with socialism in the 1970s, they retained their holdings. The feudals are crafty as well as powerful. Over the years, they have used all the political tools at their disposal.

Take for example, the events of 1951. A new prime minister, Khawaja

Nazimuddin, began to promulgate land reforms that threatened to end the reign of the feudals. As an administrator in East Pakistan (present-day Bangladesh), Nazimuddin had broken up feudal estates and redistributed land to the peasants. At the same time, he tangled with the increasingly powerful Pakistani military. War with India had sent the defense budget soaring and made the military Pakistan's dominant political institution. Nazimuddin thought he could stand up to the generals and cut military spending.

Nazimuddin took on too much. The feudals egged the army into a military coup against Nazimuddin in 1953. The United States, which at the time was cultivating Pakistan as a Cold War ally, gave the antidemocratic putsch its blessing. A military dictator was installed, and the landlords cemented their relationship with their powerful military allies. Today, 70 percent of Pakistan's military officers come from the Punjab, the most heavily feudal province in the country. And later military dictators like Ayub Khan and Zia ul Haq helped create a new set of feudals by distributing state land to military cronies.

Sometimes the feudals' exercise of political power has been open and brutal. In the early years following independence, reformist politicians in the province of Punjab attempted a land redistribution program that would have taken portions of the largest feudal estates and distributed them to peasant farmers. The feudals, short on political influence, resorted to brute force. They simultaneously withdrew their produce from the markets, creating a man-made famine. The politicians backed down.

Since then the feudals have been more subtle. Ayub Khan tried to institute land reform in 1959. He fixed the ceiling on land holdings at 200 hectares of irrigated land. Zulfiqar Ali Bhutto further reduced the ceiling to 60 hectares in 1972 and tried to limit it further in 1977. But the feudals found ways around these land reforms, in effect rendering them irrelevant. They registered pieces of their land in the names of their family members and fictitious names of peasants. Feudals were also able to keep the land by converting it to orchards, nurseries, and game preserves. But when reformers became too insistent, the feudals were not afraid to use brute force. With the feudals' backing, the army launched a coup against Bhutto, removed him from power, and hung him. The new military dictator, Zia ul Haq, reversed Bhutto's attempted reforms.

Most of the time, however, the feudals do not need the military's help to dominate Pakistan. During periods of democracy (democratic governments and military governments have each ruled for roughly half Pakistan's history), the feudals have been more than capable of protecting their own interests. This may seem surprising, since curbing the feudal landlords' power would obviously benefit the majority of Pakistanis. Surely some enterprising politician could take them on?

But keep in mind the landlords' nearly absolute economic power over the peasants who work their land. The feudals allow small sharecroppers, called *haris*, to farm allotted portions of their vast holdings. Usually, a *hari* gives half his product to the landlord as tribute. On top of this, many landlords provide loans to the *haris* for seeds and equipment, and then charge punitive rates of interest. The *haris* must therefore give up nearly everything they earn. A *hari* tills the soil at his landlord's pleasure; at any moment, he may be thrown from the land and left with nothing. This gives the feudals, in essence, a cadre of political followers who dare not disobey their orders. Indeed, many feudal fiefdoms are despotic miniature kingdoms, complete with criminal courts and even jails, in case the workers get out of hand. Consider the Legharis, one of Pakistan's preeminent families, who lead an ethnic Baluch tribe of half a million people. The Legharis own an estimated 1,215 hectares of land, which is worked by their predominantly landless tribesmen. Their feudal home in the rural town of Choti is a walled compound with a famed garden full of peacocks. And the Legharis feel no need to share their wealth. Choti has 50,000 people, but only one ten-bed clinic.

In short, near-total economic dominance has given the feudals great political power, even during periods of democracy. The evidence for this is not hard to find. From 1947 to 1970, a full 75 percent of the members of Pakistan's parliament were feudal landlords. In the most recent National Assembly (which was dissolved in October 1999 by a military coup), feudals and tribal leaders held 126 of 207 seats.

Consider the case of Benazir Bhutto. Today she is known world-wide for her struggle to promote democracy and human rights in Pakistan. Indeed, she has been a tireless campaigner for women's rights in a Muslim country, who has suffered years of imprisonment for her political convictions (and for the rampant corruption she and her husband fostered).

And she is the daughter of Zulfikar ali Bhutto, the reformist president assassinated by the military in the 1970s. Yet she is also the scion of one of the country's most powerful landlord families. When she became prime minister in 1993, she appointed 17 feudals to her 39-person cabinet.

∞

So the feudals' rule may be archaic and perhaps morally abhorrent, but is it really so bad for Pakistan? It is, to an extreme degree. To see why, look at things from a feudal's perspective. In a narrow sense, the feudals' wealth and power are based on the exploitation of landless peasants. Hence the feudals generally oppose measures that would empower these peasants, such as human rights, land reform, and education. In a broader sense, because the feudals' power is based upon their continued dominance of Pakistan's economy, they generally oppose the creation of wealth anywhere else.

The feudals have both the motive and the political power necessary to sacrifice the health and welfare of their countrymen in order to promote their own interests. Sometimes the feudals are subtle. For instance, the already wealthy feudals help themselves to government subsidies on fertilizer, tube wells, and other agricultural inputs. There are also hidden subsidies on farmers' water, electricity, farm machinery, and credit. Sometimes they are more brazen. In many countries, the extremely wealthy pay a larger tax bill. Yet the feudals, though they are Pakistan's wealthiest citizens, pay almost no taxes at all. Incredibly, income on agriculture was, by law, completely untaxed for decades (despite the fact that, even today, agricultural production generates one-quarter of Pakistan's economic output.)

Eventually, the IMF and World Bank told the Pakistani government it would get no more loans until agriculture was taxed, and in 1997, the Pakistani government finally gave in. But the feudals still manage to dodge the taxman. The Leghari family, for instance, has in recent years paid a tax bill of zero. In the province of Punjab, the government collected 2 billion rupees ($40 million) in agricultural taxes, but lost an estimated 50 billion rupees ($1 billion) to tax evasion.

The consequences of this are, of course, profound. When a country's wealthiest citizens pay almost no tax, the government is starved of funds. It has little money for the necessities of stability and development: infrastructure, education, public health care, courts, police, and so on.

Pakistan spends 0.9 percent of its GDP on public health, compared to the 2.8 percent spent in Mozambique. It spends 2.7 percent on public education, compared to the 7 percent spent in Yemen. This is a recipe for a dysfunctional state. To this day, Pakistan scores among the worst in the world on development indicators such as child malnutrition, infant mortality, and illiteracy. Not only do the feudals block education spending, they also prevent their *haris* from attending schools. A study by a Pakistani social scientist revealed that feudals often commandeer local schools and use them as farmhouses. As a result, the country's literacy rate is a meager 43 percent. Even Rwanda, recently torn apart by a bloody civil war, has a higher literacy rate, 67 percent. Pakistan's illiteracy is partially a legacy of low spending, but it is also the result of misspending. While rural primary schools are especially neglected, Pakistan's elite colleges and universities are relatively well funded, to the extent that tuition in government-run institutions of higher education has increased little over the past 50 years. Of course, the people who benefit from a university education in Pakistan are primarily the children of the wealthy.

∞

Pakistan's problems are profound. Until recently, few beyond the country's borders would have cared. But in the globalized twenty-first century, Pakistan's failures have international consequences as they are exported across the globe.

Thanks to the bankruptcy of the state education system, a parallel system of education has arisen. These are the *madrasas*, or Islamic schools, which gained international infamy since September 11. Over half a million pupils, most of them Pakistani and most of them poor, are currently studying in the world's *madrasas*. Not only do these schools provide education, but food and shelter as well. It is little wonder that victims of the feudal system have sought refuge within their walls.

Madrasas, often financed by wealthy foreign donors, including the government of Saudi Arabia, tend to promote a particularly harsh, intolerant version of Islam. They attract not only Pakistanis, but foreigners in search of religious education. It was in Pakistani *madrasas* that the brutal Taliban regime of Afghanistan was born. And it was in Pakistani *madrasas* that many al-Qaeda members were educated. The *madrasas* are the breeding grounds for the brand of militant Islam that is gaining strength in Pakistan and has done much to destabilize other states.

The answer to this problem is not for the West to pump Pakistan full of aid. Foreign aid has done little good for Pakistan in the past. Considered a crucial Cold War ally, the country received an estimated $37 billion in grants and loans between 1960 and 1990. Indeed, over the past four decades it has received more aid than any poor country except India or Egypt. But this money has done far less good than it should have. While the feudals wield the power behind the throne, the money is simply misused. (For example, it has been spent on universities that serve the country's landlord elite instead of on basic education.) Pakistan's problem is not poverty; its problem is that its landlord class often outright opposes economic and social development.

So long as the feudals are so powerful, it is doubtful that foreign aid will do the Pakistani people much good. The structural problems that feed terrorism and instability in South Asia will not abate. And the feudals seem to be going nowhere. As Mumtaz Bhutto, uncle of Benazir and brother of Zulfikar, once said, "This is a country of landlords. I come from a feudal family and make no apologies for that. Unless they can do away with agriculture and industrialize Pakistan completely, people here are stuck with me."

BRAZIL

October 2000: Across Brazil, farmers have abandoned their fields and taken to the streets, demanding emergency loans from state banks. Simultaneously, trade unions are marching on the capital, Brasilia. They have two demands: higher wages and a halt to the intended privatization of the state bank of Sao Paulo (a privatization that has already been postponed ten times). Meanwhile, in the northeastern state of Pernambuco, 4,000 police are on strike and have surrounded a government building. Their main demand is higher pay. Elsewhere, militant peasant farmers have forced the federal government into tense negotiations. A month before, the landless peasants had forcibly seized President Fernando Enrique Cardoso's country estate.

If it sounds like chaos, it is. But it's controlled chaos. October 2000 was a rather ordinary month in Brazilian politics. One thing that must be said for Brazil's many special interest groups is that they are not shy. In Brazil, all the usual suspects are well represented. Some countries have militant farmers or militant union leaders or militant government bureaucrats. Brazil has militant everything. As Charles de Gaulle put it: "Brazil is the country of the future and will always be." Brazil has tremendous natural resources; a land mass more than twice the size of Europe; a population more than twice the size of Germany. This is a country with great-power potential. And yet, between 1960 and 1990, even Egypt experienced faster growth in per capita income. Today, Brazil has achieved a level of per capita output that is roughly equivalent to the United States at the beginning of the last century. Close to 40 percent of the population still lives below the poverty line. How does so much potential translate into such weak performance?

To understand Brazil, look first at the constitution. Written recently, in 1988 (the seventh constitution since Brazil achieved independence), it mirrors the problems of the country as a whole. It is one of the longest constitutions in the world, with 160 pages and 245 articles. Many of the articles are themselves lengthy documents. Article 5, for instance, contains 77 items. The reason for this extraordinary length is that Brazil's constitution specifies rights and privileges for every special interest group one could imagine: everything from details of public pension plans, to the setting of interest rates, to how much revenue should be transferred to the states, to rules protecting government workers from being fired, to requirements that union members pay dues, to the privileges of rural landlords. The constitution, like the country itself, is dominated by special interests.

The steps Brazil must undertake to achieve growth and lift the masses out of poverty are by now well known. Undertake land reform. Reform the pension system. Realign educational spending. Overhaul the tax system. Scale back the public sector. These are not simply the prescriptions of foreign experts. Most Brazilian politicians acknowledge the need for each of these measures. Indeed, the country's leaders, both dictators and presidents, have repeatedly tried to implement these reforms. But in most cases, they have failed. The lesson of Brazilian history is that knowing what is right is not the same as getting it done.

∞

Like Pakistan, Brazil started with a postcolonial land distribution problem—indeed, one of the most inequitable in the world. Some 58,000 large estates swallow up roughly 45 percent of the country's total arable land. At the other end of the spectrum, 2.9 million small and medium-sized farms are crammed onto just 2 percent of the land.

This no doubt sounds familiar. And indeed, as in Pakistan, Brazil's landlords are a formidable presence in politics. They successfully fought off several post-World War II attempts at land reform—before the military dictatorship, during military rule (from 1964 to 1985), and since the return of democracy. Repeated attempts to scale back their privileges have been stymied. President Fernando Collor tried to enact reform via presidential decree. The congress subsequently overruled the decree. The lightly populated rural states dominated by the landlords have disproportionate representation in the Brazilian legislature.

But this is not another Pakistan. Brazil's landlords fiercely protect their privileges, but Brazil has long since developed past the point where a feudal class dominates the government and economy. While Pakistan's economy is one-third agricultural, farming accounts for only 7 percent of Brazil's output. While two-thirds of Pakistan's people still live in rural areas, more than 80 percent of Brazilians live in cities. Which is not to say that unequal distribution of land is without consequences. The landholding pattern encourages the urban migration of the landless peasants, creating urban slums, the idling of millions of acres of farmland, and the persistent rural violence of landless movements attempting to seize this unutilized land.

But the real importance of Brazil's landlords is in what they represent: severe inequality and the relentless struggle to preserve that inequality by political means. Over the years, landlords have fought repeatedly and successfully to protect the existing unequal distribution of land. This is a recurring pattern—perhaps the most important pattern—in Brazilian politics.

∞

Consider Brazil's government spending on social welfare issues (pensions, health, housing, and education). Only 8 percent of this spending reaches the poorest 20 percent of the population. In other words, 92 percent of social welfare expenditure in Brazil targets the better off. The pension system is one example. Brazil is, relatively speaking, a young country—only 5 percent of the population is over the age of 65. Yet Brazil's pension outlays somehow consume about 12 percent of GDP. So where does all this money go? Half goes to former government employees—10 percent of the workforce, 2.9 million people. The system is, quite literally, designed to be abused. Public-sector pensions average $5,000 in the judicial branch and $2,700 in the legislative branch (average per capita income is only about $3,000). The payments are not need-based, and state workers can collect multiple pensions if they hold multiple jobs.

In short, pension spending in Brazil, by targeting primarily well-off civil servants, actually increases rather than alleviates inequality. And this inequality has been vigorously defended. When, facing a growing budget deficit, the Brazilian government put forward a pension reform bill in 1996, it was amended beyond all recognition. In fact, it was not until overspending pushed Brazil to the brink of a financial crisis in 1998 that significant reforms were finally passed. Even then, the public sector workers managed to protect their unequal slice of the pie. Farsighted government employees had written pension protection into the Brazilian constitution. Hence, when the government finally succeeded in passing pension reform legislation, the Supreme Court duly ruled it unconstitutional.

On to education. At first glance, Brazil's record in this area—especially recently—seems impressive. Literacy rates have reached 86 percent, not excellent but not terrible. Brazil spends 4.7 percent of its GDP every year on education—the second-highest ratio in Latin America, after Mexico. But only 37 percent of the population aged sixteen to eighteen is enrolled in secondary school. And only 33 percent of the students who enter first grade remain in school through eighth grade. Beyond basic literacy training in primary school, there is a sudden and precipitous drop in achievement.

Once again, the story is inequality and government intervention that enhances this inequality. The problem is not *how much* money is spent. The problem is *where* that money is spent. Fully a quarter of the education budget goes to Brazil's system of public universities. But in a poor country like Brazil, only 2 percent of the population—mainly children of the rich—attend these schools. According to a 1995 World Bank study, the poorest 20 percent of the Brazilian population receive 16 percent of total education spending, while the richest 20 percent of the population (who, not incidentally could afford to pay for their own schooling) enjoy the benefit of 24 percent of spending. An OECD and UNESCO study of eighteen developing countries revealed that Brazil spends a higher ratio of its education monies on universities compared to primary and secondary schools than any other country in its survey, apart from Paraguay. Once again: inequality, in this case of educational achievement, is enhanced by government policy.

Which brings us to the taxation system. A dull subject to be sure—except perhaps in Brazil, where, in 1995, an investigation found that 40 percent of the country's 460 millionaires reported incomes of $18,000 or less. As in Pakistan, agricultural income usually finds itself outside the tax net. This privilege might long ago have been abolished but for the fact that Brazil's wealthiest citizens, while no longer landlords, use this loophole to disguise and shelter their income from taxation. Rich Brazilians also employ the more typical practices of setting up shell corporations to hide their wealth and disguising personal income as corporate income. Some simply bribe the tax collectors.

Unable to collect from the rich, the government must take from the poor. The system relies heavily on indirect taxes, such as consumption taxes. Since the poor spend much more of their income on consumption, they pay a disproportionate amount of the taxes. In addition, the Brazilian system taxes wages heavily and lets capital gains—a major source of income for the rich—off relatively lightly.

A tax system that makes the rich richer and the poor poorer: a situation so clearly unjust has spawned many attempts at reform. In 1985, the Ministry of Finance tried to raise tax rates, especially on capital gains. Business lobbies, in alliance with bureaucrats, torpedoed the change. The ministry tried again in 1987 to impose a progressive tax on all types of income. Again it was blocked. Further attempts at tax reform were defeated in 1991, 1994, 1995, and 1998.

And finally, there is the bureaucracy. Brazil's formidable state sector includes 27 top-level agencies, 300 lower-level agencies, 100 interministerial councils, and 560 public enterprises. Odd, one might think, that government employment would be so popular. After all, government jobs are notoriously poorly paid.

Yet most Brazilian state governments spend 70 percent of their revenues on personnel costs. Some spend as much as 90 percent. Public-sector payrolls consume a whopping 12 percent of GDP. Many of those on the state payrolls do not do much to earn their pay. Indeed, many of those who collect government paychecks do not bother to show up for work. (And remember that a government job also guarantees a very generous pension.) Government jobs, especially of the no-work variety, are a perk distributed by politicians to their supporters, families, and friends. Successive Brazilian governments have attempted to get a handle on the problem. Several have appointed "antibureaucracy czars" whose sole mandate is to trim the bureaucracy. But most attempts are ineffective. Even former President Cardoso, struggling to pull through in the aftermath of the recent currency crisis, was repeatedly thwarted in his attempts to confront the public sector.

∞

Brazil is a democracy—and a relatively lively one at that. All questions of promoting long-term growth aside, state promotion of inequality obviously runs counter to the direct and immediate interests of the majority of Brazilian voters. So how does such a system survive? Look first to the constitution. Its 160 pages provide powerful protection for the inequalities we have just described. The privileges of landlords, pensioners, university-goers, rich taxpayers, and civil servants are specified in excruciating detail. Moreover, changing the constitution is a monumental task—it requires a three-fifths majority vote in both houses of the legislature, *twice.*

This is a product of some visionary thinking by the country's interest groups. When the new constitution was drawn up shortly after the end of military rule, the special interests realized this was the chance of a lifetime. Scholar David Fleischer conducted a detailed analysis of the backgrounds of the members in the constituent assembly. He found that ninety-one of the deputies, the largest single voting bloc, were loyal to the landlords. The second-largest bloc represented civil servants. And so on.

It is therefore unsurprising that the constitution's construction is so perverse. When they completed their task, the framers of the constitution realized that, despite its many good points, special interest meddling had made the document unworkable. They therefore scheduled a mandatory five-year review, so that problems could be fixed. But by the time five years had elapsed, the special interests had only increased their political influence. Attempts to review the federal system, institute tax and Social Security reform, and overhaul the political system were all shot down. In fact, discussions on amending the constitution were so contentious that police had to enter the Chamber of Deputies to restore order.

Still, one might expect that pulling together a three-fifths vote to amend the constitution would not be all that difficult. After all, most of the inequalities in the constitution put a large majority of the Brazilian public at a disadvantage. But Brazil's unusual political system—while certainly democratic—hobbles attempts to bring down the special interests. Brazil's system was designed to combine the responsiveness of parliamentary democracy with a presidential leader representing "all of Brazil." Unofficially, people say that Brazil's system is an American presidency on top of an Italian parliament. In practice, voters choose a party and then their two favorite individual parliamentary candidates.

Enter the unintended consequences. Because voters select two candidates, more than one politician from the same party must always enter each race. Hence politicians are fighting their fellow party members as well as the opposition, and therefore have an incentive to differentiate themselves from members of their own party. Predictably, since members of the same party are constantly fighting each other, concepts such as unified "party platforms" simply do not work. The parties have little ideological coherence and, in fact, are little different from each other. Even party members would be hard-pressed to describe the ideological differences between the PSDB, the PMDB, and the PL. As one party leader opined wryly, "Our party is so disorganized, we can't even throw a party."

Unintended consequence number two: because politicians compete in elections essentially as individuals, rather than as the official candidate of a particular party, they are not accountable to their parties. A threat to expel a politician from the party means little. The result is a complete absence of party loyalty. In the congress of 1994 to 1998, 230 of the 513 deputies changed parties at least once during the course of their term.

Several changed parties as many as four times. The result of all this is that organizing to battle special interests is nearly impossible. Parties, even those whose leaders back reform, have extreme difficulty convincing their members to toe the party line. President Cardoso's four-party coalition seldom voted as a bloc. Indeed, Cardoso often had trouble securing the support of his own PSBD party. Hence, special interests can usually find legislators whose loyalty can be bought.

∞

In the last two decades, Brazil has made significant improvements in its traditionally severe economic mismanagement. Yet the underlying problem remains. Pensioners, unions, the public sector, the landlords, and the rich (many of these, of course, being the same people), still wage fierce political battles to defend their privileges. Economists have jokingly dubbed Brazil "Belindia"—because 20 percent of the population lives as if they were in Belgium, while 80 percent live in India-like conditions. To this day, the richest 10 percent of the population collects nearly half the country's annual income and 40 percent of the population lives at the poverty or subsistence levels. In Japan, the ratio of the richest 20 percent's share of national income to the poorest 20 percent's share is 3.4. In India, 5.7. In the famously unequal United States, 8.9. In Brazil, 25.2.

The impoverished 40 percent of Brazil's population is a large and disenfranchised group. Their conditions are appalling—so much so that Brazil's average life expectancy lags behind even India, a country with less than one-sixth of Brazil's annual income. Brazil has been fortunate in that its poor have not resorted to guerrilla violence (as in Peru or Colombia) or even terrorism (as in Pakistan). But they do protest, and the rural poor have formed a "landless movement" in which peasants occupy idle farms. Since 1970, more than 2,000 people have been killed in resulting disputes over land. Indeed, in September 2000, the army was called in to remove squatting peasants from President Cardoso's personal estate.

Morality aside, this dynamic of inequality has undermined Brazil's financial stability. Brazil's tax revenues are too small because it does not take enough from the rich, and its outlays are too large because of unnecessary spending on pensions, bureaucrat salaries, and bailouts of bankrupt state governments. This underlying structural problem has caused numerous

financial crises—in the early 1990s, in late fall of 1998, in the real devaluation of 1999. Brazil today is still teetering perilously close to yet another
crisis—the risk of an Argentina-style default on its $172 billion in external
debt. This is no small concern; Brazil's economy, while not as big as it
should be, is still a $500 billion economy compared to Argentina's $100
billion economy. Its foreign debt is more than $70 billion larger than
that of Argentina. And Brazil is home to more than two and a half times
more foreign direct investment by U.S. companies than Argentina. The
impact of a Brazilian collapse would be profound. Which is one reason to
view the election of new president Luiz Inacio Lula da Silva, a.k.a. "Lula,"
with mixed feelings. His leftist past (he led strikes against foreign-owned
automobile companies) alarmed investors. Fears of a Lula victory helped
send the value of the Brazilian real down by about 40 percent in 2002,
and the stock market down 20 percent. Yet, having come to power, Lula
has carried on with the fiscally responsible platform of his predecessor and
continued with the market reforms already in place.

What's more, Lula has taken aim at the inequality that lies at the root
of Brazil's extended malaise. Indeed, it is at the center of his platform: to
end Brazil's "historical legacy of inequality and social exclusion." This is
an agenda with the potential to transform Brazil. Lula has made many of
the right noises: promises of land reform, tax reform, and social security
reform, and a vow to keep a lid on spending. He also wants to overhaul
the way organized labor is structured to cut down on the number of
bogus unions. He has achieved some successes, notably a long-delayed
pension reform. But grand promises have been broken before in the
crucible of Brazilian special interest politics. If the vested interests win
these battles, they ensure that Brazil will remain, always, the "country
of the future."

POWERS BEHIND THE THRONE DEFINED

Pakistan and Brazil suffer mightily but they do not suffer alone. Every
country has its special interests: farmers in France, the gun lobby and
sugar growers in the U.S., the labor unions in Venezuela, the military in
Chile, state-owned enterprise workers in China. Why does this phenomenon—the rise of minority groups with strong political influence—cut
across continents, cultures, political systems, and generations?

This question was famously answered by scholar Mancur Olson, who called his insight "the theory of collective action." Fundamentally, it explains why it is difficult for large groups of people to act together, even when it is in their obvious best interest to do so. Consider a mass of people with a common problem—say, for instance, the Brazilian taxpayers who are paying for the exorbitant pension benefits of a few civil servants. It is in the taxpayers' obvious best interest to stop the pension payments. With overwhelming numbers on their side, one might think this would be easily accomplished.

But there is what Olson called the "free rider" problem. Those who travel to the Brazilian capital to lobby the congress to abolish pension payments will bear all of the costs of fixing this problem, in terms of time and effort and risk. Yet they will enjoy only a small portion of the benefits. After all, everyone's tax bill, including their own, will be slightly reduced. At the same time, people who decide not to travel to the capital and instead stay at home—the free riders—will enjoy the exact same portion of the benefits, the same reduced tax bill. So the rational choice is to stay home and be a free rider. The problem is obvious, the solution is obvious, and the individual taxpayers are probably quite angry. But it is not a problem that they can solve alone.

Small groups have crucial advantages where free riders are concerned. First, small groups are easier to police; they can identify any free riders and force them to take action, or exclude them from any benefits the rest of the group receives. In addition, small groups often have advantages of cohesion: very clear common interests, or a common religion or ethnicity. Perhaps even more importantly, consider the sharing of benefits. For a large group, the collective benefits are greater but the individual benefits are smaller. If the pension payments are eliminated, the total reduction in tax payments is huge, but individual taxpayers gain only a small refund on their bills. This situation is reversed for a small group. If pension payments continue, each individual pensioner will enjoy a large annual pension check. The size of this pension check alone probably justifies a lobbying effort, even if some other pensioners are free riders.

Once a group is large enough, the benefits of action, while great, are too thinly distributed. The free riders are too hard to exclude. In this case, rational members of the group tend to become free riders. As a result, large groups—that superficially seem to have a great power by virtue of their superior numbers—can be paralyzed into inactivity. Fundamentally, this insight explains why, throughout history and around the world, the masses are so often victimized by an elite few. It is, in a sense, the ultimate conspiracy theory.

POWERS AND PROSPERITY

Unfortunately, many economic reforms come up squarely against the collective action problem. While they promote the general welfare, they do so by benefiting the vast majority of people only a little, while hurting a few people a lot. Removing import tariffs, for instance, will hurt employees of protected industries by causing jobs to be lost and factories to go bankrupt or move overseas. In the aggregate, consumers will tend to gain more than these employees lose because huge numbers of people will each be paying a little bit less for the imported goods. But each consumer gains individually only a little. Similarly, the cessation of subsidies will be noticed greatly by subsidy recipients, but only a little by taxpayers.

This is a "benefit distribution" problem along the lines of the "time distribution" problem discussed in the last chapter. A small group of people would suffer greatly, and so have a powerful incentive to act. The large number of people, who are already likely to have difficulty organizing, would each benefit only a little. Machiavelli observed the same phenomenon in practice: "[R]eform makes enemies of all those who profit by the old order and only lukewarm defenders in all those who would profit by the new." The presence of tariffs and subsidies in even the most advanced economies of North America, Western Europe, and Japan provides powerful testimony to the universality of this problem. But there is a qualitative difference between the landlords of Pakistan, whose power undermines their country's prosperity, and the farmers of France, who collect (admittedly expensive) annual subsidies. The odd subsidy or trade barrier is one thing. The ability to hobble government tax collection and the educational system is quite another.

The impact of the "powers behind the throne" on a country's prosperity depends on which special interest groups have the greatest influence. Not all interest groups are bad for prosperity, and some even promote good policies. The important questions are: "Who are the powers behind the throne?" "What do they want?" "How great is their influence?"

Entrenched elites (such as Pakistan's landlords) tend to be the most destructive kind of special interest groups because of the sheer scope of their ambition. Most interest groups are looking for some kind of hand-out (pensioners in Brazil) or specific policy favoritism (Miami Cubans). This can be expensive—rich countries, the members of the OECD, spend an estimated total of $300 billion per year on subsidies for their farmers, which is more than the entire annual economic output of all of Africa. But if other public policies are good, the subsidies they demand need not undermine a country's prosperity.

Entrenched elites, on the other hand, tend to oppose good economic policy. Since their wealth depends on the status quo, they may indeed actively oppose economic growth. They will almost certainly oppose economic reforms such as stronger taxation systems, increased focus on basic education, development of impartial courts and a functioning legal system, and the like. The Philippines, where fifteen families own nearly half the country's farmland, is an example. The landlords there derive their wealth and power from the landless peasants who work their vast estates and dutifully support their political ambitions. Hence they oppose measures—such as taxation and education reforms—that are critical for development, but which would undermine their wealth and power. Business elites can also become entrenched interests—for instance, also in the Philippines, the cronies of President Marcos, who enjoyed government-protected monopolies in key industries. Although business groups in general tend to favor, at the very least, economic stability, these entrenched elites actively opposed market-opening economic reforms that would have introduced competition into their government-protected markets. (The presence of these entrenched elites is a major reason for the Philippines' underperformance compared to many of its Southeast Asian peers.)

But not all special interests are bad for a country's economy. Export-oriented businesses, for instance, may lobby for government subsidies, such as low-interest loans or tax breaks. But unlike a business selling to the domestic market, which can profit tremendously from government protection, an export-oriented business that competes in unforgiving foreign markets must ultimately succeed on its own business merits.

Political connections cannot help overseas. Hence export-oriented businesses tend to lobby for exactly the policies that promote prosperity—stable economics, a sensibly valued exchange rate, and well-regulated domestic markets so they can have access to world-class suppliers.

∞

But what gives the special interests their power? All countries, after all, have special interests—and some countries succeed in making good policy despite them. One factor that accompanies the power of special interests is inequality. A high degree of inequality—often a legacy of a country's colonial history (e.g., the creation, by Portuguese colonists, of immense plantations in Brazil)—tends to foster extremes of special interest dominance, because, almost inevitably, money purchases power. In democratic systems, money can finance political campaigns and buy the loyalty of politicians. In authoritarian systems, the wealthy are often cultivated as political allies, because they can mobilize resources to fend off challengers or support an incumbent.

In both Brazil and Pakistan, a high degree of inequality, bestowed by colonialism, empowers special interests—creating entrenched elites with an interest in maintaining the status quo and preventing political and economic development. Contrast this to the experience of the most successful Asian countries, notably Japan, Korea, and Taiwan. These countries all instituted aggressive land reform programs that resulted in some of the world's most equal distributions of income. This reduced the likelihood of total dominance by an interest group opposed to development. For countries like Pakistan, it is hard to imagine much progress without some way of insulating policymaking from special interest influence.

Another crucial factor in determining the influence of special interests is the structure of the political system. Some systems inadvertently empower special interests at the expense of the majority. Brazil's political system, for instance, undermines coherent political parties that could take on special interests and allows certain interest groups (notably state governors) to exert extraordinary leverage.

Israel is another case of the political structure increasing the power of special interests. Israel's story is especially clear because, although the country has been an economic success, a well-intentioned political reform has caused a sharp decline in the quality of the country's policymaking. The name of this reform was the Direct Election Law. Passed in 1992 and first implemented with the 1996 election, the law allowed voters to cast two ballots—one for a party and one for a prime minister. The law's designers reasoned that if Israel's prime ministers had a direct mandate from the people, they would have more executive power, thereby limiting the ability of small parties to disrupt and destabilize governments.

The opposite occurred. Before 1996, Israeli governments were always formed around large parties that controlled at least 40 seats in the 120-seat Knesset. Just one or two further coalition partners were required to reach the magic number of sixty-one seats. But in the 1996 election, the first after the new law was implemented, the two largest parties barely won a majority, capturing only sixty-six seats between them. And in the 1999 elections, the largest parties won only forty-five seats between them, a full sixteen short of a majority. These consequences were unexpected but logical. Israeli voters had responded to the law by casting their prime ministerial vote for a centrist candidate and their party vote for the faction that best matched their personal affiliation—be it political, religious, ethnic, or class. The plethora of parties that then took power reflected Israel's deep divisions—hawk versus dove, Arab versus Jew, Ashkenazi versus Sephardic, Russian-born versus native-born, secular versus orthodox.

The change in the electoral system was a boon for Israel's special interest groups. The result was policy dictated by these interests. Ehud Barak's "shatter-proof" ruling coalition of 1999 included the Shas party, whose spiritual leader admitted that his only reason for joining the coalition was to obtain funds to bail out the Sephardic Orthodox religious school system, which was running a deficit of 100 million shekels. The coalition also included the National Religious Party, which likewise sought money for its religious academies. Yisrael B'Aliyah, the Russian immigrant party, was in because it wanted rent subsidies for new arrivals. The Meretz Party joined to win cheaper water for farmers and more money for public housing. The threat of each of these parties to abandon the coalition gave them great leverage. In addition, they were fully prepared to sacrifice stability for their narrow interests. Indeed, a minister from Shas famously stated, "If I have to threaten the peace process in order to help Talmud

Torah [religious] education, this is legitimate." Not surprisingly, funding to such causes as the Shas educational system and mortgage subsidies to Russian immigrants soon came to consume an incredible 30 percent of Israel's budget (higher even than defense spending).

As Hanan Sher wrote, "Hundreds of thousands of Israelis receive direct transfer payments from the state in one form or another—tens of thousands of large families [mostly in the ultra-Orthodox community], 209,000 students at over 2,000 ultra-Orthodox yeshivas, 200,000 old-age pensioners, almost 150,000 recipients of 'income maintenance,' 144,000 beneficiaries of general disability payments, 23,000 women who get guaranteed alimony payments from the government. There are also indirect transfers, in the form of the heavily subsidized services for the almost 250,000 residents of the settlements in the West Bank and Gaza." The Direction Election Law, a reform to Israel's political system, has helped make the country a special interest paradise.

∞

The case of Japan is quite different but equally illuminating. Japan is one of the world's greatest success stories. Alone among non-Western countries, it has joined the ranks of the world's industrial powers. And yet, since 1990, its economy has stagnated, government debt has risen to the highest in the rich world, and the country's banking system has lurched from crisis to crisis. This stark difference is hard to explain—there has been no obvious change in Japanese politics. The ruthlessly meritocratic bureaucracy, which guided Japan's rapid growth, is as sharp as ever. Surely, given past performance, Japan's bureaucrats could devise policies to overcome whatever challenges the country now faces?

But this is another story about special interests. Little has changed on the surface of Japanese politics—the Liberal Democratic Party, or LDP, has retained power almost without interruption since the end of World War II. Yet behind the scenes, there has been a crucial change in the political system that has dramatically increased the power of special interests. Specifically, politicians have gained control over policymaking.

Admittedly, this political change has been ongoing for decades. The bureaucracy, which made most policy in Japan following the end of World War II, gradually ceded power to politicians from the LDP.

This was a slow process, as politicians struggled to assert themselves by becoming specialists in certain policy issues. But in the 1990s, the pace of change increased dramatically. As recently as 1994, politicians wrote only 18 of the 75 bills submitted during the ordinary Diet session (24 percent of the bills), and the bureaucrats wrote the rest. But by 1999, politicians wrote 60 of 124 bills (48 percent). This quick shift was driven by a succession of dramatic events. A series of corruption scandals led to the resignations of both the governor of the Bank of Japan and the Ministry of Finance's top bureaucrat during the same week. In February 1994, the Ministry of Finance pushed Prime Minister Morihiro Hosokawa into raising the consumption tax from 3 to 7 percent. This tremendously unpopular move choked off economic recovery and fed a rising popular backlash. Partially as a result, the LDP, which had governed Japan almost without interruption since the end of World War II, was forced briefly into opposition. This, and the backlash against the bureaucrats, unhinged the traditional policymaking process.

That politicians are increasingly in charge may seem a good thing for Japan's democracy. But the problem is that the LDP, still running the country, represents Japan's most conservative interest groups. The LDP started out serving agricultural interests (an astute electoral strategy, since at the end of World War II, 50 percent of the population depended on farming). As the economy grew and the agricultural sector shrunk, the party added small-scale retail stores and the construction industry to its support base. This allowed the LDP to win elections consistently.

But, to borrow a famous phrase, the LDP represents "old Japan"—rural areas, farmers, the construction industry, small-scale retail, and the elderly—when the "new Japan," the parts generating economic growth, are the service sector, export businesses, and urban areas. The LDP is still firmly beholden to "old Japan." Indeed, in a recent upper-house election, the LDP won not a single seat in urban areas such as Tokyo and Osaka.

The special-interest groups of "old Japan" are among the most protected and uncompetitive sectors in the economy. Subsidies and price supports make up roughly 75 percent of all farm income, and public works spending accounts for about 8 percent of Japan's GDP, compared with 2 percent in the U.S. and between 2 and 4 percent in Western Europe. The fact that the LDP represented these groups mattered relatively

little when bureaucrats wrote critical policies. Overregulation of the retail sector and protection of farmers fostered economic inefficiencies, but
the bureaucrats made Japan work. For decades, Japan's basic fiscal and
monetary policies were quite competent, and Japan's average inflation
rates and budget deficits from 1970 to 1990 were roughly equivalent to
those of the U.S.

But with the change in Japan's political system, the special interests
are increasingly in charge of the most crucial policies. The result has been
policies that refuse to acknowledge reality, and indeed threaten the global
economy. Bank bailouts and excessive deficit spending have pushed
Japan's national debt to more than 140 percent of GDP. At the same
time, economic reforms have been shelved or diluted. One problem that
has seized the world's attention is deflation. The phenomenon of falling
wages and prices has helped fuel Japan's banking crisis and hobbled its
growth. But consider, for a moment, the interest of some of the LDP's
core supporters—the rural elderly. For these people, retired or close to it
and living off savings (chiefly stashed in time deposits rather than stocks)
falling prices are, on balance, a good thing. Faltering growth is a small
price to pay when the real value of one's savings is constantly growing.

There may be severe global consequences if the LDP's policies push
Japan into the financial crisis that many predict is still ahead. Whether
this happens or not, Japan's changed fortunes are further testimony to
the impact the political system has on the power of special interests.

VESTED INTERESTS POSTSCRIPT: THE CRISIS MANDATE

This is quite a litany of misdeeds. But even countries with extreme special
interest problems, such as Brazil and Pakistan, have had their good years.
In the early 1990s, for instance, the Brazilian congress passed constitutional amendments breaking up state-controlled monopolies and easing
restrictions on foreign direct investment. In 1998, the congress passed
(partial) pension reform and, in 1999, limited runaway state spending.

The secret to such (unfortunately brief) periods of success is, surprisingly enough, political and economic crises. Many things change during
and after such crises. First, a sudden economic downturn will likely
drive public anger in a J-curve pattern. Political leaders must suddenly

worry about their ability to maintain public order and fend off political opposition. In this case, making policy decisions that will bring about economic recovery suddenly becomes a higher priority than pleasing narrow interests.

Second, a crisis can force a country to follow the guidance of international lenders such as the International Monetary Fund or World Bank. Pakistan in 1993 and Brazil in 1999 asked for international help to avoid debt default and, in return, the lenders demanded better economic policies.

Finally, a crisis may simply mean that policies benefiting special interests are simply no longer possible. In 1998, for instance, the Brazilian government was effectively out of money. It could no longer pay elaborate pensions. Hence the pension law had to be changed. A crisis means that a government no longer has any space in the budget for the extra favors that special interest groups are skimming off the top. This sentiment was expressed concisely by Indonesian Minister of Mines and Energy Mohammad Sadhi: "Bad times make for good policies and vice versa."

India's experience in 1991 illustrates the "crisis mandate" in action. Up to that time, India had traditionally followed a state-led development model. Fiscal and monetary policies were notoriously bad. Fragile governments made up of multitudes of tiny parties (the current government is a twenty-five party coalition) were unable to stand up to the country's many special interest groups. A minister in an earlier eighteen-party coalition government memorably compared the government to the *kalpaturu vriksha*, a mythical Hindu tree of plenty: "Stand in its shade," the minister said, "and the tree will give you anything you ask of it. Just ensure the tree isn't felled." In 1991, though, the country lurched into a balance-of-payments crisis. High petroleum prices raised import bills, while the fall of the Soviet Union resulted in a drastic reduction in foreign aid. Soon, the government was running out of foreign exchange. With less than two weeks of import cover left, a humbled Prime Minister P.V. Narasimha Rao and Finance Minister Manmohan Singh were forced to go hat in hand to the IMF. Under these circumstances, the political will for economic reform finally materialized: first, because the IMF demanded it, and second, because the crisis-wracked government was simply unable to continue its existing policies. Reforms dismantled parts of the public sector, cut through some of India's legendary bureaucratic red tape, dramatically reduced import barriers, and significantly cut tax rates.

Of course, one might expect that once the crisis has passed, the government would return to its bad old habits. The special interest groups in Brazil and India reasserted themselves once the danger of economic collapse in those countries receded, and reform progress was slowed dramatically.

Which leaves many cynics waiting hopefully for the next crisis.

CHAPTER THIRTEEN

The Visible Hand

GOVERNMENT INTERVENTION

"That government is best that governs least."
THOMAS JEFFERSON

"Better the occasional faults of a Government that lives in a spirit of charity than the constant omission of a Government frozen in the ice of its own indifference."
FRANKLIN DELANO ROOSEVELT

LIKE MOST WHO TAKE EXTREME POSITIONS, BOTH JEFFERSON and Roosevelt got it wrong; or, more probably, they overstated their points for rhetorical effect. Jefferson's principle of "a government that governs least" has been put into practice (however inadvertently) many times in human history, almost always with tragic results—the ungoverned anarchy of Somalia and the ungoverned economic plunder of Yeltsin's Russia, to name two examples.

The other side of that coin is just as tarnished. Governments that—in a "spirit of charity"—have taken responsibility for maximizing the public welfare have suffered more than "occasional faults." They have tended to produce extraordinary political and economic disasters—the totalitarianism of Stalin's U.S.S.R. and the creeping dysfunction of Castro's Cuba, for instance.

Some governments do too little and some governments do too much.

Disagreements over the proper role of the state versus the role of the market continue to foster heated intellectual battles. Arguments promoting the merits of U.S.-style hands-off capitalism, as opposed to increased government intervention, and vice versa, are made with intense passion. But—at a more fundamental level—governments can pursue either option and achieve either great success or great failure. The famously interventionist French government, the all-powerful Singaporean "nanny state," and the famously hands-off U.S. government have all nurtured prosperity in their countries. None are perfect, but these governments have done some fundamental things right and avoided some fundamental errors.

Whichever style one prefers, states or markets, there are powerful political dynamics unleashed when a government intervenes in the economy. These can result in the curbing of growth or the destruction of existing prosperity. One country that has suffered more than its fair share of such disappointments is Turkey.

TURKEY

"...it is one of our main principles to interest the State actively in matters where the general and vital interests of the nation are in question, especially in the economic field, in order to lead the nation and the country to prosperity in as short a time as possible..."
MUSTAFA KEMAL ATATURK

The decline of a great empire is inevitably a humiliating process. By the end of the nineteenth century, the Ottoman Empire—which at its peak stretched from Hungary to Iraq—had become the proverbial "sick man of Europe." The unwieldy bureaucracy failed in its attempts at modernization and the Ottoman government was bleeding money. The Empire's most lucrative domains were seized by expansionist European powers. By 1875, the Ottomans had gone so deeply into debt that they defaulted on payments to European creditors.

The harsh result was the creation of a Public Debt Administration in Istanbul in 1881, representing the interests of investors in Ottoman government securities. The Administration, controlled from Paris and London, dictated much of the Ottoman budget and economic policymaking. This was analogous to an International Monetary Fund reform program—but far worse. The Europeans had no desire to restore the Ottoman economy to health, or to promote the Empire's economic development. They simply wanted their money back. By the beginning of the twentieth century, the Ottoman Empire's main industries were under foreign control and the agricultural sector failed to produce even enough wheat to feed the population. "Foreigners" (Greeks, Armenians, and Jews) controlled much of the Empire's financial sector and owned more than 90 percent of the industrial establishments that employed more than ten workers.

The final collapse of the Empire was triggered by World War I. The Ottomans—eager to spite their main creditors—allied with Germany and Austria against the Allies. This was a mistake. The hapless Ottoman armies were overwhelmed by British, French, and Russian soldiers. By the time the war ended, the Ottoman Empire had lost virtually all of its foreign territories, the ruling sultan had been forced to sign a one-sided peace deal, and European armies had occupied much of its territory, including Istanbul. It was a moment of extraordinary humiliation. A centuries-old empire spanning continents had been demolished by modern European nation-states. First economic decline; then economic dependency; and finally military occupation and political subservience. This process was keenly observed by an ambitious Turkish army officer named Mustafa Kemal.

∞

Born to a modest family, Mustafa Kemal would in his lifetime come to be known, immodestly but accurately, as "Ataturk"—literally, "father of the Turks." To this day it is nearly sacrilegious in Turkey to criticize him. His face adorns every Turkish banknote. In 1920, Mustafa Kemal was a brilliant Ottoman officer who had won many battles but returned to an Istanbul occupied by the French, British, and Italians. The Greeks, taking advantage of the Ottoman political and economic collapse, had launched an invasion deep into Anatolia. The hapless Ottoman sultan offered no resistance.

This was too much for Mustafa Kemal and his fellow officers. Under the banners of "Independence or Death" and "For the Turk, freedom is his life," Mustafa Kemal led a military revolt. With amazing capability, his soldiers fought all comers—the invading Greeks, the occupying allied troops, even the remnants of the Ottoman government. By 1923, the band of upstart Turks had won their freedom. But Mustafa Kemal knew this was, at best, a brief window of opportunity. Europe's great powers were hungrily eyeing the Ottoman leftovers. Mustafa Kemal knew his only hope was to create a new Turkish nation: a modern state capable of facing off against the Europeans. He had no interest in piecemeal reforms, as attempted by the so-called "Young Turks" in the waning days of the Ottoman Empire. Mustafa Kemal deposed the sultan, abolished the Islamic caliphate, closed Islamic schools and courts, and decreed that the Turkish language would be written in Latin characters instead of Arabic script. He thus brought the Ottoman Empire to an irrevocable end and gave birth to modern Turkey.

But not without a fight. Ottoman holdovers still had some power. The chief Islamic leader called for Mustafa Kemal's assassination. Rumors circulated of a military plot to depose him. An opposition political party arose, gaining significant public support and organizing bloody riots against Mustafa Kemal's rule. Then, in 1925, the Kurdish minority launched a separatist rebellion. At this point, Kemal had seen enough. He used this opportunity to crush his opponents, Kurdish and otherwise. He invoked emergency powers and set up military tribunals that sentenced more than 500 people to death. By 1934, when parliament passed a law requiring Turks to take surnames, there were no (audible) objections when Mustafa Kemal chose for himself the name "Ataturk."

∞

Ataturk had two priorities. First, to create a strong and centralized state in place of the bumbling Ottoman bureaucracy; second, to create an independent state that would never contract the Ottoman disease of dependency on foreign credit or capital. (Ataturk had disparaged the failing Ottoman Empire as "a colony of foreigners.")

To do this, Ataturk invoked what he called the "New Turkish Economic School." No one was quite sure what this meant; but his vision became clearer when he ordered the Turkish government to buy out the foreign-owned railways and tobacco monopoly. He then created his own locally owned monopolies in tobacco, alcohol, sugar, matches, and explosives. In 1924, Ataturk founded the Business Bank, a national financial institution that ultimately displaced the foreign-owned banks. Ataturk said, "Our nation has crushed the enemy forces. But to achieve independence we must observe the following rule: national sovereignty should be supported by financial independence."

In 1929, the Treaty of Lausanne expired. Under its provisions, the occupying European powers had, among other things, forced Turkey to open its markets to their goods. Ataturk announced that his new economic policy was "statism" and he raised import barriers against foreign products, with effective tariff rates reaching 200 percent. In 1934, Ataturk rolled out his first five-year plan. (Thus making Turkey the first country to follow the U.S.S.R. in adopting a state-planning model.) The Turkish government constructed fifteen state-owned factories to produce textiles, glass, and paper. This was the beginning of the "State Economic Enterprises," such as Sumerbank, which makes everything from cloth to shoes, and Etibank, an enormous mining concern.

By his death in 1938, Ataturk had accomplished many of his goals. He had created a powerful state that dominated the Turkish economy and ruled through central planning. He had also created a financially independent state by kicking out foreigners and replacing foreign owner-ship with government ownership. Turks today are intensely proud of his legacy. Most feel Ataturk resurrected Turkish dignity following the humiliating Ottoman decline. But the new government, once inserted into the economy, was not so easily removed.

∞

This was a government that lived in Roosevelt's "spirit of charity." A constitution drawn up in 1961 codified this. Article 37: The state shall "provide land for those farmers who have no land." Article 41: Economic life "shall be regulated in a manner consistent with...the principle of full employment." Article 48: "The State is charged with the duty of estab-lishing...social insurance and social welfare organizations." Article 49: "It is the responsibility of the State to ensure that everyone leads a healthy life both physically and mentally, and receives medical attention."

Put negatively, the Turkish government's "visible hand" was inserted in almost every aspect of Turkish life, creating a fundamentally politicized economy. Ataturk's Business Bank, provider of capital to favored companies, came to be known as the "Bank of Politicians." Companies with close connections to the political elite benefited tremendously, growing into sprawling conglomerates straddling unrelated industries. Sabanci, Koc, Dogus, and Eczacibasi are all conglomerates—flourishing to this day—that got their start under Ataturk. Koc Holdings, for instance, operates in 10 main industries—everything from automobiles to supermarkets—and includes 108 companies. The Sabanci conglomerate notes proudly that it does business in the "the industrial, financial, commercial, and agricultural sectors." The Turkish government grew so domineering in its outright control of key sectors and influence that Turks began to refer to it as *devlet baba*—the "father state."

The powerful state that Ataturk had created to make his country invulnerable would become Turkey's Achilles heel. As political analyst N. Beriker-Atiyas would eventually write: "It is evident that [Turkish] politics in general has been reduced to a game of capturing public resources and then redistributing them through legal and illegal means."

What the Turkish story illustrates is not simply the perils of central planning. Since Ataturk, Turkey has seen both committed state planners and eager market reformers come and go. Rather, the Turkish case makes clear the fundamental distortions that result from political intervention in the economy. This dynamic, unleashed when the government becomes a major economic actor but continues to make decisions in the service of political goals, hobbles Turkey's economic development to this day.

∞

At first, the problems of Turkey's super-state were blindingly obvious. Forty years after Ataturk's death, the inefficiencies of state planning had brought the economy to the verge of collapse. The state-led economy imploded in a foreign-exchange crisis that caused widespread shortages, triple-digit inflation, and violent riots. The Turkish army threw out the civilian government and imposed martial law.

Eventually, this crisis brought to power the iconoclastic Turgut Ozal, a committed market reformer. When civilian rule was (partially) restored in 1983, Ozal took the prime ministership with a mandate to dismantle the state-run economy. Declaring himself a convert to free enterprise, Ozal freed prices, devalued the exchange rate, and reduced subsidies. He reduced the barriers to imports that had kept out foreign goods. Privatization triggered an inflow in foreign capital and the inflation rate dropped to between 30 percent and 40 percent per year.

But Ozal accomplished all this by substituting one type of government intervention for many others. This was not necessarily his fault. Government control of the economy had created huge constituencies addicted to state largesse. Many Turks simply expected state jobs, state loans, and state subsidies. A full stop to this would have meant political suicide for Ozal's administration.

So Ozal, while privatizing and liberalizing, fed the "father state" in other ways. One example was so-called "fund politics." "Funds" were extra-budgetary expenditures that were designed to buy off politically important constituencies. "Parking lot funds," "help the poor funds," even "soccer team funds" were distributed across Turkey. Researchers Oyuz Oyan and Ali Riza Aydin documented the existence of 134 such funds and noted that many more remained hidden. These off-budget funds were one reason that, even though the official fiscal deficit averaged a relatively manageable 3 percent of GDP during the 1980s, the Turkish national debt ballooned from $13.5 billion in 1980 to $40 billion in 1989. By the end of the 1980s, inflation had again bounced up to 70 percent, partially because of government overspending.

This addiction to state spending is a legacy that Turkey has yet to shake off. The government had to use roughly a quarter of its spending just to pay the wages of public-sector employees—a ratio that is double the average for wealthy industrial countries. This is because the "father state" is extraordinarily generous in handing out jobs. By the late 1990s, there were 2.7 million public-sector employees, according to TESEV, an Istanbul-based think tank. The government, despite privatization, also continued to run many state-owned enterprises. These enterprises—in Turkey known as State Economic Enterprises, or SEEs—dominated crucial industrial sectors: Turpras in oil refining; Tekel, tobacco and alcohol; Petkim, the petrochemicals industry; and Erdemir, iron and steel. These were often run to serve political goals and were thus staggeringly inefficient. TTK, the government-owned coal-mining company, somehow managed to employ 19,000 people, only a third of whom were actually miners. TKK lost the most of all the SEEs—in 2000, $370 million, and in 2001, $210 million.

Struggling to meet huge wage bills, bail out inefficient SEEs, and distribute large off-budget funds, Turkey's government lurched from one economic crisis to another during the 1990s. In 1993, public-sector borrowing reached a staggering 17 percent of GDP and inflation hit 73 percent. The predictable result was a financial crisis and a 76 percent devaluation of the lira. In the wake of the crisis, nominal interest rates hit 320 percent and GDP declined more than 5 percent. The experience was repeated—following the Russian ruble devaluation and a disastrous earthquake—in 1998. In 1999, Turkey's economy again contracted by 5 percent.

∞

But these were only the obvious problems. The Turkish government's overspending was legendary but perhaps not insurmountable. For one thing, as a key U.S. ally, Turkey had access to extensive international bailout funds almost at will. So foreign investors were willing to forgive a little government excess. Indeed, by 1999, investors viewed the Turkish economy with near-euphoria. In that year, aggressive privatization programs were slated to bring in $5 billion. The government sold stakes in high-profile firms including Petrol Ofisi, a chain of gas stations, and Tupras, the oil refiner. These sales were free of the corruption allegations that had derailed previous privatization attempts. At the same time, an aggressive anti-inflation program had taken inflation from triple digits to below 40 percent. The elusive goal of single-digit inflation seemed to be within reach. Prime Minister Bulent Ecevit, leading an unexpectedly effective coalition government, had promised an ambitious program of privatization, fiscal tightening, and responsible monetary policy anchored by a gradually declining fixed exchange rate. The IMF declared its firm support for these programs and agreed to provide generous loans. The European Union announced that Turkey was an official candidate for membership. Turkey's stock market soared by a staggering 177 percent in 1999. From 1999 to its peak in early 2000, the main market index rose by 650 percent.

But this euphoria overlooked Turkey's underlying dynamics of politicized economics. Investors received some uncomfortable reminders when the Turkish government attempted to "privatize" Turk Telekom. Oddly, the privatization deal offered only a 20 percent stake with limited management rights, with all strategic decisions requiring government approval. Understandably, the deal failed to attract any investor interest. It soon emerged that the sticking point was the MHP, the second-largest party in the ruling coalition. The MHP had gained control of the communications ministry and therefore of Turk Telekom. And Turk Telekom, a major employer, was a superb engine for distributing patronage to political supporters. The MHP had no intention of giving up its prize possession. Foreign investment was welcome as long as the foreigners did not have the power to fire anyone. Investors were not interested and the privatization failed.

This was followed closely by trouble with another high-profile privatization: Turkish Airlines, which also fell under communications ministry jurisdiction. The MHP had been winning political points by refusing to allow the airline to increase fares following fuel price increases. The MHP agreed to privatize the airline but only on the condition that fares remained unchanged. Considering that discounted fares had contributed to the airline's $167 million loss in 1999, potential investors were not interested in that deal either.

But the real problem, the problem that was about to trigger a financial crisis, was the banks. At first blush, government-controlled banking lacks the glamour of state-owned enterprises or even off-budget "funds." But keep in mind that banks can lend out many times the money put into them. And, until the banks actually collapse, this is "lending," not "spending." In theory, at least, the money will be paid back. In short, banks are machines that, almost magically, create money—a dangerous implement in a politician's hands.

Turkey's state banks, on the orders of Ataturk, were set up with the express purpose of funding home-grown and locally owned industry. Following the letter if not the spirit of this decree, Turkey's politicians began to shower their constituents with subsidized loans. The Ziraat Bank, for instance, extended easy credit to farmers. The Halk Bank was used to finance small and medium-sized firms. These loans were directed by politicians, and rarely met commercial criteria. Not surprisingly, the state banks soon began to rack up tremendous losses not revealed on questionable accounting statements. By the 1990s, these hidden losses were growing to the point that they threatened to overwhelm the government's ability to bail the banks out.

In the wake of a previous financial crisis, in 1994, Turkey had no choice but to ink agreements with the IMF on budget and state-owned enterprise reform. Turkey's politicians reluctantly agreed to the IMF conditions, shutting themselves out of two of their favorite means of distributing patronage—the off-budget "funds" and the state-owned companies. Hence they turned to more subtle instruments, notably the state-owned banks Ziraat and Halk, and opened the floodgates for sub-sidized loans. When Prime Minister Ecevit's coalition came together, the first order of business was to draw up a document detailing which state bank each party would control. After a few years of heavy politicized lending, analysts estimated that the country's public-sector banks were $20 billion in the hole. Yet the coalition partners refused to let go of their patronage machines. The ANAP, the smallest party in the coalition, was especially adamant in resisting reform.

The government was also fiddling with banks in the private sector. Well-connected businessmen were allowed to set up banks from which they subsequently stole. Of the six new private banks created immedi-ately after the 1991 elections, all six failed within a decade. The govern-ment also turned a blind eye as well-connected bankers borrowed large amounts from foreign lenders and then lent this money to the Turkish government at extremely high interest rates. In fact, the banks made so much money from lending to the government that in 1999, the practice generated 88 percent of the profits of Turkey's 500 biggest firms.

∞

By November 2000, Turkey's ongoing structural problems had festered into a crisis. During the month of November, overnight interest rates shot from below 100 percent to 1,950 percent. Foreign capital swiftly left the country and the stock market was soon nearly half off its peak.

But Turkey is no ordinary emerging market. Turkey sits at the inter-section of Europe and Asia; it is the most democratic Islamic country; it is a member of NATO. As U.S. Deputy Secretary of Defense Paul

Wolfowitz wryly observed, "The end of the Cold War has transformed Turkey from a country of enormous strategic importance into a country of enormous strategic importance." The International Monetary Fund, under heavy U.S. pressure, surprised the markets with a generous $7.5 billion rescue package, making the money almost immediately available with few strings attached. This had an almost magical calming effect. Overnight bank rates were soon down below 200 percent, and the stock market rallied.

But three months later the economic mess was still festering. Morgan Stanley described a "black hole" in the balance sheets of Turkey's public-sector banks. Estimates of the cost of cleaning up the failed banks, including the private- and public-sector institutions, ranged as high as a quarter of Turkey's GDP. A well-connected financier was caught on videotape carrying a suitcase bulging with cash en route to fleeing the country.

In February 2001, Prime Minister Ecevit burst out of a meeting with Turkey's president, angrily denouncing the president in statements to the media. What actually happened in the meeting is a matter of some dispute. Apparently, Ecevit, knowing that his coalition partners had their fingers in the public pie, had stalled on corruption investigations, especially in the banking sector. The president criticized the delays and threw a copy of the constitution across the table to emphasize his point. "We installed you, and we can remove you," a government minister reportedly retorted. Things went downhill from there.

Investors, fearing a political crisis, pulled $5 billion out of the country in one day. In two days the stock market was down by 63 percent. The government, unable to defend the currency peg, was forced to let the lira float, and it promptly plummeted by 30 percent.

But again Turkey would get a bailout. This time the IMF came to the rescue with an even larger $15 billion package. And thus, the world was called upon, and responded, to bankroll the "father state's" bad habits. The loans to Turkey will in theory be paid back, so the world's taxpayers will not feel the hit in their wallets. But this is clearly not a healthy or sustainable relationship. Turkey's dependence on bailouts seems to be growing, and—especially in the wake of Turkey's failure to support the U.S. war on Iraq—these bailouts may suddenly stop. Observers hope that the extent of Turkey's recent financial crisis will force greater reforms and, indeed, there is some evidence that this is happening. But Turkey's legacy of government intervention will be hard to shake off.

Ataturk would no doubt turn over in his grave. A Turkey dependent on foreign loans to stay afloat? A disquieting thought for a man who witnessed the collapse (and sell-off) of the Ottoman Empire. But it was, ironically, Ataturk who inserted the Turkish government into the economy. And the government's highly politicized intervention has plagued Turkey ever since.

TURKEY AND MOTOROLA

One notorious example of a company caught up in Turkey's odd kimchi is Motorola. Motorola entered Turkey in the mid-1990s, eager to exploit a hot market for mobile phones. Its market entry strategy was "vendor financing": Motorola would loan money to local companies, which would buy equipment and build networks. One of its big local partners was the Uzan family, which controlled a conglomerate active in banks, construction, printing, and media. On Motorola's dime, the Uzans built a mobile phone company called Telsim, running up debts of $1.8 billion by 2000. Motorola's only collateral was in the form of shares of Telsim stock.

Then the Turkish economy suffered its economic crisis and the Uzans missed a $728 million payment on their loan from Motorola. When Motorola went looking for its collateral, it found the Uzans had transferred Telsim's assets to a Turkish foundation—making these assets, by law, off limits to foreign companies. And the Uzans diluted Motorola's shares so the company went from owning three-quarters of Telsim stock to one quarter. Motorola, trying to get its money back, bypassed Turkish courts and filed international suits alleging racketeering, extortion, and corporate computer hacking. So far Motorola (and Swedish telecom company Nokia, in similar straits) have managed to seize two Uzan-owned corporate jets—one in France and one in Germany—as well as property in Manhattan, London, and Germany. But this covers only part of the damages, and Motorola must also deal with class action lawsuits from its shareholders for stock price fluctuations related to the Telsim debacle.

Part of the problem is the Uzans' misbehavior, but a major cause of Motorola's misfortune is—indirectly—Turkey's political dynamics. Of course, this includes the financial crisis that caused the Uzans to miss the payment in the first place. But just as important were several fundamental misunderstandings. To Western eyes, ownership of a major business conglomerate spells legitimacy—a mark of good business practices carried out in the public eye and under legal scrutiny. But in Turkey, recall, the conglomerates grew via state-directed lending. Ownership of a huge business indicates outstanding political connections, not necessarily upstanding management. In fact, the Uzans have a long history of fleecing investors, including Franklin Templeton's Emerging Markets Fund. When a judge in New York inquired as to why Motorola entered "into this venture given the already dubious history of the Uzans," Motorola replied that it had further considered the Uzans legitimate because they had been awarded a cellular license from the Turkish government. This was either another misunderstanding or horrendous naïveté. In Turkey's politicized economy, a government license does not necessarily indicate legal probity but rather, again, good connections. Thus did Motorola dramatically misread its potential business partner. Such are the dangers of Turkey's kimchi.

The Dynamics of Government Intervention

The fundamental problem with government involvement in the economy can be stated rather simply. In almost every case, a government plays the twin roles of rule maker and referee in a country's economy. The government makes the laws, and it enforces them. So it is only natural that havoc results when the referee starts playing the game. The referee's team—no matter how lacking in ability—would be all but guaranteed to win.

Economic games, equally rigged, are played daily in economies around the world. For decades, Turkey's state-owned enterprises were guaranteed to win, and well-connected owners of private conglomerates enjoyed extraordinarily unfair advantages. The problem, of course, was that many of these winners were not good at the games they were playing. (Or rather, they were only good at the political games.)

This is not to say that the government should never play an economic role. Theorists from the days of Thomas Hobbes and Adam Smith have acknowledged "market failures" that demand government intervention.

The classic and least controversial example is the matter of "public goods," which the market will under-provide. These types of goods are unusual because it is impossible to exclude people from their benefits. Consider the national defense, for instance. All persons living within a country's borders benefit from a strong national defense, whether they pay for it or not. Hence it is impossible to "privatize" defense—a private army, unable to exclude those who did not pay their bills, would fail to make money. Another "market failure" occurs when there are externalities—benefits for those other than the buyer—for certain types of goods. Education is one example. Everyone benefits from living in a more educated society, not just those who are educated. But deciding what is a public good and what is not is far from easy. There is general agreement on defense and, to some extent, primary and secondary education. Beyond these realms, even like-minded governments disagree. In the U.S. the post office is public; in the U.K. it is private. In the U.K. health care is (largely) public; in the U.S. it is (largely) private.

∞

The economic catastrophe of the Great Depression caused political leaders to see market failures everywhere. All over the world, state-owned enterprises (SOEs) sprang up and got into the business of building cars, mining coal and iron, and producing steel. In Tunisia, Egypt, Ethiopia, and Burma, for instance, the state came to control over 60 percent of the manufacturing sector. At the same time, the "welfare state" became increasingly popular. Put another way, people began to think that poverty was another "market failure" that the government needed to correct. (Surely, it was said, in a society without poor people, everyone would benefit, at least, from the reduced crime.) Governments provided pensions, unemployment insurance, disability benefits, and so on. In the U.S., spending on subsidies and transfers reached 2 percent of GDP in 1937; 6 percent of GDP by 1960; and 13 percent of GDP by 1997. In the U.K., transfers and subsidies now consume about a quarter of GDP.

Despite Turkey's dire history, not all of its government intervention was a disaster. There is nothing inherently wrong with state ownership—although it is hard to do right. The government can be both the referee and a player in the economic game. If the managers and employees of a state-owned enterprise are incentivized properly, and have no more influence over the rules and the refereeing than any other enterprise, then state-owned companies can work. Singapore's highly interventionist government made its economy run smoothly. The United States Postal Service has its problems, but is generally effective. Until recently, the Venezuelan state-owned oil company, PDVSA, had an excellent reputation for professionalism and results.

But government intervention in the economy creates powerful temptations, and politicians are not known for either morals or willpower. Government economic intervention usually lowers the walls between the players and the referees to dangerous levels. Instead of being run efficiently, state-owned enterprises are all too often asked to meet political goals: maximize employment (especially for the government's supporters); provide investment for politically important regions; and delight consumers, especially through the provision of utilities such as electricity and gas, at prices far below the cost of production.

Even when it becomes obvious that these strategies are serious money-losers, problems are rarely corrected. When the referee is playing the game, no matter how ineptly, the state-owned enterprises always seem to win. Indeed, many state-owned companies have been granted legal monopolies. Facing no competition whatsoever, they could be as inefficient as they liked. Some of the most egregious examples occurred in the communist countries. When the Soviet Union fell, it was discovered that many "profitable" enterprises were actually engaged in "value subtraction." In other words, the value of the steel, plastic, glass, and other raw materials that the state firms used in production was actually greater than the value of the shoddy products they produced. On a less extreme scale, these problems were repeated around the world. The World Bank reports that between 1978 and 1991, the losses accumulated by state-owned enterprises in low-income countries averaged 2.3 percent of the countries' GDP. The Tanzanian government, for example, spent one and a half times as much on subsidizing loss-making state-owned companies as it did on public health.

The situation with government intervention in social welfare is not much better. It's simply impossible to insulate "optimal" government intervention from political pressures. Governments tend to direct their spending on public goods such as "education" and "health" towards specific items, such as urban hospitals and prestigious universities, which differentially benefit the better off. A further ironic twist is that these types of "public" goods—universities and hospitals, for example—are all goods or services that the private sector is relatively successful at providing. And in many countries, government intervention in education is "captured" by the rich and powerful. In Africa, spending per student is forty-four times greater on higher education than on primary schooling. In Venezuela, just 31 percent of the education budget goes to basic schooling. (To be sure, not all countries get it wrong. In South Korea, 84 percent of the education budget goes to primary and secondary education.) Something similar occurs with subsidies and price controls. Governments put price caps on everything from real estate to electricity to agricultural products, ostensibly to help the poor. But wealthy people tend to benefit from price controls even more than the poor do. In Asia, Latin America, and Africa, for instance, the poor generally do not own motorized vehicles—so it is the wealthy who benefit from cheap fuel. In South Asia, 90 percent of subsidies actually go to the relatively well off.

Again, this is not to say that government ownership or regulation is inherently bad. There are many examples of relatively successful state-directed economies. Japan's Ministry of International Trade and Industry, Korea's Economic Planning Board, Thailand's so-called "Gang of Four" (the Ministry of Finance, the Budget Bureau, the central bank, and the National Economic and Social Development Board), and Indonesia's Bapennas (the planning agency), all helped to engineer extremely rapid growth. These agencies set up incentive programs, provided loans, and handed subsidies to industries deemed crucial for growth. Economists argue about whether these countries grew despite, because of, or irrespective of their governments' interventions. But the evidence of decades of rapid growth is that while such government intervention did harm in many instances, it helped in many others.

Yet worldwide, the balance of evidence shows that government intervention in the economy creates temptations for political meddling that are difficult to resist. This is true on even the simplest level. Statistical surveys reveal that, in general, the more people a government employs, the lower their average pay is likely to be. The less government workers are paid, the more likely they are to attempt to supplement income through corruption. The more a government intervenes in the economy, the more opportunities there are for corruption. The more closed an economy is—through import barriers, regulated exchange rates, and the like—the more corrupt the country is likely to be. The more subsidies a government hands out, the more likely civil servants are to become corrupt. Human nature being what it is, the presence of temptation—again, not in every country, but on the average—tends to lead to misbehavior.

In the end, this is the main argument against excessive government intervention in the economy. The government should stick to the economic roles of referee and rule maker. While this may sound like a prescription for the rollback of the state, it is not; in too many countries, as it turns out, the government is not doing enough in these roles. The trick is not to abolish the state but to do a few crucial things right.

CHAPTER FOURTEEN

"When England Sneezes..."

EXTERNAL SHOCKS

"When England Sneezes, Scotland catches a cold."
SUNDAY TIMES, APRIL 26, 1998

"If Russia sneezes, Brazil catches a cold."
U.S. BANKER, AUGUST 1999

"Remember the saying that when America sneezes, Israel catches a cold."
JERUSALEM REPORT, APRIL 9, 2001

"When Russia catches a cold, Germany sneezes."
FINANCIAL TIMES, JULY 13, 1998

"When Brazil's economy sneezes, Latin America catches a cold. When Latin America catches a cold, the U.S. reaches for the medicine cabinet. And when the U.S. feels sick, well..."
THE INDEPENDENT, FEBRUARY 1, 1999

"The last two decades have shown that if any country in the world sneezes, Latin America catches pneumonia."
NATIONAL BUREAU OF ECONOMIC RESEARCH, JANUARY 17, 2001

FROM THE TEQUILA EFFECT (CONTAGION FROM MEXICO) TO THE Samba Effect (contagion from Brazil), from the Russian debt default to the Asian financial crisis, the 1990s were a decade of highly contagious financial maladies. Above all, contagion is a sign of globalization. Increasing interconnectedness in terms of capital and trade flows, communications, and labor migration has linked different countries' fates to each other. Nothing illustrated this point more clearly than the rapid worldwide spread of financial contagion from the various emerging market crises of the 1990s.

This is only one example of an "external shock." Outside forces have always had a profound influence on the stability or instability of states. These forces range from military threats (Iraq versus Kuwait, Pakistan versus India) to International Monetary Fund reform programs (the Philippines, Mexico) to declines in oil prices (Venezuela, Russia) to pressure from the European Union (Italy, Slovakia). No country is an island, even when it comes to its own stability. The impacts of international relations and events are varied and profound.

ARGENTINA

Argentina was a star emerging market in the mid-1990s, attracting billions of dollars in foreign direct investment and enjoying an astounding 60 percent expansion of its economy between 1990 and 1998. The inflation rate fell from the hyperinflation of the late 1980s all the way down to 4 percent in 1994, the lowest in Latin America. During this extraordinary period, Argentines saw their average incomes increase by 42 percent. Domingo Cavallo, the architect of this prosperity, was in some danger of being canonized as a saint.

But in 2002, Argentina's currency lost half its value; four presidents came and went in a single month; riots and demonstrations spread across the country; and the country defaulted on $85 billion of its $155 billion public debt—the largest debt default in world history. Argentina's banking system was frozen, its currency regime in shambles, and its economy mired in a four-year recession. By defaulting on a loan repayment to the World Bank, Argentina joined an exclusive club that includes such international luminaries as Iraq, Zimbabwe, and Liberia.

A crucial point must be made about this extraordinary reversal of fortune: Argentina did not "deserve" its fate. Some unfortunate dynamics were involved—obstructive special interests and an interventionist government. But the mistakes that Argentina's leaders made—chiefly, failing to reign in government spending—did not justify its currency crisis, debt default, and economic collapse. Political leaders in other countries (and for that matter, in Argentina in past decades) have pursued far worse policies with far milder effects. More than anything else, Argentina was caught, economically speaking, in the wrong place at the wrong time. The crucial dynamic here is of external shocks.

∞

The policy innovation that (temporarily) produced an Argentine boom was called "convertibility." The brainchild of the country's now-infamous economy minister, Domingo Cavallo, convertibility was implemented in 1991 during the administration of President Carlos Saul Menem. Menem was an unlikely reformer, an Argentine of Syrian ancestry who was a fast-talking playboy. He was elected in 1989 on a left-wing ticket, promising to protect the poor and downtrodden. He was also a Peronist (an heir to the legacy of the legendary Juan Peron); a man of extraordinary charisma; a champion of the labor unions; and a proponent of populist economic policies that helped to undermine Argentina's prosperity.

Once in office, Menem embarked on a radical and successful market reform program. The centerpiece, convertibility, was a currency board system that pegged the value of the Argentine peso to the U.S. dollar at a 1:1 ratio. This was no garden-variety currency peg. Every peso in the economy would be backed by a dollar held by the central bank, putting the country's policymakers into a brutal straitjacket: no control over exchange rate policy and no control over monetary policy. Considering the country's history, convertibility was a good thing. At a stroke it all but eliminated the risks from economic mismanagement—no more risk from inflation and no more risk from devaluation. The central bank would be unable to print money indiscriminately. After a lag, inflation plummeted from thousands of percent per year to single digits. Against the opposition of trade unions, Menem put Argentina's state-owned enterprises into private hands. Foreign dollars flowed into the economy. Between 1991 and 1997, Argentina's growth rate leapt to an annual average of 6.1 percent—the kind of rate associated with East Asia's economic miracle, not slow-growing

Latin America. Menem had fulfilled his promise to help the poor, not by redistributing wealth, but by creating it.

But convertibility also put Argentina in a very vulnerable position. This was not immediately obvious in the early 1990s, as the economy boomed and foreign investment poured in. But Menem and Cavallo had unwittingly placed Argentina atop active international economic faultlines; global economic conditions were about to shift, crushing Argentina with all the implacable brutality of tectonic plates.

∞

The first rumblings were felt in late 1994, when Mexico experienced another of its periodic currency crises. This one has since been dubbed the "first financial crisis of the twenty-first century," in part because of the rapid and global spread of its effects.

Argentina, like much of the rest of Latin America, was soon suffering from the "Tequila Effect." Jittery foreign investors had noticed some alarming similarities between Argentina and Mexico. Like Mexico, Argentina had a fixed exchange rate and a current account deficit. Like Mexico, Argentina was dependent on short-term foreign capital. Like Mexico, Argentina had a weak banking system. And like Mexico, Argentina had a woefully low domestic savings rate. Like vultures to carrion, the speculators descended upon Argentina. The Argentine stock market fell to 43 percent off its 1994 close. Argentines with no desire to be left holding a depreciated currency lined up outside banks to change their pesos into dollars. They shipped a total of $8 billion, some 15 percent of all deposits, out of the country. The result was a cash crunch. Each peso taken out of the country was a peso removed from the money supply. The effect was similar to a hawkish central bank tightening the monetary supply to slow down an economic boom. But Argentina was not in a boom. Its economy was already struggling. Hence capital flight made an ugly downturn worse. Unemployment hit 18 percent. A record 146 companies went bankrupt in a single month in 1995. This prompted high-profile foreign investors like Barton Biggs, the managing director of Morgan Stanley Asset Management, to feel "a little queasy about Argentina." Biggs noted, "It is a difficult time to have a currency board when the economy is contracting."

As the economy contracted by 4.6 percent in 1995, foreign exchange reserves dwindled to just $5 billion—only enough to pay for two months of imports. Soon Argentina's country risk premium (the interest rate bond investors demanded to compensate for increased risk of default) rose to levels that threatened its ability to borrow on international capital markets to meet debt-financing needs. At some point, the country would be paying such high interest rates in order to obtain additional lending that further borrowing would only drive it deeper into a hole.

But Argentina did not reach this point. The International Monetary Fund and the World Bank helped out with a bailout package. International commodity prices stayed high, so Argentina earned a lot of money from its exports of paper, iron, minerals, and agricultural products. On top of this, the country benefited from currency stability and economic growth in its gargantuan neighbor, Brazil. High consumer demand in Brazil helped Argentina's exports grow by 33 percent in the first six months of 1995 alone. Argentina's policymakers also tweaked labor laws to allow for more temporary workers, restructured the banking system, and tightened fiscal policy, all policies that delighted international investors. The country's economy bounced back with a ferocity that few had expected. By the end of 1995, Argentina's foreign exchange reserves had been restored to pre-crisis levels. The economy grew by 4.3 percent in 1996. Employment rebounded as well.

∞

Argentina's policymakers took the wrong lessons from this. Instead of realizing that they sat upon the international economic equivalent of the San Andreas fault, they congratulated themselves for having built an earthquake-proof house. This was short-sighted; but at the time, of course, Argentina had made a spectacular comeback.

What the Mexican crisis should have demonstrated was that, because of the currency board, Argentina had no independent monetary policy, and this in effect locked the country into its dangerous position. Consider the implications. As the U.S. economy slid toward recession in 2001, Federal Reserve Chairman Alan Greenspan famously cut interest rates 11 times, bringing them down from 6.5 percent to 1.75 percent in the space of just one year. Argentina had no such option. Because of the currency board, the country's interest rates were tied to those of the United States. The straitjacket also applied to exchange rate policy. Many emerging markets—Mexico in 1994 and South Korea in 1997, to take two examples—recovered strongly after devaluing their currencies. One reason is that a devalued currency means cheap exports and therefore usually an export boom. Argentina could not devalue. To become more competitive, either Argentina's prices would have to fall or its productivity would have to rise. (And unfortunately, due to the country's restrictive labor laws, productivity was unlikely to rise. Indeed, Argentina's productivity growth was negative throughout the 1990s.) All of this meant that external conditions could cause economic disaster.

∞

Bad policies did not cause Argentina's crisis. But good policies could have prevented it. However, the moment of opportunity was overlooked. Between 1993 and 1998, Argentina's economy grew by a robust average of 4.4 percent per year. Yet during those years, the government debt expanded dramatically.

One reason for government overspending was the power of special interests. In Argentina, provincial governments wield tremendous influence. Partly this is because the constitution mandates decentralization—a reaction to the country's ugly experience with authoritarian military regimes. Partly this is because it is hard to win a congressional election without the support of the local provincial governor, so national legislators end up beholden to local governments. The result is that, even when provincial governments misbehave, the Argentine government finds it hard to crack down. The province of Corrientes under Governor Raul Romero Feris, for instance, ran up a debt of nearly $1.5 billion, in part by handing out jobs to political supporters. The central government was unable to clamp down on Romero Feris because it needed the provincial governors to deliver crucial congressional votes. The governors, for their part, did not want to stop spending because public discontent in many provinces, especially in the poor interior of the country, was rising as inefficient industries were privatized or shut down. There were other problems—an expensive pension program, weak tax collection, and President Menem's attempts to buy public support for an unconstitutional third term. But the crux of the issue is that the Argentine government was unable to cut spending. Under Menem's successor, three different economy ministers held power in one month: each was ejected when they attempted to cut spending.

This was a mistake of staggering consequence. If, between 1993 and 1998, the Argentine government had improved its overall budget balance by 2 percent of GDP, it would have cut its debt burden nearly in half. By 1998, the debt to GDP ratio would have been around 21 percent—an eminently manageable burden.

Instead, overspending continued apace. The central government's budget deficit was kept within fairly responsible limits—only about 1.5 percent of GDP per year. But most of the irresponsible spending in Argentina was taking place in the provinces. Adding in provincial government spending, the overall budget deficit was closer to 3 percent of GDP. Still, not terrible. But as economist Michael Mussa pointed out, between 1993 and 1998, Argentina's government debt increased from 29 to 41 percent of GDP. This does not match with official budget deficit statistics. In other words, not only was Argentina's government running a large deficit during an economic boom, it was also secretly spending additional "off-budget" funds.

∞

And so, when the global tectonic plates shifted again, Argentina was soon unbalanced by its unwieldy debt burden. In July 1997, the Thai baht collapsed. The devaluation of the Thai currency set off a round of financial crises. One by one, the currencies of Malaysia, Indonesia, and South Korea began to fall.

For international investors, this was a shock. For three decades, South Korea had been among the fastest-growing economies in the world; now the country was suffering a financial meltdown. Investors began to see potential crises lurking in every corner. After sending over $100 billion in portfolio investment to emerging markets in 1995 and 1996, foreign investors began to pull their money out. In 1997, net capital flows to emerging markets actually turned negative. Investors were especially wary of any country that had South Korea's particular economic weaknesses: a fixed exchange rate, a current account deficit, and an unsteady banking sector.

Argentina fit the bill closely enough. Capital stampeded out of the country. Argentina's country risk premium soared from 361 to over 800 basis points. Argentina was forced to delay a global bond issue it had planned to finance its debt.

But the real damage from the Asian financial crisis only became clear over time. The downturn in the East Asian economies meant a decline in global demand. In turn, that caused a slump in commodity prices, a serious problem for Argentina. Commodities comprised a full 60 percent of Argentine exports and much of the international investment into Argentina, which helped fund the country's current account deficit, was in the commodities sector. In 1994, for instance, billionaire financier George Soros became Argentina's largest livestock owner by buying agricultural company Cresud.

Then came the Asian Crisis. Prices for wheat fell 45 percent between May 1996 and December 1997. Prices for soybeans fell 20 percent. Prices for copper, gold, and oil also collapsed. Argentina's current account deficit climbed from 1.9 percent of GDP in 1996 to 3.8 percent of GDP in 1997. Then, in August 1998, Russia defaulted on its international debt obligations. International investors became even more skittish.

But Argentina was, ultimately, done in by the Brazilian real devaluation of 1999. The problem was not simply financial contagion but something even more fundamental. Until January 1999, Brazil and Argentina had both pegged their currencies to the U.S. dollar. But then Brazil, unable to control spending and, like Argentina, suffering as a result of both the Asian and Russian contagions, saw its real suffer a devastating speculative attack. In January 1999, it devalued by 40 percent. Argentina's position was suddenly nearly unsustainable. Argentina sent a full 30 percent of its exports to Brazil, including 60 percent of its manufactured exports. Now, after the devaluation, Argentina's exports to Brazil were suddenly 40 percent more expensive. In the ten months after the real crash, Argentina's vehicle exports to Brazil fell by 50 percent. Foreign companies like Fiat and Ford shut down auto plants in Argentina and cut loose a slew of workers.

Brazil's post-crash rebound only emphasized the hopelessness of Argentina's position. With a devalued currency, Brazilian assets were suddenly cheap. The foreign direct investment that Argentina so desperately needed flooded into Brazil instead. Multinational corporations poured $30 billion into Brazil in 1999. Indeed, consulting firm A.T. Kearney identified Brazil as the world's third most popular destination for foreign investors, behind only the U.S. and China. It was almost as if Brazil was taunting Argentina with the recovery that was just out of its reach. "Abandon convertibility," seemed to be the lesson, "and all this can be yours."

∞

Argentina's leaders refused to give in. This was not necessarily irresponsible; to abandon convertibility would have caused untold economic damage (as it eventually did). When foreign investors asked if Argentina would ever abandon its peg to the dollar, Senator Luis Molinari once said, "This is a heavy issue. It is like questioning the virginity of the virgin Mary." One government official quipped, "When you are married to Sharon Stone, you do not require an exit route." But the U.S. dollar might not have been the right match for Argentina (in sickness and in health). This was because of another global tectonic shift. For several years the dollar was the darling of world markets. Despite a gaping U.S. current account deficit, the dollar climbed by 39 percent against other currencies in the six years up to 2001, hitting a 15-year high in July 2001. This rise tracked the meteoric fortunes of the U.S. economy. Argentina was haplessly dragged along on this rise. The country desperately needed a cheaper currency, but the U.S. dollar was only going up. Like a Hollywood marriage, this was destined for a dramatic end. (The dollar has since plummeted, as all fundamentals suggested it would—but too late for Argentina.)

By 2000, a series of emerging market crises—affecting Mexico, Asia, Russia, Brazil, and Turkey—made investors demand higher interest rates for Argentina's debt, the debt that the government had missed its opportunity to pay off. The debt service burden began to rise until interest payments were costing Argentina four times the amount earned by exports. That amounted to a whopping 20 percent of government spending. In 1999, the interest rate spread on Argentine sovereign debt was about 550 basis points above U.S. Treasuries. At this level, the government could theoretically pay its debt, by generating a budget surplus (before debt payments) of about 3 to 4 percent of GDP. By early 2001, the spread was fluctuating as high as 1050 basis points. In order to pay these interest rates, the government would have needed to generate a primary budget surplus of 8 percent of GDP. This was inconceivable for any government, much less Argentina's.

The International Monetary Fund refused to lend any more money. Argentines were withdrawing nearly $1 billion per day from the banking system, and much of this money was being sent out of the country. Foreign exchange reserves were plummeting. Facing a financial collapse, the government was forced to close the banks. Riots spread from the provinces to Buenos Aires. Stores were looted and banks were vandalized. Efforts to restore order claimed the lives of thirty people and, finally, the government fell. Argentina defaulted on its debt and devalued the peso. Convertibility was finished.

This catastrophe was, at least partly, the result of poor policy choices, particularly in terms of debt reduction. These failures created an ultimately fatal vulnerability. But Argentina was primarily a victim of external shocks. An incredibly strong dollar, a drying up in capital flows to emerging markets, collapses in commodity prices, and a devaluation in neighboring Brazil were a fatal mix.

∞

The largest sovereign debt default in world history does not go unnoticed. A great many foreign investors and lenders were caught up in Argentina's political dynamics. AT&T took a huge charge against its balance sheet, and Xerox lost three cents of earnings per share. General Motors wrote off $97 million due to the peso devaluation. Some of this was due to direct government action. The U.S. Department of Energy noted that after devaluing the peso, "the [Argentine] government imposed a freeze on utility tariffs, holding them at their peso-denominated rate, thus passing the cost of devaluation on to [foreign-owned] utility companies...[This] has severely impacted the natural gas and electricity industries, causing many companies to announce heavy losses or debt default in 2002." U.S. exporters sold $4.7 billion worth of goods to Argentina as recently as 2000. With their economy in turmoil, demand for these goods collapsed; and with the devaluation of the peso, many companies that had ordered U.S. goods were unable to pay. Aon Trade Credit estimated that total credit and political risk insurance claims (chiefly insurance against default by buyers) may reach $500 million as a result of the crisis.

Hardest hit were the banks. British banks Lloyd's and Barclays both reported a rise in bad debt provisions for 2002 as a result of the Argentine crisis. Spanish banks BBVA and Banco Santander Central Hispano wrote off $1.42 billion and $1.49 billion respectively. American banks had $21 billion in Argentine exposure in late 2001, when the crisis struck, and J.P. Morgan, Citigroup, and FleetBoston Financial faced billions of dollars in losses (Citigroup over $1 billion, FleetBoston slightly less than that). Canadian Scotiabank, France's Credit Agricole, the Italian IntesaBci, and the German WestLB Group all abandoned Argentina completely.

Fortunately, Argentina's default was a slow-motion crisis. The global shifts that crushed Argentina were devastating. But they unfolded gradually. Many companies saw the crisis coming and took precautions. Still, Brazil saw its prospects worsened by Argentina's collapse, and Uruguay, suffering recession and a banking-sector collapse, was forced to restructure its $11 billion sovereign debt. Globalization helped bring Argentina's problems to the world.

CENTRAL AND EASTERN EUROPE

Not all external shocks are negative. Indeed, some can set in motion extremely positive political dynamics that would not otherwise exist.

The countries of Central and Eastern Europe (CEE), following the collapse of the Soviet Union and the fall of the Berlin Wall, were suddenly free to go their separate ways, and this they did. Serbians voted for a policy of ethnic cleansing. Much of the rest of Yugoslavia collapsed into ethnic and religious violence. Albania's economy disintegrated into bizarre pyramid schemes and near-anarchy. Russia found itself in the thrall of gangsters and kleptocrats. Likewise Ukraine, which had elected a thuggish president. Freed from Soviet oppression, many Eastern European states floundered. From labor unions to gangsters to ethnic nationalists, many newly empowered groups competed for control—often at the expense of their country's stability.

But a few countries, instead, did stunningly well. The Czech Republic, Poland, and Hungary have been star performers, and Slovakia at least respectable. What separates them from their off-track peers? One factor above all: the desire to join the European Union (EU).

For the Czech Republic, there was never any question about the pursuit of a European identity. From the moment the Berlin Wall fell, the country's destination was clear. In both democratic and market-oriented reforms, the Czech Republic has been a hare among its many tortoise-like neighbors. This is the richest CEE state and, indeed, Czechs consider membership in Europe to be almost a birthright, while the decades of Soviet oppression are seen by many as a ridiculous accident of history.

But membership in "Europe" is not so easily achieved. Europe—or more specifically, the EU—is not simply an ideal, it is an exclusive club with elaborate rules and membership privileges. The Copenhagen requirements of 1993 necessitate that EU aspirants ensure democracy, the rule of law, respect for human rights, the protection of minorities, and a functioning market economy. Even more demanding is compliance with the *Acquis Communautaire*: more than 80,000 pages of the laws, standards, and norms that are in force around the EU. Aspirants to the EU must ratify and then implement all thirty-one chapters of the *Acquis*. This is a rigorous and intrusive process—each year the EU evaluates the aspirants, rendering judgments that are public and often humiliating. But then, European Union membership is a valuable prize. For one thing, there can surely be no more powerful symbol of the achievement of a truly "European" identity. There are material benefits as well. Within the European Union, goods, services, capital, and people move freely, creating a 375 million-person, $7.8 trillion economy. In addition, the EU devotes at least a quarter of its annual budget to "structural funds" that are designed to help underdeveloped countries and regions catch up to the pack. Countries such as Ireland, Greece, and Spain have benefited immensely from EU aid.

As the most Western of the Easterners, the Czech Republic has sometimes considered EU membership to be a sure thing. Indeed, in its annual evaluation of the Czech Republic in 1994, the EU reported, "Confident of its progress toward meeting the obligations of EU membership, the Czech Republic has at times shown signs of reluctance to acknowledge difficulties and seek a collaborative approach in resolving them." But the Czech Republic has been willing to jump through the EU's many hoops, because it fears not necessarily exclusion, but rather the humiliation if one of the tortoises (Poland, Hungary, or worst of all, Slovakia) got into the EU first.

Hence, the goal of "Europe" has provided for the Czechs not only a destination, but also a very detailed map for reaching it. When the country has wavered from its course—facing a currency crisis in 1997 and an unstable minority government from 1996 to 1998—the exhaustive and very specific demands of European membership have worked to keep policy generally on track.

Realizing that the 1997 crisis put their country's claim to have a functioning market economy at stake, Czechs overwhelmingly turned their backs on populism and voted for Vaclav Klaus as prime minister, an economist who idolized Chicago School free market economics and Margaret Thatcher. Klaus took this electoral mandate and initiated a radical two-stage privatization process. When complete, more than 80 percent of the Czech Republic's economic output came from the private sector. Shortly after, when no party could achieve a majority in the Czech legislature, the pace of reform slowed dramatically. The response from the EU was a torrent of criticism. Once again, realizing what was at stake, Czechs were spurred into action. The Social Democrats, taking power in July 1998, methodically reviewed the EU criticisms, sketched out legislation that would remedy the situation, and drew up a timetable for passing laws. Parliament convened for marathon sessions under fast-track procedures. As a result, foreign investment in the Czech Republic doubled between 1998 and 2000. As Stefan Wagstyl of the *Financial Times* put it: "For most of the elites of Eastern Europe, EU accession is the aim which unites former Communist and anticommunist alike. It is the goal on which even the most fractious of the many coalition governments can agree. It shows the way forward to people who might otherwise have found it difficult to find a route map in the wreckage of the communist past."

∞

Nowhere is this more clear than in Slovakia, which by 1998 was very much off-course. Since 1994, a rabid Slovak nationalist named Vladimir Meciar had been prime minister. Meciar had started his career as a boxer, then became a lawyer, then a politician. He was every bit as combative as his career choices would indicate. He had played a key role in inspiring the country's secession from the Czech Republic in 1993, called the "Velvet Divorce." Meciar played to Slovaks' worst instincts. He tapped their frustration about poverty, unemployment, and the relative success of the

Czech Republic. His coalition allies, during his premiership, were the quasi-fascist Slovak National Party. He set about undermining Slovakia's democratic institutions, weakening the Parliament and the constitutional court. He used the secret service as a tool to crush his opponents, attacking the media, the labor unions, and disloyal local governments. His economic policy was no better. He used Slovakia's privatization process to transfer state assets to his cronies and ordered state-owned banks to finance his supporters' enterprises. By 1998, Slovakia's budget deficit was soaring and the current account deficit had reached a dangerous 10 percent of GDP.

The EU's 1997 evaluation of Slovakia was about as blistering as bureaucrats ever get. The official report lambasted the "instability of its institutions, their lack of rootedness in political life, and the shortcomings in the functioning of its democracy." Slovakia was singled out among the ten Eastern European applicants as the only country to have failed to meet the political criteria for EU entry. This was a tremendous shock to the Slovaks, who had always considered themselves among the more advanced CEE states. Yet here was a public declaration that Slovakia might fail to join the EU with the first round of applicants in 2004. The fact that their country had already failed to qualify for NATO membership in 1997 helped to convince the Slovaks that this was a real threat.

The report propelled Slovakia's opposition into action. Previously divided opposition movements suddenly found common ground. With the EU report as the rallying cry, Mikulas Dzurinda, the opposition leader, told Slovaks that Meciar was destroying their European identity. This had a powerful effect on the 70 percent of Slovakia's population that supported EU entry. Meciar was thrown from office in the 1998 elections. The new government, headed by Dzurinda, moved swiftly to repair the damage. His first trip abroad was to visit the European Commission in Brussels. Some worried that the new four-party coalition government—an awkward joining of the political left and right—was too broad to tackle serious reforms. But minds were focused on the goal of EU membership. Government spending was cut, the current account deficit reigned in, and the privatization process was put back on track. An independent judiciary was established. The rights of ethnic Hungarians and Gypsies were protected. The banking system was restructured and privatized. The secret service was brought under strict control. The constitution was amended to clarify and strengthen checks and balances.

Fast forward to 2002. Again, Slovaks went to the polls. Again, Meciar was a candidate for prime minister. And again, the European Union made it clear that Slovakia's candidacy would be seriously damaged if Meciar came to power. Under EU pressure, Slovaks gave Meciar's HZDS party only 19.5 percent of the vote—its worst-ever performance. After Dzurinda took power in his second term as prime minister, the EU confirmed that Slovakia remained on course for entry. Sure enough, the country was given an official invitation to join Europe in the first round of new member accessions.

∞

Hungary's story is more like that of the Czech Republic. Hungary has never wavered from the goal of joining the EU—but it has often needed reminders of the right roads to travel. Hungarians actually began reforming in 1987—before the fall of communism. Both of the country's main political parties, the Socialist party and the right-of-center Fidesz party, vehemently support EU accession. So do the majority of Hungarians. In a 1997 referendum on EU accession, a whopping 85 percent of Hungarians voted in favor.

But there were problems. Thanks to post-World War I map-drawing, some 3.5 million ethnic Hungarians live outside Hungary. During the 1990s, as Yugoslavia was dissolving into ethnic bloodshed, ethnic Hungarians living in Romania and Slovakia were feeling insecure. Hungarian politicians saw an opportunity. By drumming up nationalist sentiment, they could gain support from all sections of Hungarian society. Rumblings of a "greater Hungary" movement sounded frighteningly similar to the "greater Serbia" policies of Slobodan Milosevic that had ripped apart the Balkans.

The EU was not amused. Brussels issued a blunt warning to Hungary, as well as to Romania and Slovakia, that if they did not resolve the issue, the chances for EU membership were slim. Hungary's politicians quickly retreated. By 1996, they had signed treaties with both Romania and Slovakia, resolving the border issues and guaranteeing protection for ethnic Hungarians.

On the economic front as well, EU pressure kept Hungary on track. The country's economic policy degraded in the 1990s to the point that government overspending had pushed Hungary's external debt to crisis levels. The currency was dangerously overvalued, driving up the current account deficit. The country's leadership, led by a prime minister who had once been a communist, seemed unrepentant and recalcitrant. But in the face of EU criticism, the government took drastic action. State spending was slashed. The currency was devalued. Inflation and external debt were both brought under control. The banking system, which had become a mess, was cleaned up. Ailing banks were consolidated, restructured, and recapitalized. Foreign banks were invited to invest and indeed took a dominant position in the sector.

These were not easy choices. Opposition politicians took potshots from the sidelines. But the government more or less stayed on course, and the privatization process attracted significant foreign investment. Throughout the latter half of the 1990s, Hungary registered impressive 4 to 5 percent GDP growth. Foreign companies such as Audi, IBM, Suzuki, GE, and Ford set up shop in the country.

Professor Laszlo Csaba, a scholar at a Budapest think tank, marveled at this accomplishment: "In France, Germany, and Italy, far smaller adjustments have produced much greater protests. This is proof that Hungarians don't believe serious political or economic alternatives [to EU membership] exist." Perhaps this is the reason that Hungarians are the most enthusiastically pro-Europe of all aspirants.

∞

Poland has been perhaps the most aggressive reformer, famously conducting a bold experiment with a "shock therapy" program of rapid economic liberalization that proved to be an extraordinary success. Poland's economy more than doubled in size between 1992 and 2000. During the second half of the 1990s, the Polish economy grew by an average of 5.5 percent per year, including some years of growth above 7 percent. Poland has sold roughly $12 billion worth of state assets and attracted over $40 billion in foreign investment.

The goal of EU membership provided powerful impetus for this stunning performance. A solid majority of Poles backs the country's accession to the EU. Poland's mainstream political parties are uniformly pro-EU. Poland's prime minister, Leczek Miller (a former Communist) has said that there have been two great moments in Polish history. The country's conversion to Christianity 1,000 years ago was the first. The second was its sixteenth-century empire that stretched from the Baltic to the Black Sea. EU accession, he suggested, would be the third.

That said, Poland also provides a cautionary tale. Poland has a vocal anti-Europe minority with deep skepticism about Europe's intentions. Poland's admission to the EU has been especially controversial within the EU because of both its relative poverty and its sheer size. The biggest hurdle is agriculture, which still employs roughly a quarter of all Poles. Free movement of labor is another problem. The EU worries that thousands of Poles will flock to Western Europe as soon as the borders open. Then there is the issue of land sales to foreigners, which provoked a popular outcry so loud that policymakers had to backtrack. The Self-Defense Party has used guerrilla tactics—both in parliament and on the streets—to protest EU-backed agricultural reforms. The party's support is greatest among farmers who fear they will lose out as part of the EU. Ironically, success has made dealing with this kind of dissent harder. Now that EU membership has been achieved, politicians can no longer use this goal to justify painful reforms; policy has been slipping, and Standard and Poor's recently put the country's sovereign ratings on negative watch.

It is no coincidence that left-of-center governments have won elections in the Czech Republic, Poland, and Hungary, and that Vladimir Meciar still retains a significant following among Slovaks. Large portions of these countries' populations have not benefited from EU-backed reforms. These people often fear what EU membership will bring. Still, the EU is a powerful source of external pressure on these countries. The goal of EU membership, with its very specific roadmap and signposts, kept these countries on track—dramatically so in the case of Slovakia, and more subtly elsewhere. That is a highly beneficial external shock.

THE DYNAMICS OF EXTERNAL SHOCKS

Reading the papers, it's not hard to conclude that international relations are the crux of politics. International summits tend to receive high-profile coverage, and coverage of even the threat of war can border on hysteria. In truth, local political dynamics are at least as important, but—as the cases of Argentina and Eastern Europe suggest—external shocks can profoundly influence a country's fortunes.

One type of shock is created by military threats, the impacts of which at first blush seem obvious. The goal of military action is often the overthrow of a government ("regime change" in today's parlance). Lopsided wars can destabilize the loser with stunning speed, as in the cases of Iraq versus Kuwait, Rwanda versus the Congo, and the U.S. versus Afghanistan and Iraq. But the impacts of most military conflicts (limited wars or stalemates, as opposed to swift defeats) are far more subtle and unexpected. For instance, it is ironic but true that foreign military threats tend to drastically increase the political power of the military in the *threatened* country. For instance, in the first years after its independence, Pakistan, which was then waging war with India, put 85 percent of its government budget into military spending. As a result, even as Pakistan's generals were losing battle after battle with India, they were winning battle after battle at home. Taking the lion's share of government funding, Pakistan's military grew (relatively) stronger as the rest of the government atrophied. It was not long before the generals were powerful enough to launch a successful military coup. In effect, the Indian military threat helped to turn Pakistan into a military regime.

Similar examples are found around the globe. Rich soldiers tend to develop a taste for power. In fact, research by Talukder Maniruzzaman has demonstrated that the more military aid a country receives, the more likely it is to experience a military coup and the longer a military government is likely to stay in power. Consider the case of Turkey, for instance, or Bangladesh, Ethiopia, Iraq, and many others. A military fattened by foreign aid tends to become the strongest political institution in a country.

Military governments are rarely successful rulers. Soldiers tend to run authoritarian regimes that do a poor job of dealing with public discontent. Relatively enlightened military rulers—some would point to Augusto Pinochet in Chile and others to the Turkish military—are the exception, not the rule. Even worse, military rulers tend to promote conflicts. Without a conflict, there is little reason for the military to stay in power, or consume its large share of government spending. Hence, generals are rarely peace-makers, and are often warmongers.

∞

Military conflict is an old (though ongoing) example of the shocks that can result from global interconnectedness. The newest story may be financial contagion. It is difficult to exaggerate the extent of the damage caused by the devaluation of the Thai currency in 1997. The contagion from this single event spread to Indonesia, Malaysia, the Philippines, and South Korea; from there to Brazil; then to Russia and Turkey; and finally to Argentina. "Finally" is, of course, the wrong word—in the wake of the Argentine collapse, neighboring Uruguay's economy began to implode. Prior to this extraordinary chain of events, one might have assumed it possible for Thailand—with an economy half the size of Belgium's—to disappear entirely from the face of the earth without much of a notable effect on global commerce. The fact that Thailand's currency collapse instead unleashed a domino effect that toppled emerging markets around the world is testimony to the fact that global markets are connected more tightly and in more ways than many had ever realized.

To be sure, economic contagion is nothing new. Whenever the U.S. economy has suffered a downturn, for example, Canada usually suffered a downturn as well, because so many of its exports go south. What is new is the massive volume of trade, investment, and lending that connects the world's economies. World merchandise trade expanded from $58 billion in 1948 to $6.2 trillion in 2000; foreign direct investment, from just $57 billion in 1982, to $1.3 trillion in 2000. The result is that everybody does business with everyone else, given a few degrees of separation. (Argentina relied on financing from foreign banks, many of which lent generously to Russia, which exports oil to Asia, which suffered a financial crisis—and thus the fallout from Asia eventually touched faraway Argentina.)

Another type of financial contagion is portfolio contagion. This type of contagion also comes in many forms. Its simplest variant occurs when investors who have taken losses in one market sell shares in another market to cover their losses. In addition to trading with and lending to Southeast Asia, Western countries had invested a great deal in Asian stock markets. When these investments went sour, banks and hedge funds often sold shares in unrelated markets in order to pay margin calls. South Africa is perhaps the most famous victim of this problem. South African markets plunged during the Asian financial crisis, for no obvious reason—the country had generally sound fundamentals and no significant economic links with Southeast Asia. But South Africa did have highly liquid stocks—in other words, it was easy to sell South African shares. Hence investors seeking to cover their Asian losses often sold their South African holdings.

Third and finally, there is "pure" financial contagion—defined cynically as "contagion for no good reason at all." Countries suffering from the economic crises of their neighbors are quick to condemn international investors for confusing apples and oranges. There is probably some truth to this; many investors, fleeing in panic from the Thai currency crash, may not have taken the time to note the crucial differences between Malaysia and Thailand—specifically, Malaysia's relatively manageable foreign borrowings. However, "pure" contagion can also represent a rethinking of investors' expectations. During the bursting of the dot-com bubble in the United States, for instance, the conspicuous failure of a few high-profile companies to generate any profits helped investors realize that other Internet companies faced an equally bleak future. Similarly, Thailand's collapse helped investors realize that there were unsustainable bubbles in other Asian economies—Malaysia's property sector, for example.

∞

Why are some countries so prone to catching the "Asian flu" or awakening with a "Tequila effect" hangover, while others escape relatively unscathed? (Chile, for example, has generally managed to avoid the fate of its imploding neighbors.) Many factors expose a country to external shocks. A dependence on commodity exports is one. Prices of commodities—oil and gas, minerals, agricultural products—tend to be set on world markets and tend to cost the same everywhere, whether in Lagos or London or Los Angeles. Something that happens at the far end of the earth—say, increased coffee production in Vietnam—can influence other coffee-producing countries all around the world. Commodity price declines played a role in worsening the financial crises in Indonesia (oil), Russia (also oil), and Argentina (agricultural products and minerals).

This is not a new story. Oil price declines were a major factor spurring the 1978-1979 revolution in Iran.

An even more contemporary vulnerability to contagion is created by a dependence on foreign financing. Private borrowers in the Asian crisis countries, for instance, had taken out large short-term loans from foreign banks, usually denominated in dollars. When the currencies declined, the loans could no longer be serviced and the financing dried up. Sudden and devastating crises followed. The Argentina case was in some ways similar: its government had been floating bonds in international markets in order to finance its growing debt, but the effect was largely the same—it had become dependent on foreign financing to manage its debt burden. When this financing was unavailable, a debt default was the result.

Foreign financing problems suggest a counterintuitive insight. In a world of volatile global capital flows, the countries with the best performance today are increasingly likely to go bust tomorrow. Good economic performance, as in Asia and Argentina, attracts foreign lenders and portfolio investors. But this foreign financing creates vulnerability to external shocks. Today's bubble is tomorrow's financial crisis.

Another factor creating vulnerability to external shocks deserves special mention: the issue of "transparency." Browsing through back issues of the *New York Times*, one finds that from 1980 to 1995, roughly 65 articles per year mention "transparency," nearly all of these in reference to art or design. In 1996 the number increases somewhat, to 79 articles. Then with Thailand's crash in July 1997, the frequency jumps dramatically, to 98 articles. And in 1998—with the Asian financial crisis in full swing—more than 140 articles mention the word.

Loosely speaking, a lack of transparency means that crucial information is hidden from view. In the Asian financial crisis, for instance, poor accounting standards allowed Asian banks and companies to disguise their true financial health. Even more crucially, the Thai government dramatically misreported its foreign exchange exposures. More recently, the failure of energy trading company Enron to disclose its true financial performance created a stock price bubble and then shocking collapse. A lack of transparency is dangerous because markets that depend on guesswork are extremely volatile. During the Internet bubble in the U.S., for instance, investors were guessing how profitable dot-com business models would prove, because the technology was completely new. Of course, their guesses about the future turned out to be dramatically wrong, the bubble burst, and the market suddenly collapsed.

A similar process was at work in Asia. Foreign investors were certainly foolish and gullible, in some respects. They believed that Asian companies and banks were healthy and investing their money wisely. In reality, much of the money was lent to the well connected and went to dubious property speculation. The foreign investors were forced to rely on guesswork because Asian markets were not transparent. When some important guesses turned out to be wrong, the markets took a vicious turn.

A similar process took place in Mexico. In 1994, the country was in the run-up to a presidential election. On the surface, the country appeared stable and investors assumed that the political monopoly of the long-ruling PRI remained intact. The Mexican government actively obscured looming economic problems by failing to report its foreign exchange holdings for some seven months, as these holdings were being dramatically depleted. A guerrilla war and the assassination of the PRI presidential candidate cast doubt on this mirage of normalcy. At the time, all investors had to go on was their instincts about Mexico. And they assumed the worst. Net portfolio capital flows turned sharply negative. Eventually this triggered a financial crisis.

∞

But all of these negative examples should not obscure the fact that some external shocks can benefit a country tremendously. History provides some dramatic examples. The occupation of Germany and Japan by the victorious Allied powers helped to launch those countries toward stability and prosperity. Although America's attempts to influence South Vietnam were a stunning failure, the net effect of American pressure on South Korea can probably be judged a success.

The contemporary version of this foreign pressure is World Bank and International Monetary Fund reform programs. After India suffered a balance of payments crisis in 1991, for example, the IMF pressured the country to adopt market reforms. These reforms created a growing class of business leaders who, in turn, agitated for more reform. The case of the EU's influence on Central and Eastern Europe is another example.

EU pressure has helped prevent the kind of infighting among elites that has destabilized many postcommunist countries. In short, external shocks can drive positive political dynamics, producing success in the most unlikely places.

EXTERNAL SHOCKS POSTSCRIPT:
GLOBALIZATION'S UNEXPECTED CONNECTIONS

Chaos theory studies systems that exhibit complex but ultimately predictable behavior. The weather is one example: it's fairly predictable over a few hours, less predictable over a few days, and mostly unpredictable beyond that. This does not mean that the weather is random and therefore unpredictable. Rather, it means that weather patterns are so complex that small errors in prediction are magnified over time to the point that, beyond a few days, predictions are almost totally meaningless. This principle is expressed in the famous claim that "a butterfly flapping its wings in China could cause a hurricane in New York." Not knowing about the butterfly, one might fail to predict the hurricane.

As with the weather, so with politics. Consider the remarkable story of coffee in the 1990s. Throughout much of the 1980s, coffee cost about $2 per pound—enough to earn coffee producers like Brazil, Colombia, and Kenya a healthy profit. Exports of coffee beans from these countries generated large amounts of foreign exchange. Then, in 1994, an unexpected frost in Brazil destroyed much of the country's crop. The price of coffee soared. At $2.40 a pound, the Colombians and Kenyans were now making money hand over fist.

Wafting from those high-priced beans came the sweet smell of opportunity. At the time, Vietnam was working with the World Bank and International Monetary Fund to restructure its postcommunist economy. The country produced only about 1 million bags of coffee per year—but with its climate and cheap cost of labor, not to mention foreign aid and guidance, Vietnam had the potential to become a major player in the coffee market. With sky-high prices in 1994, this seemed like a good idea.

Coffee plantations take about four years to begin large-scale production. So, right on time, four years after the development program began, Vietnamese coffee hit the market. Major investments had allowed

Vietnam to become an almost instantaneous key player in that market, tripling its coffee production over the five years from 1994 to 1999, and surpassing Colombia to become the world's second-largest coffee producer. With Vietnam on the market, the supply of cheap robusta beans grew from an average of 27 million sacks between 1992 and 1996 to 43 million sacks in 2001. Total coffee production reached an all-time high of 115 million bags that year.

Up to this point, everything had gone as planned. But when Vietnam's beans hit the market, the result was a massive global oversupply. The oversupply triggered a theoretically predictable, but generally unexpected, collapse in the price of coffee. The price of a pound of coffee fell from over $2 to 95 cents in December 1999 and to 45 cents in October 2001—the lowest level in 36 years. In many parts of the world, coffee prices have fallen below the costs of production.

The proverbial butterfly had flapped its wings. At this point, the hurricane hit, and it hit all over the world. There are seventy coffee-growing countries, all earning basically the same price for their beans, and they all suffered—from Nicaragua to Indonesia, from Ethiopia to Colombia. In India, coffee growers staged massive protests demanding government support for their industry. In Mexico, many of the country's 3 million coffee workers went bankrupt, and large numbers of the newly unemployed migrated illegally into the U.S. Kenya and Tanzania experienced a surge in the number of AIDS cases as former coffee farmers abandoned their rural communities, often leaving their wives behind, and moved to the cities. In Nicaragua, drug smuggling increased dramatically as coffee growers lost their traditional source of income. In 2001, Colombia earned roughly 30 percent less from its coffee exports than in the previous year. An estimated 560,000 families are involved in cultivating coffee in Colombia and many of them, searching for alternatives, switched to coca growing.

And all of this because of Vietnam—and decisions made with IMF and World Bank support. Call it chaos theory in action.

∞

Another story of unexpected connections was triggered by the global migration of labor. Poor countries, with not enough jobs to satisfy their own citizens, have exported their labor force to richer countries. Many of these laborers support a family back home. Much of what these people earn is sent back to the countries they come from, as so-called "remittance income." What started as a trickle has today become a flood, resulting in a huge and unexpected source of funds for the poorest countries. In 2001 alone, $72.3 billion was remitted by migrant workers, according to the World Bank. Migrant laborers in the U.S. alone sent home $28.4 billion. Indeed, total annual remittances now exceed the amount of foreign aid received by the developing world.

These numbers are not necessarily large from a rich-world point of view. But to a developing country, the remittances are a huge transfer of wealth. Mexico, for instance, receives $10 billion every year from its expatriate workers in the United States. Indeed, an astounding one-third of the population of the Mexican state of Zacatecas now resides in the U.S. Nepalese expatriate workers who are mostly employed in India and the Persian Gulf send home remittances equal to 13 percent of Nepal's GDP and 50 percent of the country's foreign exchange earnings. In Albania, a quarter of the workforce works abroad, predominantly in Greece: each year they send home roughly $500 million, or 17 percent of their country's GDP. Ecuador earned $1.4 billion in 2001 from the 400,000 Ecuadorian workers abroad—mostly in the U.S. and Spain. Morocco earned $3.3 billion in 2001 from its overseas nationals, mostly working in Europe. Bangladesh earned an estimated $2.1 billion that year. South Africa, as the largest African economy, attracts a huge number of migrant laborers; according to a survey, three quarters of all Mozambican families have at least one family member working there.

But the world's premier exporter of labor is the Philippines. In the 1970s, the country began to promote the idea of working overseas as a way to earn foreign exchange and bring down chronically high unemployment. By 1982, 110 countries had recruited workers from the Philippines. Currently, roughly 10 percent of the country's population, some 7.5 million people, works overseas, earning an estimated $6.4 billion in 2001. Filipinos work in the construction industry in Saudi Arabia, entertain in Japanese nightclubs, work as nannies and maids in Hong Kong, serve in hospitals in the U.S. and Europe, and teach in Africa.

This is an extraordinary source of income, but it is also vulnerable to external shocks. Millions of Somalis have escaped starvation because of the remittance income from overseas Somali workers. But in the wake of September 11, the U.S. closed down Somalia's main money transfer company, Al Barakat, accusing it of having links to Usama bin Laden and the al-Qaeda organization. To many Somali towns that, according to United Nations estimates, earn roughly 40 percent of their income from remittances, this U.S. action was devastating.

The boom and bust in the Persian Gulf had far wider effects. As oil wealth poured into the region during the 1970s, millions of Arabs followed the money to work in jobs ranging from university professors to construction workers. Egypt supplied 43 percent of these migrant laborers in the Gulf, who sent home $3.3 billion in remittances in 1984 alone. Unofficial estimates put the figure closer to $10 billion per year—making remittance income Egypt's largest source of foreign exchange. But then, in the mid-1980s, oil prices came crashing down. Saudi Arabia earned $120 billion from oil exports in 1980 but only $43 billion in 1985. The result was a mass exodus of migrant workers—roughly 1 million Arabs working in the Persian Gulf returned to their countries in the mid-1980s. Egypt, Jordan, Sudan, and Yemen were especially hard hit. Jordan's economy went into recession. Yemen is estimated to have lost about 5 percent of its annual GDP growth. In 1983, Yemen exported a paltry $10 million worth of goods, but earned about $1.2 billion from its overseas labor force.

Then came the Gulf War. All told, remittance earnings in the Gulf countries declined $23 billion in 1990 and 1991. The resulting economic pain was felt from India and Pakistan to Sri Lanka, Bangladesh, and the Philippines. Indeed Pakistan could no longer finance its current account deficit and suffered a balance of payments crisis, ending up in an IMF reform program.

More recently, the U.S. economic downturn has had repercussions throughout Latin America. The Immigration and Naturalization Service estimates that 60 percent of the funds remitted annually from the U.S. is sent to Central and South America and the Caribbean. Nicaragua derives 16.2 percent of its GDP from remittance income; El Salvador, 13.8 percent; Jamaica, 13.5 percent, the Dominican Republic, 9.3 percent, and Honduras, 8.5 percent. Nicaragua estimates that, because of the U.S.

downturn, it might lose 30 to 40 percent of the $800 million it receives every year in remittances. The Dominican Republic has recently suffered a sovereign rating downgrade. Remittance income is an unexpected boon—indeed, a more stable source of income than portfolio capital flows, notes the World Bank—but unexpected connections are not without their risks.

Economic Potential Energy

INSTITUTIONS

IN THE LAST TWO DECADES, A GREAT REVOLUTION HAS TAKEN place. This revolution involved no tanks or soldiers, guerrillas or riots. This was a revolution in our understanding of what makes countries work. The revolutionaries in this case were not Maoists or Islamists but rather scholars: Douglass North (who won a Nobel Prize for his efforts), Oliver Williamson, William Baumol, and Hernando de Soto, to name a few.

The revolutionary insight these scholars have produced, stated simplistically, is that no matter how excellent a country's economic policies, how educated and skilled its people, how plentiful its natural resources, or how high its level of development aid, that country will not grow prosperous in the absence of good institutions—stable property rights, strong enforcement of contracts, transparent and consistent regulation, and so on.

Like many great insights, this one seems obvious in retrospect. But for decades this principle was ignored. Foreign aid agencies poured billions of dollars into mega-projects (dams, roads, railways) in the developing world, expecting to launch economic growth. They were genuinely shocked when their policies did not trigger dramatic development and, what's worse, many of the recipient countries slipped backwards into even greater poverty.

The fundamental insight of institutional economics is that people respond to incentives, and these incentives are shaped by institutions. People by nature are innovative and pursue prosperity. The question is, will they pursue their own prosperity by stealing state assets, organizing a guerrilla revolt, attempting to collect bribes, or—just perhaps—by starting a successful business? By and large, people choose the path that seems most likely to yield success for themselves and their families. In some countries, people pour their energy into developing innovative high-tech products. In other countries, people pour their energy into developing innovative convoluted scams. Both may require brilliant insights, perhaps, but they will have spectacularly different results in terms of generating prosperity. The prospective gains to be had from either approach are determined by institutions.

"Institutions" in this case does not mean hospitals or universities. Rather, institutions here are "the rules of the game," the constraints on human behavior—including laws, regulations, and customs—running the gamut from highly formal rules (the U.S. Constitution) to quite informal rules (how to behave at the dinner table). These rules are sometimes broken (people steal; people run red lights; the occasional cretin will use the salad fork for the main course). But on balance, people tend to obey the rules, because it requires less mental effort to do so (or they are punished for disobedience), and therefore institutions tend to persist over time.

A country's labor and capital are a mass of economic potential energy. The question is, how will this energy be spent? On economically creative activity or on economically destructive activity? In the countries that go down the former path, wealth will be created and the population as a whole will gradually become rich. In the countries that go down the other route, a few people will get rich but national wealth will stagnate and the vast majority will remain desperately poor.

RUSSIA

In 1991, Russia stood on a precipice contemplating a long and essentially irreversible leap into the unknown. The greatest centrally planned economy in history, in which markets and private property officially did not exist, was about to be abolished. The Communist Party, which had completely dominated the government for roughly seven decades, was about to be outlawed. What kind of system would replace these all-powerful institutions, which had run politics and the economy for so long that only a handful of Russians had experienced anything else? Nobody knew.

At the same time, Russia stood poised to make a powerful leap. This was no postcolonial "least-developed country" attempting to pull itself up by its bootstraps; this was a country with a 99 percent literacy rate and an abundance of skilled labor, natural resources, and high technology; a country that had exported its politics around the world and built a space station. It had the undivided attention of the world's greatest economic minds; access to foreign aid and loans (admittedly given stingily at first); and its own brilliant and well-trained home-grown economic talent (Yegor Gaidar and Grigori Yavlinsky to name just two). Russia also had no shortage of role models to choose from. Taiwan and South Korea had proved that it was possible to leap from poverty to prosperity in a single generation; Japan and Germany had proved it was possible to recover quickly from a devastating political and economic catastrophe; China had proved that it was possible to undertake a postcommunist transition at extraordinary rates of economic growth.

So it was with great expectations that Russia's leaders launched an aggressive program of economic reform. Price controls would be abolished, industries privatized, and restrictions on economic activity lifted. In fits and starts, this is in fact what happened. Between 1991 and 1996, roughly 18,000 of Russia's industrial enterprises were privatized. In a few short years, Russia's private sector grew from near insignificance to account for close to 90 percent of the country's industrial production.

But that was 90 percent of a rapidly shrinking pie. As is now well known, Russia's market reforms unleashed an economic disaster. Over the course of the 1990s, the Russian economy contracted by nearly 50 percent. Between 30 and 40 million Russians fell below the poverty line. Infectious diseases such as tuberculosis became major public health threats. Alcoholism rose dramatically. The life expectancy of the average Russian actually fell, from 69 years in 1990 to 64 years, and to only 57 for males, toward the middle of the decade. And after all this, and despite more than $70 billion in international aid, at the end of the 1990s, Russia suffered a financial crisis and defaulted on its foreign debt repayments.

A difficult transition was expected, but this was a shock. What about Russia's highly educated workforce? The outdated but extensive industrial base? The well-developed infrastructure? The famed scientists? How could it be that all of this productive potential, instead of being unleashed by market reform, could instead have been wasted?

There are of course many causes. No story this complex has a single villain. But the story can be told simply, and it revolves around institutions. At bottom, halfway reforms created an institutional environment in which Russia's productive potential—human brilliance, industrial might, and rich resources—were, to a large degree, not simply unused, but actually misused. Many Russians, from ordinary factory workers to the captains of industry, had tremendous incentives to do things that were profoundly destructive to their country's economic well-being. And this is indeed what they did.

Institutions are crucial everywhere, yet in few cases is the story as clear as in Russia. Countries with poor institutions tend to remain impoverished. Fundamentally, it is hard to account for the absence of something—in this case, economic growth—especially considering that poor countries tend to have many other problems (political instability, bad economic policies, crippling debt). The Russian case is very different. Educated, urbanized, resource-rich, industrialized Russia had a lot to lose, and it lost it dramatically, suddenly, and very obviously. Over the course of the 1990s, an estimated $300 billion of the country's wealth was simply looted and sent abroad to Swiss bank accounts and the like. Unlike most stories about institutions, this one is dramatic.

∞

Many have pointed out that Russia has never had a tradition of private property. In Western Europe, even in medieval times, kings were said to obey the principle of "unto kings belongs the power of all things and unto individual men, property," from the Roman philosopher Seneca. This was the uncrossed line that separated enlightened monarchs from tyrants. Russia's czars, on the other hand, had no such qualms about private property. Their absolute rule included de facto possession of all the lands and riches of their domains. Commoners and nobles alike served only as tenants of the czars' property. When the Soviets took power in 1917, any ambiguity about property under the czars was eliminated via the outright abolishment of private property and private enterprise. Some brief experiments with markets were erased by Stalin's uncompromising collectivization program. State ownership and central planning were the economic order for the next fifty years.

And this was what Premier Mikhail Gorbachev inherited in the late 1980s, but when he did it was on the verge of economic collapse. Remarkably, Soviet planners came up with a "500-day Plan" for "instant capitalism." In a country with no tradition of private property, which had been dominated by central planning for as long as anyone could remember, this was quite a leap. Gorbachev shied away from making the leap. Under the heading "*perestroika*," he implemented dramatic but only partial reforms. Some prices were freed but many remained state-controlled. Some restrictions on private enterprise were lifted but some subsidies remained in place. Some private property rights were created but others (notably for ownership of land) remained in state hands. This was a formula for disaster; Gorbachev's halfway reforms opened tremendous loopholes through which Russia's state assets were simply stolen.

Take but one example. Prices of commodities remained state-controlled, while regulations on private business activity were lifted. This created an extraordinary opportunity, one that managers of state-owned enterprises were generally unable to resist. In the early 1990s, the state-controlled price of a ton of crude oil was 30 rubles—roughly the same as the market price of one pack of Marlboro cigarettes. With foreign trade liberalized, enterprise managers could buy Russian oil from state firms at the state-controlled price of 30 rubles and then sell this oil abroad at market prices, pocketing millions of dollars in the process. In 1992, attempts to close this loophole by reformers under the leadership of Yegor Gaidar were rebuffed by powerful state enterprise managers, politicians, and government officials, who were growing rich off the embezzlement scam. Scholar Anders Aslund estimates that the total take from reselling underpriced natural resources approached $24 billion—an incredible 30 percent of Russia's annual economic output.

One more example. In the early 1990s, the central bank had come under the control of a hard-line antireformer named Viktor Gerashchenko. Gerashchenko suddenly realized he had the power to distribute loans to anyone he wanted, at whatever interest rates he chose. Money does not grow on trees, as the saying goes, but it does grow in central bank vaults.

Gerashchenko made friends quickly by handing out credits directly to state enterprises, often with no expectation of repayment, at hugely negative real interest rates. For Gerashchenko and his cronies, it was a temptation too lucrative to resist. In 1992 alone, the central bank handed out credits worth 32 percent of Russia's annual output. Geraschenko was dubbed "the worst central banker of any major country in history" by Harvard professor Jeffrey Sachs.

Thankfully, many of these loopholes were closed by the mid-1990s, but extraordinary damage had already been done. Aslund estimated the total amount plundered via these kinds of parasitic economic activities at nearly 80 percent of Russia's GDP in 1992 alone. This was not just unproductive, it was profoundly destructive. The theft of natural resources diminished national wealth, and cheap central bank credits unleashed hyperinflation. But the most infamous Russian scam was still to come: the "loans-for-shares" deal of 1994.

This was by no means the first theft of state resources, and probably not the worst, but for sheer unashamed avarice it was breathtaking. For instance, through one loans-for-shares deal, business tycoon Mikhail Khodorkovsky, in effect, acquired the Yukos oil company for $159 million. That was a mind-boggling discount. In 1999 alone, Yukos produced crude oil worth roughly $8 billion on world markets. The company's 11.5 billion barrels of proven reserves were roughly equivalent to those held by British Petroleum prior to its merger with Amoco, when British Petroleum was valued at $85 billion. Hence, $159 million for Yukos was, as some called it, the "sale of the century."

The actual "loans-for-shares" scheme was convoluted enough to defy simple explanation. The Russian treasury, short on cash, took out loans from leading private banks and gave shares in state-owned companies to these banks as collateral. When the government defaulted on the loans, the banks gained the right to sell the shares at auction. At first this sounds like a convoluted privatization scheme—but the complex deals were actually rigged. The loans to the government were structured in such a way that the government was almost certain to default. The auctions were set up in such a way that the banks could choose to whom they sold the shares and keep the prices low, and the business tycoons who provided the loans in the first place almost always walked away with the shares at the end. In short, what had happened was an elaborate scam to transfer the chief assets of Russia's state-owned enterprises to well-connected business tycoons at knock-down prices.

∞

Thus the "oligarchs" stepped onto the Russian scene. The oligarchs were the tycoons who came to control vast business empires straddling banking, industry, and the media, often by exploiting loopholes created by partial reform. Khodorkovsky, for instance, was a leader of the Soviet youth organization who, in the confusion of the late 1980s, managed to obtain worthless accounting rubles, then convert them into real rubles, and then convert those rubles into dollars. Vladimir Potanin, a former Soviet bureaucrat, used his connections to win control of a state bank and then convinced Russian government ministries to do all their banking with him.

It is tempting to single out the oligarchs as the great villains of the Russian collapse. And, to be sure, many Russians did. With their fur coats, gaudy cars, and ostentatious villas, the oligarchs look like the picture of evil to a Russian struggling to make ends meet. But the oligarchs were just responding to the perverse incentives that weak institutions created. The oligarchs could have invested in revitalizing poorly performing Soviet enterprises, but there was little prospect of reward if they followed that course. The far more lucrative route was to exploit connections, government weaknesses, and contradictory regulations in order to strip state-owned assets and build business empires and Swiss bank accounts with the proceeds. As Chrystia Freeland, the *Financial Times* Russia bureau chief for much of the 1990s, put it: "In a country of corrupt bureaucrats, weak legal guarantees for investment, and taxes that are both impossibly high and haphazardly imposed, the oligarchs' tactics actually constitute the only rational business strategy. In short, for all their myriad sins, the oligarchs are merely a symptom of Russia's disease, not the disease itself."

∞

Why did Russia's best and brightest gravitate towards scams, which—at least in theory—carry the possibility of dire punishment, when they could have invested in building legitimate businesses? First, scams offered the possibility of staggering rewards (as the oligarchs demonstrated). Second, it was extremely hard to make a "real" business work.

Ironically, during the transition from state planning to "free markets," the size of the Russian government actually expanded. Between 1992 and 1998, more than 1.2 million bureaucrats were hired, almost 2 percent of the total labor force. These jobs did not pay well—in fact, at some points when the government ran short of funds, they hardly paid at all—but they offered excellent opportunities for collecting bribes. In 1991, the All Union Research Institute of the Soviet Interior Ministry estimated that half the income of an average government functionary came from bribes. As the bureaucracy expanded, Russian companies could expect almost a visit a day from one of the sixty-seven different government agencies responsible for supervising business. In many cases the pretext of regulation was all but abandoned in favor of out-and-out extortion. As oligarch Mikhail Smolensky put it, the officials who issue licenses and permits "practically have a price list hanging on the office wall." By one assessment, petty bribery alone accounted for 20 percent of business costs in Russia.

This was not the only obstacle to legitimate business. The Russian tax code was complex, contradictory, and easily manipulated. Roughly 200 different levies were on the books. Oligarchs simply bribed tax collectors to avoid making payments, and small businesses without connections faced extortion from government officials. All the bribery and bureaucracy made it extremely difficult to run a (legitimate) company. Entrepreneurs starting up new businesses had to deal with as many as thirty government agencies to obtain vital permits and approvals. Russian managers spent a third of their time dealing with government officials—even in infamously bureaucratic El Salvador, that figure wasn't more than 12 percent. The predictable result was that Russians did not start businesses. In 1999, the number of legally registered enterprises was about one for every fifty-five people, compared with one for every ten people in Poland and Hungary.

∞

What businesses did exist were deliberately run inefficiently, because managers had powerful incentives to run them that way. For years after the end of communism, Russia's state-owned enterprises existed in a bizarre state of limbo that scholars Clifford Gaddy and Barry Ickes memorably dubbed Russia's "virtual economy." By 1997, 40 percent of all tax payments to the Russian government, and 50 percent of all payments among state enterprises, were made in barter rather than cash. A Russian commission set up to investigate this bizarre phenomenon found, "An economy is emerging where prices are charged which no one pays in cash; where no one pays anything on time; where huge mutual debts are created that also can't be paid off in reasonable periods of time; where wages are declared and not paid; and so on…"

The commission found that the country's largest enterprises conducted 73 percent of their business in barter. The reason for this quasi-medieval shift in the Russian economy was that the real prices of goods and services had to be disguised. If cash appeared at any point in the business process—whether as wages, taxes, payments to suppliers, and so on—then the real value of the goods was revealed. What Russia's state enterprises were hiding was that many of them were "subtracting value"—the goods they produced were nearly worthless or, at least, worth less than the value of the labor and raw materials that went into making them. By conducting most transactions in barter (at arbitrary rates of exchange) this destruction of value could be disguised. To the casual observer, it looked like a "real" economy (people were working; products were shipping). But in actual fact nothing of value was being done. This was especially true in the defense sector of the Russian economy, which went into free fall after the collapse of communism.

The management consulting firm McKinsey conducted an extensive study in 1999 of business management practices in Russian industries ranging from steel and cement to confectionery, hotels, and software. They repeatedly found that a lack of resources was not the problem—Russian firms had the talent and the capital to succeed. McKinsey reported that even the notorious value-destroying state-owned companies could be brought up to 65 percent of U.S. productivity levels with "limited upgrade investments" and better management.

However, McKinsey found that Russian companies' overall productivity rates were only at 19 percent of U.S. levels. Tellingly, since the fall of the U.S.S.R., productivity levels in the "virtual economy" of state-owned enterprises had actually declined by roughly 50 percent. Roughly a quarter of Russia's industrial capacity was in obsolete value-destroying assets whose productivity would have been higher if they simply ceased operation. Perhaps most surprisingly, what new investment was being made was also extremely inefficient. New assets brought online after 1992 had an average of only 30 percent of U.S. productivity levels—only about 10 percent better than the companies built under communism.

Across the economy, in a variety of industries, McKinsey found that Russian firms were deliberately operating and making investments in an unproductive fashion. Almost invariably the reason was that a lack of productivity was rewarded by a poor institutional environment. In the steel sector, loss-making firms were excused from paying their energy bills, their largest single production cost. Hence the better-run firms were punished for their success by being forced to subsidize the energy bills of the loss-making firms. In confectionery, inefficient firms did not have to pay taxes; hence, they were actually more profitable than their well-run foreign competitors. In residential construction, contracts went to the best-connected companies regardless of productivity, and often on the condition that the companies not lay off excess workers. In food retailing, the larger and more efficient a store was, the higher the tax rates it had to pay and the more intrusive the regulation it faced. Responding predictably to this incentive structure, Russian firms were obligingly inefficient. In industry after industry, the most productive firms were often the least profitable firms. With perhaps some exaggeration, McKinsey estimated that Russia could improve its annual economic growth rate by 8 percent per year by removing these distortions.

∞

Indeed, much of the business done in Russia was actually criminal. Throughout the 1990s, restrictions on business activities were removed, but new capitalist institutions—competent regulatory agencies, commercial laws, and independent courts, which make and enforce the rules of legitimate economic activity—had not yet been created. Companies were not held to regular disclosure announcements. Dividends and proxy voting were unregulated. Shareholders were kept in the dark about the companies they were invested in. Hence the scale of fraudulent corporate activity dramatically increased. A pyramid scheme called MMM defrauded Russian investors of perhaps $2 billion. In 1999, the newly privatized Yukos oil company forced its subsidiaries to sell it oil at $1.70 a barrel, when the market price was about $15; Yukos paid a total of $408 million for something that should have cost $3.6 billion. It then exported about a quarter of that oil to world markets, essentially siphoning off about $800 million in thirty-six weeks.

Instead of taking deposits and making loans on market criteria, Russia's banks concentrated their efforts on obtaining government subsidies, trading in government debt, and getting their hands on government assets through crooked privatizations. These activities were far more lucrative than legitimate banking could have been in the Russian environment. The banks also became the center of oligarch business empires. They were tightly linked to affiliated companies and sometimes even owned by affiliated companies, for which they functioned as illegitimate treasury departments, infusing cheap credit and channeling profits offshore. Making use of connections to corruptible government bureaucrats, the banks often simply stole public funds. Some $512 million in government funds deposited in a bank affiliated with Vladimir Potanin simply disappeared. At around the same time, billions of dollars in government deposits intended for the reconstruction of Chechnya also vanished.

There is always a demand for law and order, and when the government cannot provide it, others will step in to fill the void. The infamous "Russian mafia," with an estimated 35,000 members by 1995, ran more than just the usual prostitution, gambling, and drug rackets. Colorful thugs with nicknames like "Sylvester," "Baboon," and "the Jap" eventually worked their way into banks, real estate markets, and the stock exchanges. Infamous mobsters like Vladimir "The Poodle" Podiatev came to control political and business empires; in his city of Khabarovsk, Podiatev even ran his own political party and television station.

Russia's mafia grew powerful partially because it was needed. Businesses—such as restaurants, kiosks, and cafes—paid protection money, which kept them free of petty crooks and even meddling government officials. It was a rough version of justice. Unlike the state, the mafia could enforce contracts. Unlike the state, the mafia could ensure payment of tribute. And unlike the state, the mafia was obeyed. According to government statistics, roughly three-quarters of all Russian businesses and commercial banks paid protection money—equivalent to between 10 percent and 20 percent of their turnover, and half their profits. One estimate is that organized crime oversaw commercial transactions comprising 40 percent of the turnover in goods and services by 1993. As oligarch Mikhail Smolensky put it, "The only lawyer in this country is the Kalashnikov. People mostly solve their problems in this way. In this country, there is no respect for the law, no culture of law, no judicial system—it's just being created."

Then there were the infamous "share dilution" schemes. In 1997, for example, the privatized oil company Sibneft issued 44 million new shares in its production company. Rather dull financial news, one might think, except that the shares were issued at below-market prices to affiliates of Sibneft, and the affiliates then transferred the shares back to the parent company. The result of this complex transaction was to expropriate the stakes of Sibneft's other owners, by diluting their equity by 75 percent.

Foreign investors famously bore the brunt of many of these deals. In 1994, representatives of U.K.-based TransWorld Metals were attending a stockholders' meeting in Siberia for the Krasnoyarsk Aluminum Smelter, one of the world's largest aluminum producers. TransWorld owned 20 percent of the smelter, but when its representatives arrived at the meeting, they found that their names had simply been expunged from the shareholders' register and they no longer owned anything. An equally famous case was that of BP Amoco. In 1997, it invested $571 million into Sidanko, Russia's fifth-largest oil company. Shortly thereafter, BP lost much of the value of its investment as Sidanko was put into bankruptcy and its assets transferred to Russian companies in dubious proceedings. Not all of these things were actually illegal, according to Russian law— but then again, that is exactly the point. During the "lost decade" of the 1990s, the Russian institutional environment often rewarded inefficiency, duplicity and outright theft.

∽

Considering the depth of Russia's economic disaster—an almost 50 percent economic contraction and $300 billion shipped overseas—villainous characters and actions of dubious morality were certainly easy to find in the 1990s. Some have blamed the economic chaos on supposed defects in the Russian character, or the oligarchs or the Mafia. But Russia's "lost decade" involved a wide spectrum of society: mobsters, bankers, oligarchs, bureaucrats, politicians, managers of state-owned enterprises in industries ranging from oil to finance to steel. The sudden and widespread plunder and misdirection of energy and resources that followed the fall of Communism took more than a few bad apples. Fundamentally, it was driven by powerful incentives to which many of Russia's best and brightest responded. The best opportunities were in unproductive activity and even outright theft. And that, on a grand scale, is what took place.

BOTSWANA

In the fall of 2001, a Japanese economist learned that Moody's, the international bond-rating agency, was threatening a dramatic downgrade of Japan's sovereign bonds, from an "Aa3" rating to "A2," indicating an increased risk that the Japanese government would be unable to pay its debts. The economist flipped through his most recent Moody's sovereign ratings report.

His finger ran down the page. So Japan would be rated as more risky than France and Spain, he mused. Rated lower than Singapore, Sweden and the U.K. Below Belgium, Italy, Portugal, Botswana.

Botswana? Some hurried Internet research ensued. Botswana, it turned out, was a landlocked southern African country with neighbors including war-torn Angola and crisis-stricken Zimbabwe. The Japanese economist was dumfounded. Japan rated lower than Botswana? Japan was the second-largest economy in the world. Japan gave development aid to Botswana. The story soon hit the media, and it was big news. Talk show hosts and editorialists never tired of repeating the incredible comparison. Moody's analysts were hauled before the Japanese parliament to explain themselves. Amidst all the sound and fury, an important question went unasked: how did things in Botswana get so good?

That's not an easy question to answer, but Botswana has had an extraordinary run. Over the past thirty-five years, it has enjoyed the highest average annual rate of per capita economic growth (7.7 percent) of any country on earth, over the same period in which average per capita incomes in sub-Saharan Africa actually declined. Its current per capita income (adjusted on a purchasing-power parity basis) is $6,600, roughly equivalent to that of Brazil and four times the African average.

Those familiar with the mining industry might protest that this is not so amazing. After all, Botswana is the world's largest diamond producer. But diamonds have not helped other countries such as Sierra Leone, Angola, and the Congo, which currently rank among the world's poorest and most violent places. And Nigeria, with far more wealth in the form of oil, remains a disaster. Add to this the fact that Botswana is small, land-locked, and tropical, factors that, in combination, are hardly a formula for success. When Botswana became independent in 1966 it had a total of 12 kilometers of paved roads and 100 secondary-school graduates.

In short, there is something quite remarkable about Botswana. According to scholars Daron Acemoglu, Simon Johnson, and James A. Robinson, the secret of Botswana's success is its institutions. In essence, they argue that what is really important is to understand what happened *before* Botswana's diamonds were found. Typically, a huge discovery of natural resources does nothing good for a country. Rulers enrich themselves, creating a patronage regime that maintains power by handing out wealth to a few favored cronies (Nigeria). Or the discovery launches a civil war, as rival groups battle for control of the wealth (Angola). Or, if large enough, the resources completely fund the government budget, excusing the rulers from the need to collect taxes or maintain public support (Saudi Arabia). Natural resource wealth is rarely a blessing.

Botswana avoided these fates because it had uniquely good institutions that ensured the diamond wealth was channeled into productive uses. Instead of destabilizing the country, the funds from diamonds launched Botswana on a growth takeoff. Good institutions ensured that the gains from the diamonds were shared widely amongst the country's political elite, instead of ending up in the pockets of a chosen few. This growth takeoff soon launched a virtuous circle, all too sadly absent in most of Africa. Once the economy started growing rapidly, people could see that the system was working. Hence even those who felt they deserved a bigger share of the riches were less inclined to compromise that system.

∞

The first of these good institutions was built upon the tribal system of the Tswana peoples, from whom the name "Botswana" is derived.

The Tswana migrated from modern-day South Africa to the territory that would become Botswana in the eighteenth century. They lived in large settlements and raised cattle as their principal source of livelihood. Tswana society was virtually unique among southern African cultures in that adult male Tswana could actively participate in the political process through popular assemblies called *kgotla*. In the *kgotla*, tribesmen discussed communal issues, suggested solutions to problems, and debated methods to better society. They could openly criticize their chiefs and the king. The king also adjudicated court cases through the *kgotlas*.

Contrast this with, for instance, Somalia. Somalia at independence seemed in some respects to have bright prospects. Almost uniquely among postcolonial African nations, its people had a common history, culture, religion, and language, rather than a cobbled-together collection of unrelated ethnicities. It also had a relatively less-destructive experience with colonialism (of which, more later). But Somali culture—like most others in Africa—lacked the consultative *kgotla* assemblies and instead divided the country into competing clans. These clans, following independence, became warring factions in an ongoing battle over resources.

There were other Tswana countries in Southern Africa. Lesotho, for instance, is culturally identical to Botswana. Yet it has enjoyed none of Botswana's success. Unlike Botswana, Lesotho's traditional institutions were all but wiped out by colonialism. After a series of wars, the British in Lesotho followed a typical colonialist policy: divide and rule—favoritism to a few local elites—to prevent local groups from banding together against the occupying power. This elevation of favored elites in Lesotho undermined the *kgotla* consultative process and made the country's rulers (backed by the British army) accountable to no one. The country's first post-independence ruler, Chief Lebua Jonathan, orchestrated a military coup when elections went against his party.

This was a story repeated across Africa. There is strong statistical evidence that countries that were heavily colonized for the purpose of resource extraction are more likely to be impoverished today. Essentially, political institutions designed to extract wealth tended to persist even after colonialism ended. When the colonists left, the institutions were simply taken over and run to the benefit of African elites. Indeed, Acemoglu, Johnson, and Robinson estimate (with perhaps some exaggeration) that this "colonial institutions" variable may account for as much as three-quarters of the income gap between former colonies.

Botswana was more fortunate. In the first part of the eighteenth century, the Tswana tribes united—a rarity in Africa—to keep out the Boers. The British eventually colonized the territory in 1885—mostly because of its strategic location—but Britain did not impose direct rule. As Britain's high commissioner wrote at the time: "We have no interest in the country...except as a road to the interior; we might therefore confine ourselves for the present to...doing as little in the way of administration or settlement as possible." Cecil Rhodes repeatedly tried to get control of the territory, but three chiefs from different Tswana tribes journeyed to London, received an audience with Queen Victoria, and persuaded her to preserve their autonomy. As a result, Tswana traditional institutions—crucially the *kgotla*, which allowed citizens to criticize their rulers—were preserved from precolonial times up to independence.

At independence, Botswana's only significant industry was cattle ranching. Inauspicious, one might think, but this had highly positive unexpected consequences. Cattle are large but mobile assets, must be transported over long distances to be sold, and are vulnerable to theft. In other words, the business of cattle ranching tends to give rise to difficult property and contractual disputes. Hence, newly independent Botswana focused heavily on developing institutions to protect private property rights, specifically the rights of cattle owners. (No surprise, since roughly two-thirds of the members of Botswana's early national assemblies were "large or medium-size cattle owners.") When the diamond wealth arrived, the strong institutions helped to ensure that wealth transferred to the public was not simply stolen by the government or appropriated by more powerful groups.

Contrast this experience with, for instance, that of Ghana. Ghana's elites, since colonial times, had grown rich off gold. Hence Ghana's elites had little interest in setting up institutions of private property. As a result, when wealth from gold and coffee flowed into the country, it tended to end up in the hands of a few leaders and cronies and to trigger endless battles over redistribution.

But these property institutions, and traditional consultative assemblies, could easily have been swept aside. Fortunately, Seretse Khama, Botswana's first postcolonial president, made a series of excellent choices. First, he refused to turn the government bureaucracy into a patronage mechanism. Most newly independent African countries booted Europeans out of the civil service in a fit of nationalism. This process of "indigenizing" the bureaucracy was all too often an excuse to promote cronies to positions of power. In Botswana, however, Khama was determined to maintain the British system of appointment based on merit. Hence, for decades after independence, expatriates kept their jobs and foreign advisers and consultants were heavily relied upon. As a result, according to a study of Botswana conducted in the 1980s, "probity, relative autonomy, and competency have been nurtured and sustained" in the civil service.

Second, when diamond revenues first became significant in the 1970s, Khama transferred the subsoil property rights from his own tribe (the Bangwato) to the government. This defused the potential for tribal conflicts over resources and, just as critically, helped ensure that the distribution of diamond revenues was governed by the country's superior property rights institutions. A contrary decision to have kept the diamond revenues for his own tribe would almost certainly have unleashed a disaster. There were other good choices: reducing the power of tribal chiefs in favor of the government, and negotiating better terms for minerals agreements, for instance. These decisions by Khama and subsequent leaders helped Botswana to make the best of the resources and institutions it had.

∞

Since independence, Botswana has been, essentially, a one-party state. The Botswana Democratic Party (BDP) has ruled the country uninterrupted since 1965. The BDP also runs the only daily newspaper. In general, however, the BDP has shown a willingness to tolerate and respond to public criticism. It allows several weekly newspapers that are highly critical of the government. Rather than clamping down on opposition, the BDP makes an effort to appease critics. Before a 1974 election, the government launched the Accelerated Rural Development Program, which invested heavily in rural infrastructure. This investment was not simply a handout. Botswana has made "efficient" social investment primarily in basic infrastructure, education, and health.

Indeed, the government has behaved very much as though it is observed by a watchful public. The balance of payments has usually been kept in surplus, inflation has rarely exceeded 10 percent per year, and investment usually averages 20 to 30 percent of GDP. Botswana has never once been forced to ask the IMF for a structural adjustment loan. Amazingly, when Botswana could not sell diamonds for six months in the early 1980s because of deteriorating international market conditions, no budget cuts were required. The government had saved enough, and managed its accounts well enough, to cope. Few rich countries could achieve such a feat.

Of course, the country is not without failings. Literacy rates of 75 percent are not world-class. Ethnic minorities, such as the San, are not treated equally. Wealth inequality is huge as diamond revenues are distributed widely among the elites but not among the public at large. Much of the credit for Botswana's steady rate of growth goes to DeBeers for its shrewd management of the world diamond market. Most seriously, Botswana failed dramatically to implement good policies for dealing with AIDS. Recently, the country has made an about-face and adopted one of Africa's most aggressive AIDS-fighting programs—but more than one-quarter of all Botswanans are already thought to be infected. This is a looming disaster. But these important problems do not make Botswana any less exceptional. In a region littered with states failed and failing, Botswana stands out.

THE DYNAMICS OF INSTITUTIONS

In 1986, a Peruvian economist named Hernando de Soto wrote a book called *The Other Path*. It was an economics book, but it had relatively little to say about inflation rates, technology, budget policies, capital investment, and the other things people tend to think about when they figure out economic growth. Perhaps the best way to describe de Soto's work is through a famous experiment he conducted. He and his researchers bought two sewing machines and attempted to set up a small sewing shop in Lima. They discovered firsthand that the process of legally registering their small business took 289 days, required the full-time labor of four people, and in the end cost more than $1,200 (roughly equivalent to 30 months of pay at Peru's minimum wage). That was before they could even begin legally to sew.

De Soto found a similar phenomenon in housing. In Peru, obtaining permission to build a house on state-owned land took a full six years and eleven months. The team had to go through 207 administrative steps in 52 government offices to build the house. Obtaining a legal title to the land required an additional 728 steps. De Soto also showed how in the Philippines, obtaining permission to build a home required 168 steps involving 53 public and private agencies; that process took as long as 25 years.

At its root, de Soto's book was about institutions. It was about how, in impoverished Peru, there were more than 500,000 laws and executive orders governing economic activity. These oppressive regulations, and the bureaucracy and corruption they fostered, sapped the energy of the Peruvian people, particularly the poor, and prevented this energy from being turned to economically creative activity. This probably sounds true but obvious. The dead hand of over-regulation is a famous enemy of politicians on the right and has been for some time. As former U.S. President Ronald Reagan put it: "The government's view of the economy could be summed up in a few short phrases: If it moves, tax it. If it keeps moving, regulate it. And if it stops moving, subsidize it."

But de Soto was saying something more profound. That burdensome regulation was a drag on Peru's businesses was obvious; what interested de Soto was the fact that Peruvians ran small businesses anyway. Peru's poor had homes. They had jobs. They even had savings. But because of oppressive regulation, these economic activities were not "legal." In other words, they took place in the "informal sector." The savings were stuffed under mattresses. Sewing shops were hidden in private homes. Houses were built and occupied without formal title. De Soto found, for instance, that 53 percent of Peruvian city dwellers and 81 percent of those living in the countryside were living without formal title to their land or homes. In the Philippines, 57 percent of urban Filipinos and 67 percent of rural residents lived in unregistered housing.

The crux of de Soto's argument was not that regulations slowed business activity but rather that the poor were deprived of property rights. They could set up businesses, but because the businesses were "illegal" they had no way to enforce contracts with suppliers or customers, no way to borrow against the value of their business, and nowhere to turn if assets were stolen. They could build homes. But without legal title to their land, they had no way to obtain mortgages or establish credit histories. This was not simply a result of over-regulation, but also of dysfunctional legal systems and corrupt government bureaucracies.

De Soto's point was that because of poor institutions, a tremendous reserve of economic potential energy was left to rot. De Soto estimated that the combined savings of the poor in the developing world totaled roughly forty times all of the foreign aid poor countries have received worldwide since 1945. In other words, the poor were in full possession of the means to alleviate their own poverty. But the institutions that would allow them to make these savings economically productive simply did not exist. "Markets and capitalism are about property rights," de Soto said in an interview, "...and what we've forgotten, because we've never examined the poor—we've sort of thought the poor were a cultural problem—is that the poor don't have property rights."

This claim was revolutionary because it suggested that developing countries already had much of what they needed to succeed. Economists had traditionally focused on a lack of something as the reason for many countries' continued poverty—not enough capital, perhaps, or education. Foreign aid was supposed to provide what these countries lacked. But de Soto was saying that countries had reserves of economic potential energy, but they had simply failed to unleash it. It was an intuitive argument, but one that was in many ways alien to the vast majority of economic theory.

What de Soto wrote in the early 1980s was not ignored, but neither was its importance fully recognized. Perhaps de Soto was right in practice. But it was hard to say what was most important. Surely absence of education, or lack of capital, or even poor macroeconomic policies were the real problem? Without a theory on which to rest his observations, de Soto could only go so far. The world of development economics continued to focus on foreign aid and economic policy advice.

TRANSACTION COST ECONOMICS

But the theories that would eventually support de Soto's work were already being created. In fact, the first shot in this revolution had actually

been fired decades earlier, by Ronald Coase. The importance of this first
shot was by no means obvious at the time. Coase had simply pointed out
that transacting (buying and selling) is difficult and costly. Consider a
transaction so familiar in the U.S. that it is taken for granted. Something
catches an individual's fancy in a catalog. He sends money in the mail
and in a few days receives the item. This transaction requires several
leaps of faith. The buyer sends the money before receiving the product
(running the risk of theft) and without ever having seen the item (running the risk of deception). These kinds of transactions are possible only
because of sophisticated institutions—consumer protection bureaus,
credit card companies, contract laws, and more recently, seller ratings
on eBay. Without these institutions, such distant transactions could not
take place.

Coase pointed out that all market transactions are costly—including
costs of gathering information ("Is the product a lemon?") and costs
of enforcement ("Will the dealer simply take my money and run?").
Coase was actually most interested in explaining why companies exist.
Since transacting is expensive, it sometimes makes more sense to avoid
transacting with outside parties altogether by forming a company and
bringing all the transactions under one roof. In the process of making
this argument, he inadvertently launched a new discipline, called "transaction cost economics."

The application of Coase's insight to poverty in Peru is probably
not immediately obvious. Indeed, the observation that transactions are
costly simply did not fit into standard economic models of markets and
firm behavior. Most transaction costs were simply assumed away by the
standard economic supposition that people are rational actors. Coase's
point was accepted but generally ignored.

But there was a puzzle that Coase's insight would eventually help solve.
There were many successful countries in the world. By the late 1980s, these
included a few countries in Asia such as Hong Kong, Singapore, South
Korea, and Taiwan, that had leapt to prosperity in a single generation. The
puzzle was to understand why these countries had succeeded and other
poor countries remained poor. After all, people generally seek prosperity,
and the models of Europe, North America, Japan, and emerging Asia
offered a path to prosperity. So why did so much of the rest of the world

fail to "catch up?" Were these poor countries missing something crucial, such as the right climate, religion, culture, or resources? Or was something else going on?

The man who did the most to identify the "something else," and won a Nobel Prize for his efforts, was Douglass North. As early as the 1970s, he and other scholars had begun to outline a "transaction cost view of economic history." Yet it would not be until the 1990s that his ideas were fully developed. Above all else, North sought to explain why people, in their search for prosperity, persisted—often for decades or even centuries—in doing things that were economically unproductive or even destructive.

North's explanation is perhaps best understood through an example—the souk (or *suq*)—a traditional North African and Middle Eastern market that has existed for thousands of years and still exists today. This type of traditional market has counterparts around the world. Its basic characteristics are very familiar—prices are rarely posted and are always subject to bargaining; goods and services are nonstandardized and of widely varying quality; and all sales are final. This is an extremely inefficient way to do business. Every transaction requires endless searching for the appropriate merchant and then endless haggling over the terms of the sale.

But North was not just making a point about inefficiency. He was making a point about incentives. People pursue prosperity, but in souk economies, the best way to do this is to be a better haggler. While there are gains to be had from creating better products, the people getting rich in the souk are those who can consistently buy shoddy products and sell them at the best prices. The merchants make their money by knowing more than the buyers about the real quality of a product and haggling to get the best price possible. In other words, the economic energy of the people in the souk economy is not simply left untapped, it is actually misdirected. From an economic point of view, all of this haggling does little good. It redistributes rather than creating wealth. But for individual merchants, this is the best way to get rich, so they keep doing it.

The way to break out of this cycle of inefficiency is for incentives to arise that drive positive institutional change. In early modern Europe, the existence of long-distance trade created incentives for some merchants to do things differently. Trade over long distances required formal instruments to create trust—people would not pay for goods sight unseen with no way to ascertain their quality, or even ensure that their payments would not be stolen. In the traditional souk, the incentives were to trick the customer. In long-distance trade, the incentives were to create better ways to do business fairly in order to gain access to larger markets. Innovations that supported the growth of trade included the charging of interest on loans, the creation of bills of exchange, and the development of standardized weights and measures. With each innovation, the potential markets for trade grew and so did the incentives to do business even more efficiently. Historians have tracked how, in early modern Europe, the best trade laws traveled from country to country along with merchants and their goods. Over hundreds of years, the inefficient souk evolved into the system of set prices, standardized goods, and specialized contract law that exists today. And in the process, tremendous wealth was created, as opposed to being endlessly redistributed, that led to the rise of the Western world.

The point is that better institutions unleashed Europe's economic potential energy. This energy came not from resources of labor or capital that were given to Europe or resources stolen from elsewhere, but rather resources that Europe already had that were simply being misused. As scholar William Baumol put it, innovation drives economic growth. Innovation creates better technologies, better ways of organizing, better ways of doing business. It is this innovation that helps a country use its resources ever more productively so that it becomes rich. Fundamentally, Baumol points out, people are innovative everywhere. When institutions are good—including the rule of law, property rights, and enforcement of contracts—people have incentives to innovate in ways that power growth. When institutions are bad, people instead innovate better ways to seize public resources, create government-protected monopolies, or profit from crime, as Russia's misfortune so powerfully demonstrated.

∞

By the late 1980s, it was widely accepted that North and his fellow scholars were onto something. But there was little real-world evidence to back them up. It was an elegant theory, a new way of looking at history, but with questionable relevance to the real problems of developing-country poverty. By the end of the 1990s, though, the data had begun to come in. In 1997, as the focus of its annual *World Development Report*, the World Bank compiled data on political and economic institutions in ninety-four industrial and developing countries over a period of thirty years. This included quantitative political and economic data as well as a survey of the experiences of 3,600 firms in 69 countries.

The results of this study strongly supported North's argument. The World Bank found that countries with weak governmental institutions saw their per capita income grow only about half a percentage point per year over the 30-year period covered by the study, compared to an average of 3 percent per year for countries with strong institutions. The bank also found a strong link between economic institutions and levels of growth and investment.

One of the institutions the World Bank analyzed was the civil service or government bureaucracy. Bureaucracies with effective rules and restraints, greater competitive pressures, and greater monitoring by the public tended to perform better. The bureaucracies of East Asia—notably Singapore, Japan and Korea—did many things well, especially merit-based recruitment and promotion. In other countries, bureaucrats would be paid very little but given ample opportunities to collect bribes. In the bribe-prone Philippines, for example, the wages of civil servants were just 25 percent of private-sector wages. In bribe-resistant Singapore, public-sector workers received 114 percent of equivalent private-sector wages.

Another institution analyzed by the World Bank was the legal system. In many countries, the courts were subject to political manipulation. More than 70 percent of entrepreneurs in developing countries counted judicial unpredictability as a major problem in their business operations. Efficiency was another concern. In Brazil and Ecuador, it took 1,500 days to try the average case, against 100 days in France. This made the legal system essentially unusable. India's courts, for instance, were found to be fair and the justices competent. But the legal system was so slow that there were 28 million cases pending in the courts, and the average case took 20 years to resolve.

In addition to law enforcement, the World Bank found that the laws themselves were often a problem. In successful countries, the World Bank found that laws were clear, enforced, and also transparent. But almost 80 percent of entrepreneurs in former Soviet states complained that rules and policies were changed haphazardly. Businesspeople could not count on rules and regulations remaining in place. Sixty percent of entrepreneurs in former Soviet states, the Middle East, and Africa complained of constant government changes and policy surprises.

But perhaps the most crucial institution was property rights. In successful countries, clear laws and strong judicial enforcement protected the right to use an asset, the right to permit or exclude its use by others, the right to collect the income generated by the asset, and the right to sell or otherwise dispose of the asset. Without these laws, as Hernando de Soto argued, businesses were hobbled. Eighty percent of entrepreneurs in Latin America, Africa, and the former Soviet Union were skeptical that their governments would protect their personnel and property. The World Bank cited the example of Thailand to show how good property rights enforcement could unleash economic potential energy. In two separate land-titling initiatives, Thailand issued more than 4 million title deeds between 1985 and 1997. In the immediate wake of this initiative, Thai farmers increased their borrowing by 27 percent because, suddenly, they were able to use their land as collateral. These farmers poured much of this money into productive investments, to the extent that titled land was more productive than untitled land by an average of 12 to 27 percent.

Before and since the World Bank study, researchers have churned out a steady stream of evidence that institutions are critical to growth. Every year the World Economic Forum, in its *Global Competitiveness Report*, reports more survey data showing a strong link between good institutions and economic performance. More such studies come out every day. Scholars Philip Keefer and Stephen Knack found strong econometric evidence that both political and economic institutions help explain the divergence between rich and poor countries. Independent judiciaries, a system of checks and balances between branches of government, and policy predictability and continuity were especially crucial. Other studies are smaller-scale. The World Bank has just issued a study showing that secure and transferable property rights for land dramatically increased investment in productive technologies on Ethiopian farms.

Every country has economic potential energy. In some cases (Russia), a country is obviously blessed with tremendous resources; in others (Japan) the potential is harder to see. But in the long term, as the saying goes, what matters is not the size of the resources but how they are used. Tremendous economic potential may be squandered—as in the case of Russia—or applied to extraordinary effect. It all depends on the incentives people face. If they have incentives to haggle, they will haggle. If they have incentives to build better products, they will build better products. And these incentives are in large part determined by institutions.

"Eating Big Macs Doesn't Make it McChina"

"China is like a black box where both optimists and pessimists can find proof to support their expectations."
WILLIAM GREIDER, *ONE WORLD, READY OR NOT*

MANY WOULD CLAIM THAT POLITICS IS UNPREDICTABLE. EVEN economic behavior—an area putatively driven by the commercial logic of dollars and cents—is regarded as difficult to predict, and economic forecasters are frequently and spectacularly wrong. Politics is infinitely more complex, with its passions, ideologies, and moral concerns, its idiosyncratic leaders and disruptive power struggles. Not to mention that, practically speaking, a country's future course may at any moment be disrupted by unexpected developments: the assassination or sudden death of a leader; a currency crisis in a neighboring country; the crashing of jet planes into the World Trade Center. Surely the forecasting of such phenomena is impossible.

Fair enough; there will never be a perfect political forecast. And yet, at the very least, risk assessments are possible. Consider the case of the United States. Certain factors are unforeseeable—terrorist attacks or political assassinations, for instance. But we can assess structural factors that exist in the U.S. today and tend to change only slowly over time, such as its well-established rule of law, strong checks and balances in the government, a political system with popular legitimacy, policymaking institutions (such as the central bank) that are strong and independent, effective government agencies from the FBI to the FDA, and so on. These structural factors enable the United States to weather unexpected shocks—attempts to impeach the president, ferocious race riots, a presidential vote too close to call, terrorist attacks on New York and Washington—and maintain both political stability and competent economic policy. Certainly, one can imagine scenarios under which these structural factors erode or are overwhelmed. Indeed, this is one of Hollywood's favorite pastimes. But the point is that because of these structural factors, the United States is far less vulnerable to many of the political dynamics outlined in this book—corruption, rising discontent, dangerous opposition, succession crises, faltering state power, entrenched interests, and so on.

But in addition to their usefulness in assessing risks, the principles addressed here also apply to the art of forecasting, even if such forecasts will inevitably be imperfect. Understanding political dynamics can help in making predictions about politics that turn out to be right. The authors of this book, for instance, made the following predictions based on principles that should by now be familiar:

"Many factors might interrupt the possibility of a smooth transition to the post-Suharto era, including mounting Muslim commitments and anger at the domination of the economy by Chinese-born businessmen. But the single most likely factor is widespread and skyrocketing anger at the corruption of the ruling family...The real issue is the anger of ordinary Indonesians about the absence of a level playing field for them."
JOURNAL ARTICLE ON INDONESIA, "INDONESIA ON THE BRINK,"
JULY 1996 (MARVIN ZONIS)

"Alberto Fujimori bases his legitimacy on two accomplishments: saving Peru from economic ruin and crushing the Shining Path guerrilla insurgency. Now that the economy has hit a trough and guerrilla violence has ended, Fujimori's appeal is considerably diminished. Peruvians blame him for the economic downturn, and many oppose his third presidential term. Political unrest may therefore be imminent."
COUNTRY REPORT ON PERU, JANUARY 1999 (DAN LEFKOVITZ)

"[The Venezuelan public has] bought into a...powerful myth that Chavez has promoted. They believe their country possesses extraordinary oil wealth that has been stolen by a corrupt political elite...In sum, they believe that Chavez's undemocratic anticorruption drive will deliver quick, material benefits to the entire nation. This, of course, is untrue... To grow rich will require decades of hard work, not the mere redistribution of money. Hence supporters of Chavez will soon be greatly disappointed. This bodes ill for Chavez and the country's stability."

COUNTRY RISK SUMMARY FOR VENEZUELA, SEPTEMBER 1999 (SAM WILKIN)

To be sure, attempts to predict politics often unravel in the face of unexpected human behavior or unforeseen complexities. But there are better guesses and worse guesses. And because extensive academic research has shown that political stability correlates with market movements, economic growth, losses to direct investors, and financial crises, it pays to make the best guess possible.

Up to this point this book has roamed the world in search of the best examples to explain the various principles of political dynamics—Egypt for social change, Indonesia for the J-curve, Iran for state power, Uganda for leadership, Argentina for external shocks, and so on. But to fulfill the book's stated goal—to explain what makes countries stable or unstable and why it matters—it makes sense to focus on a single country, and demonstrate how all the principles apply to that one country's stability. For this, there is no better candidate than China.

CHINA

Why China's stability matters to the world needs little explanation. As Singapore's Lee Kwan Yew put it, "It is not possible to pretend China is just another big player. This is the biggest player in the history of man." Except in terms of population, this may sound like an overstatement—but China does have the potential to reshape the international political order. In purchasing power parity terms (meaning that exchange rates are adjusted to reflect relative price levels), China is already the second-largest economy on earth. Where economic power goes, eventually, military power often follows. Many have envisioned a future in which China challenges the U.S. for global dominance.

This strategic interest in China is perhaps second only to business interest. As of 2002, China has become the single biggest recipient of foreign direct investment in the world, surpassing America. Jack Welch, former chairman of General Electric, said, "If you want to be the world leader in your industry, you must be the leader in China." According to Phil Murtaugh of Shanghai General Motors, China is "the most promising market in the world...It has by far the highest growth potential of anywhere in the world, and that's why we're here and why everybody else wants to be here." A clearly giddy James Cayne, CEO of Bear Stearns & Co., has said: "China is the most exciting thing I've ever seen." By the end of 1996, twelve U.S. companies had more than $100 million invested in China: Motorola, Arco, Coca Cola, Amoco, Ford, United Technologies, PepsiCo, AT&T/Lucent, GE, General Motors, Hewlett Packard, and IBM.

On top of all this, China fascinates because it defies conventional labels. It is a nominally communist state that has nevertheless enjoyed some of the most rapid economic growth of any country in history. It is an authoritarian state but one in which people enjoy increasing personal freedoms. Somehow, China has enjoyed dramatic success while defying much of the conventional wisdom on market reform and democratization. (As China scholars Daniel Burstein and Arne de Keijzer put it, "Eating Big Macs doesn't make it McChina.") China and its workings, and the political dynamics that will determine its future, make for the ultimate case study. There is no more significant, or practical, way to apply an understanding of how and why the kimchi matters than in analyzing China.

MAINTAINING STABILITY

China's record on stability, since the beginning of economic reform in the early 1980s, is admittedly imperfect—the bloodshed at Tiananmen Square left a lingering stain. But compared with China's record before reform, it is exemplary. Mao Zedong ran a spectacular scapegoating regime, leading bloody campaigns against intellectuals, capitalists and even the Communist Party itself. But since 1980, the fear and repression of the Mao years has been, to a significant extent, replaced by a new ruling bargain, between the Party and at least some segments of Chinese society. This new bargain has meant political stability, the possibility of greater personal liberty, the growth of private business, and rising prosperity.

Before the era of economic reform, the Communist Party's grip on society at large was brutal and direct. In a communist system, economic decisions are made according to political criteria, not market criteria. It does not matter what is efficient and what is inefficient: the most incompetent managers can be promoted for their political loyalty; the most unproductive enterprises can be showered with funds if they please the Party. This forms a repressive sort of ruling bargain. Those who are loyal to the Party would reap economic rewards. Those who show disloyalty risk being sent to the countryside for reeducation and forced labor. Market reforms would cause this arrangement to collapse. If efficiency matters, should the gifted manager whose Party loyalty is only lukewarm nevertheless be promoted? If efficiency matters, should the talented entrepreneur who has never given a thought to communist doctrine be sent off for reeducation? The decisions needed for the maintenance of political control would in many cases directly undermine economic productivity, and vice versa. If the Party's new goal was to promote growth, would that mean the end of its political dominance?

With fewer and fewer economic decisions made on political criteria, Party membership was no longer a ticket to prosperity. So the Chinese people began to ignore the Party. Party membership among college students fell from 23,000 in 1982 to 16,000 in 1990, even as the total number of students increased dramatically. Similarly, Chinese with an entrepreneurial bent left the party to seek their fortunes in private business, and new entrepreneurs did not bother to join. By late 1988, only about 1 percent of self-employed workers were party members. In Shenzen, as of 1995, of more than 13,000 private enterprises, only 17 had basic-level party organizations.

Worse yet, the Party's attempts to bring the elites of the postreform era into its ranks were thrown into disarray by the bloodshed at Tiananmen Square. While only 5 percent of China's general population belonged to the Communist Party, almost 40 percent of college teachers and administrators did. Yet students and academics were the leaders of the

Tiananmen uprising. At the same time, the loyalty of business leaders was thrown into question by the high-profile actions of Wan Runnan of Beijing's Stone Corporation, who contributed support to the demonstrators. The intellectuals and the capitalists—even if they were Party members—clearly could not be trusted. Following the uprising, there was a crackdown, and business owners were forbidden from joining the Party. This had the effect of further diminishing the Party's influence over private business. Obviously, business owners, who were now suspect and prevented from joining, would try to prevent their workers from setting up Party organizations. The Communists were losing their grip.

China's Communist leaders found an ingenious solution to their problems. Academics call it "state corporatism," and it has now been enshrined in Chinese law—in draft form in 1989, and the final version in 1998. The Chinese government created or licensed associations for nearly every conceivable social or professional group: organized laborers, students, writers, scientists, churches, and even business owners. These associations are exclusive. If there are two organizations for a single profession, interest, or activity, one is usually forced to disband. And membership is generally compulsory. For instance, when one obtains a license to operate a business, one is forced to enroll in a business association. Each association must in turn register with the government and have a Party or government body as its supervisor. This is not as direct a means of control as under the previous system, but the Party (which controls the funding and staffing of these associations) is once again able to monitor society at large. Better yet, these associations encourage people to buy into the political system. When they have problems with taxes or licenses, for instance, upstanding members can appeal to their associations for help, and be duly rewarded with Party assistance. Membership—and good behavior—has its privileges.

This new strategy has been extraordinarily successful in gaining the loyalty of the country's business elites. In the late 1990s, scholar Bruce Dickson conducted a random-sample survey of owners of medium- and large-scale private enterprises in eight Chinese counties. To a large extent, China's capitalist elites felt the "state corporatist" organizations advanced their interests. Most reported that they would try to solve problems by appealing to these associations; a huge majority believed the business associations represented their interests; most believed that the business associations could influence the implementation of government policies at local levels. This is not democracy, but these businesspeople, at least, felt they were represented in Chinese politics.

Against this backdrop, some of the other surprising findings from Dickson's survey make a lot of sense. For instance, these business elites valued stability above all else. Strikingly, 58 percent said the government's top priority should be maintaining social stability, even at the expense of economic development. (Even government and Party officials, asked the same question, were less obsessed with stability—61 percent selected economic development as a more important goal.) In short, perhaps unsurprisingly, entrepreneurs were extremely happy with top-down, government control: 97 percent agreed that "measures to further deepen economic reform should be initiated by party and government leaders, not by society." Indeed, Dickson's detailed analysis of the survey results found that the longer entrepreneurs had been in business, the more they bought into the existing political system. "The longer the entrepreneurs have been in business, the more likely they have been a candidate for village chief or village council; the more likely they believe that...rich people should have more influence in policymaking, that what is good for business is good for the community, and that diversity of individual views and groups is a threat to stability."

This again highlights another (by now familiar) point. Wealth is often a powerful driver of political stability. While the Communist Party continues to produce the economic policies and political stability that allow the Chinese people to preserve and enhance their wealth, it is likely to retain the support of the newly rich. There may be a desire for more outright, democratic representation, but not at the expense of stability. This is not to say that business loyalty to the Party is blind or unthinking, but for business elites at least, there is a ruling bargain that works.

In 2001, in a speech marking the eightieth anniversary of the founding of the Communist Party, President Jiang Zemin publicly recommended lifting the ban on admitting entrepreneurs into the Party, and this became official policy in 2002. Here, the top leadership was actually a bit behind the times. Many local Party leaders had already taken matters into their own hands, reclassifying private businesses as collective or joint stock enterprises, and thus allowing their owners to be recruited as Party members. Others had simply ignored the ban; as many as one-fifth of private entrepreneurs were reported to have already joined the Communist Party.

DELIVERING GROWTH

All of this may explain how China's leaders were able to implement dramatic reforms while maintaining political control in the process. Many mysteries, however, remain unsolved. First and foremost: the unavoidable conclusion that, by standard principles of economics, China's two decades of rapid growth should not have occurred at all.

Even as its economy was expanding, China's economic institutions were deeply flawed and pouring vast sums into maintaining loss-making enterprises in order to maintain employment and stability. The highly politicized legal system, corrupt bureaucrats, and vague and contradictory commercial laws did next to nothing to protect property rights and contracts. The Chinese government was massively and inextricably involved in the economy, running state-owned enterprises that generated the majority of industrial production. And on top of this, there were powerful entrenched interest groups that profited tremendously from the old state-controlled economic order, including managers of public enterprises and Communist Party officials. Yet somehow the Chinese government managed to implement market reforms and convince its people to work productively, unleashing economic potential energy rather than looting state assets.

The secret of China's success, as pointed out by scholar Yingyi Qian, has been reform policies that both serve the interests of its entrenched elites and unleash its economic potential energy. To do this, China's economic reforms have been, to say the least, unorthodox. They have not followed the standard script dictated by the IMF or World Bank. But given China's unique kimchi, they have worked.

The most famous of these reforms was dubbed "growing out of the plan" by scholar Barry Naughton. Rather than attempting Russian-style shock therapy, the Chinese leadership essentially froze the level of production under central planning and simultaneously implemented reforms to allow free market production to grow rapidly. This allowed growth and reform while simultaneously protecting entrenched interests. Inefficient managers who sold into the plan at favorable prices were allowed to continue to produce and sell the same amounts of goods they had been selling. But the amounts specified by the plan were virtually frozen in the 1980s, and any surplus production, over and above the amounts the plan demanded, could be sold onto the free market, at market prices. This meant that the entrenched interests were happy—they could still produce and sell at artificial state-set prices. But they also had incentives to do better. This had exactly the desired effect. Plan production and sales of coal, for example, increased only slightly from 329 million tons in 1981 to 427 million tons in 1989. But free market production and sales of coal shot from 293 million tons to 628 million tons over the same period. Similar stories unfolded in other industries. In 1978, 97 percent of total retail sales were dictated by central planning; by 1989, only 31 percent.

Another such reform, equally ingenious, was the creation of local government firms. Again, this was unorthodox. Local governments were allowed to create and operate new companies and keep the revenues they generated as either local tax revenues or to reinvest in their companies. This had an extraordinary effect. Between 1979 and 1993, most new firms entering the Chinese market were not private firms, or state-owned enterprises run by the central government, but local government firms. In fact, by 1993, firms owned by local governments accounted for 42 percent of national output, compared with only 15 percent for the private sector.

Certainly, creating *more* state-run firms as part of an economic reform program is unusual to say the least. But this reform worked because firms owned by local governments were able to navigate China's difficult institutional environment. It did not matter as much that China's legal system failed to protect property rights and contracts—local governments, with control over local courts and law enforcement, could protect their own. Hence local government firms were able to overcome problems of arbitrary regulation and predatory taxation that would hobble private companies. At the same time, because these firms were locally owned, they did not succumb to many of the problems that plague national state-owned enterprises. The local government firms were forced to sell into nationwide free markets and were forced to compete on market terms. Furthermore, the local government firms were a key source of local government revenues. Local governments were required to remit a relatively fixed amount of revenue to the central government each year; any amount they generated over and above this—whether through taxation or by running their local firms—the local governments could keep. Hence local governments had every incentive to run their firms as "profitably" as possible, in order to generate revenues.

One final example of China's unorthodox reforms came in banking. Banking reforms adopted in 1978 allowed Chinese citizens to create bank accounts anonymously, without presenting IDs or registering their real names. At first this seems bizarre; anonymous bank accounts are an invitation to crime and corruption. But anonymous bank accounts also offer protection from corrupt or greedy government regulators. The Chinese government was able to collect revenues—from the banks themselves, based on aggregate deposits—but it was unable to target specific individuals with illegal taxes and the like. Hence, China's rich had every incentive to "hide" their money in the state banking system, in sharp contrast to Russia, where profits were quickly sent offshore. Thus China's banking system grew rapidly, despite the country's weak institutions. The ratio of bank deposits to GDP exploded from 6 percent in 1978 to 65 percent in 1998.

There were many other reforms as well, but the guiding principles were the same—to unleash economic potential energy, even in unorthodox ways, while keeping the vested interest groups happy. This allowed China's leaders to execute the transition from communism at remarkable rates of growth.

Although admittedly sketched in broad terms, these are some of the dynamics that have allowed China to produce stability and growth for more than two decades. But what about the future? Are there political dynamics that could cause this to unravel? Will China continue to move in the direction in which its leaders are pushing, or will dramatic and unintended consequences unfold?

Not every principle discussed thus far comes into play here. Ethnic conflict, for instance, is unlikely to affect China's stability, although it certainly may occur in Tibet or Xinjiang. But what follows, in assessing China's prospects, sums up the principles in the book.

SOCIAL CHANGE

Any attempt to characterize social change in China will inevitably be understated. China's last fifty years have been punctuated by the most extraordinary kinds of social upheaval: the communist revolution that toppled the republican government; the disastrous Great Leap Forward industrial push that caused widespread famine in the countryside, leaving at least 20 million dead; the Cultural Revolution, in which ideological battles decimated the political leadership, tore apart China's social fabric, and erased a decade of potential development; and the 1978 ascension of Deng Xiaoping and the launching of economic reform. Even this last, seemingly most gentle social change, has been wrenching—a popular expression in China's fifth largest city, Shenyang, is that since the launching of economic reform, and the celebration of previously demonized capitalist virtues of profit and individual enterprise, it is as if "heaven and earth have changed places."

This political dynamic has had the greatest effect on the poor—who, in many cases, despite China's overall rapidly rising wealth, are actually newly poor. Workers in state-owned enterprises were the labor elite of the communist years; they were the Communist Party's core supporters. These workers ate from the so-called "iron rice bowl": cradle-to-grave welfare benefits, provided by the government, including lifetime employment, health care, education for their children, and cheap food. Industrial laborers were divided into *danwei* (work units), a subdivision of their state-owned enterprises, which determined where one worked, lived, and often married. But in this new era of economic reform, millions of these most-privileged workers have been laid off—as many as 70 million by some estimates. From labor elite to the bottom of the socioeconomic ladder.

Added to this is the phenomenon of mass migration. China's peasants have always been poor, but now there is a new kind of poverty, a rootless poverty, with as many as 120 million Chinese criss-crossing the country in search of work. Between 1992 and 1995, while China's GDP grew at 9 percent per year, average personal income actually fell in the rural provinces of Anhui, Guizhou, Ningxia, and Xingjiang. Population growth and technological change have contributed to a huge surplus in farm labor. As a result, rural Chinese have flocked to cities in record numbers. Because of China's system of residency and work, migrants to cities often had no official status and therefore received no benefits. They became the "floating" population. Their children were not entitled to attend school and health care was difficult to receive. The increase in urban migrants led to social problems, such as a noticeable increase in crime. In large cities such as Shenyang, migrants and the newly jobless can be seen hawking their possessions in the markets, and women are increasingly being forced into sex work.

This tremendous social disruption has led to unfocused political action. There were an estimated 100,000 protests in 1999, the most recent year for which statistics are available. The largest recent incidents included the April 1999 rallies by the Falun Gong religious sect that took place in 30 cities; a rally of 15,000 miners in February 2000; the demonstration by 20,000 farmers that led to five days of rioting in Jiangxi province also in 2000; and a protest by an estimated 10,000 miners that disrupted a railway line in Jilin province in July 2001. The political dynamic of social change tends to leave people searching for an ideology to make sense of their lives and explain their problems (as radical Islam did for many in Egypt and the rest of the Middle East). To date, no such ideology has presented itself in China. (Communism, the obvious candidate, is already the government's official ideology.) Hence, confused Chinese have sought comfort elsewhere. One alternative has been the well-publicized (yet still mysterious) Falun Gong, or "Buddhist Law." The sect—perhaps implausibly—claims 70 million adherents in China, who practice its breathing exercises while studying the teachings of its New York-based leader, Li Hongzhi (who has, among other things, claimed to have the ability to turn invisible). Similarly, membership in underground churches has exploded. By some estimates, there are now 30 million Chinese Christians—half of whom belong to unauthorized congregations. While there were 200 unauthorized churches in Beijing in 1996, there are now an estimated 1,000. Membership in cults, mystical movements, and religions has swelled.

Thus far this desire for comforting ideologies to assuage the pain and confusion of social change has had little direct impact on Chinese politics. But it is a concern for the future.

CORRUPTION

Social change chiefly affects the poor, who are inevitably less politically powerful. Perhaps even more crucial is the dynamic of corruption, which has the potential to separate the Communist Party from the middle classes who, crucially, now support it.

Authoritarian politics and economic openness are always an uneasy mix. Sometimes the result is Singapore, leading the world in probity. But more often the combination of government officials who are above the law, a tame press, poorly paid civil servants, and wealthy businesspeople results in sleaze. In recent years, China has had spectacular problems with corruption. One notable scandal involved a dollar smuggling ring in Fujian, which transported cars, oil, cigarettes, and other goods with an aggregate value of roughly $6 billion before it was discovered. A large number of Communist Party members turned out to be involved, and several were executed. Senior officials, including the wife of Beijing party secretary Jia Qinglin, were also implicated.

With its unrestrained power and influence in economic affairs, the Party itself has also been infected with corruption. In 1995, Beijing mayor Chen Xitong became the first Politburo member to be fired for a corruption scandal. Mu Sui-Xin, the popular mayor of the northeastern industrial city of Shenyang, was imprisoned on corruption charges and later died in jail. A document produced by the Communist Party noted that a full 98 percent of senior officials had relatives in key posts in either the public or private sectors. According to the study, in cases of fraud of over $600,000, 78 percent of the suspects were related to senior party officials.

Corruption has resulted in extraordinary hardship for Chinese peasants. Local officials are notorious for preying on already impoverished villagers with a variety of dubious taxes, fees, tolls, fines, and levies. For instance, one villager interviewed by the U.S. public television program *Frontline* told of checkpoints set up on roads where officials would collect mysterious vehicle taxes and confiscate the automobiles of those who could not pay. Every year, the fines would get more creative—recently, officials had visited in search of "irrigation project labor fees." This outright theft fuels public anger. In August 2000, near Fengcheng, close to the capital of Jiangxi province, angry farmers began protesting the actions of corrupt government bureaucrats who had actually torn down the homes of those peasants who could not or would not pay illegal taxes. As the riot spread, peasants ripped down the homes of government officials in retaliation. The rioting traveled from village to village, ultimately involving an estimated 20,000 farmers.

But where this dynamic may have its greatest impact is on the middle class. These people (especially business owners, as noted) are likely to support the Party as long as China's government maintains stability and promotes economic growth. But if—as in the Philippines—corruption becomes an impediment to most businesspeople, stacking the deck against those who are prosperous, educated, and ambitious, these people may turn against the government. This poses a real threat, as the middle classes can mobilize great political power. Corruption always undermines the legitimacy of the political and economic system. An opinion poll asked Chinese throughout the country, "How many people have reached wealthy status through 'normal' means?" Almost half the respondents checked the "Not too many" option, and 11 percent checked "Virtually none."

Indeed, this dynamic helped drive China's most dramatic recent incident of instability, Tiananmen Square. Many of the students who joined the protests were angered by the corruption of the Party elite. A chart that was circulated at the demonstrations listed the children of Communist Party leaders who held ministerial positions. In the words of Tian Jiyun, a vice premier at the time of the uprising, "A lot of stories circulate these days about cabals of the 'princes' [children of Communist Party officials], the 'secretaries,' and the 'son-in-laws,' and it makes people sick. The Party's fallen very low. If we can't get the Party in order, will never get rid of corruption and turmoil will always be with us."

The risk is that the Communist Party, in its attempts to co-opt businesspeople by providing them with favors and even Party membership, will create a "crony capitalist" elite. This dynamic tends to build momentum on its own. The new elite, those with political influence, will tend to resist reforms that could reduce their political influence, exacerbating the problem. Thus political favoritism only increases, and likewise corruption and the difficulty of reform.

This process is by no means inevitable. Reforms promoting transparency and accountability can defuse this trend. The Party is very aware of the problem, and many of the examples cited above were uncovered by its own internal investigations. The Party's introduction of local democratic elections is one response to corrupt local officials. But corruption is nevertheless a political dynamic that the Communist Party's current strategies are likely to promote.

OPPOSITION

The most notable feature of political opposition movements in China is that there are none—at least none of significance. The Chinese Democratic Party has been brutally quashed. The quasi-religious Falun Gong has been weakened by government crackdown. Other than that, there are Tibetan activists and Muslim guerrillas in Xinjiang, but neither movement poses a threat to Party control.

The reason for this is not hard to find. China's Communist Party is both competent and utterly ruthless in its suppression of any and all opposition. Any independent institution—governmental, military, religious, or cultural—is potentially a threat to the Party's power. The army could attempt a coup; a religious movement could attempt a revolution (as has happened in Chinese history); a business leader could fund an opposition group; a labor union could organize strikes; an independent legislature or judicial system could take decisions against the Party's interests. While liberalizing the economy, the Party has sought to retain oversight of everything from the courts to the local Catholic Church, through the practice of "state corporatism."

That said, the possibility for opposition movements is growing, as the Party loses its monopoly on the flow of information. Until recently, a rigorously censored press and media helped the Party ensure that the population understood the world as China's leaders saw fit. This is decidedly no longer the case. For one thing, China now runs a negative balance on its tourism account—the Chinese spend more traveling outside China than non-Chinese spend traveling in China. More and more citizens experience noncommunist systems personally and directly. In addition, TV satellite dishes are now widely, and inexpensively, available. Furthermore, text messaging on cell phones—China is now the world's largest cell phone market—has become widespread.

The potential political impact of this has already been amply demonstrated. The 1989 Tiananmen Square uprising was coordinated spontaneously, via telephone, fax, and shortwave radio. The Falun Gong managed to spread its message using fax, email, Internet chat rooms, and now text messaging through cellular phones. During the recent SARS epidemic, the Chinese government initially issued spurious data on the number of cases. But the World Health Organization issued conflicting data, which were publicized on Voice of America and the BBC. Over the next several days, hundreds of millions of text messages were sent across China on cell phones. China's government was forced to abandon its policy of denial and began issuing accurate information. Even if the Party remains determined to suppress opposition, the increasingly free flow of information diminishes its ability to do so.

THE J-CURVE

With all this in mind, consider that China is on the upward slope of the "inverted J." China experienced a phenomenal average GDP growth rate of roughly 10 percent per year between 1981 and 2001. This has meant rapidly rising incomes. Measured in purchasing power parity, China's average income per head has soared by 800 percent over the past 25 years.

Nothing in the analysis so far suggests that this growth will suddenly stop. However, if it does stop, there is the significant potential for a J-curve effect. This is especially crucial given that, as we have noted, so much of the Chinese ruling bargain is based on "delivering the goods." Much of Chinese society seems willing to accept that, as Premier Zhu Rongji put it, "Historical experience has told us that nothing can be accomplished without stability." China's new elite is willing to accept that only the unopposed rule of the Communist Party can deliver stability, which legitimates the Party's monopoly on power. "China is not ready for democracy," is an often-heard refrain. However, should the Party fail to deliver growth, or fail to deliver stability, this justification evaporates and the ruling bargain would be imperiled. Given the example of Indonesia—catastrophic violence after years of dictatorial stability—China's location on the upward slope of the "J" seems worth bearing in mind.

SUCCESSION

Lest this sound too alarmist, note that China is no one-man state like Iran under the Shah or Yugoslavia under Tito, without whom stability will collapse. The Communist Party's political organization is sophisticated, and the leadership, centered in the Communist Party standing committee, has grown more collective since the days of Mao. It is not one person who has all the power, but rather one group. This decreases the odds that the death, departure, or mental dysfunction of a single key individual will wreak catastrophe. China's government and bureaucracy produce substantial state power.

That said, China is vulnerable to the dynamics of succession. A crucial reason that China has done so well over the past two decades is excellent leadership. China's government cannot run itself (as was the case in the U.S., when Washington was obsessed with the Monica Lewinsky scandal). There are few checks and balances, institutions are subservient to the leadership, and there are no opposition parties to oppose and check faulty policies. Hence China under a less competent leader is likely to do significantly less well. In this, considerable risks inhere.

Perhaps more importantly, as Henry Kissinger put it, "No communist country has solved the problem of succession." Current president Hu Jintao, recognized as an extraordinarily able technocrat, was, nonetheless, reportedly elevated to the standing committee of the Politburo by Deng Xiaoping with the offhand remark, "Hu's not bad." Political power is gained and held not through formal processes—although these do exist—but through the informal exercise of political influence. It took Deng Xiaoping three attempts to put a successor in place. He was forced to purge his first two choices, Hu Yaobang and Zhao Ziyang. Hu's downfall was a push for democratic reforms and early retirement for the previous generation of leaders; Zhao's mistake was meeting with the Tiananmen Square protestors and apologizing for the actions of the Communist Party.

This insecurity of leadership makes retiring leaders reluctant to leave the stage. Deng Xiaoping willingly stepped down as the president of China, but held on to his post as chairman of the Central Military Commission, through which he exercised power for many more years. In emulation, former President Jiang Zemin has just surrendered his posts as president and secretary general of the Communist Party to Hu Jintao, but also like Deng, he is holding on to his command of the armed forces.

All of this helps create the potential for power struggles or a destabilizing transition. Despite the Party's elaborate hierarchy and collective leadership, the lack of a succession process increases the possibility that its stability will be undermined by an extralegal power struggle, as has occurred more than once since the Communists took power.

GOVERNMENT INTERVENTION

Amidst all of China's economic policy successes, there has been one dramatic failure—the state-owned enterprises (SOEs). The government approached the problem ingeniously. It tried to replace direct subsidies to the SOEs with loans from the banking system with the intention of "growing out of" state ownership, just as it had grown out of central planning. This did not work. Instead of gradually forcing the SOEs to become more efficient, the banks, under political pressure and knowing that SOEs effectively enjoyed a government guarantee, continued lending to loss-making firms. More recently, the SOEs have started lending to each other, in a practice called "triangular" lending. Most of these loans will never be repaid. State banks have thus far poured more than $600 billion of public savings into the SOEs. Standard and Poor's estimates that up to half of the loans in China's banking system may be nonperforming and that the state banks are technically insolvent. Furthermore, by 1998, the SOEs were consuming an estimated 64 percent of total bank lending in China, depriving the private sector of much-needed capital.

Attempts to deal with this problem, for instance by creating asset management companies that are charged with the disposal of bad loans, have not always worked. Edward Steinfeld studied the case of Central China Non-Ferrous Metals (CCNFM), which is hugely loss-making, as it must support schools, hospitals, and even a police force for its 9,500 employees. Lending to CCNFM was taken over by an asset management corporation, but little changed as the asset management corporation had no authorization to hire, fire, or change the running of the company.

The reason that these institutional changes have failed to solve the SOE problem is that fundamental relationships remain unaffected. Thus far 25 million workers have been laid off; but a further 25 to 40 million are estimated to be superfluous. Hence any true attempt to reform the SOEs will dramatically increase unemployment among people who were formerly "labor elites." This is a major threat to China's stability. The other unchanged relationship is that the Communist Party has retained control over the appointment of SOE managers, and therefore over running these firms. Party officials worried about stability have pressured the banks to lend and prevented the asset management companies from making real changes. To be sure, painful reforms including layoffs and salary reductions have been undertaken, but the slow pace has meant more bad loans and more economic problems. Already, the IMF estimates that reforming the SOEs may cause China's public debt to rise to more than 100 percent of GDP.

Again, this is a dynamic of which China's leaders are well aware. If not for the potential consequences for stability, the leadership might privatize every SOE tomorrow. But here again, current strategies have the potential to undermine the banking system, and therefore continued economic growth. Added to the even more fundamental problem of "crony capitalism" noted above, this dynamic will likely have a role in determining China's future.

EXTERNAL SHOCKS

China's economy is large enough to be relatively insulated from external shocks. The most dramatic demonstration of this was during the Asian financial crisis of the late 1990s. At the time, Asian economies absorbed nearly 60 percent of China's exports and provided 70 percent of its direct investment. But given the size of China's overall economy, some stimulative government spending was enough to keep growth on track. Even as other Asian economies melted down, Chinese growth continued at over 7 percent during the crisis years.

Nevertheless, China is vulnerable to shocks such as a sharp decline in foreign direct investment. In recent years, China has been spectacularly successful in attracting foreign money. Direct investment has soared from relatively insignificant amounts in the 1980s to more than $50 billion today—making China the largest recipient of foreign direct investment in the world, an incredible achievement for a developing economy. Even as global FDI flows declined in 2002, investment in China continued to grow.

This investment is not solely responsible for China's recent growth; indeed, it is not massive when compared to the size of the Chinese economy. (FDI provides only 10 percent of China's total investment.) Yet a sharp decline in foreign investment would likely worsen any instability or economic downturn. If the Chinese economy declines sharply, investment—in part driven by expectations of China's future growth—is also likely to decline. More seriously, if China experiences significant political instability, followed by heavy-handed repression, not only is investment likely to decline, but many foreign-owned facilities in China would face pressure to shut down. Hence any economic or political problems afflicting China are likely to be exacerbated by external shocks.

This is also true regarding the issue of Taiwan. The desire to reunify with Taiwan, by force if necessary, is a constant feature of Chinese politics. It seems inconceivable that China would now make any attempt to seize Taiwan by force. To do so would imperil economic ties with two of its biggest trade and investment partners, the U.S. and Japan, and potentially bring about a military confrontation with United States. Even if China could defeat the Taiwanese military, the operation would be unimaginably costly, both directly and in terms of disrupted international ties. China's leadership does not seem prone to such extraordinary miscalculations.

Again, however, this external shock could add fuel to a crisis. China's leaders have found nationalist rhetoric to be a useful distraction—as recounted in the case of the anti-U.S. protests leading up to the anniversary of the bloodshed at Tiananmen Square. Facing a sharp downturn in growth, or determined domestic opposition, China's leaders might turn to nationalism to rally support. This would be very costly in economic terms. But as elsewhere noted, for instance in Zimbabwe, political logic can drive desperate leaders to destructive actions.

CONCLUSION

None of this is to say that China is doomed to fail. Rather, we offer this analysis to demonstrate the intention of this book: to aid the reader in identifying the political dynamics that produce or undermine stability;

and the dynamics that well-intentioned policies may produce; and the unintended consequences that may result.

Thus we end this book where we started, with the belief that understanding the kimchi, that is to say the local political dynamics of different countries, is critically important to the success of international business and foreign policy in an era of globalization. China has worked well for the last two decades, but it has done so through policies that have unleashed positive dynamics despite being far from orthodox. These policies have also unleashed negative dynamics—a financial system bankrupt in reality and the powerful possibility of the Chinese people refusing to accept the Party's monopoly. Whether China continues to work will be determined by the unfolding of these dynamics, tugging the country in unintended directions, and the ability of strong institutions, good policy, and good fortune to resist them. This China Passage, as it might be called, is breathtakingly challenging; it's difficult to imagine it can be smoothly navigated.

As we wrote this book, we came to a number of broad conclusions:

First, we recognize the indisputable truth in the claim that colonialism did extraordinary damage to much of the developing world—although not in the simplistic way that is often contended. Whether some of the atrocities perpetrated by colonial regimes create a moral responsibility that persists to the present is open to debate. Much of the rhetoric about colonialism—that the rich countries continue to oppress poor countries even to this day—is certainly false. Most of this rhetoric is scapegoating intended to distract attention from problems developing-country governments have created for themselves.

Still, a crucial cause of the continued poverty in much of the developing world is the institutional structures created as a result of colonialism, both in terms of politics and economics. The assets of a good colony are the liabilities of an independent country. Many ethnic and religious conflicts were created by colonial regimes, via the arbitrary drawing of borders or the promotion of favored locals. Many entrenched interest groups were established by colonial governments and remain the powers behind the throne to this day. Indeed, it is a very rare developing country whose political and economic institutions were not warped by colonialism in a way that makes economic development extraordinarily difficult.

Second, equality matters. A theme that has emerged again and again is that excessive inequality hobbles development. Often, money buys power, regardless of the form of the political system, so a rich elite is able to rig the system to preserve its privileges and, in the process, prevent economic growth. Crony capitalists shut down markets to prevent competition to their businesses. Agricultural landlords disrupt the provision of public goods, even such basic public goods as education, in an effort to preserve their political and economic power. The result is a dysfunctional political dynamic. This is emphatically *not* to say that outright redistribution of wealth always, or even often, works. Attempts to redistribute wealth tend to degenerate into even worse cronyism. But high levels of inequality, reinforced by entrenched interests, always present risks to stability and growth. It is paradoxical but nonetheless true that the rich are often the enemies of economic growth and market economics.

Third, today's unstable boom is tomorrow's crisis. The principle of the J-curve is that countries that boom and then go bust are often more unstable than countries that never boom at all. There are certainly opportunities in developing markets—the list of best-performing stock markets of the last ten years is dominated by developing countries: China, Turkey, Bangladesh, Kenya, Poland, and Jamaica, among others. However, investors should always beware of countries that are fundamentally unstable yet (temporarily) doing extraordinarily well.

Fourth, aid poorly given is often worse than no aid at all. U.S. aid has fostered the unnatural survival of many corrupt regimes, which can then distribute handouts to maintain support. Development aid given to countries with good policies can increase growth and alleviate poverty. But "strategic" aid given to key allies can be a disaster. When the kleptocratic regimes that receive this aid eventually collapse, the resulting public anger is often directed against their foreign sponsors.

Fifth, attempts to promote economic development must take the kimchi into account. The evidence is strong that free markets and liberal democracies are the best way to promote prosperity and stability. These systems are extraordinarily successful in the production of legitimacy and the unleashing of economic potential energy. However, just because the end goal is known does not make it easy to get there. China, for instance, produced rapid economic growth with highly unorthodox policies—not just authoritarianism, but also government-owned enterprises and anonymous bank accounts. Indeed, declaring that the shortest distance between two points is a straight line, and making policy on this basis, is sometimes disastrous. Attempts at orthodox economic reforms in Russia unleashed highly destructive political dynamics. The shortest distance to the end goal of prosperity may not be a straight line, but rather may require some twists and turns to take account of a country's unique kimchi. As China scholar Yingyi Qian put it, "The real challenge of reform facing transition and the developing countries is not so much about knowing where to end up, but about searching for a feasible path toward the goal."

Sixth and finally, to repeat, the kimchi matters. What emerged again and again in our research is that "one size fits all" solutions do not work. Attempts to see the world as a single nation do not work. Attempts to impose standardized economic reform policies do not work. Attempts to label countries simplistically as allies or enemies do not work. In the less globalized world of yesterday, the costs of these mistakes were bearable. But with every advance in technology that brings us closer together, the fallout from these errors grows larger and more painful. Local political dynamics have a way of undermining even the most commercially astute international business strategies and the most well-intentioned foreign policies. These political dynamics and their unintended consequences cannot be ignored. Economic reforms must take into account vested interests and institutions. Foreign policy and development aid must take into account the mechanics of ruling bargains. And most importantly, global businesses, as they seek to bind the world closer together, must take into account the kimchi, if they are to profit and to bring prosperity to us all.

Notes

The Kimchi Matters—An Introduction

Page xv: Microsoft would make a $20 million investment in Hangul & Computer: Belinda Raband and Assif Shameen, "Brickbats for Bill," *Asiaweek,* November 10, 2000.

Page xv: Microsoft's plan: Calvin Sims, "How Korean Pride Rallied To Save a Software Maker," *New York Times,* August 15, 1999.

Page xv: 80 percent, 15 percent: ibid.

Page xvi: "There have been many who, having something to put into words...": translated by Gari Leydard, 1966: 29–57, in *The Korean Alphabet: Its History and Structure,* Young-Key Kim-Renaud, ed., University of Hawaii Press, 1997, p. 2.

Page xvi: "Koreans are in great need of their own letters:" from Hun Min Jong Um, the Royal Rescript which presented Hangul to the Korean people, in *A History of Korean Alphabet and Movable Types,* Ministry of Culture and Information, Republic of Korea, p. 8.

Page xvii: This likely makes Korea the only country on earth...: John H. Koo, "Language," in *An Introduction to Korean Culture,* by John H. Koo and Andrew C. Nahm, Hollym International Corp., 1997, p. 103.

Page xvii: A survey of Korean college students: "Collegians Want to Resemble Hyundai's Chung J.Y. Most," *Korea Times,* May 23, 2000.

Page xviii: Microsoft's software was unable to represent certain archaic words and expressions: Calvin Sims, "How Korean Pride Rallied to Save a Software Maker," *New York Times,* August 15, 1999.

Page xviii: "It was probably the first time that an entire nation...:" D.H. Oh, managing director of IDC Korea, quoted in ibid.

Page xviii: "Hangul 815:" Laxmi Nakarmi, "Pulling Back from the Brink," *Asiaweek,* May 26, 2000.

Page xviii: "The movement toward a truly integrated global economy...:" C.J. Silas, Phillips Petroleum Company, quoted in "Free Trade or Competing Blocs?," *The Executive Speaker,* November, 1992.

Page xviii: "We treat the world as a single nation:" CEO of Gillette quoted in Fareed Zakaria, "The New American Consensus; Our Hollow Hegemony," *New York Times,* November 1, 1998.

Page xviii: "The world economy has become a single stage...:" Deputy Secretary of State John C. Whitehead from: "Global Economic Integration," Department of State Bulletin, January 1989.

Page xx: According to the World Trade Organization, world merchandise trade has expanded from $580 billion in 1973...$1.8 trillion...$6.2 trillion in 2000: World Trade Organization, International Trade Statistics 2001.

Page xx: In 1975, only 8 percent of countries had open capital markets; by 1997, a full 28 percent did: Thomas L. Friedman, *The Lexus and the Olive Tree: Understanding Globalization,* Farrar, Straus, and Giroux, 1999.

Page xxi: last remaining British investor in Belarus: "Challenged, Feebly," *Economist,* July 26, 2001.

Page xxii: an estimated $225 billion, $100 billion: http://www.imf.org/external/np/vc/2003/021003.htm

Page xxiii: Ambrose Bierce observed dryly: quoted in Moises Naim, "A Complex and Enduring Globalization," *Financial Times,* August 5, 2002.

Part I: Discontent

Page 1: 100 countries, home to 3.6 billion souls: United Nations estimate cited in Samuel Brittan, "Liberal Imperialism is a Dangerous Temptation," *Financial Times,* April 11, 2002.

Chapter One—"We Practically Own Everything...": Corruption

Page 4: "Americans...have always had a sense...:" David Brooks, "The Triumph of Hope over Self-Interest," *New York Times,* January 12, 2003.

Page 5: its manufacturing sector had grown by 12 percent per year during the 1950s: "A Question of Faith," *Economist,* May 7, 1988.

Page 5: He jailed opposition politicians...: " ibid.

Page 5: first Swiss bank account: "Ferdinand Marcos; Giant Reduced by his Own Greed," *Financial Times,* November 29, 1989.

Page 5: a tiny, close-knit elite...: William Branigin, "'Crony Capitalism' Blamed for Economic Crisis," *Washington Post,* August 16, 1984.

Page 6: Rodolfo Guenca: Robert A. Manning, "The Philippines in Crisis," *Foreign Affairs,* Winter 1984/1985.

Page 6: involvement in at least five communications companies: Samuel Senoren, "Unveiling the Marcos Corruption," *Financial Times,* April 2, 1986.

Page 6: Marcos personally headed twenty-five of these: Jeff Gerth, "The Marcos Empire: Gold, Oil, Land, and Cash," *New York Times,* March 1, 1986.

Page 6: Sadlemi: ibid.

Page 18: "We practically own everything in the Philippines:" Tony Tassell, "Mrs. Marcos in Legal Fight to Get $13bn.," *Financial Times,* December 8, 1998.

Page 6: properties in New York City worth some $350 million: Paul Taylor, "Marcos Invested Heavily in U.S., Says Investigators," *Financial Times,* February 27, 1986.

Page 7: Foreign banks lent primarily to those businesses that had arranged government loan guarantees: Chris Sherwell, "Why Confidence Drained Away," *Financial Times,* September 19, 1984.

Page 7: "foreign exchange shortage:" ibid.

Page 7: When Marcos's daughter got married, Mark Fineman, "Early Promise Faded; 20 Years of Marcos: Few Gains Seen," *Los Angeles Times,* February 2, 1986.

Page 7: grotesque projects: Robert A. Manning, "The Philippines in Crisis," *Foreign Affairs,* Winter 1984/1985.

Page 7: "Well, some are smarter than others:" Imelda Marcos quoted in, William Branigin, "'Crony Capitalism' Blamed for Economic Crisis, *Washington Post,* August 16, 1984.

Page 8: the opposition took the opportunity to air its claims in public: Marites Danguilan-Vitug, "Filipino Opposition Loses Bid to Oust Marcos, But Wins Victory by Creating Publicity," *Christian Science Monitor,* August 15, 1985.

Page 8: "wasted because of misallocation of crony-type projects:" Jaime Ongpin, quoted in William Branigin, "'Crony Capitalism' Blamed for Economic Crisis," *Washington Post,* August 16, 1984.

Page 8: Marcos permitted family and friends to avoid taxes: Fox Butterfield, "Marcos's Fortune: Inquiry in Manila Offers Picture of How it was Acquired," *New York Times,* March 30, 1986.

Page 8: vote-buying, ballot-rigging, ballot-snatching, and voter intimidation: "No Service to Democracy," *Financial Times,* February 10, 1986.

Page 9: he stole a total of $10 billion: "A Question of Faith," *Economist,* May 7, 1988.

Page 9: disco shoes, gowns and dresses, jewels, and gallons of perfume: Richard Gourlay, "Imelda's Shoes Inhabit a National Shrine," *Financial Times,* February 25, 1987.

Page 9: the SEC filed a complaint against GTE: Jeff Gerth, "Questions Arise about Graft," *New York Times,* November 20, 1985.

Page 9: Hiring such a person was not unusual: Jeffrey Kanige, "Defense in Marcos Bribery Case: It's Just Business," *New Jersey Law Journal.* April 19, 1993.

Page 9: golfing buddy: "Aquino v. Westinghouse Looks like Another Epic 'Thrilla in Manila,'" *Financial Times Energy Newsletters—Power Asia,* March 13, 1989.

Page 10: The Aquino government alleged: Jeffrey Kanige, "Defense in Marcos Bribery Case: It's Just Business," *New Jersey Law Journal,* April 19, 1993.

Page 10: "bagman" and "frontman:" Greg Rushford, "Aquino Lawyers: Documents Back Bribes to Marcos; Westinghouse Denies Charges; Asks U.S. Judges in N.J. to Dismiss Suit," *New Jersey Law Journal,* June 6, 1991.

Page 10: $40 million in cash and $60 million in electrical power generating equipment: Settlements; Reached Before Trial, *National Law Journal,* February 5, 1996.

Page 10: Cojuangco drove his Mercedes: Antonio Lopez, "The Marcos Cronies Come Back," *Asiaweek,* July 31, 1998.

Page 11: An unlikely combination of left-wingers and businesspeople: Sangwon Suh and Antonio Lopez, "Unbowed under Mire," *Asiaweek,* October 27, 2000.

Page 11: "This issue is trust…:" Corazon Aquino quoted in Jonathan Sprague and Antonio Lopez, "The Battle Lines Form," *Asiaweek,* September 3, 1999.

Page 12: dramatic examples of hyper-corrupt rulers: Tom Masland and Jeffrey Bartholet, "The Lost Billions," *Newsweek,* March 13, 2000.

Page 13: Empirical evidence has found a direct link between high levels of corruption and low levels of foreign direct investment and economic growth: Paolo Mauro and Shang-Jin Wei, "Corruption and Growth," *World Bank Working Paper,* 1997.

Chapter Two—The Cake: Ethnic Conflict

Page 17: religious and ethnic conflicts…are often described as age-old and intractable: Lloyd Rudolph and Susanne Hoeber Rudolph, "Modern Hate," *New Republic,* March 22, 1993.

Page 18: most ethnic and religious groups have managed to get along peacefully: ibid.

Page 18: Scholar Raufu Mustapha conducted a study: Raufu Mustapha, 1992, cited in Okwudiba Nnoli, *Ethnicity and Development in Nigeria,* United Nations Research Institute for Social Development, 1995, pp. 33–34.

Page 18: Prior to the arrival of the British…: Nnoli, pp. 29–30.

Page 19: They quite naturally turned to those who spoke the same language: ibid., pp. 39–40.

Page 19: Yoruba, Igbo, and Hausa began to form ethnic kinship associations: ibid., p. 40.

Page 19: they offered temporary shelter: Pade Badru, *Imperialism and Ethnic Politics in Nigeria, 1960–1996,* Africa World Press, 1998, p. 6.

Page 19: According to scholar Okwudiba Nnoli: Okwudiba Nnoli, *Ethnicity and Development in Nigeria,* United Nations Research Institute for Social Development, 1995.

Page 19: According to a 1960 study by researcher Peter Kirby, cited in Nnoli, p. 28.

Page 20: It was also anti-Southern and anti-Igbo: ibid., p. 39.

Page 20: The first major incident: ibid., p. 90.

Page 20: the World Bank contended: cited in: "Fissiparous Folk," *Economist,* January 15, 2000.

Page 20: development plan that devoted most of the budget to the North: ibid., pp. 108–112.

Page 20: "The Northernization Policy does not only apply…": Sir Ahmadu Bello, quoted in Isaac O. Albert, "Chapter 7: The Sociocultural Politics of Ethnic and Religious Conflicts," in Ernest E. Uwaizie, Isaac O. Albert, Godfrey N. Uzoigwe, eds., *Inter-Ethnic and Religious Conflict Resolution in Nigeria,* Lexington Books, 1999, p. 73.

Page 21: the government's relatively meager revenues were generated primarily by international sales of cocoa: Nnoli, p. 125.

Page 21: this just meant more jobs, more contracts, more loans: ibid., p. 184.

Page 21: Enter some opportunistic politicians…: ibid., pp. 114–122.

Page 21: Voter intimidation, ballot theft, and the like were widespread: ibid., p. 110.

Page 21: coup d'etat…: ibid., p. 130.

Page 21: a wave of violence against Igbo…: ibid., p. 135.

Page 21: "return match:" Albert, p. 74.

Page 22: more than 50,000 Igbos were killed: Nnoli, p. 137.

Page 22: Biafra expelled Northerners: ibid., pp. 137–138.

Page 22: the case of the Wawa…: ibid., pp. 180–201.

Page 22: Nigeria has gone from two regions…: ibid., pp. 148–149.

Page 23: Soon rival ethnic groups…began to fight over the newly valuable farmland: ibid., pp. 221–223.

Page 23: property valued in the millions was destroyed: ibid., p. 224.

Page 23: social services…are often nonexistent: ibid., p. 212.

Page 23: per capita income of only $290 per year: World Bank, World Development Report 2003.

Page 24: keeping the Niger Delta underdeveloped: Norimitsu Onishi, "Deep in the Republic of Chevron," *New York Times,* July 4, 1999.

Page 24: 40 percent to the oil companies, 60 percent to the government: Norimitsu Onishi, "Left Behind: As Oil Riches Flow, Poor Village Cries Out," *New York Times,* December 22, 2002.

Page 24: an estimated $50 billion: Norimitsu Onishi, "Deep in the Republic of Chevron," *New York Times,* July 4, 1999.

Page 24: the Delta's 7 million citizens live in appalling conditions…: Norimitsu Onishi, "Left Behind: As Oil Riches Flow, Poor Village Cries Out," *New York Times,* December 22, 2002.

Page 24: militants shut down half of the country's oil production: ibid.

Page 24: highest premium in the world: William Wallis, "Militants Demand Fair Play: The Delta," Survey-Nigeria, *Financial Times,* March 30, 2000.

Page 24: "The development of the people…:" quoted in Norimitsu Onishi, "Nigeria Combustible as South's Oil Enriches North," *New York Times,* November 22, 1998.

Page 24: "Our government cannot assist us…:" quoted in Norimitsu Onishi, "Deep in the Republic of Chevron," *New York Times,* July 4, 1999.

Page 24: The siege ended when Chevron Texaco agreed to a long list of demands…: Norimitsu Onishi, "Left Behind: As Oil Riches Flow, Poor Village Cries Out," *New York Times,* December 22, 2002.

Page 24: an estimated $53 million per year: William Wallis, "Shell Takes Action to Counter Criticism," *Financial Times,* February 22, 2001.

Page 25: Chevron now faces a U.S.-filed lawsuit: David Buchan and Patty Waldweir, "Shell Fails to Prevent Trial on Abuses in Nigeria," *Financial Times,* March 27, 2001.

Page 25: A boycott by German consumers caused sales...to fall by 30 percent: Sara Minogue, "Sustainable PR," *Strategy,* November 4, 2002.

Page 25: Shell Oil is no wilting violet: "Petroleum and Principles," *Financial Times,* July 26, 2002.

Page 25: The results are reviewed every year in annual reports: "The Power of Publicity," *Economist,* December 5, 1998.

Page 25: suing Shell in American courts: "Shell Execs Face Questioning in Nigeria Lawsuit," *Energy Compass,* January 23, 2003.

Page 26: razed the town of Odi: Norimitsu Onishi, "Left Behind: As Oil Riches Flow, Poor Village Cries Out," *New York Times,* December 22, 2002.

Page 26: The cause of the conflict was forgotten...: Muhammad Tawfiq Ladan, "Chapter 9: The Role of Youth in Inter-Ethnic and Religious Conflicts: The Kaduna/Kano Case Study," in Ernest E. Uwaizie, Isaac O. Albert, Godfrey N. Uzoigwe, eds., *Inter-Ethnic and Religious Conflict Resolution in Nigeria,* Lexington Books, 1999, pp. 103–104.

Page 26: A committee...found that the causes...were economic: ibid., p. 105.

Page 27: Nigerian oil is free of sulphur: Roger Cohen, "Rich, Oil Poor: A special report; High Claims in Spill Betray Depth of Nigerian Poverty," *New York Times,* November 20, 1998.

Page 27: Africa's share in U.S. oil imports is expected to rise: Norimitsu Onishi, "Left Behind: As Oil Riches Flow, Poor Village Cries Out," *New York Times,* December 22, 2002.

Page 28: Susan Olzak unearthed this pattern in statistical research: Susan Olzak, *The Dynamics of Ethnic Competition & Conflict,* Stanford University Press, 1992.

Page 28: A study comparing black-white relations in the U.S. and Brazil: Marvin Harris, *Patterns of Race in the Americas,* Walker, 1964.

Page 28: Studies have found similar patterns among Hindus and Muslims in India: Asghar Ali Engineer, "Remaking Indian Muslim Identity," *Economic and Political Weekly,* April 20, 1991.

Page 29: A study by the World Bank: Paul Collier, *Economic Causes of Civil Conflict and Their Implications for Policy,* June 15, 2000.

Page 29: A study of postcolonial Africa: Johnson, Slater, and McGowan, 1984, p. 646, cited in J. Craig Jenkins and Augustine J. Kposowa, "Explaining Military Coups

D'Etat: Black Africa, 1957–1984," *American Sociological Review,* 1990. Vol. 55. December, p. 861–875.

Page 29–30: This political logic…has unfolded in countries around the world: Robert Bates, "Ethnic Competition and Modernization," *Comparative Political Studies,* January 1974, p. 471.

Page 30: "market-dominant minorities:" Amy Chua, *World on Fire,* Doubleday, 2003.

Page 30: political dynamics…can create terrific ethnic and religious hatred where none had existed: Lloyd Rudolph and Susanne Hoeber Rudolph, "Modern Hate," *The New Republic,* March 22, 1993.

Page 30: Ashutosh Varshney sought to answer this question…: Ashutosh Varshney, "Ethnic Conflict and Civil Society: India and Beyond," *World Politics* 53, April 2001.

Chapter Three—Neon Allah: Social Change

Page 34: land reform reduced farmers' holdings to tiny tracts: Afaf Lufti Al-Sayyid Marsot, *A Short History of Modern Egypt,* Cambridge University Press, 1985, p. 141.

Page 34–35: in 1952, only 42,485 Egyptians were attending institutions of higher education; by 1977, that number had grown to 500,000: Geneive Abdo, *No God But God: Egypt and the Triumph of Islam,* Oxford University Press, 2000, pp. 116–122.

Page 35: in 1991, the average engineer earned 336 Egyptian pounds per month, doctors 332 pounds, and lawyers 292 pounds—all less than $100: ibid., p. 82.

Page 35: items such as refrigerators, television, or a car: Arlene Macleod, *Accommodating Protest,* Columbia University Press, 1991, p. 34.

Page 35: sitt-al-bayt: ibid., pp. 45–59.

Page 35: Only 8 percent of Egyptian women say that working outside the home is acceptable or good according to Islam: ibid., p. 94

Page 35: women seen walking alone…: ibid., p. 63.

Page 36: 15,000 Egyptian troops: Abdo, pp. 20–21.

Page 37: membership in religious associations has soared: Marsot, p. 138.

Page 37: A rare sight in the 1960s: Abdo, p. 13.

Page 37: 90 percent of young people…: Cairo Center for Criminal and Social Studies, cited in Abdo, p. 28.

Page 38: "Anyone who helps a regime that is opposing Islam…: "Egypt: Staying Away," *Economist,* February 19, 1994.

Page 38: An assault on a tour bus: "Tourism Reels after Terror Attack: Militants Gun Down 18 Greek Visitors Outside Cairo," *Financial Times,* April 19, 1996.

Page 38: 20 percent falloff in tourist business: Mark Huband, "Killings Highlight Role of Economic Reform," *Financial Times,* November 19, 1997.

Page 38: $1 billion in tourist revenue: "Heaven or Hell?" *Economist,* March 20, 1999.

Page 40: profound psychological stress: Marvin Zonis, "Self-Objects, Self-Representation, and Sense-Making Crises: Political Instability in the 1980s," *Political Psychology,* Vol. 5, No. 2, 1984, pp. 267–285.

Chapter Four—"They Transform Themselves into Tigers": The J-Curve

Page 42: docile and industrious: Satish Mishra, "Chaotic Indonesia is Waiting for 'Messiah,'" *Jakarta Post,* November 4, 2002.

Page 42: "tropical Islam:" Teresa Poole, "Suharto Aims to Woo Islamic Moderates," *The Independent,* May 5, 1992.

Page 42: unruly and unproductive: Satish Mishra, "Chaotic Indonesia is Waiting for 'Messiah,'" *Jakarta Post,* November 4, 2002.

Page 42: "I am not an economist...:" Sukarno quoted in John Andrews, "The Extended Family; Two Fathers; Sukarno and Suharto, *Economist,* August 15, 1987.

Page 43: the persona of a traditional Javanese king: "Indonesia. What price stability?," *Economist,* August 3, 1996.

Page 43: 52.8 million...21.9 millon: World Bank, Social Policy and Governance in the East Asia Region, Social Indicators, www.worldbank.org/eapsocial/sector/poverty/povcwp2.htm.

Page 44: Suharto's three sons and three daughters...: "The Family Firm," *Economist,* July 26, 1997.

Page 44: $100 in 1970 to around $900 in 1996: "Indonesia. What price stability?," *Economist,* August 3, 1996.

Page 44: 52.8 million...21.9 million: World Bank, Social Policy and Governance in the East Asia Region, Social Indicators, www.worldbank.org/eapsocial/sector/poverty/povcwp2.htm.

Page 44: with the poor just as likely to attend school as the rich: Kathleen Beegle, Elizabeth Frankenberg, Duncan Thomas, "Measuring Change in Indonesia," A project of RAND in collaboration with UCLA and the Demographic Institute of the University of Indonesia, May 1999, p. 39.

Page 44: 11 percent, 62 percent, 65: World Bank, World Development Indicators, 1998.

Page 46: 128 percent, 136 percent: James Levinson, Steven Berry, Jed Friedman, "Impacts of the Indonesian Economic Crisis: Price Changes and the Poor," February 21, 2001.

Page 46: 700 ruppiah per hour...500 ruppiah per hour: Beegle, Frankenberg, Thomas, p. 57.

Page 46: half-finished skyscrapers dotted the Jakarta skyline: John Maxwell, "This Complex Crisis," *Inside Indonesia No. 60,* October–December 1999.

Page 46: people scavenged for roots...: Richard Lloyd Parry, "Indonesians Live in Fear of New Wave of Unrest," *The Independent,* June 3, 1998.

Page 46: three meals per day to two: Nicholas D. Kristof with Sheryl WuDunn, "Of World Markets, None an Island," Global Contagion Series, *New York Times,* February 17, 1999.

Page 47: "They look friendly..." Seth Mydans, "Newly Jobless (and Newly Angry) Upset Indonesia," *New York Times,* January 29, 1998.

Page 47: 30,000 students converged on the parliament building: "Indonesia Awakes to the Post-Suharto Era," *Economist,* May 23, 1998.

Page 47: Suharto apologized...: ibid.

Page 47: Matsushita traded in Indonesia for Vietnam: Zhai Jingsheng, "Indonesia Under Pressure to Improve Investment Climate," *Xinhua General News Service,* September 7, 2002.

Page 47: More than thirty Korean firms closed their facilities: ibid.

Page 47: a third of the 300 shoe manufacturers: Rowan Callick, "Indonesia's Dangerous Isolation," *Australian Financial Review,* November 2, 2002.

Page 48: 38 percent of Nike shoes...26 percent: Matthew Moore, "An Industry in Strife," *The Age,* November 23, 2002.

Page 48: Proctor and Gamble...: Robert Go, "Multinationals are Moving Production to Other Developing Countries, *Straits Times,* December 23, 2002.

Page 49: "...while one man may rebel...:" David Gilmour, "Far-Flung Battle Lines," *Financial Times,* September 7, 2002.

Page 50: "J-Curve effect:" James Davies, "The 'J Curve' of Rising and Declining Satisfaction as a Cause of Some Great Revolutions," in Graham Davis and Ted Robert Gurr, eds., *Violence in America: Historical & Comparative Perspectives,* Bantam Books, 1970.

Chapter Five—Toppling Punto Fijo: Opposition

Page 56: fly to Miami for a weekend of shopping: Alexandra Starr, "Washington Diarist," *New Republic,* May 20, 2002.

Page 58: 91 percent, 78 percent: Alfredo Keller & Asociados, "Revisión de las bases de la cultura política de los venezolanos," *Análisis mensual.* Caracas: Febrero de 2000, cited in Janet Kelly, "Thoughts on the Constitution: Realignment of Ideas about the Economy and Changes in the Political System in Venezuela," Prepared for delivery at the 2000 meeting of the Latin American Studies Association. Hyatt Regency, Miami. March 16–18, 2000.

Page 59: Voter turnout was…95 percent…30 percent: Michael McCaughan, "Populist Ex-Soldier Wants to Bring Radical Changes to his Country and his Region: The Election of Hugo Chavez is Creating Great Expectations Among, and Beyond, the Poor of Venezuela," *Irish Times,* January 4, 1999.

Page 59: per capita oil revenues of $330 per year…$9,000: *CIA World Factbook 2003.*

Page 59: 20 percent poorer: Ricardo Hausmann, "Chavez Must Yield to Election Calls," *Financial Times,* January 18, 2003.

Page 59: approval rating…35 percent: Richard Lapper and Andy Webb-Vidal, "As Chavez's Grip Tightens, Oil-rich Venezuela Moves Towards 'Castro Communism,'" *Financial Times,* February 6, 2003.

Page 60: "El Pantaletaxo:" Anna Husarska, "Hugocentric: Caracas Dispatch," *New Republic,* June 25, 2001.

Page 60: "Caserolas Contra Chavez:" Alexandra Starr, "Washington Diarist," *New Republic,* May 20, 2002.

Page 60: "The worse they look…": Andy Webb-Vidal and James Wilson, "Spreading Political Crisis in Caracas Leaves a City Divided: Venezuela's Three-week Strike Leaves Areas Where Opposing Camps Fear to Tread," *Financial Times,* December 21, 2002.

Page 60: economy contracted by 10 percent…17 percent: "A Divided Country Self-destructs," *Economist,* January 18, 2003.

Page 60: American Airlines suspended several flights: Christina Hoag, "Venezuela Strike Hurts Some U.S. firms; Businesses Have Had to Close; Airlines Trim Flights," *Milwaukee Journal Sentinel,* January 21, 2003.

Page 60: Microsoft, IBM, Ford Motor Company, Shell, Coca Cola, Oracle, and Avon: Paul Tharp, "U.S. Firms Shut Factories in Strike-Torn Venezuela," *New York Post,* January 21, 2003.

Page 61: U.S. crude oil supplies fell 14 percent…26 percent: Virginia Baldwin Gilbert and Patrick L. Thimangu, "Fuel Prices Soar With No Fall in Sight As Crude Nears 2-Year High," *St. Louis Post-Dispatch,* February 8, 2003.

Page 62: anti-Tamil riots: Rohan Gunaratne, "International and Regional Implications of the Sri Lankan Tamil Insurgency," Lecture, *Voice of Sinahla,* October 1998.

Page 62: over 20,000 Sri Lankans: ibid.

Page 63: 100,000 Tamils fled the country: David Osler, "Tigers Seek Legitimacy: How One of the World's Most Feared Guerilla Organizations Runs a Fleet of General Cargoships in its Spare Time, *Lloyd's List,* March 20, 2000.

Page 63: fifty-four countries: Dushy Ranetunga, "Prabhakaran and Tamil Separatism," *Island,* March 29, 2000.

Page 63: $2.75 million per month: Peter Chalk, quoted in Nirmal Ghosh, "LTTE's Global Shadow Economy Behind Violence," *New Straits Times,* May 24, 2000.

Page 63: One bank in the Jaffna Peninsula…: "There is Another Country," *Economist,* August 18, 2000.

Page 63: roughly $4 million: Peter Chalk, quoted in Nirmal Ghosh, "LTTE's Global Shadow Economy Behind Violence," *New Straits Times,* May 24, 2000.

Page 63: the Tigers set up a plethora of legitimate businesses: MR Narayan Swamy, "The Tamil Tigers Prove Ferocious, With Help from Abroad," *International Herald Tribune,* June 19, 2000.

Page 63: 200,000 Tamils: Patricia Chisholm, "Death in the Night; a Community Grieves over a refugee's Murder," *Maclean's,* November 23, 1998.

Page 63: 10,000 former guerillas: Paul Kaihia, "Banker, Tiger, Soldier, Spy; a Tamil Immigrant's Arrests Masks a Tale of International Intrigue," *Maclean's* August 15, 1996.

Page 63: Several known leaders: ibid.

Page 64: a 6 percent annual tax: ibid.

Page 64: $22 million per year: "When a War Comes to Our Shores," *Toronto Star,* September 28, 2000.

Page 64: LTTE arms procurement officer: Peter Chalk, "Liberation Tigers of Tamil Eelam's (LTTE) International Organization and Operations—A Preliminary Analysis," Commentary No. 77, A Canadian Security Intelligence Service Publication, March 17, 2000.

Page 64: ten ships: David Osler, "Tigers Seek Legitimacy: How One of the World's Most Feared Guerilla Organizations Runs a Fleet of General Cargoships in its Spare Time, *Lloyd's List.* March 20, 2000.

Page 64: The ships were registered in Panama...: ibid.

Page 64: The Indian army once seized: ibid.

Page 64: TNT and RDX: ibid.

Page 64: The LTTE fielded an army of three brigades and a guerilla cadre...: Rohan Gunaratne, "International and Regional Implications of the Sri Lankan Tamil Insurgency," Lecture, *Voice of Sinahla,* October 1998.

Page 65: thirty foreign tourists: Christopher Thomas, "Colombo Bombs Injures Britons," *London Times,* October 16, 1997.

Page 65: The Tigers run their own customs and tax collection service...: Amy Waldman, "Sri Lanka Faces the Divisions Within," *New York Times,* January 8, 2003.

Page 65: Sri Lanka's economy contracted by 1.4 percent: Paul Tighe, "Sri Lankan Government, Tamil Rebels Open Peace Talks in Thailand," *Bloomberg News,* September 16, 2002.

Page 65: government spending on energy...were all preempted: Paul Tighe, "Sri Lankan Government, Tamil Rebels Open Peace Talks in Thailand," *Bloomberg News,* September 16, 2002.

Page 65: The World Bank estimates...2 percent per year: Sadanand Dhume, "The Cost of War," *Far Eastern Economic Review,* June 1, 2000.

Page 65: attack on the U.S.S. Cole: Amy Waldman, "Masters of Suicide Bombing," *New York Times,* January 14, 2003.

Page 66: Authorities...have located and frozen Tiger bank accounts...: "Smiles that Conceal the Worries," *Economist* July 20, 2002.

Page 66: Bush issued an executive order blocking assets...: "Tamils Sued for Peace after Funds Cut Off," UPI, July 23, 2002.

Page 66: "We will seriously consider renouncing armed struggle...:" Somini Sengupta, "Sri Lanka Rebel Voices Hope for End to 18-Year War," *New York Times,* April 11, 2002.

Page 66: The main road...has been reopened: "The Tigers Comes out of his Lair," *Economist,* April 13, 2002.

Page 67: Workers...went without pay for months at a time: Gerry Gendlin, "The Collapse of Russia," *Précis,* MIT Center for International Studies, Volume X Number 5, Spring 2001.

Page 67: life expectancy...dropped from 69 years...: Alexander Pochinok, Labor and Social Development minister, cited in Gendlin.

Page 69: three-quarters of the population…: Stephan White, Richard Rose, Ian McAllister, *How Russia Votes,* Chatham House Publishers, 1997, p. 132.

Page 69: "against the two candidates:" Marie Mendras, "Yeltsin and the Great Divide in Russian Society," *East European Constitutional Review,* Spring/Summer 1996, Volume 5, Number 2/3, p. 54.

Page 71: 5.7 percent of the popular vote: Inga Mikhailovskaya, "Russian Voting Behavior as a Mirror of Social-Political Change," *East European Constitutional Review,* p. 60.

Page 72: a recent study by the World Bank: Paul Collier and Anke Hoeffler, "Greed and Grievance in Civil War," *World Bank,* May 2000.

Page 72: 50,000 soldiers, $500 million per year: ibid.

Page 73: Political Risk Services…in a disarmingly honest assessment: William D. Coplin, Michael K. O'Leary, and Tom Sealy, *A Business Guide to Political Risk For International Decisions,* Political Risk Services, 1991.

Chapter Six—Tony Blair's Gay Gangsters: Channels for Discontent

Page 77: $460, 44 percent, 35 percent: The World Bank, *World Development Report 2003*

Page 77: quasi-feudal system: Lloyd I. Rudolph and Susanne Hoeber Rudolph, *In Pursuit of Laskshmi,* The University of Chicago Press, 1987. p. 50.

Page 78: 600 distinct political parties: P.P. Rao, "National and State Parties," *The Hindu,* October 10, 2000.

Page 79: election results are widely seen as legitimate: Rudolph and Rudolph, p. 89.

Page 79: 59 percent of Indians: "The Maturing of a Democracy," *India Today,* August 31, 1996.

Page 79: "At village after village that afternoon…:" Pankaj Mishra, "The Other India," *New York Review of Books,* December 16, 1999, p. 99.

Page 80: per capita income is $25,920: The World Bank, *World Development Report 2003.*

Page 80: 448 public protests and 425 assemblies for political purposes…518 and 479: Sangwon Suh and Yulanda Chung, "Radicals Rising," *Asiaweek,* December 8, 2000.

Page 80: "There is simply no other way…:" ibid.

Page 81: more than one million voters: Martin Lee, "The Slow Squeeze on Hong Kong," *Washington Post,* September 12, 1997.

Page 81: 16 percent of Hong Kongers wanted to see him stay in power: David Lague, "The Will of the People Unheard," *Far Eastern Economic Review,* April 11, 2002.

Page 81: the largest demonstration since the 1989 protests: "Hong Kong Vows Not to Back Down on Civil Servant Pay Cuts," *Deutche Presse-Agentur,* July 8, 2002.

Page 81: "Anti-Subversion Law:" Michael Dorgan, "Hong Kong Frets New China-based Laws May Curb Freedom of Press, Religion, Speech," *Knight Ridder Washington Bureau,* December 30, 2002.

Page 81–82: "excite disaffections against the Central People's Government…:" ibid.

Page 82: tens of thousands took to the streets: ibid.

Page 82: Ten foreign banks voiced concerns: ibid.

Page 82: "Jewel of Africa:" "The Poll That Bob Stole—Zimbabwe's Future," *Economist,* March 16, 2002.

Page 82: mesmerizing public speaker: Peter Gourevitch, Letter from Zimbabwe, "Wasteland: Comrade Mugabe is Clinging to Power, and Taking His Country Down with Him," *New Yorker,* June 3, 2002.

Page 82: one of only five countries…: Tony Hawkins and James Lamont, "A Bitter Harvest: With Real Wages Lower Than at Independence and Food Shortages Looming, Robert Mugabe is Gambling Everything on Next Year's Election," *Financial Times,* August 18, 2002.

Page 82: its healthcare system was ranked dead last among 191 countries: ibid.

Page 83: spent most of the money himself: "It's a Bleak House in Zimbabwe This Christmas," *Africa News,* December 22, 2000.

Page 83: "We might very well demand two ears…:" Robert Mugabe quoted in Peter Gourevitch, Letter from Zimbabwe, "Wasteland: Comrade Mugabe is Clinging to Power, and Taking his Country Down with Him," *New Yorker,* June 3, 2002.

Page 83: 20,000 civilians: ibid.

Page 83: focused on the South African bogeyman: Gary Younge, "Comrade Bob," *Guardian,* September 4, 2001.

Page 84: colonists forcibly removed blacks from their homes: Rachel L. Swarns, "After Zimbabwe's Land Revolution, New Farmers Struggle and Starve," *New York Times,* December 26, 2002.

Page 84: "cannot continue to exist…:" Robert Mugabe quoted in R.W. Johnson, "This is Mugabe's Secret—He's Turned Into a Replica of Ian Smith, *Times* (London), June 24, 2000.

Page 84: "Keep your England…:" Robert Mugabe quoted in James Blitz and James Lamont, "African Leaders Hit at Blair on Zimbabwe," *Financial Times,* September 3, 2002.

Page 84: "trapping tankers on the high seas:" Robert Mugabe quoted in R.W. Johnson, "This is Mugabe's Secret—He's Turned Into a Replica of Ian Smith, *Times* (London), June 24, 2000.

Page 84: "lower than pigs and dogs:" Robert Mugabe, quoted in "Ex-president Loses Gay Sex Case Appeal," *Guardian,* May 30, 2000.

Page 84: "the gay government of the gay United gay Kingdom:" Robert Mugabe quoted in David Thomas, "In Praise of Peter Tatchell," *Daily Mail,* March 7, 2001.

Page 84, "We are being told we must accept gay rights…:" Robert Mugabe quoted in "How the People Have Learned to Despise the Man They had Loved like a King," *Express,* January 18, 2000.

Page 85: "Jews in South Africa…:" Robert Mugabe, quoted in Tim Butcher, "'Jewish Plot' Denounced by Mugabe," *Daily Telegraph,* September 4, 2001.

Page 85: "The wrongs of the past must be forgiven and forgotten…:" Richard Dowden, "The Zimbabwean Leader Espouses Violence—Yet He is Also a Man of Learning," *Financial Times,* March 4, 2002.

Page 85: legislation was passed allowing the government to seize land: "Zimbabwe MPs Pass Law to Seize Land," *Financial Times,* March 20, 1992.

Page 86: Tsvangirai is a known for his casual dress and straight talk….: Mercedes Sayagues, "Zimbabwe; Profile: 'Public Enemy Number One in a Rumpled Suit, *Africa News,* March 6, 1998.

Page 86: the MDC rallied Zimbabweans: Peter Gourevitch, Letter from Zimbabwe, "Wasteland: Comrade Mugabe is Clinging to Power, and Taking his Country Down with Him," *New Yorker,* June 3, 2002.

Page 86: "greedy, greedy, greedy colonialists…:" Rachel L. Swarns, "Criticized by the West, Mugabe Is a Hero to Many," *New York Times,* September 6, 2002.

Page 86: over 1,600 farms have been invaded: "Harare Lists More Land for Expropriation," *Financial Times,* June 30, 2001.

Page 86: veterans harassed factories…: "Zimbabwe's International Image Says it All," *Zimbabwe Independent,* April 20, 2001.

Page 86: nearly all the 4,500 white farmers: Rachel L. Swarns, "Criticized by the West, Mugabe Is a Hero to Many," *New York Times,* September 6, 2002.

Page 86: an estimated quarter of a million jobs were lost: "Queues Give Lie to Mugabe's Claims: Empty Shelves Contradict the President's Belief in Zimbabwe's Economic Resilience," *Financial Times,* September 11, 2002.

Page 86: exports dropped by 40 percent: ibid.

Page 86: inflation ran to triple digits: Tony Hawkins and James Lamont, "A Bitter Harvest," *Financial Times,* August 18, 2002.

Page 86: tourism…all but dried up: Michael Holman, "Zimbabwe's Loss, Mozambique's Gain," *Financial Times,* September 5, 2002.

Page 86: crops of tobacco, citrus, beef, and flowers: Tony Hawkins, "Problems Point to 2003 Being Crunch Year for Zimbabwe," *Financial Times,* December 30, 2002.

Page 86: Food production fell by a third: ibid.

Page 87: neither free nor fair: "The Poll that Bob Stole—Zimbabwe's Future," *Economist,* March 16, 2002.

Chapter Seven—The World's Most Powerful Man: State Power

Page 92: his visage stared down…: Marvin Zonis, *Majestic Failure,* The University of Chicago Press, 1991, p. 112.

Page 92: Shahanshah, King of Kings, and the Aryamehr: ibid., p. 261.

Page 92: *A Bullet for the Shah: All They Had to Do was Kill the World's Most Powerful Man*: Alan Williams, *A Bullet for the Shah,* Popular Library, 1976, cited ibid., p. 61.

Page 92: "Iran, because of the great leadership of the Shah…:" Jimmy Carter, quoted in Ashraf Pahlavi, *Faces in a Mirror,* Prentice Hall, 1980, p. 198, cited ibid., p. 239.

Page 92: U.S. Defense Intelligence Agency…predicted: ibid., p. 268.

Page 92: SAVAK maintained tight control: ibid., p. 107.

Page 92: $25 billion by 1974: ibid., p. 77.

Page 92: "White Revolution:" ibid., pp. 72–75.

Page 92: claimed dominion over time itself: ibid., p. 81.

Page 93: factions with the army loyal to Tudeh were purged: Nikki R. Keddie, *Roots of Revolution,* Yale University Press, 1981, p. 144.

Page 93: troops stormed the religious schools: ibid., p. 158.

Page 93: when a guerrilla uprising struck: Zonis, p. 68.

Page 93: SAVAK ordered newspapers to celebrate the Shah: Zonis, p. 62.

Page 93: SAVAK agents infiltrated opposition groups: Keddie, p. 144.

Page 93: the Iranian regime was complicit in human rights violations: ibid., p. 144.

Page 93: A Plan Organization was duly established: ibid., p. 147.

Page 93: 45 percent of the oil revenues…were diverted: ibid., p. 148.

Page 93: in order to import, export, or expand: ibid., p. 171.

Page 94: visitors to Tehran were impressed: ibid., p. 169.

Page 94: Cheap credit was extended to large firms: ibid., p. 171.

Page 94: The PO devoted much of its resources: ibid., p. 148.

Page 94: the government generally neglected to build local irrigation systems: ibid., p. 148.

Page 94: The endless credit supply to large-scale domestic enterprises…: ibid., p. 151.

Page 94: Prices for essential commodities such as grain skyrocketed: ibid., p. 149.

Page 94: Rural peasants began to flood into the cities: ibid., p. 167.

Page 94: the Shah withdrew: Zonis, p. 91.

Page 94: "no longer functioning:" ibid., p. 256.

Page 94: "The country is lost…:" Prime Minister General Gholem Reza Azhari, quoted in Zonis, p. 256.

Page 95: Black Friday: ibid., p. 248.

Page 95: the Shah shied away from using force: ibid., p. 249.

Page 95: crowds roamed the streets burning symbols: ibid., p. 251.

Page 95: more than $4 billion in losses: Julia Malone, "Future Unclear for Those Multimillion-Dollar Suits against Iran," *Christian Science Monitor,* Midwestern Edition, January 2, 1981.

Page 95: U.S. citizens living in Iran: J. Stempel, *Inside the Iranian Revolution,* 1981, 161 in Alan Epstein, "Foreign Expropriation Losses of Personal Assets: Should a Deduction Be Allowed Under Internal Revenue Code Section 165(c) (3)?" *The Tax Lawyer,* 40 Tax Law. 211, Fall 1986.

Page 95: OPIC, the U.S. government political risk insurer, had a $1 billion book of business…: David Tuller, "What's New in Insurance: Insuring Companies far From Home," *New York Times,* April 22, 1984.

Page 96: Race riots: Beng-Huat Chua, *Communitarian Ideology and Democracy in Singapore,* Routledge, 1995, pp. 81–84, cited in R. Ph. Le Blanc, *Singapore: The Socio-Economic Development of a City-State:,* Erasmus University, 1984, p. 6.

Page 96: an attractive location for manufacturing: ibid., p. 75.

Page 96: a program to control population growth: ibid., p. 81.

Page 96: the government spent an incredible amount…on education: ibid., p. 57.

Page 96: Mass transit was also good: U.S. Department of State. Fiscal Year 2001, Country Commercial Guide: Singapore.

Page 97: the civil service selection process was highly meritocratic: Todd Crowel and Andrea Hamilton, "The Next Generation," *Asiaweek,* November 13, 1998.

Page 97: civil servants were given excellent salaries: ibid.

Page 97: no one was exempt from scrutiny: Sheila McNulty, "Singapore MP Jailed for Graft," *Financial Times,* June 9, 1999.

Page 97: Singapore ranked as the fifth least corrupt country in the world: Transparency International Corruption Perception Index, 2002.

Page 97: fully 75 percent of Singaporeans: R. Ph. Le Blanc, p. 81.

Page 97: The state minutely directs economic activity: U.S. Department of State, Fiscal Year 2001, Country Commercial Guide: Singapore.

Page 97: Spitting, chewing gum, and watching pornography: "Plenty to Do," *Economist,* May 14, 1998.

Page 97: Taxis were equipped with bells: "A Tale of Two Systems," *Economist,* July 9, 1994.

Page 97: Gates are left unlocked: Steven Frank, "Singapore: Who's Laughing Now?" *Asiaweek,* October 25, 1996.

Page 97: motorcyclists leave their helmets: Rohit Jaggi, "Experiment Works for Most People," Survey—Singapore, *Financial Times,* April 11, 2001.

Page 97: caning is the punishment for thirty different offenses: U.S. Department of State, Bureau of Democracy, Human Rights, and Labor, Singapore: 1999 Country Report on Human Rights Practices, February 25, 2000.

Page 97: did not even try to contest 55 of the 84 seats: Douglas Wong, "Ready for debate and democracy," Survey—Singapore, *Financial Times,* April 12, 2002.

Page 98: the Internal Security Act: U.S. Department of State. Fiscal Year 2001, Country Commercial Guide: Singapore.

Page 98: Reporting usually conforms to the government line: ibid.

Page 98: Public assemblies must be state-sanctioned: ibid.

Page 98: In 1997, the prime minister warned voters: ibid.

Page 98: more than 92 percent of the people are literate: World Bank, *World Development Report 2003*.

Page 98: 3.6 deaths per 1,000 live births: *CIA World Factbook 2002*.

Page 98: $24,740: World Bank, *World Development Report 2003*.

Page 98: Ninety percent of Singaporeans own their own homes: Neal R. Pierce, "Singapore City-state will Survive Troubles," *Baltimore Sun,* June 1, 1998.

Page 98: the island's last strike was in 1986: U.S. Department of State, Fiscal Year 2001, Country Commercial Guide: Singapore.

Page 98: such world-class companies as Singapore Airlines…: John Burton, "Champions who do not find victory: Corporate Expansion," Survey—Singapore, *Financial Times,* April 12, 2002.

Page 99: venture capital firms are springing up: Sumathi Bala, "Chips are down as jobless rate rises: Economy," Survey—Singapore, *Financial Times,* April 12, 2002

Page 99: "Goh-bachev:" John Burton, "Cracks Appear in Corporatist Model Nation, Survey—Singapore, *Financial Times,* April 12, 2002

Chapter Eight—Good Leaders and Bad: Quality of Leadership

Page 105: the economy grew a whopping 4.2 percent…5.6 percent…1.6 percent…4.5 percent: Quest Economics Database, *Americas Review,* World of Information, December 20, 1999.

Page 106: 72 percent of Americans say 1998 was a good year: Robert J. Samuelson, "Washington Disconnected," *Newsweek,* January 11, 1999.

Page 106: the Treasury Department…was dealing effectively with…the Russian ruble devaluation…: Gerald Baker, "Economic Crisis Averted," *Financial Times,* December 30, 1998.

Page 107: some twenty ethnic groups: Ian Livingstone, Chapter 3: "Developing Uganda in the 1990s," *Developing Uganda,* Holger Bernt Hansen and Michael Twaddle, eds., James Currey (publisher), 1998, p. 10.

Page 107: convoluted political institutions: John Mukum Mbaku, *Africa in the Twenty-First Century: Which Way Forward?,* The John S. Hinckley Lecture, Weber State University, 2000

Page 107: bizarre arrangement: Phares Mutibwa, *Uganda Since Independence,* Africa World Press, 1992, p. 26.

Page 107: Obote promoted and relied on…Idi Amin: Rita M. Byrnes, ed., *Uganda: A Country Study,* Federal Research Division, Library of Congress, Research Completed 1990.

Page 107: "in the interest of national unity…:" Mutibwa, p. 39.

Page 107: Obote forced the new constitution through parliament: Library of Congress report.

Page 108: penetrate the religious establishment and the trade unions: Mutibwa, p. 36.

Page 108: troublesome Buganda region: Library of Congress report.

Page 108: "Move to the Left:" Mutibwa, p. 69–70.

Page 108: Bureaucrats…could not decipher…: Library of Congress report.

Page 108: quickly replaced competent ministers: Akiiki B. Mujaju, "Domestic Incoherence and External Intervention in Africa: The case of Uganda," *Makerere Political Science Review,* Vol. 1, 1997. pp 22–42.

Page 109: Uganda's economy plummeted…4.4 percent…62 percent…930…300: Ian Livingstone, Chapter 3: "Developing Uganda in the 1990s," in *Developing Uganda,* Holger Bernt Hansen and Michael Twaddle, eds., James Currey (publisher), 1998, p. 3.

Page 109: he uprooted 750,000 people…killed as many as 300,000…taking…the national treasury with him: Library of Congress report.

Page 110: Museveni also made a 180-degree turn on economic policies: Michael Twaddle and Holger Bernt Hansen, "Chapter 1: The Changing State of Uganda," in *Developing Uganda,* Holger Bernt Hansen and Michael Twaddle, eds., James Currey (publisher), 1998, p. 7.

Page 110: growth averaged…6.9 percent: World Bank, World Development Report 2003.

Page 110: he reduced inflation from 230 percent….to 0 percent: Paul Collier and Sanjay Pradhan, "Chapter Two: Economic Aspects of the Transition from Civil War," in *Developing Uganda,* Holger Bernt Hansen and Michael Twaddle, eds., James Currey (publisher), 1998, p. 27.

Page 110: The economy grew at a rate of 7.2 percent…housing boomed…: Collier and Pradhan, pp. 28–32.

Page 110: the once bustling black market…disappeared: Bill Berkeley, *The Graves Are Not yet Full,* Basic Books, 2001 p. 23.

Page 110: a full 40 percent of Uganda's annual budget: Declan Walsh, "Impressive Ugandan Leader Faces Toughest Test in Today's Election," *Irish Times,* March 12, 2000.

Page 110: The poverty rate fell from 56 percent…to 44 percent: Simon Appleton with Tom Emwanu, Johnson Kagugube, and James Muwonge, "Changes in poverty in Uganda, 1992–1997," Centre for the Study of African Economies Working Paper Series, Working Paper 106, May 1999, p. 16.

Page 110: Consumption per capita rose by 16.5 percent: ibid., p. 8.

Page 110: a 1990 survey…34 percent…said "peace"…: Collier and Pradhan, p. 33

Page 110–111: Museveni breached African etiquette by openly discussing sexual behavior…: Denise Johnson, "Uganda's Frank Talk Averted the worst; Strong, Engaged Leadership Produced an Education That Paid Off," *Minneapolis Star Tribune,* October 8, 2000.

Page 111: the infection rate dropped from 15 percent of the population to 8 percent: ibid.

Page 111: "The stability of Uganda hinges on one man…:" Billy Okadimiri, quoted in Berkeley p. 236.

Page 112–113: Guests at his inauguration speech included…members of the Apartheid regime: Martin Meredith, *Nelson Mandela,* St. Martins Press, 1998, p. 520.

Page 113: "…in spite of my criticism of Mr. de Klerk…:" ibid., p. 506.

Page 113: "He created a way for the Afrikaner community to participate…:" "Proving that One Man Can Make a Difference," *U.S. News and World Report,* May 24, 1999.

Page 113–114: Tunisia's economy grew by over 4.7 percent per year: World Bank, *World Development Report 2003.*

Page 114: three quarters of Tunisians lived in a home…: Francis Ghiles, Survey—Tunisia, *Financial Times,* July 27, 1994.

Chapter Nine—After Tito—Tito: Succession Threat

Page 117: a civil war had claimed a tenth of Yugoslavia's population: Mirko Tepavac, "Chapter 3: Tito's Yugoslavia," *Yugoslavia's Ethnic Nightmare,* Jasminka Udovicki and James Ridgeway eds., Lawrence Hill Books, 1995, p. 58.

Page 117: making the creation of Yugoslavia an historical inevitability: Christopher Bennett, *Yugoslavia's Bloody Collapse,* New York University Press, 1995, p. 54.

Page 118: Tito responded by sending 30,000 troops to crush the uprising: ibid., p. 55.

Page 118: He gave in to many of their demands for autonomy…: ibid., p. 71.

Page 118: federal aid comprised three quarters of Kosovo's budget: Richard West, *Tito and the Rise and Fall of Yugoslavia,* Sinclair Stevenson, 1994, p. 342.

Page 118: the Croatian republic's politicians demanded more autonomy…: Bennett, p. 73.

Page 118: He went on national TV and accused Croatia's leadership of pandering to nationalism…: West, p. 300.

Page 118: he purged prominent Croatian politicians…: Bennett, p. 74.

Page 119: Tito succeeded in creating a genuine "Yugoslav" identity: ibid., p. 64

Page 119: The evening news was broadcast from a different republic or province each day: Milan Milosevic, "Chapter 5: The Media Wars," *Yugoslavia's Ethnic Nightmare,* Jasminka Udovicki and James Ridgeway, eds., Lawrence Hill Books, 1995, p. 105.

Page 119: A huge personality cult arose around Tito…: Stevan K. Pavlowitch, *Tito— Yugoslavia's Great Dictator: A Reassessment,* Ohio State University Press, 1992, p. 75.

Page 119: a person of any ethnicity could travel from one end of the country to the other without being harassed: Mirko Tepavac, "Chapter 3: Tito's Yugoslavia," *Yugoslavia's Ethnic Nightmare,* Jasminka Udovicki and James Ridgeway, eds., Lawrence Hill Books, 1995, p. 58.

Page 119–120: Scholar Gavriel Ra'anan tried to lay out the qualifications…: Gavriel D. Ra'anan, *Yugoslavia after Tito,* Westview Press, p. 45.

Page 120: a new constitution…containing 406 articles, 100,000 words, and 205 pages: Pavlowitch, p. 79.

Page 120: keeping Tito alive as long as possible…: ibid., pp. 85–86.

Page 120: Sloganeers dutifully churned out pithy mottos…: ibid., p. 88.

Page 120: Foreign debt surpassed $20 billion: Slavko Curuvija and Ivan Torov, "Chapter 4: The March to War (1980–1990)," *Yugoslavia's Ethnic Nightmare,* Jasminka Udovicki and James Ridgeway eds., Lawrence Hill Books, 1995, p. 74.

Page 120: "Tito and the Eight Dwarves:" Pavlowitch, p. 87.

Page 121: Milosevic visited Kosovo…: Curuvija and Torov, p. 82.

Page 121: peacekeeping operations in Bosnia had cost $2.4 billion…and in Kosovo, $1.9 billion: George C. Wilson, "Peacekeeping Saves Cents, Makes Sense," *National Journal,* March 30, 2002.

Page 122: Italy's national income has grown fivefold and individual income fourfold: Percy Allum, "Italian Society Transformed," *Italy Since 1945*, Patrick McCarthy, ed., John A. Davis, general ed., Oxford University Press, 2000, p. 10.

Page 122: the incredible dominance of the Christian Democratic Party…: Frederic Spotts and Theodore Wieser, *Italy, A Difficult Democracy*, Cambridge University Press, 1986., p. 15.

Page 123: Amitore Fanfani, Giulio Andreotti…: ibid., pp. 15–16.

Page 123: a total of 1,331 ministerial and sub-cabinet jobs…152 oft-reappointed people held almost two-thirds of these; and 31 people were reappointed….they held 489 jobs: study by Mauro Calise and Renato Mannheimer, cited ibid.

Page 123: a well-practiced constitutional process kicks in: ibid., p. 106.

Page 125: The military action cost American taxpayers $1.5 billion: Harry Johnston, "Why the U.S. Shouldn't Be Out of Africa," *Palm Beach Post*, December 22, 1996.

Page 125: the factions squabbled for three days over the words "We the undersigned:" Mark Turner, "Somali Talks Put Diplomats' Skills to Test," *Financial Times*, November 20, 2002.

Page 125: Somalis are not traditionally strict Muslims…: "Into the Vacuum," *Economist*, September 22, 2001.

Page 125: The United States…has frozen the assets…and held talks with warlords: Mark Turner, "Strife-riven Somalia Moves Centre-stage," *Financial Times*, December 12, 2001.

Page 126: "When I used to travel…:" Jerry Rawlings, quoted in Danna Harman, "Days Wane for African Big Men," *Christian Science Monitor*, December 27, 2002.

Page 127: Prince Bandar Bin Sultan…once recalled his reaction…: Evan Thomas and Christopher Dickey, "The Saudi Game," *Newsweek*, November 19, 2001.

Page 130: President Akayev married off his son to the daughter of President Nazarbayev: "A Worrying Vote," *Economist*, February 26, 2000.

Page 130: surreal state-of-the art tennis complex: Robert Rand, "Backhands and Bombs," *New Yorker*, October 22, 2001.

Page 130: Niyazov traces his family tree back to Noah: Ehud Ya'ari, "A Golden Opportunity among Muslim Friends," *Jerusalem Report*, May 21, 2001.

Page 130: renamed some days of the week and months of the year…: Ilan Greenberg, "When a Kleptocratic, Megalomaniacal Dictator Goes Bad," *New York Times*, January 5, 2003.

Page 130: "President for Life:" "Dream On," *Economist*, January 8, 2000.

Page 98: Nazarbayev has…transferred more than $1 billion: Edmund L. Andrews, "Spotlight on Central Asia is Finding Repression, Too," *New York Times,* April 11, 2002.

Page 131: the combined oil and gas deposits of the five Central Asian "stans" plus Azerbijian: Richard Butler, "A New Oil Game, with New Winners," *New York Times,* January 18, 2002.

Page 131: Karimov…receives invitations to the Oval Office: Todd S. Purdum, "Uzbekistan's Leader Doubts Chances for Afghan Peace," *New York Times,* April 14, 2002.

Chapter Ten—Fujishock: The Ruling Bargain

Page 134: We believe the credit for the first use of "ruling bargain" in this way—to understand what makes a nondemocratic country stable or unstable—goes to Daniel Brumberg.

Page 135: As dissected by scholar Joshua Teitelbaum…: Joshua Teitelbaum, *Holier Than Thou,* Washington Institute for Near East Policy, 2000.

Page 135: "protect the principles of Islam, enforce its Sharia…:" Gregory Gause, *Oil Monarchies,* Council on Foreign Relations Press, 1994, p. 106.

Page 135: Saudi Arabia's modern government bases the country's official constitution on the Koran…: ibid., p. 111.

Page 135: "Custodian of the Two Holy Mosques:" ibid., p. 30.

Page 136: "money is the great lubricant:" Judith Miller, *God Has Ninety-Nine Names,* Simon & Schuster, 1996 p. 84.

Page 136: between 1974 and 1990, the government spent $800 billion…: ibid., pp. 84–126.

Page 136: Students received $270 per month: ibid., p. 87.

Page 136: annual population growth rate…was 2.8 percent…1.2 percent…0.2 percent: World Bank, *World Development Report 2003.*

Page 136: the population was 9.8 million…14.9 million: ibid.

Page 136: In 2001, [the population was] 21.4 million: Teitelbaum, p. 6.

Page 136: prices peaked around 1982 at roughly $42 per barrel…$10…$20: Gause, pp. 82–83.

Page 136: per capita income of $15,810: Teitelbaum, p. 6.

Page 137: students had no choice but to take their education in the predominantly religious Saudi educational system: , p. 7.

Page 137: the unemployment rate…may be as high as 25 percent: "western sources" cited by Teitelbaum, p. 6.

Page 137: a shanty town of 60,000 sits near the Kuwaiti border: "dissident sources" cited by Heidi Kingstone, "Trouble in the House of Saud," *Jerusalem Report,* January 13, 2003.

Page 137: The 1999 budget enforced a hiring freeze, a 30 percent cut…: Teitelbaum, p. 117

Page 137: "The boom period is gone for good and…we have to become used to a different lifestyle…:" Crown Prince Abdullah quoted ibid., p. 118.

Page 137: King Fahd has one son who lives in a $300 million palace…: Miller, p. 87.

Page 138: The royal family invests the kingdom's money in interest-bearing instruments…: Teitelbaum, p. 18.

Page 138: Wahhabis have always separated themselves…: Liesl Graz, "The Turbulent Gulf," in Nawaf E. Obaid, "The Power or Saudi Arabia's Islamic Leaders," *Middle East Quarterly,* St. Martin's Press, 1992.

Page 138: "only those who lead by God's book,"…"No claim on our obedience…:" Juhayman bin Muhammad al-'Utaybi, quoted in Teitelbaum, p. 20.

Page 138: Usama bin Laden reportedly offered to rally his own Islamist troops to defend Saudi Arabia…: Eric Rouleau, "Trouble in the Kingdom," *Foreign Affairs,* July–August 2002.

Page 139: four hundred…ulama….sent a petition to the king…: Gause, p. 34.

Page 139: "Memorandum of Advice:" ibid., 35.

Page 139: "Awakening Shaykhs"…: Teitelbaum, pp. 56–60.

Page 139: "Our religion was not meant to be only confined to corners of a particular mosque…:" Salman bin Fahd Al-'Awda, quoted ibid., p. 60.

Page 139: they did not go quietly…: ibid., p. 58.

Page 140: "It is never acceptable that Christians and Jews are wandering freely…:" militant group, Kata'ib al-Iman, quoted ibid., p. 60.

Page 140: an informal poll conducted by Interior Minister Nayef…: cited by Miller, p. 125.

Page 141: his aim to abolish the Saudi regime and divide the entire Arabian Peninsula…: Teitelbaum, p. 79.

Page 141: Bin Laden is personally popular in Saudi Arabia: Eric Rouleau, "Trouble in the Kingdom," *Foreign Affairs,* July–August 2002.

Page 141: most of the September 11 hijackers came from the 'Asir: Thomas L. Friedman, "The Saudi Challenge," *New York Times,* February 20, 2002.

Page 142. 80 approval rating: "Peruvians Accept Fujimori's New Authority," Agence France Presse, April 7, 1992.

Page 142: the economy actually contracted by a third…inflation reached…40 percent per month: "The Dark Side of the Boom," *Economist,* August 5, 1995.

Page 142–143: civil war…cost the lives of 30,000 Peruvians and cost $25 billion and cost $25 billion: David Adams, "Blast May Herald Rebels' Return," *St. Petersburg Times,* March 22, 2002.

Page 143: abolished capital controls, freed the currency, and rapidly privatized state-owned industries: "The Dark Side of the Boom," *Economist,* August 5, 1995

Page 144: inflation was brought down to double digits in 1992 and to around 8 percent by 1995: ibid.

Page 144: Peru grew…tops in the world: "Peru: Americas Review 1998," *Americas Review,* World of Information, March 1998.

Page 144: The impoverished Southern Andean states…saw the greatest poverty relief, 75 percent, from 55.1 percent to 49.6 percent, by 36 percent: Kenneth M. Roberts and Moises Arce, "Neoliberalism and Lower-class Voting Behavior in Peru," *Comparative Political Studies,* April 1998.

Page 144: 3,102 deaths due to political violence…only 297: Country reports on human rights practices for 1994. U.S. Department of State, 1995.

Page 148: as scholar Hossein Mahdavy noted: see Hossein Mahdavy, "Patterns and Problems of Economic Development in Rentier States: the Case of Iran," in *Studies in the Economic History of the Middle East,* M.A. Cook, ed., Oxford University Press, 1970.

Page 148: "no representation without taxation:" Gause, p. 79.

Chapter Eleven—Clockwork Crises: The Instability Trap

Page 158: Student radicals took over campuses…: Timothy Kessler, *Global Capital and National Politics,* Praeger, 1991, pp. 5–21.

Page 158: "tragic complacency of previous regimes"…"Shared Development,"…: ibid., pp. 21–26.

Page 158: bad economics…: ibid., pp. 5–26.

Page 159: Inflation shot up, thanks to out-of-control government spending…: ibid., pp. 25–26.

Page 159: the nominal exchange rate…had been set at the same value since the 1950s: ibid., p. 27.

Page 159: "the little rich Mexicans…:" Luis Echeverria, quoted in Solis, 1981, cited in ibid., p. 28.

Page 159: "We're not going to devalue anything here…:" Jose Lopez Portillo, quoted in Jorge Castaneda, *Perpetuating Power,* The New Press, 2000, p. 34.

Page 159: the peso collapsed, falling by 60 percent: ibid., p. 27.

Page 159: Mexican businesspeople…founded…the Coordinating Enterprise Council: ibid., p. 28.

Page 159: President Lopez Portillo set about winning back business support…: ibid., p. 29.

Page 160: Portillo slashed the budget deficit from 9.9 percent of GDP to 6.7 percent: ibid., p. 29.

Page 160: oil production tripled to 2.4 million barrels per day…: Alan Riding, "Getting Mexico Moving Again," *New York Times,* July 4, 1982.

Page 160: the public sector deficit skyrocketed from 7.3 percent of GDP to 12.5 percent in 1981: Caroline Atkinson and Christopher Dickey, "Oil Boom Accelerated Mexico's Economic Bust," *Washington Post,* August 28, 1982.

Page 160: Mexico….borrowed approximately $52 billion: Alan Riding, "Getting Mexico Moving Again," *New York Times,* July 4, 1982.

Page 160: an estimated $17 to $23 billion left the country: Kessler, p. 35.

Page 160: Mexicans had stashed $25 billion in assets in Texas alone: Federal Reserve study, cited in Kessler, p. 35.

Page 160: a pitched battle over who would succeed Lopez Portillo…: Castaneda, p. 51.

Page 161: "birds of ill omen never win:" ibid., p. 45.

Page 161: with a budget deficit in excess of $20 billion: Alan Riding, "Taming Mexico's Passion for More," *New York Times,* September 12, 1982.

Page 161: "like a dog," Lopez Portillo: cited in Kessler, pp. 34–35.

Page 161: U.S. government…extended a $600 million line of credit: Jonathan Ferguson, "Mexico's Dilemma: Starvation Versus Economic Collapse, *Toronto Star,* March 22, 1987.

Page 161: Lopez Portillo nationalized fifty-nine private banks: Alan Riding, "Taming Mexico's Passion for More," *New York Times,* September 12, 1982.

Page 161: Treasury Secretary James Baker III, "Brady Bonds:" Peter Marber, *From Third World to World Class,* Perseus Books, 1998, pp. 53–57.

Page 161: De la Madrid…set up a generous subsidy scheme to repair some of the damage Mexican businesspeople had suffered…24 percent, 10 percent: Kessler, pp. 53–65.

Page 162: abandoned the PRI for the right-wing National Action Party: ibid., p. 6.

Page 162: PAN won control of several large cities: "How the Ruling Party Keeps Mexico Surprisingly Calm," *Business Week,* October 1, 1984.

Page 162: This boost in spending pushed inflation over 100 percent: Jonathan Ferguson, "Mexico's Dilemma: Starvation Versus Economic Collapse," *Toronto Star,* March 22, 1987.

Page 162: "We have cut spending right down to the bone…:" Carlos Salinas, quoted in Castaneda, pp. 66–67.

Page 162: the U.S., the IMF, and the World Bank rushed in: ibid., p. 69.

Page 163: Salinas…adhered rigidly to fiscal discipline…: Marber, p. 188.

Page 163: Salinas privatized state industries, deregulated…: Rudiger Dornbusch, Ilan Goldfajn, Rodrigo Valdes, "Currency Crises and Collapses," Brookings Institution Papers on Economic Activity, 2: 1995, p. 237.

Page 163: Euromoney magazine: Sebastian Edwards, "The Mexican Peso Crisis: How Much Did We Know? When Did We Know It?," Working Paper 6334. National Bureau of Economic Research Working Paper, December 1997, p. 4.

Page 163: over half of all investment headed for Latin America, a total value of $91 billion: Edwards, p. 8.

Page 163: The current account deficit rose to 6.8 percent of GDP…, and 8 percent: Jeffrey Sachs, Aaron Tomell and Andres Velasco, "The Collapse of the Mexican Peso: What Have We Learned?," Harvard University and NBER, Session on Mexico: May 6, 1999.

Page 163: "The president who devalues is devalued:" Lopez Portillo, quoted in Kessler, p. 110.

Page 163: in the early part of 1994, an Indian uprising in the southern state of Chiapas….: ibid., p. 109.

Page 163: Salinas spent $10 billion defending the peso's value: Edwards, p. 17.

Page 163: showering money on districts where the PRI faced the most significant opposition: Dornbusch, Goldfajn, Valdes, p. 240.

Page 163: the Central Bank extended $8 billion in domestic credit in March and April: Sachs, p. 29.

Page 163: This just worsened the gaping current account deficit: ibid., p. 38.

Page 164: Citicorp still had an estimated $5 billion invested in Mexico: James R. Kraus, "Citi Having Rough Road in Latin Loans," *The American Banker,* October 13, 1995.

Page 164: American portfolio investment…was estimated at $1 billion, with another $2.2 billion in the Mexican debt market: Lisa Barnsten and Patrick Harverson, "U.S. Investors Nurse Bruises From Peso Crisis," *Financial Times,* December 30, 1994.

Page 164: the Mexican stock market lost an astounding half of its value: Stephen Fidler, "Slow Recovery After Tequila Effect," *Financial Times,* January 25, 1996.

Page 164: The United States ultimately extended $50 billion in bailout funds: Dornbusch, Goldfajn, Valdes, p. 241.

Page 164: considering the 2,000 mile border… prospect of fervent anti-Americanism…: Paul Krugman, "The Tequila Effect," *USA Today,* May 5, 1997

Page 164: Argentine stocks lost 7.5 percent…, 28 percent, 26 percent, and 20 percent: Stephen Fidler, "Slow Recovery After Tequila Effect," *Financial Times,* January 25, 1996.

Page 165: Scholar Mancur Olson explained this phenomenon: see Mancur Olson, "Dictatorship, Democracy, and Development," *American Political Science Review,* Vol. 87, No. 3, September 1993.

Page 168: Thailand's economic difficulties—a current account deficit at 8.1 percent of GDP: William Barnes, Survey—Thailand, The Economy," *Financial Times,* December 5, 1996.

Page 168: short-term debt totaling $41 billion, a 40.7 percent increase: Ted Bardacke, "Moody's in Downgrade of Thai Debt," *Financial Times,* September 4, 1996.

Page 168: Chavlit was forced to back down: Ted Bardacke, "High Price of Democracy: The New Thai Government Aims to Dispel Accusations of Corruption With The Promise of a New Constitution," *Financial Times,* December 3, 1996.

Page 168: In an effort to gain favor and ward off challenges, the prime minister gave contracts…: "Part of a Long Tradition," *Financial Times,* December 5, 1996.

Page 168: The financial crisis quickly spread: John Ridding, "Caught in the Asian Smog," *Financial Times,* October 25, 1997.

Page 168: "The governments with political strength to do the unpleasant…:" Lee Kwan Yew, quoted in "Southeast Asia Finds Fiscal Discipline Will be an Unsavoury Dish: The Region's Economic Crisis Means Growth is No Longer the Only Issue at Stake for the Politicians: Social Peace," *Financial Times,* October 31, 1997.

Chapter Twelve—Powers Behind the Throne: Entrenched Interests

Page 170: an estimated 35 percent [of Cubans] voted for Clinton: William Schneider, "Elian Gonzalez Defeated Al Gore," *National Journal,* April 28, 2001.

Page 170: el voto castigo: ibid.

Page 170: "Elian Gonzalez Defeated Al Gore:" ibid.

Page 171: the top five percent....owns 64 percent of all Pakistan's farmland: Abdus Sattar Ghazali, *Hegemony of the Ruling Elite in Pakistan,* Eagle Books, October 6, 2000.

Page 171: 1997 study... cited by Sreedhar, "Pakistan's Economic Dilemma," www.nyu.edu/globalbeat/southasia/06181998sreedhar1.html, June 18, 1998.

Page 172: Nazimuddin had broken up...: Akbar S. Ahmed, "Social Structures and Flow," *Foundations of Pakistan's Political Economy,* William James and Subrato Roy, eds., Sage Publications, 1992, p. 112.

Page 172: the United States...gave the antidemocratic putsch its blessing: ibid.

Page 172: 70 percent of Pakistan's military officers come from the Punjab: B. Raman, "Pakistan's Army Within the Army," Asiafeatures.com, June 30, 2000.

Page 172: Ayub Khan and Zia ul Haq helped create a new set of feudals: Shada Islam, "Lords of Misrule," *Far Eastern Economic Review,* May 20, 1999.

Page 172: man-made famine: Ayesha Jalal, *Democracy and Authoritarianism in South Asia,* Cambridge University Press, 1995.

Page 172: They registered pieces of their lands in the name of their family members: Shada Islam, "Lords of Misrule," *Far Eastern Economic Review,* May 20, 1999.

Page 173: *haris*: ibid.

Page 173: consider the Legharis: Tim McGirk, "The Feudal Curse," *Time,* February 3, 1997.

Page 173: a full 75 percent of the members of Pakistan's parliament....: Ghazali.

Page 126: 126 of 207 seats: Shada Islam, "Lords of Misrule," *Far Eastern Economic Review,* May 20, 1999.

Page 174: Bhutto...appointed 17 landlords to her 39-person cabinet: ibid.

Page 174: hidden subsidies: Parvez Hassan, *Pakistan's Economy at the Crossroads,* Oxford University Press, 1998, p. 71.

Page 174: Leghari family...has in recent years paid a tax bill of zero: Tim McGirk, "The Feudal Curse," *Time,* February 3, 1997

Page 174: the government collected 2 billion rupees...but lost 50 billion rupees: Shada Islam, "Lords of Misrule," *Far Eastern Economic Review,* May 20, 1999

Page 175: Pakistan spends 0.9 percent of its GDP on public health...2.8 percent...2.7 percent...7 percent: *United Nations Human Development Index 2001.*

Page 175: A study by a Pakistani social scientist, cited in Paul Blustein, "In Pakistan's Squalor, Cradles of Terrorism," *Washington Post,* March 14, 2002.

Page 175: literacy rate...43 percent...67 percent: World Bank, World Development Report 2003.

Page 175: half a million pupils: Paul Blustein, "In Pakistan's Squalor, Cradles of Terrorism," *Washington Post,* March 14, 2002.

Page 175: over the past four decades, it has received more aid than any poor country: ibid.

Page 176: "This is a country of landlords....:" Mumtaz Bhutto, quoted in Shada Islam, "Lords of Misrule," *Far Eastern Economic Review,* May 20, 1999.

Page 178: 2.9 million small and medium-sized farms, 2 percent of the land: Amaury de Souza, "The Social Agenda at Century's End," *Brazil under Cardoso,* Susan Kaufman Purcell and Riordan Roett, eds., Lynne Rienner Publishers, 1997, p. 78.

Page 178: several post-World War II attempts at land reform: Lincoln Gordon, *Brazil's Second Chance,* Brookings Institution Press, 2001, p. 126.

Page 178: Collor...tried to enact reform via presidential decree...: Kurt Weyland, *Democracy Without Equity,* University of Pittsburgh Press, 1996, p. 113.

Page 179: 12 percent of GDP: Barry Ames, *The Deadlock of Democracy in Brazil,* University of Michigan Press, 2001, p. 276.

Page 179: Public-sector pensions average $5,000 in the judicial branch...$2,700...$3,000: de Souza, p. 85.

Page 179: a pension reform bill...was amended beyond all recognition: Economist Intelligence Unit, *Brazil Revisited,* 1999.

Page 179: Literacy rates have reached 86 percent: Gordon, p. 133.

Page 179: 37 percent of the population aged sixteen to eighteen: de Souza, p. 65.

Page 180: only two percent of the population...attends these schools: "Cramming Them In," *Economist,* May 11, 2002.

Page 180: According to a 1995 World Bank study: cited in de Souza, p. 71.

Page 180: an investigation found that 40 percent of the country's 460 millionaires: cited in Jack Epstein, "Tax Reform Now!" *Freedom Magazine,* Latin Trade, April 2001

Page 180: shell corporations: ibid.

Page 180: the system relies heavily on indirect taxes: Weyland, p. 124.

Page 180: business lobbies...torpedoed the change: ibid., p. 110.

Page 180–181: Brazil's formidable state sector includes 27 top-level agencies…300…100…and 560: ibid., p. 60.

Page 181: most Brazilian state governments spend 70 percent of their revenues on personnel costs: *Country Report, Brazil,* World of Information January 23, 2001.

Page 181: Public-sector payrolls consume a whopping 12 percent of GDP: "A Sorry State," *Economist,* March 27, 1999.

Page 181: many of those who collect…do not bother to show up: Gordon., p. 160.

Page 181: "antibureaucracy czars:" Ieda Siqueria Wiarda, "Chapter 9: Brazil: The Politics of Order and Progress?," *Latin American Politics and Development,* Howard J. Wiarda and Harvey F. Kline, eds., Westview Press, 1990, p. 192.

Page 181: Scholar David Fleischer conducted a detailed analysis: cited in Javier Martinez Lara, *Building Democracy in Brazil,* Macmillan Press, 1996, p. 70.

Page 182: a mandatory five-year review…police had to enter the Chamber of Deputies to restore order: ibid, p. 187.

Page 182: an American presidency on top of an Italian parliament: "Gatecrashing the Honeymoon," *Economist,* February 8, 2003.

Page 182: "Our party is so disorganized, we can't even throw a party:" Ames, p. 187.

Page 182: 230 of the 513 deputies changed parties at least once: Economist Intelligence Unit, "Brazil Revisited," 1999.

Page 183: the richest 10 percent of the population collects nearly half the country's annual income…: ibid.

Page 183: In Japan…3.4…5.7…8.9…25.2: World Bank, World Development Indicators, 2000, Table 2.8.

Page 183: Brazil's average life expectancy lags behind even India: Gordon, p. 137.

Page 183: Since 1970, more than 2,000…: *Country Report, Brazil,* World of Information, January 23, 2001.

Page 184: the value of the Brazilian real down about 40 percent…20 percent: Raymond Colitt, "Brazil's Savers Swept up in Lula's Reforming Zeal," *Financial Times,* February 17, 2003.

Page 184: overhaul the way organized labor is structured: ibid.

Page 185: scholar Mancur Olson: see Mancur Olson, *The Logic of Collective Action: Public Goods and the Theory of Groups,* Harvard University Press, 1971.

Page 186: Machiavelli: see Niccolo Machiavelli, *The Prince.*

Page 188: Japan, Korea, and Taiwan…all instituted aggressive land reform programs that resulted in some of the world's most equal distributions of income: Gustav Papanek, "The New Asian Capitalism: An Economic Portrait," in Peter L. Berger, and Hsin-Huang Michael Hsiao, eds., *In Search of an East Asian Development Model,* Transaction Books, 1988. p.33.

Page 189: "shatter-proof:" Judy Dempsey, "Barak Builds Himself a Shatter-proof Coalition," *Financial Times,* July 7, 1999.

Page 190: "Hundreds of thousands of Israelis receive direct transfer payments from the state…:" Hanan Sher, "Jerusalem on the Rio de la Plata?" *Jerusalem Report,* January 28, 2002.

Page 191: 18 of 75 bills, 60 of 124 bills: Kishiko Hisada, "Nonprofit Groups Join Politicians To Challenge Bureaucrats," *Asahi Shimbun,* November 15, 1999.

Page 191: accounts for about eight percent of GDP: Mamoru Ishida, "Reform Delays Discouraging," *Japan Times,* September 23, 2002

Page 192–193: "Crisis Mandate:" see: Peter Gourevitch, *Politics in Hard Times: Comparative Responses to International Economic Crises,* Cornell University Press, 1986; Stephen Haggard and Robert Kaufman, eds., *The Politics of Economic Adjustment: International Constraints, Distributive Conflicts, and the State,* Princeton University Press, 1992; John Keeler: "Opening the Windows for Reform: Mandates, Crises, and Extraordinary Policy-Making," *Comparative Political Studies* 25, and Aaron Tornell, "Are Economic Crises Necessary" in Rudiger Dornbusch and Sebastian Edwards, eds., *Reform, Recovery, and Growth,* University of Chicago Press, 1995.

Page 193: "Bad times make for good policies…:" Mohammad Sadli, quoted in David Dixon, Tom McCawley, and William Wallis, "Windfall Dilemma of the World's Poorer Oil Exporters," *Financial Times,* October 20, 2000.

Chapter Thirteen—The Visible Hand: Government Intervention

Page 196: the Ottomans…defaulted on payments to European creditors: Erik J. Zurcher, *Turkey A Modern History,* I.B. Tauris & Co., p. 88.

Page 196–197: the Administration…dictated much of the Ottoman budget and economic policymaking: Dietrich Jung, with Wolfango Piccoli, *Turkey at the Crossroads,* Zed Books, 2001, p. 48.

Page 197: the Ottoman Empire's main industries were under foreign control: Helen Chapin Metz, ed., *Turkey: A Country Study,* Library of Congress Report, Research completed January 1995.

Page 197: "Foreigners"...controlled much of the Empire's financial sector: Zurcher, pp.89–90.

Page 197: the Ottoman Empire had lost virtually all of its foreign territories: Albert Hourani, *The History of the Arab Peoples,* Harvard University Press, 1991, pp. 315–316.

Page 198: The chief Islamic leader called for Mustafa Kemal's assassination: Jung, with Piccoli, p. 68.

Page 198: Rumors circulated of a military plot: Feroz Ahmad, *The Making of Modern Turkey,* Routledge, 1993, p. 57.

Page 198: He invoked emergency powers and set up military tribunals: ibid., p. 58.

Page 198: "a colony of foreigners:" Ataturk, quoted ibid., p.93.

Page 198–199: He then created his locally owned monopolies: Zurcher, p. 204.

Page 199: Ataturk founded the Business Bank: Ahmad, p. 96.

Page 199: his new economic policy was "statism:" Anne O. Krueger, "Government Failures in Development," *Journal of Economic Perspectives,* Volume 4, Number 3. Summer 1990. p. 14.

Page 199: Thus making Turkey the first country to follow the USSR: Z.Y. Hershlag, *Turkey The Challenge of Growth,* 2nd Edition, E.J. Brill, 1968, p. 6.

Page 199: Sumerbank: Ahmad, p. 98.

Page 199: A constitution drawn up in 1961 codified...: Elie Kedourie, *Politics in the Middle East,* Oxford University Press, 1992, p. 120.

Page 200: "Bank of Politicians:" Ahmad, p. 96.

Page 200: conglomerates...that got their starts under Ataturk: *Middle East Review, Turkey: Review,* World of Information, September 13, 2001.

Page 200: Koç Holdings: *Country Report, Turkey: Economy,* World of Information, February 8, 2000.

Page 200: The Sabançi conglomerate notes proudly: Sabançi, quoted in "Fingers Crossed," *Economist,* June 8, 2000.

Page 200: "It is evident that [Turkish] politics in general has been reduced...:" N. Beriker-Atiyas, "Kurdish Conflict in Turkey: Issues, Parties and Prospects," *Security Dialogue,* vol. 28, 1997, pp. 439–452.

Page 201: the inflation rate dropped to between 30 percent and 40 percent per year: Zurcher, p. 311.

Page 201: Researchers Oyuz Oyan and Ali Riza Aydin documented…: cited in Ahmad, p. 191.

Page 201: the official fiscal deficit averaged…3 percent of GDP: Helen Chapin Metz, ed., *Turkey: A Country Study,* Library of Congress Report, research completed January 1995.

Page 201: the Turkish national debt ballooned from $13.5 billion to $40 billion: Zurcher, p. 307.

Page 201: inflation had again bounced up to 70 percent: ibid., p. 311.

Page 201: according to TESEV: cited in David Barchard, "Drive to Modernize and Serve as Market Economy: Reforming the Bureaucracy," Survey—Turkey, *Financial Times,* July 25, 2002.

Page 201: Tupras, Tekel, Petkim: *Country Report. Turkey: Economy,* World of Information February 8, 2000.

Page 201–202: TKK…somehow managed to employ 19,000…: Leyla Boulton, "The Battle to Keep the State at Bay," *Financial Times,* January 15, 2002.

Page 202: 76 percent devaluation: Helen Chapin Metz, ed., *Turkey: A Country Study,* Library of Congress Report, research completed January 1995.

Page 203: the airline's $167 million loss in 1999: Leyla Boulton, "Ankara to Keep Golden Share in THY Sell-off," *Financial Times,* December 14, 2000.

Page 203: Ziraat Bank, Halk Bank: "Financial Crisis Highlights Need for Reform," *Financial Times Survey,* July 13, 2001.

Page 204: questionable accounting statements: C. Emre Alper and Ziya Onis, "Financial Globalization, the Democratic Deficit and Recurrent Crises in Emerging Markets: The Turkish Experience in the Aftermath of Capital Account Liberalization," *Emerging Markets Finance and Trade,* Volume 39, Number 3, 2003.

Page 204: opened the floodgates for subsidized loans: ibid., p. 10.

Page 204: a document detailing which state bank each party would control: Serhan Cevik, "Turkey: Challenging Statism and Crony Capitalism," Morgan Stanley Global Economic Forum, www.morganstanley.com

Page 204: $20 billion in the hole: Alper and Onis, p. 19.

Page 204: Of the six new private banks…six had failed within a decade: ibid., p. 19.

Page 204: well-connected bankers borrowed large amounts from foreign lenders and then lent this money to the Turkish government at extremely high interest rates: ibid., p. 11.

Page 204: 88 percent of the profits: "Fingers Crossed," *Economist,* June 8, 2000.

Page 204: stock market was soon nearly half off its peak: "Turkey and the IMF: Take Ten Billion," *Economist,* December 7, 2000.

Page 205: the International Monetary Fund...surprised the markets with a generous $7.5 billion rescue package: ibid.

Page 205: Morgan Stanley described a "black hole"...: Cevik.

Page 205: A well-connected financier was caught on videotape: "On the Brink Again," *Economist,* February 22, 2001.

Page 205: "We installed you, and we can remove you:" Leyla Boulton and Quentin Peel, "Turkish Turmoil," *Financial Times,* February 21, 2001.

Page 205: The government....was forced to let the lira float: "On the Brink Again," *Economist,* February 22, 2001.

Page 206–207: Turkey And Motorola: the principal source for this section was Barbara Rose, "Motorola's Fraud Lawsuit a Story of Global Intrigue," *Chicago Tribune,* February 16, 2003.

Page 207: "into this venture...:" New York judge, quoted in David Glavin, "Motorola, Nokia to Win Judgment in Lawsuit," Bloomberg News, reprinted in *Chicago Sun Times,* February 20, 2003.

Page 208: All over the world, state-owned enterprises sprang up...: Anne O. Krueger, "Government Failures in Development," *Journal of Economic Perspectives,* Volume 4, Number 3, Summer 1990.

Page 208: In the U.S., spending on subsidies and transfers reached 2 percent...6 percent...13 percent: "The Future of the State," *Economist,* September 20, 1997.

Page 209: "value subtraction:" ibid.

Page 209: The Tanzanian government...spent one and a half times as much: World Bank, *World Development Report: The State in a Changing World,* Oxford University Press, 1997, p. 53.

Page 210: urban hospitals...which differentially benefit the better off: ibid.

Page 210: In Venezuela, just 31 percent of the education budget...In South Korea, 84 percent: ibid., p. 53.

Page 210: These agencies set up incentive programs, provided loans, handed subsidies: ibid., p. 83.

Page 210–211: The less government workers are paid...: ibid., p. 10.

Page 211: the more closed an economy…the more corrupt: Paolo Mauro, "Why Worry About Corruption?" *Economic Issues 6,* International Monetary Fund Publication Services, February 1997, p. 4.

Page 211: The more subsidies a government hands out, the more likely civil servants are to become corrupt: ibid., p. 5.

Chapter Fourteen—"When England Sneezes:" External Shocks

Page 213: "When England Sneezes…:" Stephan McGinty, "Cool Caledonia," *Sunday Times,* April 26, 1998.

Page 213: "If Russia Sneezes…:" Jeffrey Marshall, "Risk Management Takes on New Dimensions," *U.S. Banker,* August 1999.

Page 213: "When America Sneezes, Israel catches a cold:" Judy Maltz, *Jerusalem Report,* April 9, 2001.

Page 213: "When Russia catches a cold, Germany sneezes," Frederick Studemann, "Russia's Troubles Fuel Fears of Germany Business Community," *Financial Times,* July 13, 1998.

Page 213: "When Brazil's economy sneezes…:" "The Global Crisis: Latin America: Samba Effect Follows Tequila Tumble," *The Independent,* February 1, 1999

Page 213: "The last two decades have shown…:" Kristin Forbes and Roberto Rigobon, "Contagion in Latin America: Definitions, Measurement, and Policy Implications," *National Bureau of Economic Research Working Paper 7885,* September 2000.

Page 214: [Argentina] defaulted on $85 billion of its $155 billion public debt: Alan Beatie, "IMF Debt Deal for Argentina Provokes Revolt," *Financial Times,* January 25, 2003.

Page 216: They shipped a total of $8 billion: David Pillings, "Guarded Optimism Bolsters Argentina," *Financial Times,* December 18, 1995.

Page 216: "a little queasy about Argentina…,"…"It is a difficult time to have a currency board…:" Barton Biggs, quoted in David Pilling, "Argentina Combats Mexican Wave," *Emerging Investor,* January 9, 1995.

Page 217: Argentina earned a lot of money from its exports of paper, iron….: David Pilling, "Rallying around the Flag of Exports," *Financial Times,* January 30, 1996.

Page 217: the economy grew by 4.3 percent: Ken Warn, "Rising Red Ink Blots Expectations," *Financial Times,* September 9, 1997.

Page 218: productivity growth was negative throughout the 1990s: Sebastian Edwards, "This Argentine Scheme," *Financial Times,* January 21, 2002.

Page 218: the governors....did not want to stop spending: Manuel Pastor and Carol Wise, "From Poster Child to Basket Case," *Foreign Affairs,* November/December 2001.

Page 218: an expensive pension program…: "A Decline without Parallel: Argentina's Collapse," *Economist,* March 2, 2002.

Page 219: improved its overall budget balance by 2 percent of GDP: Michael Mussa, "Argentina and the Fund: From Triumph to Tragedy," *Institute for International Economics,* March 25, 2002.

Page 219: "off-budget" funds: ibid.

Page 219: After sending over $100 billion: Geoff Dyer, "Brazil Rebounds," *Financial Times,* June 2, 2000.

Page 219: net capital flows to emerging markets actually turned negative: Martin Wolf, "Time for Plan B in Argentina," *Financial Times,* October 30, 2001.

Page 220: Argentina's country risk premium soared from 361 to 800 basis points: Ken Warn, "Argentina's Basic Instincts Say: Stick with the Dollar," *Financial Times,* May 5, 1998.

Page 220: Argentina was forced to delay a global bond issue: ibid.

Page 220: George Soros became Argentina's largest livestock owner: Ben Christie, "Commodities and Agriculture: Argentine Mining Industry Looks for a Silver Lining," *Financial Times,* February 8, 2000.

Page 220: Prices for wheat fell 45 percent, prices for soybeans fell 20 percent: Ken Warn, "Argentina's Basic Instincts Say: Stick with the Dollar," *Financial Times,* May 5, 1998.

Page 220: Argentina's current account deficit climbed from 1.9 percent to 3.8 percent: ibid.

Page 220: Argentina's vehicle exports to Brazil fell by 50 percent: Mark Mulligan, "Time for Consolidation as Sector Slows Down," Survey—FT Auto, *Financial Times,* December 3, 1999.

Page 220–221: Multinational corporations poured $30 billion into Brazil: Geoff Dyer, "Brazil Rebounds," *Financial Times,* June 2, 2000.

Page 221: consulting firm AT Kearney identified Brazil as the world's third most popular destination: cited in Richard Lapper, Survey—Latin American Finance, *Financial Times,* March 19, 2001.

Page 221: "This is a heavy issue…:" Luis Molinari, quoted in Richard Lapper, "Pessimism Trap Puts a Damper on Growth," Survey—Argentina, *Financial Times,* September 26, 2000.

Page 221: "When you are married to Sharon Stone…:" anonymous government official, quoted in Ken Warn, "Argentina's Basic Instincts Say: Stick with the Dollar," *Financial Times,* May 5, 1998.

Page 221: the dollar climbed by 39 percent…: Barry Riley, "For a Few Euros More," *Financial Times,* July 14, 2001.

Page 221: the interest rate spread on Argentine sovereign debt was about 550 basis points…1050 basis points…8 percent of GDP: Michael Mussa, "Argentina and the Fund: From Triumph to Tragedy," *Institute for International Economics,* March 25, 2002.

Page 222: AT&T took a huge charge: Peter Thal Larsen, "AT&T Faces Charges after Latin Abandon," *Financial Times,* October 22, 2002.

Page 223: Lloyd's and Barclays both reported a rise in bad debt provisions: Jane Croft, "Bad Debt Provisions Give Banks Testing Time," *Financial Times,* February 28, 2003.

Page 223: American banks had $21 billion in Argentine exposure: John Barham, "Devaluation, Default, Depression," *LatinFinance,* February 2002.

Page 223: JP Morgan, Citigroup, and FleetBoston Financial…: Richard Lapper, "Banks Count Cost of Stake in Argentina," *Financial Times,* May 13, 2002.

Page 223: Canadian Scotiabank, France's Credit Agricole…: Colin Barraclough, "That Sinking Feeling," *Newsweek,* August 19, 2002.

Page 224: "Confident of its progress towards meeting the obligations of EU membership…:" EU report cited by Robert Anderson, "EU Membership: Preparations Come but Slowly," Survey—Czech Republic, *Financial Times,* December 1, 1997.

Page 225: Vaclav Klaus…idolized Margaret Thatcher: Anthony Robinson, "Survey—Czech Republic," *Financial Times,* December 19, 1994.

Page 225: The Social Democrats…methodically reviewed the EU criticisms…: Robert Anderson, "Pace Quickens as More Chapters Open," Survey—Central and Eastern Europe, *Financial Times,* October 24, 2000.

Page 225: Parliament convened for marathon sessions: Robert Anderson, "Fierce EU Criticism Stings Feuding Czechs Into Action—and Despite Concerns About Stability, Slovakia is Fast Catching Up," Survey—Central and Eastern Europe, *Financial Times,* October 24, 2000.

Page 225: "For most of the elites of Eastern Europe, EU accession is the aim…:" Stefan Wagstyl, "Tentative Steps to Closer Union," Survey—Central and Eastern Europe, *Financial Times,* November 10, 1999.

Page 226: He used the secret service as a tool to crush his opponents…: Robert Anderson, "A New Begging for Slovakia as Meciar Steps Down," *Financial Times,* November 3, 1998.

Page 226: "instability of its institutions, their lack of rootedness in political life…" 1997 EU evaluation of Slovakia, cited in Robert Anderson and Stefan Wagstyl, "EU Membership is the Top Priority," Survey—Slovakia, *Financial Times,* May 25, 2000.

Page 226: Slovakia was singled out among the 10 Eastern European applicants: Robert Anderson, "Facing Isolation in the Heart of Europe," *Financial Times,* October 28, 1997.

Page 226: the 70 percent of Slovakia's population that supported EU entry: Robert Anderson and Stefan Wagstyl, Survey—Slovakia, *Financial Times,* May 25, 2000.

Page 227: Slovaks gave Meciar's HZDS party only 19.5 percent of the vote: Robert Anderson, "EU Hails Centre-Right Victory in Slovakia," *Financial Times,* September 24, 2002.

Page 228: "In France, Germany, and Italy…:" Laszlo Csaba, quoted in Anatol Lieven, "Hungarian Banks Stronger after Braving Pain of Reform," *Financial Times,* September 11, 1997.

Page 228–229: Poland's mainstream political parties are uniformly pro-EU: *Economist,* Survey of Poland, October 27, 2001.

Page 229: Poland's prime minister…has said that there have been two great moments in Polish history…: "Survey of Poland," *Economist,* October 27, 2001.

Page 229: The Polish leaders…showed their domestic audience that they were not selling out: Preston Keat, "Countries Lifted by EU Decision," *Financial Times,* December 20, 2002.

Page 230: research by Talukder Maniruzzaman: Talukder Maniruzzaman, "Arms Transfers, Military Coups, and Military Rule in Developing States," *Journal of Conflict Resolution,* Vol. 36 No. 4, December 1992, pp. 733–755.

Page 231: World merchandise trade expanded from $58 billion in 1973…$1.8 trillion… $6.2 trillion in 2000: World Trade Organization, International Trade Statistics 2001.

Page 236: Vietnam…tripling its coffee production: Claudia Carpenter, "Coffee Plunges as Report Shows a Surge in Brazilian Exports," *Bloomberg News,* September 4, 2001.

Page 236: the supply of cheap robusta beans grew from an average of 27 million sacks….43 million sacks: Yadira Ferrer, "World Coffee Glut to Stretch to 2003, *Inter Press Service,* December 6, 2001.

Page 236: Total coffee production reached an all-time high of 115 million bags: Commodity Report—Coffee, *African Review of Business and Technology,* November 15, 2001.

Page 236: 95 cents in December 1999: Juan Forero, "The Caprice of Coffee," *New York Times,* November 8, 2001.

Page 236: 45 cents in October: Commodity Report—Coffee, *African Review of Business and Technology,* November 15, 2001.

Page 236: In Mexico, many of the country's 3 million coffee workers went bankrupt: Dudley Althaus, "A Brewing Disaster in Mexico," *Houston Chronicle,* May 7, 2001.

Page 236: Kenya and Tanzania experienced a surge in the number of AIDS cases: Kunal Bose, Raymond Colitt, and Andrea Mandel-Campbell, "A Crisis is Brewing in Your Coffee Cup," *Financial Times,* April 11, 2001.

Page 236: In Nicaragua, drug smuggling increased: Bruce Finley, "Fair-trade Movement Brews New Hope for Coffee Growers," *Denver Post,* October 21, 2001.

Page 236: Colombia earned roughly 30 percent less…560,000 families: John Otis, "Desperate Times Brewing," *Houston Chronicle,* November 23, 2001.

Page 237: In 2001 alone, $72.3 billion was remitted by migrant workers: World Bank, World Development Report 2003.

Page 237: Migrant laborers in the U.S. alone sent home $20 annually: ibid.

Page 237: Mexico…receives $10 billion every year from its expatriate workers in the United States: ibid.

Page 237: In Albania, a quarter of the workforce works abroad: "Bad News for the (Fairly) Good Guys," *Economist,* February 2, 2002.

Page 237: each year, they [Albanians] send home roughly $500 million, or 17 percent of their country's GDP: World Bank, World Development Report 2003.

Page 237: Ecuador earned $1.4 billion in 2001 from the 400,000 Ecuadorian workers abroad: ibid.

Page 237: Bangladesh earned an estimated $2.1 billion [in 2001]: ibid.

Page 237: Morocco earned $3.3 billion in 2001: ibid.

Page 237: three quarters of all Mozambican families have at least one family members working [in South Africa]: "A Ticket to Prosperity," *Economist,* September 2, 2000.

Page 237: the world's premier exporter of labor is the Philippines…: Pamela G. Hollie, "Filipinos Are Flocking to Take Overseas Jobs," *New York Times,* January 31, 1982.

Page 237: [Filipinos earned] an estimated $6.4 billion in 2001: World Bank, World Development Report 2003.

Page 238: millions of Arabs followed the money…: John Kifner and Judith Miller, "Wave of Arab Migration Ending with Oil Bloom," *New York Times,* October 6, 1985.

Page 238: Egypt supplied 43 percent of these migrant laborers in the Gulf…: ibid.

Page 238: Saudi Arabia earned $120 billion from oil...: ibid.

Page 238: The result was a mass exodus of migrant workers: ibid.

Page 238: Egypt, Jordan, Sudan, and Yemen were especially hard hit: ibid.

Page 238: All told, remittance earnings in the Gulf countries declined $23 billion in 1990 and 1991: joint study conducted by the Arab Monetary Fund, the Arab Petroleum Exporting Countries Organization, and the Arab Fund for Economic and Social Development.

Page 238: Nicaragua derives 16.2 percent of its GDP from remittance income...13.8... 13.5...9.3...8.5: World Bank, *World Development Report 2003.*

Chapter Fifteen—Economic Potential Energy: Institutions

Page 243: between 1991 and 1996, roughly 18,000....were privatized...from near insignificance to close to 90 percent of the country's industrial production: Daniel Yergin and Joseph Stanislaw, *Commanding Heights,* Simon & Schuster, 1998, p. 297.

Page 243: Between 30 and 40 million, infectious diseases, alcoholism, life expectancy: Alexander Pochinok, Labor and Social Development minister, from Gerry Gendlin, "The Collapse of Russia," *Précis,* MIT Center for International Studies, Volume X Number 5, Spring 2001.

Page 243: despite more than $70 billion: "Russia," *East European Markets,* July 18, 1997.

Page 244: an estimated $300 billion was simply looted: David Remnick, "Can Russia Change?" *Foreign Affairs,* January–February 1997.

Page 244: Russia has never had a tradition of private property: Richard Pipes, quoted in David Remnick, "Can Russia Change?" *Foreign Affairs,* January–February 1997

Page 245: Prices of commodities remained state-controlled, while regulations on private business activity were lifted...: from Anders Aslund, "Russia's Collapse," *Foreign Affairs,* September–October 1999.

Page 245: Scholar Anders Aslund estimates...: ibid.

Page 246: the central bank handed out credits worth 32 percent of Russia's annual output: ibid.

Page 246: Aslund estimates the total amount plundered...at nearly 80 percent of Russia's GDP: ibid.

Page 246: Mikhail Khodorkovsky...acquired the Yukos oil company..., "sale of the century:" Lee S. Wolosky, "Putin's Plutocrat Problem," *Foreign Affairs,* March–April 2000.

Page 247: The oligarchs were the tycoons...convinced Russian government ministries to do all their banking with him: Andrew Jack, "Roubles from the Rubble," *Financial Times,* March 23/March 24, 2002.

Page 247: "In a country of corrupt bureaucrats...:" Chrystia Freeland, "Not-so-Badfellas," *New Republic,* October 12, 1998.

Page 248: Between 1992 and 1998, over 1.2 million bureaucrats were hired: Anders Aslund, "Russia's Collapse," *Foreign Affairs,* September–October 1999.

Page 248: the All Union Research Institute...estimated that half the income of an average government functionary: cited in Claire Sterling, "Redfellas," *New Republic,* April 11, 1994.

Page 248: Russian companies could expect almost a visit a day: Anders Aslund, "Russia's Collapse," *Foreign Affairs,* September–October 1999.

Page 248: "practically have a price list...:" Mikhail Smolensky, quoted in David Remnick, "Can Russia Change?" *Foreign Affairs,* January–February 1997.

Page 248: petty bribery alone accounted for 20 percent of business costs: Ana Nichols, "The Grip of Corruption," *Business Central Europe,* July/August 2000.

Page 248: Roughly 200 different levies, oligarchs bribed, small businesses without connections: Anders Aslund, "Russia's Collapse," *Foreign Affairs,* September–October 1999.

Page 248: the number of legally registered enterprises was about one for every 55 people: ibid.

Page 249: "virtual economy:" from Clifford Gaddy and Barry Ickes, "Russia's Virtual Economy," *Foreign Affairs,* August–September 1998.

Page 249: By 1997, forty percent of all tax payments: ibid.

Page 249: "An economy is emerging where prices are charged...:" Karpov commission cited ibid.

Page 249: the country's largest enterprises conducted 73 percent of their business in barter: Karpov commission cited ibid.

Page 249: the real prices of goods and services had to be disguised...nothing of value was being done: ibid.

Page 249: McKinsey...conducted an extensive study of business management practices...: McKinsey Global Institute, *Unlocking Economic Growth in Russia,* McKinsey & Company, Inc., October 1999.

Page 249: McKinsey found that Russian companies' productivity rates...: ibid.

Page 250: across the economy, in a variety of industries, McKinsey found that Russian firms were deliberately operating and making investments in an unproductive fashion….: ibid.

Page 251: a pyramid scheme called MMM: Thane Gustafson, *Capitalism Russian Style,* Cambridge University Pres, 1999, p. 74.

Page 251: the newly privatized Yukos oil company forced its subsidiaries to sell it oil at $1.70 a barrel…36 weeks: Lee S. Wolosky, "Putin's Plutocrat Problem," *Foreign Affairs,* March–April 2000.

Page 251: Russia's banks concentrated their efforts on obtaining government subsidies…: Michael S. Bernstam and Andrei Sitnikov, "Ersatz Banks," Chapter 14, in *The New Russia,* Eds. Lawrence R. Klein and Marshall Pomer, Stanford University Press, 2001, p. 221.

Page 251: they functioned as illegitimate treasury departments…: "Mr. Rouble Quits," *Economist,* March 23, 2002.

Page 251: $512 million in government funds deposited in a bank affiliated with Vladimir Potanin: Lee S. Wolosky, "Putin's Plutocrat Problem," *Foreign Affairs,* March–April 2000.

Page 251: billions of dollars in government deposits intended for the reconstruction of Chechnya also vanished: Lee S. Wolosky, "Putin's Plutocrat Problem," *Foreign Affairs,* March–April 2000.

Page 251: The infamous "Russian mafia," with an estimated 35,000 members…: Gustafson, p. 143.

Page 251: Vladimir "The Poodle" Podiatev: David Remnick, "Can Russia Change?" *Foreign Affairs,* January–February 1997.

Page 251: Russia's Mafia grew so powerful partially because it was needed…: Claire Sterling, "Redfellas," *New Republic,* April 11, 1994.

Page 252: "the only lawyer in this country is the Kalashnikov…:" David Remnick, "Can Russia Change?" *Foreign Affairs,* January–February 1997.

Page 252: "share dilution" schemes: Lee S. Wolosky, "Putin's Plutocrat Problem," *Foreign Affairs,* March–April 2000.

Page 252: the privatized oil company Sibneft…: Lee S. Wolosky, "Putin's Plutocrat Problem," *Foreign Affairs,* March–April 2000.

Page 252: representatives of UK-based TransWorld Metals, were attending a stockholders' meeting in Siberia…: *Financial Times,* November 16, 1994 and *Kommersant-Daily,* November 25, 1994, cited in Gustafson, p. 69.

Page 252: BP Amoco…In 1997, it invested $571 million into Sidanko…: Michael Wines, "Spiffing Up a Dirty Business; Russia's Oil Barons Say Wildcatter Capitalism Era is Over," *New York Times,* December 28, 1999.

Page 253–258: Botswana Section: information obtained exclusively from Daron Acemoglu, Simon Johnson and James A. Robinson, "An African Success Story: Botswana," Centre for Economic Policy Research, January 30, 2002.

Page 257: a study of Botswana conducted in the 1980s…: Jack Parson, *Botswana: Liberal Democracy and the Labor Reserve in Southern Africa,* Westview Press, 1984, quoted in Acemoglu, Johnson, and Robinson, p. 18.

Page 258: Hernando de Soto's experiment, from Hernando de Soto, *Mystery of Capital,* Basic Books, 2000.

Page 259: 500,000 laws and executive orders governing economic activity: Yergin and Stanislaw, p. 250.

Page 260: "Markets and capitalism are about property rights…:" Hernando de Soto, quoted in Yergin and Stanislaw, p. 269

Page 261: Ronald Coase's theories: see Ronald Coase, "The Nature of the Firm." *Economica,* 1937, 4:386–405.

Page 262–263 Douglass North's theories: see Douglass North, *Institutions, Institutional Change, and Economic Performance,* Cambridge University Press, 1990.

Page 263: William Baumol's theories: see William Baumol, *The Free-Market Innovation Machine: Analyzing the Growth Miracle of Capitalism,* Princeton University Press, 2002

Page 264: the World Bank compiled data on political and economic institutions: World Bank, *World Development Report: The State in a Changing World,* Oxford University Press, 1997.

Page 264: half a percentage point per year over the 30-year period…: ibid., p. 32

Page 264: a strong link between economic institutions and levels of growth and investment: ibid., p. 30

Page 264: Bureaucracies with effective rules and restraints…: ibid., p. 7

Page 264: The bureaucracies of East Asia…: ibid., p. 9

Page 265: In the bribe-prone Philippines, civil servant wages were just 25 percent of private-sector wages….in bribe-resistant Singapore…: ibid., p. 94

Page 264: in many countries the courts were subject to political manipulation: ibid., p. 8

Page 264: More than 70 percent of entrepreneurs in developing countries: ibid., p. 36.

Page 264: In Brazil and Ecuador, it took 1,500 days…France…: ibid., p. 100

Page 264: India's courts…were found to be fair and competent: World Bank, *India: Policies to Reduce Poverty and Accelerate Sustainable Development,* January 31, 2000, pp. 44–45.

Page 265: In successful countries, the World Bank found that laws were clear, enforced…: World Bank, *World Development Report: The State in a Changing World,* Oxford University Press, 1997, p. 100.

Page 265: almost 80 percent of entrepreneurs in former Soviet states: ibid., p. 34.

Page 265: Sixty percent of entrepreneurs in former Soviet states, the Middle East, and Africa…: ibid., p. 36.

Page 265: Thailand issued more than 4 million title deeds…: ibid., p. 44.

Page 265: titled land was more productive than untitled land by an average of 12 to 27 percent: ibid., p. 44.

Page 265: Independent judiciaries, a system of checks and balances between branches of government…: Philip Keefer and Stephen Knack, "Why Don't Poor Countries Catch Up? A Cross-National Test of an Institutional Explanation," *Economic Inquiry,* Volume XXXV, July 1 1997, pp. 590–591.

Page 265: The World Bank has just issued a study showing that secure and transferable property rights…: Klaus Deininger, Songqing Jin, Berhanu Adenew, Samuel Gebre-Selassie, Berhanu Neg, *Tenure Security and Land-Related Investment: Evidence From Ethiopia,* World Bank, March 8, 2003.

Conclusion—"Eating Big Macs Doesn't Make it McChina"

Page 267: "China is like a black box…:" William Greider, *One World, Ready or Not,* quoted in Daniel Burstein and Arne de Keijzer, *Big Dragon,* Simon & Schuster, 1998, p. 342.

Page 269: "It is not possible to pretend China..:" Lee Kwan Yew quoted in Burstein and de Keijzer, p. 14.

Page 270: "If you wan to be the world leader in your industry…:" Jack Welch quoted in Gordon Chang, *The Coming Collapse of China,* Random House, 2001 p. 148.

Page 270: "the most promising market in the world…:" Phil Murtaugh quoted in Chang, p. 95.

Page 270: "China is the most exciting thing…:" James Cayne quoted in Burstein and de Keijzer, p. 16.

Page 270: twelve U.S. companies had over $100 invested in China: Burstein and de Keijzer, p. 50.

Page 279: As scholars Daniel Burstein and Arne De Keijzer put it: "Eating Big Macs…:" Burstein and de Keijzer, p. 99

Page 271: Party membership among college students fell…: Bruce Dickson, *Red Capitalists,* Cambridge University Press, 2003, p. 36.

Page 271: of more than 13,000 private enterprises, only 17 had basic-level party organizations…: ibid., pp. 38–39.

Page 271: While only five percent of China's general population belonged to the Communist Party…: ibid., p. 35.

Page 271–272: the high-profile actions of one Wan Runnan: ibid., p. 99.

Page 272: business owners were forbidden from joining the Party: ibid., pp. 98–99.

Page 272: further diminishing the Party's influence over private business…: ibid., p. 39.

Page 272: "state corporatism:" ibid., p. 25.

Page 272: forced to enroll in a business association: ibid., pp. 64–65.

Page 272: scholar Bruce Dickson conducted a random-sample survey…: ibid.

Page 273: Jiang Zemin publicly recommended lifting the ban on admitting entrepreneurs into the Party, ibid., p. 103.

Page 274: one-fifth of private entrepreneurs were reported to have already joined: ibid., p. 108.

Page 274: as pointed out by scholar Yingyi Qian: Yingyi Qian, "How Reform Worked in China." Draft: July 2001.

Page 274: "growing out of the plan:" Barry Naughton, *Growing Out Of the Plan,* Cambridge University Press, 1995.

Page 275: sales of coal: Qian

Page 275: creation of local government firms…: ibid.

Page 275: firms owned by local governments accounted for 42 percent…: ibid.

Page 276: Banking reforms adopted in 1978 allowed Chinese citizens…: ibid.

Page 277: "heaven and earth have changed places:" James Kynge, "Something Rotten in the Rice Bowl," *Financial Times,* June 30–July 1, 2001.

Page 277: danwei: ibid.

Page 277: as many as 120 million Chinese criss-crossing the country....Carl J. Dahlman and Jean-Eric Aubert, *China and the Knowledge Economy,* World Bank, October 2001.

Page 278: increase in crime: James Harding, "China Starts to Face Up to Rising Crime Problem," *Financial Times,* February 20, 1999.

Page 278: migrants and newly jobless can be seen hawking…: James Kynge, "Something Rotten in the Rice Bowl," *Financial Times,* June 30–July 1, 2001.

Page 278: 30 million Chinese Christians…: George Gilboy and Eric Heginbotham, "China's Coming Transformation," *Foreign Affairs,* July–August 2001.

Page 279: a multi-million dollar smuggling ring in Fujian…: "No Longer On the Run," *Asiaweek,* December 8, 2000.

Page 279: Beijing mayor Chen Xitong became the first Politburo member…: Burstein and de Keijzer, p. 205.

Page 279: the popular mayor of the northeastern industrial city of Shenynag: Burstein and de Keijzer, p. 205.

Page 279: 98 percent of senior officials…in cases of fraud of over $600,000: Melinda Liu, "Party Time in Beijing," *Newsweek,* November 25, 2002.

Page 279: "irrigation project labor fees:" Guo Xin-Min of Guo Village, interviewed by Sue Williams, "China in the Red," *Frontline,* Ambrica Productions, 2003.

Page 279–280: near Fengcheng…angry farmers…: Chang, p. 247.

Page 280: An opinion poll asked Chinese throughout the country, "How many people have reached wealthy status through 'normal' means?": cited in Burstein and de Keijzer, p. 185.

Page 280: a chart was circulated at the demonstrations: Jonathan Mirsky, "Revolution's Dark Legacy," *Asiaweek,* Jan. 19, 2001.

Page 280: "A lot of stories circulate these days…:" Tian Jiyun, quoted ibid.

Page 282: Tiananmen Square uprising was coordinated spontaneously…: Mike O'Sullivan, "Experts Say China Serving as Test Cast of Internet's Impact," Voice of America News, June 2, 2003.

Page 282: "Historical experience has told us that nothing can be accomplished…:" Zhu Rongji quoted in Chang, p. 249.

Page 283: "No communist country has solved the problem of succession:" Henry Kissinger, quoted in Chang, p. 258.

Page 283: It took Deng Xiaoping three attempts to put a successor in place: John Bryan Starr, *Understanding China,* Hill and Wang, 2001, p. 5.

Page 284: Central China Non-Ferrous Metals: study by Edward Steinfeld cited in: Richard McGregor, "Debt-laden Institutions Lighten Their Load," Survey—China, *Financial Times*, November 13, 2000.

Page 285: a further 25 to 40 million are estimated to be superfluous: estimates cited in Rahul Jacob, "China's Workers Unite in Anger," *Financial Times*, Monday May 27, 2002.

Index

Abacha, Sani (former president of Nigeria): 12

Abdullah, Crown Prince of Saudi Arabia: 137

Abdullah, King of Jordan: 151

Acemoglu, Daron (Botswana scholar): 254

Afghanistan: Saudi discontent exported to, VIII; American rebuilding of, XXIII; as non-Big-Mac state, XXIII; Egyptian militants migrating to, 37; freedom fighters, 40; US in Central Asia because of, 131; Saudi financing of jihad in, 140; Pakistani roots of Taliban regime, 175

Africa: AIDS in, XXIII, 84, 110; term "Wabenzi" coined in, 3; Nigeria (ethnic conflict), 17–27; oil in, 27; postcolonial, 29–30; Lebanese and whites in, 30; Tamil Tigers operations in, 64; Zimbabwe (channeling discontent), 82–87, South Africa, 83–85, 112–113, 124, 232, 237, 255; leaders, 79; Uganda (leadership), 106–111; GDP compared with OECD agricultural subsidies, 187; education spending, 210; motorized vehicle ownership, 210; Filipinos in, 237; Botswana (institutions), 253–258; property rights protection in, 265

Agriculture: Scientific advances in, XI, Nigerian state's involvement in, 21, 27;

in Egypt, 34; in Zimbabwe, 85–88; in Pakistan, 174, 176; in Brazil, 178; in Japan, 191; in Poland, 229

Ah Rae Ah Hangul (Korean firm): XV–XVIII, XX

AIDS: as threats from impoverished world, XXIII; in Zimbabwe, 82, 84; Clinton and AIDS vaccine, 106; in Uganda, 110–111; in Kenya and Tanzania, 236; in Botswana, 258

Akayev, Askar (president of Kyrgyzstan): 129

Albania: diaspora funding for war, 72; Kosovo, 117–118, 121; pyramid schemes in, 223; migrant labor from, 237

Aligarh (city in India): 30–31

Al-Qaeda: exploiter of globalization, XIX; Egyptians in, 38; use of Tamil Tigers as model, 65; as result of Saudi Arabia's failed ruling bargain, 140–141; Pakistani madrassas as feeding ground for, 175; Somali links to, 238

Amin, Idi (former president of Uganda): 107–109; succession practice of, 126

Angola: as oil producer, 27; war in, 253

Aquino, Benigno (Filipino opposition leader): 7

Aquino, Corazon (former president of the Philippines): rise to presidency, 8–10; indictment of Westinghouse, 10–11